THE
DEVIL'S
DIARY

THE
DEVIL'S
DIARY

Alfred Rosenberg and the

Stolen Secrets of the Third Reich

ROBERT K. WITTMAN

AND DAVID KINNEY

HARPER

An Imprint of HarperCollins*Publishers*

HarperCollins books may be purchased for educational, business,
or sales promotional use. For information, please e-mail the Special Markets
Department at SPsales@harpercollins.com.

FIRST EDITION

Designed by Jo Anne Metsch

Library of Congress Cataloging-in-Publication Data

Wittman, Robert K., and Kinney, David (David Francis).
The devil's diary : Alfred Rosenberg and the stolen secrets of the Third Reich / Robert K.
Wittman and David Kinney.
p.   cm.
ISBN 978-0-06-231901-2

1. Rosenberg, Alfred, 1893–1946—Diaries. 2. Nazis—Diaries. 3. Rosenberg, Alfred, 1893–
1946—Political and social views. 4. Hitler, Adolf, 1889–1945—Friends and associates.
5. National socialism—Philosophy. 6. Holocaust, Jewish (1939–1945)—Philosophy.
7. Germany—Foreign relations—Soviet Union. 8. Soviet Union—Foreign relations—
Germany. 9. Wittman, Robert K. 10. United States—Federal Bureau of Investigation—
Officials and employees—Biography.

DD247.R58 W58   2016
940.53/18092—dc23   2015036609

---

16 17 18 19 20   ov/RRD   10 9 8 7 6 5 4 3 2 1

For our families

Great philosophical changes need many generations to turn them into pulsating life. And even our present acres of death will someday bloom again.

—ALFRED ROSENBERG

With small steps you can stumble into mass murders, that's the bad part. Very small steps are sufficient.

—ROBERT KEMPNER

Contents

THE
DEVIL'S
DIARY

"Long live eternal Germany!" Local Nazis welcome Alfred Rosenberg (*center, hand raised*) to Heiligenstadt, Thuringia, in 1935. *(ullstein bild/ullstein bild via Getty Images)*

Prologue: The Vault

The palace on the mountain loomed over a stretch of rolling Bavarian countryside so lovely it was known as Gottesgarten— God's Garden.

From the villages and farmsteads on the meandering river below, Schloss Banz commanded attention. Its sprawling stone wings glowed a luminous gold in the sunlight, and a pair of delicately tapered copper spires rose high above its Baroque church. The site had a thousand-year history: as a trading post, as a castle fortified to withstand armies, as a Benedictine monastery. It had been pillaged and destroyed in war, and extravagantly rebuilt for the royal Wittelsbach family. Kings and dukes, and once even Kaiser Wilhelm II, the last emperor of Germany, had graced its opulent halls. Now, in the spring of 1945, the colossus was an outpost of a notorious task force that had spent the war looting occupied Europe for the glory of the Third Reich.

As defeat drew near following six punishing years of war,

Nazis all across Germany had been burning sensitive government files before the documents could be seized and used against them. But bureaucrats who could not bring themselves to destroy their papers instead hid them in forests, in mines, in castles, and in palaces like this one. Around the country, immense libraries of secrets were there for the Allies to find: detailed internal records shedding light on the warped German bureaucracy, on the military's pitiless war strategy, and on the obsessive Nazi plan to clear Europe of its "undesirable elements," finally and forever.

In the second week of April, the soldiers of General George S. Patton's Third U.S. Army and General Alexander Patch's Seventh U.S. Army overran the region. Since crossing the Rhine a few weeks earlier, the men had charged across the western reaches of the battered country, slowed only by demolished bridges, improvised roadblocks, and pockets of stubborn resistance. They passed cities flattened by Allied bombs. They passed hollow-eyed villagers and houses flying not the Nazi swastika but white sheets and pillowcases. The German army had all but disintegrated. Hitler could be dead in three and a half weeks.

Not long after the Americans arrived in the region, they encountered a flamboyant aristocrat who wore a monocle and high, polished boots. Kurt von Behr had spent the war in Paris plundering private art collections and ransacking common household furnishings from tens of thousands of Jewish properties in France, Belgium, and the Netherlands. Just before the liberation of Paris, he and his wife fled to Banz with loads of pilfered treasure in a convoy of eleven cars and four moving vans.

Now von Behr wanted to cut a deal.

He went to the nearby town of Lichtenfels and approached a military government officer named Samuel Haber. It seemed that von Behr had grown accustomed to living like royalty beneath the elaborately painted ceilings of the palace. If Haber would give him permission to stay put, von Behr would show him a secret stash of important Nazi papers.

The American was intrigued. With operational intelligence at a premium and war crimes trials on the horizon, Allied forces had been ordered to track down and save every German document they could find. Patton's army had a G-2 military intelligence unit dedicated to the task. In April alone, its target teams would capture thirty tons of Nazi files.

Acting on von Behr's tip, the Americans made their way up the mountain and through the gates to the palace to see von Behr. The Nazi escorted them five stories belowground, where, sealed behind a false wall of concrete, a mother lode of confidential Nazi documents was hidden. The files filled an enormous vault. What could not fit inside lay scattered about the room in piles.

After surrendering his secret, von Behr—apparently realizing that his gambit would not save him from the ravages of Germany's humiliating defeat—prepared to depart the stage in style. He donned one of his extravagant uniforms and accompanied his wife to their bedroom in the estate. Raising two flutes of French champagne laced with cyanide, they toasted the end of everything. "The episode," an American correspondent wrote, "had all the elements of the melodrama Nazi leaders seemed to relish."

Soldiers found von Behr and his wife slumped in their luxurious surroundings. As they examined the bodies, they spied the half-empty bottle still sitting on the table.

The couple had chosen a vintage rich in symbolism: 1918, the year their beloved homeland had been laid low at the end of another world war.

The papers in the vault belonged to Alfred Rosenberg, Hitler's chief ideologue and an early member of the Nazi Party. Rosenberg was a witness to the party's embryonic days in 1919, when bitterly angry German nationalists discovered a leader in Adolf Hitler, the bombastic, vagabond veteran of the First World War. In November 1923, on the night Hitler tried to overthrow the Bavarian government, Rosenberg marched into the Munich beer hall one step behind his hero. He was there in Berlin a decade later when the party came to power and set about crushing its enemies. He was there in the arena, fighting, as the Nazis remodeled all of Germany in their image. He was there to the end, when the war turned and the whole twisted vision fell apart.

In the spring of 1945, as investigators began leafing through the enormous cache of documents—which included 250 volumes of official and personal correspondence—they discovered something remarkable: Rosenberg's personal diary.

The account was written by hand across five hundred pages, some entries in a bound notebook, more on loose sheets. It began in 1934, a year into Hitler's rule, and ended a decade later, a few months before the war ended. Of the most important men in the highest ranks of the Third Reich, only Rosenberg, Propaganda Minister Joseph Goebbels, and Hans Frank, the brutal governor-general of occupied Poland, left behind such diaries. The others, Hitler included, took their secrets with them to their graves. Rosenberg's diary promised to shed light on the workings of the Third Reich from the perspective of a man who had operated at the very upper reaches of the Nazi Party for a quarter of a century.

Outside Germany, Rosenberg was never as well-known as Goebbels, or Heinrich Himmler, mastermind of the SS security forces, or Hermann Göring, Hitler's economic chief and commander of the air force. Rosenberg had to struggle and scrap against those giants of the Nazi bureaucracy for the sort of power that he thought he deserved. But he had the Führer's support from beginning to end. He and Hitler saw eye to eye on the most fundamental questions, and Rosenberg had been unerringly loyal. Hitler appointed him to a succession of leading positions in the party and the government, elevating Rosenberg's public profile and ensuring him far-reaching influence. His rivals in Berlin loathed him, but the rank and file of the party saw Rosenberg as one of Germany's most important figures: Here was a big thinker with the ear of the Führer himself.

Rosenberg's fingerprints would be found on more than a few of Nazi Germany's most notorious crimes.

He orchestrated the theft of artwork, archives, and libraries from Paris to Krakow to Kiev—the loot that the Allies' Monuments Men would famously track down in Germany's castles and salt mines.

In 1920, he planted the insidious idea in Hitler's mind that a global Jewish conspiracy was behind the communist revolution in the Soviet Union, and he repeated the claim over and over. Rosenberg was the preeminent champion of a theory that Hitler used to justify Germany's devastating war against the Soviets two decades on. As the Nazis prepared to invade the Soviet Union, Rosenberg promised that the war would be a "cleansing biological world revolution," one that would finally exterminate "all those racially infecting germs of Jewry and its bastards." During the first years of the war in the East, when the Germans had the Red Army pinned back against Moscow, Rosenberg led an occupation authority that terrorized the Baltics, Belarus, and Ukraine, and his ministry collaborated with Himmler's genocidal crusaders as they massacred Jews throughout the East.

Not least, Rosenberg laid the groundwork for the Holocaust. He began publishing his toxic ideas about the Jews in 1919, and as editor of the party newspaper and author of articles, pamphlets, and books, he spread the party message of hate. Later, Rosenberg was the Führer's delegate for ideological matters, and in cities and villages all across the Reich he was welcomed with bunting and cheering crowds. His theoretical masterwork, *The Myth of the Twentieth Century*, sold more than a million copies and was considered, alongside Hitler's *Mein Kampf*, a central text of Nazi ideology. In his ponderous writings, Rosenberg borrowed antiquated ideas about race and world history from other pseudo-intellectuals and fused them into an idiosyncratic political belief system. The party's local and district leaders told him they delivered thousands of speeches with his words at their fingertips.

"Here," Rosenberg boasted in the diary, "they found both direction and material for the battle." Rudolf Höss, commandant of the death camp at Auschwitz, where more than a million people were exterminated, said that the words of three men in particular had prepared him psychologically to carry out his mission: Hitler, Goebbels, and Rosenberg.

In the Third Reich, an ideologue could see his philosophies put to practical use, and Rosenberg's had lethal consequences.

"Again and again, I am swept up in a rage when I think about <u>what</u> these parasitic Jewish people have done to Germany," he wrote in the diary in 1936. "But at least I have one gratification: to have done my bit in the exposure of this treachery." Rosenberg's ideas legitimized and rationalized the murder of millions.

In November 1945, an extraordinary International Military Tribunal convened in Nuremberg to try the most notorious surviving Nazis on war crimes charges—Rosenberg among them. The prosecution case was built on the mass of German documents captured by the Allies at the end of the war. Hans Fritzsche, indicted as a war criminal for his role as chief of the Propaganda Ministry's News Division, told a prison psychiatrist during the trial that Rosenberg had played a critical role in the formation of Hitler's philosophies in the 1920s, before the Nazis rose to power. "In my opinion, he had a tremendous influence on Hitler during the period when Hitler still did some thinking," said Fritzsche, who would be acquitted at Nuremberg but later sentenced to nine years in prison by a German denazification court. "Rosenberg's importance exists because his ideas, which were only theoretical, became in the hands of Hitler a reality. . . . The tragic thing is that Rosenberg's fantastic theories were actually put into practice."

In a way, Fritzsche argued, Rosenberg carried "the main guilt of all those who sit here on the defendant's bench."

At Nuremberg, Robert H. Jackson, the chief U.S. prosecutor, denounced Rosenberg as the "intellectual high priest of the 'master race.'" The judges found the Nazi guilty of war crimes, and on

October 16, 1946, Rosenberg's life ended in the middle of the night at the end of a rope.

Over the coming decades, historians trying to understand the hows and whys of the century's greatest cataclysm would pore over the millions of documents salvaged by the Allies at the end of the war. The surviving documentation was extensive—secret military records, detailed inventories of plunder, private diaries, diplomatic papers, transcripts of telephone conversations, chilling bureaucratic memos discussing mass murder. After the trials ended in 1949, American prosecutors closed down their offices, and the captured German documents were shipped to an old torpedo factory on the banks of the Potomac River in Alexandria, Virginia. There, the papers were prepared for filing with the National Archives. Microfilms were made, and eventually most of the originals were sent back to Germany.

But something happened to the bulk of Rosenberg's secret diary. It never arrived in Washington. It was never transcribed, translated, and studied in its entirety by Third Reich scholars.

Four years after it was unearthed from the Bavarian palace vault, the diary vanished.

LOST

AND

FOUND

1949–2013

Prosecutor Robert Kempner at Nuremberg's Palace of Justice.
(U.S. Holocaust Memorial Museum, courtesy of John W. Mosenthal)

1

The Crusader

Four years after the end of the war, in Courtroom 600 of Nuremberg's Palace of Justice, a prosecutor waited for verdicts to be handed down. These would be the final judgments against the Nazi war criminals indicted by the Americans, and Robert Kempner had everything invested in the outcome.

Pugnacious, dogged, a tireless networker with a taste for intrigue, the forty-nine-year-old lawyer had gone through life with his chin jutted out, as if inviting adversaries—and there were many—to take their best shot. Though he did not stand out physically, his hairline vanishing atop his five-foot-eight-inch frame, Kempner had a personality that had a way of making people take sides. Depending on your point of view, he was either charismatic or ostentatious, dedicated or dogmatic, a champion of righteous causes or a petty boor.

Kempner had spent the better part of twenty years at war with Hitler and the Nazis, the last four in this city ruined by the Führer's megalomania and the Allies' bombs. His struggle was a singular personal story and at the same time a universal narrative: his fight for his life, his bit part in the global fight of his age. In the early 1930s, as a young police administrator in Berlin, Kempner argued that Germany should arrest Hitler and his followers for high treason before they could overthrow the republic and carry out their blueprint of terror. Within days of the party's rise to power in 1933, Kempner—a Jew, a liberal, and an avowed opponent—lost his government post. Following a brief detention and Gestapo interrogation in 1935, he fled to Italy, then France, and finally the United States, where he continued his campaign. Tapping a library of internal German documents and a network of informants, Kempner helped the Justice Department convict Nazi propagandists operating in the United States, and fed intelligence about the Third Reich to the War Department, the clandestine Office of Strategic Services, and J. Edgar Hoover's Federal Bureau of Investigation.

Then, in a plot turn ripped from the pages of a Hollywood script, he returned to his homeland and helped prosecute the very men who had dismissed him from his job, demonized him for his Jewish blood, stripped him of his German citizenship, and sent him running for his life.

After Göring, Rosenberg, and the other boldfaced names of the fallen Reich were prosecuted for war crimes in that famous international trial, Kempner stayed on in Nuremberg for twelve additional cases brought by the Americans against another 177 Nazi collaborators: doctors who performed gruesome experiments on concentration camp inmates, SS administrators who worked prisoners to death, company directors who benefited from forced labor, leaders of killing units that massacred civilians all across Eastern Europe during the war.

Kempner personally oversaw the last and longest prosecution, Case 11, nicknamed the Ministries Trial because most of the defendants had held leading posts in the government offices on

Wilhelmstrasse in Berlin. The most prominent figure on trial, State Secretary Ernst von Weizsäcker of the Foreign Office, had cleared the way for the invasion of Czechoslovakia and was shown to have personally approved the transport of more than six thousand Jews from France to the death camp at Auschwitz. The most notorious culprit was Gottlob Berger, a senior SS officer who put together a murder squad noted for its brutality. "Better to shoot two Poles too many," he once wrote about the unit, "than two too few." The most unsettling defendants were the bankers who not only financed the construction of concentration camps but also stockpiled the tons and tons of gold fillings, jewelry, and eyeglasses stripped from victims of the extermination camps.

The trial had been under way since the end of 1947, and now, on April 12, 1949, it was finally coming to a close. The three American judges walked into the courtroom, ascended to the bench, and began reading aloud from their judgment. It ran eight hundred pages; reciting it took three days. Across the room, guarded by ramrod-straight military policemen in glittering silver helmets, the Nazis listened through headphones as translators deciphered the verdicts into German. When it was all over, nineteen of the twenty-one defendants had been convicted—five of them on the landmark Nuremberg charge of crimes against the peace. Weizsäcker got seven years in prison, Berger twenty-five; the three bankers were sentenced to five to ten years.

For the prosecution, it was a major victory. After digging through the Nazi documents and interrogating hundreds of witnesses over four years, they had convicted the worst offenders and sent them to jail. They had shown the world that complicity for the Holocaust ran deep and broad throughout the German government. They had painted, as Kempner would put it, "the entire criminal fresco" of the Third Reich and reinforced Nuremberg's place in history as "a fortress of faith in international law." They had bolstered the argument for forceful prosecution of war crimes.

The verdicts were the culmination of Kempner's long campaign against the Nazi Party.

Or at least, they should have been.

Within a few years, the promise of Nuremberg would come unraveled.

All along, the trials had their detractors in Germany and America. The critics saw not justice but vindictiveness at the core of the prosecutions, and Kempner, an abrasive personality and notably aggressive interrogator, became a symbol of that perceived unfairness. Case in point was the prosecutor's sharp questioning of former Nazi diplomat Friedrich Gaus, during which Kempner threatened to hand the witness over to the Russians for possible war crimes prosecution. One of his fellow American prosecutors declared Kempner's tactics "foolish," fearing that he would "make martyrs out of the common criminals on trial in Nuremberg." Another witness cross-examined by Kempner called the prosecutor "a most Gestapo-like man."

In 1948, Kempner was drawn into a bitter public debate with a Protestant bishop, Theophil Wurm, over the integrity of the proceedings. Wurm wrote Kempner an open letter of protest; Kempner replied by suggesting that those who questioned the Nuremberg trials were in fact "enemies of the German people." As the disagreement played out in the press, Kempner found himself pilloried in German newspapers. He was caricatured as a self-righteous Jewish exile bent on vengeance.

Censure came even from U.S. Senator Joseph McCarthy, whose Wisconsin constituency included a large number of German Americans. The senator opposed Weizsäcker's prosecution, because, according to his unnamed sources, the Nazi had been a valuable undercover agent for the Americans during the war.

McCarthy said Nuremberg was hampering U.S. intelligence-gathering in Germany and told the Senate Armed Services Committee in spring 1949 that he wanted a probe into the "complete imbecility" surrounding Weizsäcker's trial.

"I think this committee," McCarthy said, "should see what type of morons—and I use that term advisedly—are running the military court over there."

By the time the last trials were over, U.S. war crimes courts had sentenced more than one thousand Nazis to prison terms. Most of them languished in Landsberg Prison, near Munich. A great many West Germans still refused to accept the validity of the Allied courts and considered these imprisoned Nazis to be not war criminals but rather victims of an illegitimate justice system. The issue grew into a major point of contention after West Germany elected its first chancellor in 1949, at a time when America, uneasy about Soviet plans in Europe, was working to rebuild its defeated foe as a loyal and remilitarized ally.

Cold War realities quickly worked to undo the accomplishments of the war crimes prosecutors.

In 1951, following a review of the sentences, the U.S. High Commissioner for Germany released one-third of the Nuremberg convicts and commuted all but five death sentences. By the end of the year, every one of the Nazis that Kempner had put behind bars in Case 11 had been released. Though the reductions were announced as a show of clemency, Germans heard a different message: The Americans were finally acknowledging that the trials had been unjust. Kempner lashed out at the decision. "Today I want to go on record with a warning that the premature opening of the Landsberg gates will loose against society totalitarian subversive forces that endanger the free world."

His warning went unheeded. American leaders gave in to political pragmatism, and by 1958 nearly all of the war criminals had been freed.

•   •   •

Kempner's fight was far from over. He had spent four years immersed in the documentary evidence of the Nazi crimes, and he knew that even after trials conducted under the klieg lights of the international press, the world still did not know the full story.

Angry about revisionist histories as the survivors of the Third Reich tried to reclaim the story of Germany under the Nazis, he took to the press to fight back. "With more or less outspoken nostalgia," Kempner wrote in the *New York Herald Tribune*, "many political writers in Germany are telling their people that Germany would have been fine if Der Führer had not gotten a little out of hand." He would have none of it. He lamented the angelic photos of Hitler in the right-wing press, the militaristic suggestions that the generals could have saved Germany from ignominy if Hitler hadn't meddled in battlefield affairs, the whitewashing efforts of the Nazi diplomats.

He called for the publication, in Germany, of the facts that had come out in Nuremberg. "This is the only way to combat the systematic poisoning of the German mind going on under our very eyes in the infant German Republic."

Not long before writing those words, however, the prosecutor had done something that ran counter to that spirit of openness. Kempner had taken important original captured German documents home with him after Nuremberg—and if any copies existed, nobody knew where they were anymore.

In his role as a prosecutor, Kempner had the power to request any documents that he wanted for the preparation of his case. On more than one occasion, questions were raised about his handling of the papers. On September 11, 1946, the chief of the Document Division wrote in a memo that Kempner's office had borrowed five documents and not returned them. "I might add that this is not by any means the first occasion on which this Division has had considerable trouble in inducing Dr. Kempner to return Library Books and documents."

In 1947, Kempner earned notoriety among the American prosecution team for his handling of the single most famous surviving document about the Holocaust. Not long after returning to Nuremberg for the second round of trials, Kempner set his staff to poring over the records of the German Foreign Office, which had been salvaged from their hiding place in the Harz Mountains and brought to Berlin. One day, an aide came across a fifteen-page document. "The following persons," it began, "took part in the discussion about the final solution of the Jewish question, which took place in Berlin, am Grossen Wannsee No. 56/58 on 20 January 1942." This was the Wannsee Protocol, which described a meeting led by Reinhard Heydrich, chief of Himmler's Reich Security Main Office, to discuss the "evacuation" of the Jews of Europe.

A few months after the document's discovery, one of the American prosecutors, Benjamin Ferencz, looked up from his desk to see Charles LaFollette storming into his office. "I'm going to kill the son of a bitch!" he yelled. LaFollette was prosecuting another of the later Nuremberg trials, this one against Nazi judges and lawyers. He had heard about the Wannsee Protocol, but Kempner would not hand it over. There was competition among the many prosecutors at Nuremberg, and Kempner presumably wanted to unveil the explosive document at the trial he was preparing to lead.

Ferencz walked over to Kempner's office to intervene. Kempner denied that he was withholding anything. Ferencz kept after him. Finally, after a bit more prodding, Kempner opened a bottom drawer in his desk and asked innocently, "Could this be it?"

LaFollette instantly realized how important the document was to his case: The Reich Ministry of Justice had sent a representative to this crucial meeting. Immediately, LaFollette stormed off to report the incident to Telford Taylor, the chief prosecutor of the trials, and demand that he "fire the bastard!" Ferencz followed behind and took up Kempner's defense. He told Taylor that the Ministries case would surely fall apart if Kempner were banished from Nuremberg, and besides, Kempner had only inadvertently kept the document to himself.

"Which nobody believed," Ferencz wrote years later in a letter to Kempner. In any event, Taylor sided with his Ministries prosecutor.

Kempner was not the only person in Nuremberg filing away original Nazi papers for his own private use. Since the end of the war, the captured documents had been shipped among military document centers, flown to Paris and London and Washington to be studied by intelligence units, taken to Nuremberg for the war crimes trials. As the files zipped across Europe, souvenir hunters found plenty of opportunities to steal something on Nazi letterhead signed by someone important under the ubiquitous party sign-off: "*Heil Hitler!*" Those responsible for the safekeeping of the documents worried in particular about the prosecution staff in Nuremberg. They feared that those who requested papers were "more influenced by private journalistic instincts than by a desire to further the cause of justice," as one army officer put it in a memo. Another observer concluded that the prosecution's Document Division at Nuremberg was doing little to keep track of the flow of records.

One key document that vanished was a memorandum by Hitler's military adjutant, Friedrich Hossbach, showing that the Führer was already plotting the conquest of Europe in 1937; prosecutors had to rely on a notarized copy during the trial. Asked about the memo by a historian overseeing the publication of captured German documents after the war, Kempner recalled seeing it and suggested that "some souvenir-hunter may have taken the original." By September 1946, administrators at one of the military document centers had stopped lending originals to the prosecution teams in Nuremberg, fearing they would never get back the one thousand pieces of evidence they had already loaned out.

Throughout the trials, the Palace of Justice in Nuremberg was awash in paper. A survey completed in April 1948 found more than sixty-four thousand cubic feet of "administrative files, press negatives and releases, a film library, courtroom recording tapes, interrogation report tapes, library books and other publications, original documents, photostats, copies of documents, document books, trial briefs, prisoner files, interrogation files, summaries of interrogation files, transcripts of all courts and staff evidence analysis."

There was so much there that officials worried about original documents being unwittingly tossed in the trash. It was, as Kempner wrote later in his memoir, "a terrible mess"—and he took advantage of the chaos.

He said he feared that potentially explosive documents would not be properly archived, so he took it upon himself to make sure they were put to good use. He acknowledged in his memoir that if some "interested and clever" researcher approached him for important documents during the trials, he might simply lay the files on his office couch and walk out the door, saying, "I don't want to know anything."

Better to have a "valuable historical asset" in the hands of a trusted associate who would report on its contents, he thought, than to leave it in the hands of government bureaucrats who may or may not let it be destroyed.

All of the original seized German documents were supposed to be returned to military document centers after the trials, but Kempner wanted to use the documents he had collected to write articles and books about the Nazi era. On April 8, 1949, a few days before the verdicts were handed down in the Ministries Trial, the prosecutor secured a one-paragraph letter from Fred Niebergall, director of the Document Division for the prosecution team: "The undersigned authorizes Dr. Robert M. W. Kempner, Deputy Chief of Counsel and Chief Prosecutor, Political Ministries Division, to remove and retain material

of an unclassified nature pertaining to the war crimes trials at
Nürnberg, Germany, for purposes of research, writing, lecturing and study." It was an unusual memo. Later, one lawyer who
worked in military intelligence had serious doubts that a man in
Niebergall's position would have signed it.

The very same day, Kempner mailed a letter to the E. P. Dutton publishing house, in New York, with a synopsis for a book
based on his Nuremberg interrogations and the documents of the
German Foreign Office, tentatively titled "Hitler and His Diplomats." He had pitched the book in January, and an editor at Dutton expressed interest and asked for more details.

It would emerge later that the book was only one of the publishing ideas Kempner had in 1949.

Decades later in his memoirs, Kempner would explain his reasoning for taking documents from Nuremberg. "I knew one
thing. If I ever wanted to write about something and had to contact archives, although I would have received nice replies, they
would be unable to find some of the material. But I had my documents."

As a justification, it fell far short. What Kempner really wanted
was an important advantage over other writers documenting the
Nazi era: exclusivity.

With his permission slip in hand, Kempner had his Nuremberg
papers packed up and—along with whatever else he had accumulated during his time as a Nazi prosecutor—shipped across the
Atlantic to his home outside Philadelphia. The delivery arrived at
the Lansdowne station of the Pennsylvania Railroad on November 4, 1949: twenty-nine boxes weighing more than eight thousand pounds.

"Hitler and His Diplomats" never came together. It seems that
Kempner got sidetracked. Instead, he found other ways to seek justice for the wrongs of the Third Reich. He opened up a law office
in Frankfurt and, among other legal work, began taking on cases of

Nazi victims suing for restitution. He represented Erich Maria Remarque, whose bestselling First World War novel *All Quiet on the Western Front* was burned and banned by the Nazis. He represented Emil Gumbel, a prominent mathematics professor at the University of Heidelberg who was forced out of his job because of his pacifist views. He represented Jews and Catholics and members of the Resistance. It grew into a lucrative line of work.

A decade after Nuremberg ended, prosecution of Nazi war criminals began anew. A 1958 trial in West Germany brought renewed attention to atrocities Germans believed they had left in the past. Ten Nazis were convicted of murdering more than five thousand Lithuanian Jews during the war, a case that spurred German justice ministers—alarmed that many perpetrators had escaped punishment after the war—to found a Central Office for the Investigation of Nazi Crimes in Ludwigsburg.

At the same time, prosecutors outside Germany brought high-profile cases to trial. In 1961, Kempner returned to the international limelight when he flew to Jerusalem to testify in the trial of Adolf Eichmann, the man who had managed the deportation of the Jews from all over Europe. In a number of high-profile trials later in the decade, Kempner appeared as attorney for relatives of the victims. He represented the father of Anne Frank and the sister of Carmelite nun Edith Stein in a case against three SS officers charged in the extermination of thousands of Dutch Jews. He represented the widow of a pacifist journalist murdered by a Nazi storm trooper in 1933. He spoke for thirty thousand Berlin Jews in the trial of a Gestapo commander, Otto Bovensiepen, who orchestrated their deportation to the East.

Kempner capitalized on the renewed attention to Nazi crimes by writing a flurry of books about those and other prominent cases for German audiences. He also published excerpts of his Nuremberg interrogations and, in 1983, his memoirs, *Ankläger einer Epoche*, or *Prosecutor of an Era*. Although Kempner had become a naturalized American in 1945, his books were not published in English, and he would always be better known in the land of his birth.

Four decades after Nuremberg, he was still at the ramparts. When Deutsche Bank bought the Flick industrial conglomerate, Kempner successfully lobbied the company to pay more than $2 million in reparations to thirteen hundred Jews who worked as slave laborers in gunpowder factories for a Flick subsidiary during the war.

The battle against the Nazis came to define Kempner. He steadfastly refused to let the world forget what the perpetrators had done. If he was told that a former Nazi did not seem like such a bad person, he would open his files to prove otherwise.

"Literally thousands of murderers still are walking the streets of Germany and the world," he told a reporter once. "How many Nazi criminals are still free? Judge for yourself." Even with all the trials after the war, only a few thousand Germans were tried for murder. "Can you tell me how some two thousand people managed to murder six to eight million? It is mathematically impossible."

Thirty, forty, fifty years after the Nazi era, he refused to let it go. It was a fight he would wage until the very end of his life.

Even as Kempner shuttled between the United States and Europe maintaining his international legal affairs, he managed a complicated home life. Though his law firm was in Frankfurt, he had become a naturalized U.S. citizen, and his primary home was still in Lansdowne, Pennsylvania, where he had settled during the war. There, he lived with his second wife, Ruth, a social worker and writer; his elderly mother-in-law, Marie-Luise Hahn; his secretary, Margot Lipton; and, during the 1950s, a son, André.

The Kempners had a secret: The boy's mother was not Ruth Kempner—as they told everyone—but Margot Lipton. Robert Kempner and the secretary had carried on an affair in 1938.

André was raised to believe that he was the Kempners' adopted son. On school records, Ruth Kempner was listed as the boy's mother. It was just simpler that way. "Simpler," Lipton said, "for Dr. Kempner." Neither André nor his older brother—Lucian, Kempner's son by his first wife—would learn the truth until many years later. Not that they didn't have suspicions. At André's wedding in Sweden, everyone marveled that Lipton and the groom looked so much alike.

The Kempner sons were too respectful to ask questions. "I just accepted what my father said," Lucian explained, "and beyond that it was not my business."

Whatever he knew, André grew up to worship his father. After he moved to Sweden with his wife to run a farm at age twenty-nine, he sent his family regular letters in meticulous script. "I just want to thank you Father for being the most wonderful Dad to all of us," he wrote after Kempner and Lipton came to visit one year. "It is never easy to tell you when I am with you, but I hope you will never underestimate the love and understanding I have for you and your work."

Beginning in the 1970s, Kempner lived in Europe full-time, splitting his time between Frankfurt, Germany, and Locarno, Switzerland. He had a heart attack in 1975—it came not long after a band of neo-Nazis protested outside his law office—and he grew too frail to travel overseas. Ruth Kempner and Lipton, still living in Pennsylvania, visited for weeks at a time, but otherwise the lawyer came to rely on yet another devoted woman.

Jane Lester was an American raised in Brockport, New York, sixty miles east of Niagara Falls. In 1937, she followed a classmate to Germany, where she taught English to those hoping to emigrate. Years later, she admitted her naïveté. She had no idea what Hitler was doing to his enemies. On Kristallnacht, when the Nazis rampaged across Germany, destroying synagogues and Jewish shops and homes in 1938, she slept soundly. The next day, she couldn't understand why the students at the language school had not shown up. She left Germany, worked in a brokerage in Buffalo, then became a typist in Washington—"a government girl," as she put it—for the Office of Strategic Services.

One day in 1945, Lester read in the *Washington Post* that translators would be needed for the war crimes trials in Nuremberg, and she went to the Pentagon to apply for a job. Soon she was headed back to Germany.

She knew Kempner by reputation; she saw him dining at the Grand Hotel in Nuremberg, where practically everyone involved with the trials retired each night. She finally met him in 1947, when he was recruiting staff for the later trials. She became his aide and often tagged along during interrogations, which seemed to alarm defendants. "They couldn't quite figure me out," she said. "The rumor had gone around that I was a psychologist." She also had the honor of being the person who translated the Wannsee Protocol into English for the American prosecutors.

After the war, she worked for U.S. military intelligence at Camp King, in Oberursel, outside Frankfurt. But she moonlighted with Kempner, who needed help translating correspondence and managing his practice. It grew into a partnership that would last for the next four decades.

"The last twenty years of his life, I was never separated, day or night, from Robert Kempner," she said. "I was his nurse, his chauffeur, his secretary." She did not say it, but she, too, had been his mistress.

Kempner and the three women in his life stayed close till the end. As Lucian put it years later: "It was all a big happy family."

Kempner's wife, Ruth, died in 1982. Toward the end of his life, he lived in a hotel outside Frankfurt, where he and Lester slept in adjoining rooms with the door open. That way she would be close if anything happened to Kempner in the middle of the night. Robert and Lucian Kempner spoke almost every day, and since the father couldn't hear well on the phone, Lester would listen along and repeat whatever he'd missed.

Kempner died on August 15, 1993, at the age of ninety-three. That week, Lipton had traveled from Pennsylvania to Germany to be with him.

"He died in my arms," Lester said. "We sat there, one on each side of him in his death room." When the doctor arrived and declared him dead, "we were in a terrible state of horror, grief, and disbelief."

The women called Lucian, who drove up from Munich with his wife and took charge of affairs.

It would not be simple. In a lifetime of research and writing and travel, Kempner had kept everything. Paintings, furniture, thousands of books, and piles of paper filled the properties he owned in Frankfurt and in Lansdowne, Pennsylvania, a Philadelphia suburb. He kept endless files of personal, professional, and legal documents: old passports, address books, childhood lesson journals, used train tickets, utility bills, ancient letters, photographs.

Lester found Kempner's will tucked away in a bag in her hotel room. It was one page, handwritten in thick black marker, barely legible. According to the document, Kempner had left everything to his two sons, Lucian and André.

But there was a catch.

Robert Kempner alongside Jane Lester, his aide and translator, during the 1948–49 Ministries Trial in Nuremberg. *(ullstein bild/ullstein bild via Getty Images)*

2

―

"Everything Gone"

Two years after Kempner's death, his loyal aide Jane Lester was still trying to figure out a way to keep his legacy alive. His status as a prominent former Nuremberg prosecutor gave Kempner cachet in postwar Germany. He was a regular presence in the press and the subject of television programs about the trials. But he was virtually unknown in the United States. Lester wanted to change that.

She decided to call a man in Lewiston, New York, named Herbert Richardson, an ordained minister and former theology professor who ran a small academic publishing company, the Edwin Mellen Press. Critics dismissed Mellen as a "quasi–vanity press cunningly disguised as an academic publishing house," a slight that Richardson disputed in an unsuccessful $15 million libel lawsuit against the magazine *Lingua Franca*. It's possible Lester had found Richardson's name somewhere in Kempner's files. In 1981, Kempner had tried to interest American publishers in his backlist, and the Mellen Press was among the publishers he contacted. Richardson explained that he ran a small outfit and could not produce a commercial edition.

"The problem is, however, that I think your books SHOULD be published in English and distributed in North America," Richardson wrote in April 1982. "This is such important information and it is tragic if it doesn't get out. But what can I do??? I am a small publisher and I can't do what I can't do."

Thirteen years later, when Lester called him, Richardson was still interested. Lester translated a portion of Kempner's memoir, and the Mellen Press published it in 1996 in conjunction with the fiftieth anniversary of the end of the first Nuremberg trial.

In March 1996, Richardson attended a reunion of Nuremberg prosecutors in Washington, D.C., where he approached a senior historian at the United States Holocaust Memorial Museum and asked about donating "a small quantity" of Kempner's papers. The documents were still in the possession of his two former assistants, Lester in Germany and Lipton in Pennsylvania. At the time, both women were in their eighties, and still very close to each other.

Two days later, the historian arranged an appointment for Richardson, Lester, and Lipton with the museum's chief archivist, Henry Mayer. Lester did most of the talking, describing Kempner's importance and the inestimable value of the papers he'd left behind. But the conversations didn't go anywhere. Mayer had arrived at the museum only two years earlier, and he was dealing with a flood of new material. He had more than enough work to do, and nothing he heard that day about this collection of papers made it sound like a high priority.

Richardson soon had another idea: He would open a facility of his own to house the papers. On September 21, 1996, he led an elaborate ceremony to mark the opening of a new Robert Kempner Collegium in Lewiston, a border town upriver from Niagara Falls. Wearing a black gown and academic vestments, he led an inaugural church service at which he sang Kempner's praises before a small group of the late lawyer's friends and supporters, including Lester and her extended family. Kempner was "one of the most courageous battlers against a state which claimed itself to be lawful but was lawless," Richardson said from the pulpit, his voice rising and falling through the half-filled church. The windows were open to let in the early autumn cool. "Robert Kempner dedicated his life to the service of justice, and sought to expose and to oppose those laws and those states that were not lawful but illegal, a state that proclaimed laws that were criminal, a state that in the name of justice committed the most heinous injustices in history." The Kempner Collegium would be dedicated to the idea that morality supersedes the law.

Tears welling up in his eyes, Richardson recalled how he had come to be part of Kempner's posthumous circle of friends. He was just another weary old man, he said, whiling away his sixties. Then Lester called, seeking his help publishing Kempner's books in English, and suddenly he was shocked out of his malaise. "A year later," Richardson told the audience, "having been carried by Jane into new projects and new visions, I have to say, she is the fountain of youth!" Then he stepped down to hand her a framed commendation. "The roving imagination and abundant energy of Jane Lester are the spiritual arms of this noble knight who is questing for the grail, risking dangers, overreaching boundaries, and embracing not only the fruits but also the nettles of life," it read. Richardson called her a "lifelong warrior for justice."

Then the visitors toured the Mellen Press, and between bites at a luncheon, Lester signed copies of the translated Kempner memoir for the guests. Afterward, the group returned to the church for a dramatic reading of some passages by an actor with an English lilt.

Lipton cut the ribbon at a little white house where a large sign had been erected out front to announce the presence of the new institution.

But inside, the shelves were bare.

The problem was that while the women had physical custody of the papers, Robert Kempner's two sons had legal custody. The Kempner sons had not yet decided what to do with the Lansdowne documents, but in 1995, they negotiated with Germany's national archives, the Bundesarchiv, to donate the files from Kempner's law office in Frankfurt. When, according to Lucian Kempner, Richardson tried to involve himself in the deal, their attorney sent him a cease-and-desist letter.

Undeterred, Richardson wrote Lucian Kempner with an offer two and a half months after opening the Robert Kempner Collegium. His new center would dedicate itself to "the collection, cataloging, publication, and study of Robert Kempner's library and papers." In exchange, Lucian would receive $20,000 up front, royalties from the republication of his father's books, and an honorary degree from Richardson's institution. "May I come to Munich in January to discuss these proposals with you?"

Lucian declined the offer.

In May 1997, Lester again called the Holocaust Museum about the Kempner Papers. This time, the museum's chief archivist, Henry Mayer, was ready to talk.

Mayer's grandfather, Heinrich Meier, a cattle farmer in Oberlustadt, Germany, had been forced out of his occupation by the Nazis. Farmers were pressured to boycott Jews from whom they had bought livestock for generations. Someone caught buying from a Jewish dealer would receive only a fraction of the usual amount from the government cooperative for their milk. Demonstrators would block attempts by Jews to sell at the marketplace. Eventually, insurance companies would not offer Jews the insurance they needed by law for their cattle. Fed up, Heinrich Meier boarded the luxury liner SS *Washington* in 1937 with his daughter and his son and left for New York. Relatives had arrived earlier, and he moved onto the same block in Flatbush. The split was irrevocable: When he arrived, he changed the spelling of his surname so it would no longer be pronounced the German way, *MY-er*, but instead *MAY-er.*

The Mayers never spoke of the Holocaust. Henry Mayer was born five years after the Second World War ended, and he learned very quickly that asking about what had happened to the Jews in the Third Reich was strictly verboten. "It was always something that you didn't bring up," he said. "You didn't talk about it."

Henry Mayer studied American history at the University of Chicago and got his master's at Wisconsin. On track to become a professor, he failed the preliminary exam for the Ph.D. program, and as he was studying for a second attempt, he decided he didn't want to be a professor after all. He dropped out of the program, moved to Washington, D.C., and in time found a job at the National Archives. The work there was engaging, but eventually it got to the point where his entire life seemed to be inventorying material and transferring records from one place to another, so when a job was offered at the newly opened Holocaust museum in 1994, he jumped at the chance.

Millions of visitors would pass through the Holocaust museum over the coming years, and the idea was that when they left, they would go out in the world "to confront hatred, prevent genocide, and promote human dignity." Before taking the elevator into the main exhibition, tour-goers were given cards describing an individual victim of Nazi persecution. The long walk through the galleries took them past images of the massacres, into a railcar of the type that transported Jews to their deaths, beneath a sign reading ARBEIT MACHT FREI—"Work sets you free"—like the one above the entrance to Auschwitz, and finally into a room filled with four thousand shoes left behind by victims of the gas chambers at Majdanek, in Poland. The museum sought to deliver a lesson in history, but also to spark questions of personal accountability: What would you have done? What *will* you do to stop the spread of hatred today?

The collection went far beyond what was exhibited in the

galleries, however. The museum held an extensive archive of materials to help researchers learn about and tell the story of the Holocaust: documents, photographs, archival recordings, oral histories, and unique artifacts.

As the son and grandson of German Jews forced out of Nazi Germany, Henry Mayer was intrinsically interested in the museum's mission. But it was not until he began working there that he discovered the full scope of his family's history.

Mayer's ancestors, named Meier and Frank, had lived for generations in and around Karlsruhe, along the Rhine River in southwestern Germany. In the 1930s, some members of the extended family fled to the United States. But many did not escape. They were caught in a Nazi dragnet in October 1940, when the Gestapo rounded up more than seventy-six hundred Jewish men, women, and children from all over the region and expelled them across the border.

The transports did not go to the east—the standard deportation route of German Jews in later years—but to the west, where they became the responsibility of the puppet Vichy regime established in unoccupied southern France after the Nazis seized the north earlier that year. The Germans had deported the Jews without warning Vichy; the French reacted by sending the trains on to internment camps, including one thrown up on the swampy outskirts of a tiny commune called Gurs, in the foothills of the Pyrenees.

The trains carrying the Jews stopped at the nearest rail station, in Oloron-Sainte-Marie, and everyone was piled into open trucks. Rain poured down in icy torrents as they rode the last stretch of their long, bitter journey. Eight hundred miles from their homes, the detainees were directed—wet, freezing, shell-shocked—to desolate rows of ramshackle barracks. Their luggage was left piled in the mud.

Social workers who visited the French-run camp as winter set in found an "unbreathable atmosphere of human hopelessness" and "an intense desire to die" among the elderly prisoners—forty percent of the deportees were sixty and older. Inside rows of barbed wire watched over by armed guards, the windowless wooden sheds were packed with people. Their barracks had no heat, no running water, no furniture. Lice, rats, roaches, and disease proliferated. "It rained and rained," wrote a prisoner. "The earth was a morass; one could slip and sink into the mud." The prisoners shared high boots for navigating the muck to go to the primitive toilets—buckets beneath open-air stands with no doors. Drifting over everything, one historian would write, was "the smell of clay mixed with the stench of urine." Prisoners were fed a diet of ersatz coffee, thin soup, and bread. There was not enough drinking water to go around, and the hunger was unrelenting. "It would take a master poet like Rimbaud," wrote a Jewish academic imprisoned at Gurs, "to render all the nuances of misery afflicting thousands upon thousands of people, men and women of all ages."

Heinrich Meier's cousins Elise and Salomon Frank did not survive to the end of 1940 in the camp; they died during the coldest winter in years.

Heinrich's brother and sister-in-law, Emmanuel and Wilhelmina Meier, and his cousin Martha Mayer spent nearly two years in the French internment camps before their time came. In August 1942, they were shipped north by rail to Drancy, a Paris suburb, where whatever possessions they still had were taken away. At daybreak on August 14, buses took Emmanuel and Wilhelmina to the train station, where guards wielding machine guns forced them into cattle cars for the journey east to "an unknown destination." Martha's transport left three days later. They found themselves among the sick and the elderly and masses of young orphans, some of them only two, three, and four years old.

After journeys of a few days, Heinrich's relatives arrived at their final destination, 850 miles east in occupied Poland: Auschwitz.

A lifetime away at the Holocaust museum, Mayer helped build, organize, and catalog a collection of more than seventy million pages. No acquisition would be as large or as complicated—or as historic, ultimately—as the Kempner Papers.

After Lester called in 1997, Mayer wrote to Lucian and André Kempner. They replied enthusiastically, and soon Lucian took charge of the matter. He believed the Holocaust museum would be the perfect place for his father's papers. "His life was the fight against Nazism." Lucian explained that the documents in question were in Lansdowne, and that Margot could arrange for them to inventory them.

As Mayer and a team of scholars drove up from Washington in August 1997, it seemed as if everything would go smoothly.

They arrived at a six-bedroom house the Kempners had bought during the war. It was at the bottom of a hill on a bend of Darby Creek. Nobody answered the door at the appointed hour. A few minutes later, Lipton returned from a walk. When Mayer introduced himself, she seemed surprised. "Who?" Her memory jogged, she led them inside and showed them where they could find the material.

It was everywhere: in Kempner's office to the left, in the room to the right, in the sunporch, in two rooms at the top of the stairs, in the basement. One of the rooms was entirely unlit, and Lipton had to fetch lightbulbs.

One of the men had been to the house before. Jonathan Bush was a lawyer and expert on war crimes trials whose résumé included stints as staff prosecutor with the Justice Department's Nazi-hunting Office of Special Investigations and general counsel for the Holocaust museum. Years earlier as a twentysomething scholar studying Holocaust reparations, Bush had come to interview Kempner. The place hadn't changed much in the years since. "It was a complete mess," he said. "I'd never seen so many boxes crammed into one house." In each room Lipton showed them, the boxes reached from floor to ceiling. Every surface was covered with files.

The four men were overwhelmed. "Now what do we do?" Mayer recalled thinking. If you had told Bush there were two thousand boxes in the house, he would not have doubted it. "Holy shit!" he thought. "How are we ever going to figure it out?"

They broke into two teams and started cataloging. They only had time enough to look over a small sampling of material to see whether Kempner had kept anything worth saving or not. In the basement they found five bookcases crowded with old volumes, including foreign-language dictionaries, Nuremberg materials, and law books dating to pre-Nazi years. Four tables held nearly thirty boxes of records on Kempner's personal finances and restitution work. In the office filing cabinets, they found file after unorganized file of letters and reports. The room was so crammed with furniture and boxes that they couldn't reach the papers contained in the glass-enclosed bookcase.

The folders made no sense; they were neither chronologically nor topically arranged. The men had to move carpentry tools, vitamin bottles, and lotions to get to the newspaper clips and bills and photographs and travel guides. They had to stand on the boxes below to reach the ones at the top. They couldn't possibly see everything that was there, Bush said. "Most boxes were behind two other rows of boxes under six other boxes."

What they did see was undeniably interesting, and historically important. Bush opened one box and was surprised to see documents showing that Kempner, bane of the Nazi war criminals, had intervened in a case on behalf of Göring's widow, Emmy; she believed she should receive her husband's government pension. Bush spotted copies of letters to and from J. Edgar Hoover. He was particularly amazed by the breadth of Kempner's papers on the war crimes trials. Copies of this material had been donated to major libraries, but it took up so much space that even institutions had gotten rid of the stuff. Kempner's archive was practically complete, Bush said. "He had *everything*."

The collection, Mayer wrote in his report after the visit, was "of enormous historical value to the study of the Holocaust." It was also in "extreme distress." Mold had colonized some of the

papers in the porch and the basement. He recommended immediately moving the papers to an interim storage area, where they
could be treated for insect infestations and reboxed.

He shared his report with Lucian, who then passed it along to
Lester and Lipton. Then the trouble started. Lipton didn't want to
part with anything.

This was where the catch in Kempner's will came into play. To
ensure that Lipton would be cared for after his death, Kempner
had stipulated that she be permitted to stay in the Lansdowne
house—along with its contents—at the expense of his estate.
Lucian and André wanted to honor that request, but they also
wanted to remove the historically important documents Kempner
had left in Lansdowne.

Not long after Mayer inventoried the papers at the house, a
letter arrived from Lipton: She was not going to give up the papers
without a fight.

"You are apparently unaware of my legal rights in this matter,"
the letter read. Kempner had given Lipton the right "to retain
possession of or to dispose of everything in 112 Lansdowne Court."
She had no problem with the museum archiving Kempner's
papers—"eventually." But she did not want to be left in a half-
empty house. "You may not appreciate the fact that, after retirement, an older person often finds a certain comfort in being
surrounded by the papers, books, photographs and artifacts which
embody their life's work," the letter read. Moreover, it was insen-
sitive of Mayer, she wrote, not to ask her whether she "would
mind your sending a truck and carting away most of the contents
of my home, where I have lived for over 50 years and where I
intend to go on living for another 30." She apparently planned to
live well past one hundred.

Lipton told Mayer she would take Lucian and the museum to
court if they proceeded with their plans. "I expect to receive, by
return mail, your apology for your failure to discuss these matters
with me and your solemn promise that you will never again pro-

pose to enter and remove from my home any of its contents without my written invitation and consent."

According to Lucian, Lipton was with Richardson and Lester in Germany when her letter was drafted, and museum officials wondered later whether the letter had actually been written by Richardson himself.

Around the same time that the dispatch arrived at the Holocaust museum, Lucian received a letter from Lipton's attorney. She would drop her objections to the removal of the Kempner Papers if he gave Lipton the Lansdowne house and everything else inside. Owning the house would have given her the option to sell it, keep the proceeds, and move elsewhere. Again, Lucian declined.

At the end of 1997, Mayer replied to Lester. "It is our intention to ensure that Dr. Kempner's intellectual legacy is preserved for future generations of scholars in an institution dedicated to the ideals for which he toiled so long and so hard." He apologized for not keeping her in the loop but noted that Lucian had asked him not to involve others in the negotiations. He promised to work with her to ensure that her own papers and possessions were not removed along with Kempner's. "We have no intention to steal, either inadvertently or intentionally, anything belonging to you."

But not wanting to stumble into litigation, the museum stood down until Lucian Kempner and Margot Lipton could work out their differences.

The wild card in the whole affair was Herbert Richardson. In his years as a teacher, students said he could be explosively angry and intimidating. He could also be a charismatic speaker, deeply captivating and full of passion. Watching Richardson hold forth, one of his students said she could understand how Adolf Hitler won over the masses.

When Richardson was told this, he sighed.

"Some compare me with Hitler, some compare me with God," he said. "How am I to reply to that?"

Richardson got his doctorate in theology from Harvard Divinity School in 1963, and taught there for five years. Though he was a Presbyterian minister, he went to work at a Catholic institution, the University of St. Michael's College, in Toronto, where he won tenure. His scholarship ran the gamut. Richardson wrote about Saint Anselm of Canterbury, abortion, the Baby M surrogate case, Joan of Arc, gays in the military. His book *Nun, Witch, Playmate,* published by Harper & Row in 1971, examined the "Americanization of sex."

He started his academic press, which was independent of the university, in 1972. The original idea was to publish dissertations of students at St. Michael's, but it soon grew into a house for scholars anywhere who could not get their work published. Richardson called his outfit a "press of last resort." In 1979, he moved it out of his Toronto basement and eighty miles south, into a building in Lewiston. The press grew slowly, eventually turning a profit and publishing several hundred titles a year on a wide range of subjects. Richardson said editions landed in research libraries all over the world, including his alma mater, Harvard.

He brooked controversy in the 1980s when he defended the Unification Church of the Reverend Sun Myung Moon and the Church of Scientology against charges that they were not new religions but instead cults.

Then, in 1991, a classroom incident threatened to upend his academic career. One day, he began shouting at his students— they were not circling their desks in an orderly enough manner— then got into a noisy argument with his teaching assistant and fired the man on the spot. Students reported the incident, university officials began monitoring Richardson's classes, and the following year he was asked to take early retirement. "Richardson's behavior," the chair of the religious studies department wrote at the time, "was a time bomb waiting to explode."

The professor refused to step aside and instead asked for a medical leave of absence. For years he had had chest pains, and he thought it was time to go to cardiac rehab at Duke University. If he continued teaching, he told friends, "I'd be dead by February." He went to Durham, but checked out of the program after only a couple of weeks—it was too expensive, he said later—and instead traveled around North America and Europe. He went to Wales, to an international outpost of the Mellen Press; to Kansas, where his father was buried; and to Southern California, where he was thinking of retiring in the desert community of Borrego Springs. He went to the Turks and Caicos Islands, where he set about establishing a Mellen University, which soon advertised academic degrees on the basis of dissertations and "life experiences" for $995. "Life is a school," Richardson said. "When you are living, you are learning."

Word got back to St. Michael's of his activities during his journeys, and when he returned, the university charged him with gross misconduct. Because he had tenure and could not be fired outright, the matter went to a highly unusual public tribunal. University officials leveled a series of charges against Richardson, from the picayune to the serious. In the end, the main allegations were that he had abused his medical leave and had misrepresented to university officials how much time he was spending at the Edwin Mellen Press.

Richardson testified before the tribunal for five days. "This public humiliation has been the most extraordinary embarrassment to me and my family," he said. "It has led to my financial ruin and my professional disgrace." He cast himself as a victim of bullying by academic colleagues. When he learned of the investigation, he said, he fell into a deep depression. "Everything on which I'd built my life for fifty years was under attack, and I could feel my being breaking under the load." He lost the case and was fired in October 1994. In its findings, the tribunal reported that it didn't believe Richardson's testimony. "His quick wit, eloquence, and mercurial personality enable him to give a persuasive gloss to self-serving half truths."

A year after this, the most tumultuous episode of his life, Herbert Richardson met Jane Lester.

In August 1998—a year after Mayer and the other museum officials inventoried Kempner's papers at the Lansdowne house—Lipton took the Kempner heirs to court over an undeveloped thirty-six-acre piece of real estate she had purchased with Ruth and Robert Kempner in 1958. After Kempner's death, she had handed it over to Lucian and André to sell, and they agreed to give her a share of the proceeds. But in 1997, when the brothers signed a contract to sell the property for $450,000, she sued, contending that she had been fraudulently misled by the Kempners' attorney and that she should receive all of the money from the sale.

Court papers show that Lucian Kempner believed Herbert Richardson had "undue influence" over Lipton and was behind the legal maneuvering. Lucian's lawyer, Kevin Gibson, told the court that Lipton had given Richardson power of attorney over her affairs, and she had been moved out of the Lansdowne home and into an adult care facility called the Lockport Presbyterian Home, twenty miles from Richardson's U.S. office in upstate New York. Gibson asked the judge to throw out Lipton's lawsuit and give Kempner's heirs permission to enter the house and remove Kempner's possessions.

At the Holocaust museum, Mayer, increasingly impatient, had been watching the messy legal proceedings from afar when, on June 23, 1999, there was a breakthrough. Gibson finally had a chance to depose Lipton. She had just turned eighty-five, and the years had taken their toll. "I don't really know where I live right now," she admitted. Asked how she knew Richardson, she replied, "I don't remember." Gibson showed her a $13,000 check drawn from the Kempner estate bank account. It appeared that Lipton had signed Lucian's name, claiming she had power of attorney. Lipton testified that she knew nothing of the withdrawal.

Gibson repeatedly asked Lipton whether she had any objections to the removal and safekeeping of Kempner's papers from the Lansdowne house, and she said she did not. "I would prefer this to be done after my death," Lipton said, "but if it has to be done now, I suppose it could be done." She also said she had no plans to return to the house, and "no reservation" to its sale. Eventually, Lipton would settle her real estate lawsuit against the Kempner heirs.

The lawyer immediately contacted the museum, which decided to move quickly. "Not only could Ms. Lipton change her mind," Mayer wrote to his colleagues, "but also the house is currently uninhabited and therefore the contents are in precarious condition." A week after Lipton's deposition, Mayer was back in Lansdowne. Gibson, the lawyer, met him there with a locksmith and a police officer to make sure that everything went smoothly.

The first thing they found when they walked inside was a revolver on a kitchen shelf. The second thing they discovered was that most of the papers they had seen two years earlier were now missing. "The house was completely empty," said Bush, the war crimes scholar who had helped Mayer inventory the house two years earlier. In the basement, bookshelves were swept clean. In Kempner's office, the filing cabinets were empty. Most of the documents on the second floor had likewise vanished. Walking through the house with their inventory from the 1997 visit, Mayer and the others marked "gone," "everything gone," and "all gone" on entry after entry. "Even the desk is gone," someone noted.

Gibson called detectives from the Lansdowne police to investigate while Bush and the others knocked on doors down the street. Neighbors reported seeing a moving truck in front of the house the week before.

Police interviewed the Kempners' longtime caretaker, Magnus O'Donnell—the family knew him as Nifty—and he told them that seven months earlier, Richardson had visited the house and, along with Lester and Lipton, sorted through the collection.

They'd packed up what they wanted, he said, and shipped the boxes to New York. Two dumpsters' worth of old clothes, furniture, and housewares were thrown away.

Investigators tracked Richardson down in Lewiston and discovered that the missing papers had been moved into the Robert Kempner Collegium, which was air-conditioned and locked. They told Richardson they were investigating how he had handled Lipton's finances and demanded that he turn the material over to the Holocaust museum. He readily agreed.

On August 3, accompanied by police, Mayer went to the collegium in Lewiston to sort through and pack up the Kempner Papers. An angry Jane Lester met them there with her attorney; Richardson was nowhere to be seen.

In 1997, Lester's phone call had restarted the museum's acquisition of the Kempner Papers. Two years later, she was outraged about how the matter had played out. Yes, they had removed the documents, she said, but only to safeguard them and ensure that the museum did not take things that did not belong to Kempner's estate.

Eventually, the delegation moved to the second floor to examine the collection. They agreed to painstakingly review each file to determine what constituted Kempner's papers and what belonged to Lester and Lipton.

It went slowly. Lester complained that the museum was invading her privacy. She told Mayer she wanted to remember his face, because one day she would write about what he was doing to her. Each time they came to a letter she had written to Kempner, she refused to part with it. There were many hundreds, dating from the 1960s through the 1980s: Lester, Lipton, and the Kempners had written to each other nearly every day when they were apart. Mayer argued that letters sent to Kempner should be considered part of his collection, and tried to keep everything he could.

All told, the Kempner collection was the largest written estate donated to the museum to date. The museum had gathered eighty-five boxes of Nuremberg files, 117 volumes of bound trial papers, sixty-eight boxes of Kempner's personal and professional papers, thirty-nine 78-rpm sound recordings, and nearly one thousand books and periodicals.

When they got the material to the museum's warehouse, north of Washington, and began studying the files in more detail, the archivists and historians started to discover Kempner's secret: For decades, his neglected house in suburban Philadelphia had been the hiding place of a large collection of original German documents—documents historians had never seen, because Kempner had taken them from Nuremberg and never returned them.

He had taken a 1944 war diary from a Waffen-SS unit in Hungary, dating to the period when six hundred thousand Jews were sent off to their deaths. He had taken a letter signed by Reinhard Heydrich, one of the architects of the Holocaust, asking Hitler where to send the cultural property seized from Austrian Jews. He had taken a document from September 1939 ordering the confiscation of all radios owned by Jews. He had taken a letter signed by Wilhelm Keitel, chief of the Supreme High Command of the German Armed Forces, from the prison in Nuremberg.

Kempner had notes for a speech Alfred delivered two days before the 1941 invasion of the Soviet Union. He had a few of Rosenberg's pencil drawings, including studies of a nude woman in repose. He had Rosenberg's personal *ahnentafel*, a family tree drawn up to prove that he had no Jewish relatives.

When they were done cataloging the collection, Mayer thought the museum had everything the Kempner heirs had donated. He thought that they had finally reached the end of the bizarre Kempner saga.

He was wrong.

Henry Mayer, senior adviser on archives at the U.S. Holocaust Memorial Museum, examines the Rosenberg diary. *(U.S. Holocaust Memorial Museum, courtesy of Miriam Lomaskin)*

3

"To Stare into the Mind
of a Dark Soul"

A few weeks after Mayer returned from his face-off with Jane
Lester in Lewiston, a noted Holocaust museum historian
named Jürgen Matthäus sent him a memo. He had good reason to
believe that something quite significant was hidden among the
cache of papers donated by Robert Kempner's heirs: Alfred
Rosenberg's diary.

In fact, the scholar wrote, he had found solid documentary
evidence in Kempner's papers: The prosecutor had admitted it
himself.

After its discovery in the palace vault, the diary made its way
to the offices of the Nuremberg prosecutors. It was not introduced into evidence during the trial, and in fact, when Rosenberg's lawyer asked to see it as he prepared his defense case, he was
told that it could not be found.

Seventy-five of the original diary pages made it to the National
Archives at the end of the Nuremberg trial, as well as copies of

another 116 pages. In the mid-1950s, a German historian named Hans-Günther Seraphim was preparing to publish them in an annotated edition when he looked over a piece Kempner had published in a German magazine called *Der Monat* in 1949 titled "The Fight Against the Church," in which Kempner reproduced a number of entries from the Rosenberg diary. Seraphim realized that the excerpts did not come from the pages in the archives, so he wrote Kempner to ask what other sections of the diary he had. The former prosecutor did not hide the truth. He said that he had about four hundred handwritten pages; he had planned to publish some of them, but, he told Seraphim, "I never got to it." Seraphim wanted Kempner to share his material so a full edition could be published. Kempner declined, but when he learned that Seraphim was going to publish an abridged edition, he suggested a footnote advising readers that Kempner had in his possession "very extensive additional materials."

Seraphim was either unaware that the document was government property or else unwilling to press the point.

Over the coming years, Kempner proceeded to quote from previously unknown entries in two of his published books. In one, he even wrote that the "secret diaries . . . are located in my own archive." But when other scholars approached him about seeing them, Kempner gave them only cagey replies.

For Henry Mayer, this was a shocking discovery. The diary was an irreplaceable document of monumental importance. Beyond the diary's inherent value as a historic artifact, scholars hoped that the missing pages held important insight about the final solution. Rosenberg and his aides had been involved in key discussions in 1941 and 1942 as the Nazis began to exterminate the Jews of Europe.

Fred Niebergall didn't have the right to give Kempner permission to borrow documents for his research, and even if he had, Kempner did not have the right to keep something like the Rosenberg diary forever.

Spurred by Matthäus's memo, Mayer did a systematic search for the missing diary in the Kempner Papers at the museum. It wasn't there.

Then, on June 25, 2001, he received a call from a man named Walt Martin, who explained that he represented a person who had in his possession some of the papers that had come from Kempner's Lansdowne home.

Mayer was perplexed. The museum had meticulously searched the house for papers when they came for the Kempner collection in the summer of 1999; what little that had been left behind, the museum had taken. They could not have missed anything. He prodded the man for information. Martin gave multiple accounts. First he said the material had been found in a dumpster outside the house. Then he said it was found in the home's sunporch.

Did these documents, Mayer asked, happen to include a diary by a man named Alfred Rosenberg?

Martin thought so. How much would it be worth? "One million, two million?"

Mayer said he would get back to Martin. Instead he called the FBI.

Robert Wittman, founder of the FBI's Art Crime Team, had made his name working undercover around the world to recover artifacts from thieves, scammers, and smugglers of every stripe. He recovered a fifty-pound crystal ball that had once graced the Imperial Palace in Beijing; it was found atop a dresser in the house of a self-described witch in Trenton, New Jersey. At a rest stop near exit 7A of the New Jersey Turnpike, Wittman conducted a sting operation against smugglers selling a seventeen-hundred-year-old piece of golden Peruvian armor. He turned up an astonishing cache of stolen Americana hidden in a modest house south of Philadelphia. That $2 million to $3 million collection included the rifle that radical abolitionist John Brown had wielded during his ill-fated attack on Harpers Ferry; a ring encapsulating a lock

of George Washington's hair; and a golden watch presented to
Union general George Meade after the Battle of Gettysburg (VIC-
TORY, the inscription declared). Wittman lured a dealer to a Philadelphia airport hotel to recover Geronimo's warbonnet. In
Madrid, he helped Spanish investigators track down eighteen
paintings, worth $50 million, by the likes of Goya and Brueghel.
He rescued Pickett's map of Gettysburg, the original manuscript
of *The Good Earth*, by Pearl S. Buck, and one of the fourteen original copies of the Bill of Rights.

Wittman was the most successful art crime investigator in the
history of the FBI, spearheading operations to recover more than
$300 million worth of cultural artifacts, and in the process bring-
ing international attention to a lucrative corner of the criminal
universe. The Bureau tallied up the financial value of every artifact Wittman discovered, but he knew that the lost objects of
antiquity were really priceless.

How could anyone put a dollar value on irreplaceable cultural
and national heritage? Salvaging stolen relics of history was what
got Wittman excited about his job.

Going to work on the case for the Holocaust museum in 2001,
Wittman joined a conference call with Mayer and Martin, intro-
ducing himself as Bob Clay, an appraiser of historic documents.
He had good reason for using his real first name: It was always
easier to stay in character if he kept the lies to a minimum.

Wittman knew from experience that he would learn more
undercover than he would from a straight FBI interrogation. By
posing as an appraiser, he would be able to tell Martin that he
needed to see the collection personally, and he would have a reason
to ask pointed questions about the provenance of the documents.

Martin told them that the Kempner heirs had hired a contractor to clean out the house in preparation for sale. That man sub-
contracted the job to his brother, William Martin, a trash-removal
contractor who said he found the documents in trash bags on the
property. How they got there was a mystery. Museum officials

"went into holes in the rat-infested basement, they looked behind walls, they searched a safe," said Kevin Gibson, the lawyer for the Kempner heirs. "And when they left, I went through it again. There were no more documents." Some of the papers looked like Nazi originals, Walt Martin said. He had hundreds of pages of German military plans, a document about exploiting the Soviet Union for raw materials after the war, some of J. Edgar Hoover's letters to Kempner, and—he hoped and believed—copies of Rosenberg's diary. He also had Lucian Kempner's old army uniform. Walt Martin said he had contacted British historian David Irving about the Kempner haul. Irving had recently lost a prolonged libel suit against author Deborah Lipstadt after she included him in a book about Holocaust deniers.

When they hung up, Wittman told Mayer to set up a date to visit Walt Martin's house outside Philadelphia and see what he really had. If Martin had the diary, Wittman could immediately take custody of it for safekeeping while he investigated whether it belonged to the government.

On October 30, Mayer and a historian from the Holocaust museum arrived at Martin's home. It was a brick row house in a neighborhood tucked into an industrial strip beside Interstate 95. The researchers found great piles of papers strewn about the little home. Some of them were still in their boxes, some of them were piled up in loose stacks. Martin smoked while they worked, the ashes from his cigarettes dropping onto the documents.

Mayer quickly determined the papers to be valuable pieces of Kempner's estate, and reported back to Wittman and his partner, Jay Heine, who were waiting outside. The agents stepped into the house and told Martin that the FBI was taking the documents as evidence until the parties could work out the tangled ownership questions.

Martin threatened to sue, and officials at the Holocaust museum debated how forcefully to press their case. Though the Rosenberg diary did not turn out to be in Martin's boxes, the jewel of the Kempner collection still loomed large in Mayer's mind. He argued for fighting Martin in court. He wanted to be sure that the museum could claim ownership of the diary if it should ever surface. Given the interest in the lost pages, Mayer did not want to see them fall into unsympathetic hands.

The museum's leadership agreed, and the entire affair ended up in federal court.

In the end, because no one could dispute Martin's story—because no one could definitively prove that museum officials had not overlooked the boxes when they came for Kempner's collection in 1999—lawyers recommended a settlement. The two parties agreed to split everything. For the second time, Mayer found himself sitting down and divvying up piles of papers Kempner had left behind. The two parties took turns selecting which documents they wanted.

One day in 2005, Martin's half of the documents went on the block at Wilson's Auctioneers and Appraisers in Chester Heights, outside Philadelphia. In as schizophrenic a sale as any, the papers of Robert Kempner, this lifelong opponent of Nazism, went up for sale alongside a Hitler Youth sport shirt, an SS belt and buckle, a Luftwaffe teaspoon, and a Nazi armband.

For Mayer and Wittman, it was a disappointing conclusion to a chase that had begun with Walt Martin's phone call to Mayer in 2001. It had become obvious that the papers Kempner stockpiled in Lansdowne had been divided, relocated, and hidden in less than optimal conditions since his death. Every time the archivist and the agent thought they had everything in hand, they learned about some new wrinkle.

More and more, the prospect of finding the lost diary was beginning to feel like the longest of long shots.

In the midst of the Martin negotiations, Mayer learned that still more of Kempner's papers had been found, hidden behind locked doors in the basement, at the collegium established by Herbert

Richardson in Lewiston, New York. Jane Lester had moved into the building, but she was laid up after falling and breaking her hip. In early 2001, her sisters found her in such deplorable condition that they spirited her away to a hospital, successfully fought to be appointed her guardians, and seized control of her finances. Her assets approached $6 million, at least some of which she held in a joint account with Richardson. At the same time, the sisters' attorneys learned of Richardson's involvement with Margot Lipton, and the courts appointed an independent guardian, Edward Jesella, a lawyer in Lewiston, to oversee her affairs. He found that Richardson had persuaded Lipton to add his name to her bank accounts in the United States and Europe, where she had more than $1 million saved. Jesella moved aggressively to take control of Lipton's finances. Richardson's attorneys threatened legal action, Jesella said, but ultimately the professor severed all contact with the woman.

In 2003, the attorney representing Lester's sisters invited the Holocaust museum to look through documents that had been removed from Richardson's building in Lewiston and placed in a storage locker in Amherst, New York. If the boxes included any papers that had been bequeathed to the museum by Kempner's heirs, the attorney told Mayer, the museum was welcome to take them to Washington.

Mayer consulted with Wittman about the new cache of Kempner Papers. Since Lester's guardians were inviting Mayer to take whatever belonged to the museum, Wittman suggested the archivist go to Amherst alone and call if he ran into any trouble.

Mayer spent a day in the storage unit, opening boxes. The diary wasn't there, either.

But the trip was not a bust. Lester's sister Elizabeth mentioned something intriguing. She had accompanied Jane to an interview with a reporter for the German newsmagazine *Der Spiegel*, and during the conversation Lester had let slip that she'd given Rosenberg's diary to someone for safekeeping.

Herbert Richardson.

•   •   •

Mayer drafted a memo for Wittman, laying out the status of the search: that the diary was stolen government property, that Kempner seemed to have had it after the Nuremberg trials, and that, according to the most recent information, Richardson had the pages in his possession. But Lester's overheard remark to a reporter was not the sort of evidence that Wittman could use to build a solid case. Besides, since Richardson divided his time between Canada and the United States, complicated international collaboration would be required if the FBI pressed its case.

The diary still had not been recovered by the time Wittman retired from the FBI in 2008. Not long after, Mayer ran into Eli Rosenbaum, who made a career of hunting down and deporting Nazis as director of the Justice Department's Office of Special Investigations. Rosenbaum offered to help, but eventually he acknowledged that he couldn't move the case forward.

Desperate, Mayer called Wittman in 2012 to see if he might take another crack at the case.

The former agent was interested. He had launched his private art-recovery-and-security consulting business, but his mission had hardly changed. He was still tracking down the unique and the priceless for clients. The difference was that as a private operator, he had the freedom to pursue cases without worrying about the limitations of international borders.

Soon after Mayer's call, Wittman took the train to Washington with his son, Jeff, who had joined the firm after college. As always, security was tight outside the monumental granite building dedicated to the memory of the Nazis' victims. Just three years earlier, an eighty-eight-year-old white supremacist wielding a .22-caliber rifle had killed a security guard at the front door. The Wittmans made their way through the metal detector and up to a fifth-floor conference room to meet with museum officials.

Wittman could relate to the museum's cause. His American father had met his Japanese mother at the Tachikawa U.S. air base during the Korean War, and after they married in 1953, they moved back to the United States and settled in Baltimore. When he was a boy, Wittman remembered, strangers would hurl epithets at his mother—"Jap! Nip!"—in public. He was stunned at the time, but eventually he would come to realize that the hatred stemmed from the war. His neighbors had suffered personal losses in the fight against the Japanese. He could see it from both sides: Wittman's father had piloted an American landing craft in the Pacific, while uncles on his mother's side fought for the Japanese army.

When Wittman considered the relocation and internment of more than 110,000 people of Japanese ancestry, most of them citizens, by the United States after the attack on Pearl Harbor, it did not take a great deal of imagination to see how Nazism spread in Germany. How easily patriotism devolved into officially sanctioned racism.

Kempner himself had said it: Even small steps in the wrong direction could put a nation on a path to catastrophe.

At the museum, Mayer outlined what he knew about the status of the Rosenberg diary, and Wittman went to work. A decade after that first call from Mayer, he was primed for the pursuit. The time had come to solve the half-century-old mystery and get Rosenberg's diary back into the public's hands.

Wittman pored over Mayer's reports on the messy donation of Robert Kempner's papers. The prosecutor's two sons had passed away, as had Lester and Lipton. But Richardson was still alive—he had turned eighty that year—so the investigation began with him. Wittman decided he would have to find the former professor and try to get him to talk. Locating Richardson was simple enough: He still worked at his academic press in Lewiston and lived across the river in Niagara Falls, Ontario. The question was whether he would cooperate. Wittman could only find out by confronting him face-to-face. No one had approached Richardson directly and told him that if he had the diary, he had no right to it and no choice but to hand it over to the government. Wittman would force the former professor to take the situation seriously.

But it was a case filled with uncertainties. What if Robert Kempner had given the diary away before he died? Or sold it? What if Lester's offhand remark had been misunderstood, and Richardson never really had the diary? Or what if he'd unloaded it once he realized that he couldn't publish it? What if he had the diary and chose to simply deny it?

In November, Wittman called Mayer about his game plan. Years in pursuit of the diary had not dimmed the archivist's enthusiasm, and he wanted to go along to see if they could put the museum back on the diary's trail. But chronic back trouble had flared up and he couldn't endure the trip, so Wittman took to the road with his son and partner, Jeff.

When they arrived in Lewiston, they discovered a sign still standing before the narrow building with white siding that Richardson owned on Ridge Street: THE ROBERT KEMPNER COLLEGIUM, it read in gold letters on a green background. But, stepping onto the porch and peering through the front windows, they could see that the building was empty, an uninhabited shell. So Wittman and his son made their way over to an unprepossessing redbrick building at the end of an industrial road on the outskirts of Lewiston's village district. This was the home of Richardson's Edwin Mellen Press, and inside, a pair of friendly employees told the Wittmans that they had just missed the professor. He was out to lunch. Come back later this afternoon and you can speak to him.

Wittman left a business card, and smiled as he thought about Richardson's reaction. As an undercover FBI agent, Wittman's role in art crime cases had been confidential; at the press conferences announcing a major recovery, he would stand in the back, out of the range of the press cameras. But after Wittman retired in 2008, he went public with a memoir, *Priceless*, and now a simple Internet search would let Richardson know that he was dealing with a former special agent with a long and successful record of hauling hidden artifacts of history back into the daylight.

Predictably, when they returned later in the afternoon, the Wittmans were met with an entirely different attitude at the Mellen Press. No one spoke to Richardson, a Mellen staffer now said, without an appointment. They would have to call ahead to set up a date, she explained. But she refused to give them the number to call. They persisted, and she finally introduced them to the director of the press, John Rupnow. He promised to set up a meeting with Richardson the following day and told them to call back later to confirm the appointment. When they called back, no one answered.

Richardson was stonewalling them. To Wittman, that signaled that he was hiding something. He knew something he was afraid to admit. If Wittman's instinct was correct, it meant Richardson had the Rosenberg diary.

Later that day, the Wittmans drove into Canada to try to approach Richardson at his home. If he wasn't there, Wittman would leave another business card. It was important that Richardson understand that he couldn't just ignore him.

But even for an experienced investigator, things don't always go smoothly. At the border, Wittman and his son hit a snag. Wittman told the border agent that he was traveling into Canada for sightseeing, since this was easier than explaining their entire mission. The Holocaust museum is a federally supported organization, and Wittman feared that any work he did on its behalf across the border would require him to ask for permission from Canadian authorities. He wanted to avoid the kind of bureaucratic red tape that would gum up the museum's pursuit of the diary for years.

Wittman's tourist cover story didn't ring true to the border agent. They didn't look like they were going to see Niagara Falls: The Wittmans were wearing business suits. The guard ordered Wittman to pull over, and he watched, annoyed but a bit amused at the absurdity of the situation, as his car was searched. In his briefcase the officers found his investigative file and peppered Wittman with questions. He tried to explain his situation, but soon border patrol, unimpressed with his arguments, was escorting him back to the New York side.

With inconvenience came inspiration. Wittman knew that Richardson commuted into Lewiston every few days. Perhaps if Richardson's car was stopped and searched a few times, as Wittman's had been, he could be persuaded to cooperate. The best way to get Richardson to give the diary back, Wittman believed, would be to keep him under steady psychological pressure.

Wittman knew from experience that patience was the key. Time was on his side. Let a guilty subject stew about the circumstances, not knowing what the investigator knows, and a psychological defense mechanism kicks in: He will almost always begin to consider worst-case scenarios.

That's when the breakthrough comes.

Once back in Philadelphia, Wittman called his close friend and colleague David Hall, an assistant U.S. attorney in Wilmington, Delaware. Hall had made a career of prosecuting weapons and military technology dealers, but he also worked with Wittman on art crime investigations, including the recovery of a pair of Picassos stolen from a gallery in Palm Beach. In one memorable case, he and Wittman had flown to Rio de Janeiro to negotiate the return of three iconic Norman Rockwell paintings. In addition to conducting his private business, Wittman worked with Homeland Security Investigations as an undercover consultant and frequently teamed up with Hall and Mark Olexa, a special agent with HSI. Wittman knew they would work with him on a case as important as the search for the Rosenberg diary.

But a few days later, when Wittman sat down at the U.S. attorney's office in downtown Wilmington with Hall and Olexa, the prosecutor wasn't immediately sold on Wittman's case. As Wittman unspooled the twisted facts, Hall's head began to spin. If he hadn't known Wittman for decades, he would have dropped the whole matter. Hall, who had been an intelligence officer in the U.S. Navy Reserve for thirty years, prided himself on cracking difficult cases. This one, he thought, sounded "like a tale told by a madman."

There was a diary that disappeared sometime between 1946 and 1949. There was a thirdhand report that Jane Lester, now deceased, had told a reporter that she had given it to a former professor in upstate New York. Above all, there were a lot of questions. If Hall had more solid information about who had the diary and where it was, he would have probable cause to justify a search warrant, and then he could simply seize the pages. But nobody could even say for sure whether the diary was in the United States or Canada or somewhere else altogether.

Still, Hall knew that Wittman had good instincts, and the prosecutor was intrigued enough to open a federal investigation. Wittman went over his action plan with Hall and Olexa. First they needed to conduct a methodical background check on Richardson. Then they needed to analyze his U.S.–Canada crossing history for patterns, and order officers at the border to pull Richardson aside and search his car. Wittman hoped the inspection—coming so soon after his own visit to the Mellen Press—would lead Richardson to believe he was under surveillance. The final step would be to interrogate the former professor about the diary and, if he did not cooperate, issue a subpoena ordering him to turn it over.

Olexa went to work. One day in December, Richardson's car was searched at the border. Two months later, investigators were ready to confront him. Hall wanted to do it at the office in Lewiston, where Richardson might offer to let agents look around. He didn't expect Richardson to turn over the diary right away. But he hoped the former professor would say something that investigators didn't already know. Olexa had learned that Richardson often visited Lewiston on Thursdays, so on February 7, he drove to Lewiston with another agent and staked out the tiny parking lot at the offices of the Mellen Press to await Richardson's arrival.

When he appeared, the agents stepped out and identified themselves. Richardson agreed to speak. He told them about how he had come to meet Lester and Lipton and how he had helped them. He said they became a tremendous burden to him, but he cared for them greatly. "I thought of this woman, these women, like my mother." Richardson said he'd helped the women recoup money from the Kempner heirs. He volunteered that he had never taken any funds out of the women's bank accounts.

Richardson did acknowledge helping bring some of Kempner's paintings from Lansdowne to Lewiston but said he had "never heard of any piece having any particular value." He denied ever handling any of the documents that had gone missing from the house in Lansdowne. "I don't think I've ever had in my possession any of Kempner's papers."

Not only did Richardson deny having the Rosenberg diary, he said he was not aware that such a journal even existed.

Unconvinced, Olexa handed Richardson a federal grand jury subpoena ordering him to turn over the Rosenberg papers, along with any other government documents in his possession. Richardson was on notice that the diary was government property and that if he had it, he would be wise to surrender it.

Before they parted, Olexa issued Richardson a piece of advice: You should hire an attorney.

A few weeks later, the affair unfolded exactly as Hall and Wittman had hoped.

Richardson's lawyer, Vincent Doyle, called the prosecutor's office to ask about the subpoena. Hall explained that he was after any and all Nuremberg trial documents, but especially the Rosenberg diary. He told Doyle that Richardson had said some things in the parking lot that Hall believed to be untrue, and he urged Doyle to personally search for the diary if possible.

A month later, on March 27, Doyle called and left a message at the U.S. attorney's office in Wilmington. Hall and Olexa happened to be together at the Immigration and Customs Enforcement office in downtown Philadelphia, and Hall used a colleague's telephone to return the call. He put Doyle on speakerphone so Olexa could listen in.

Doyle said that Richardson had some German documents, some of them bound, some of them loose, and that they were handwritten. *Does this sound like what you're after?* Hall looked at Olexa. He felt like a poker player who had drawn a royal flush. But the seasoned negotiator played it as cool as he could.

"Vince," he said, "the only way to know if that's what we want is to look at them."

On April 5, 2013, Henry Mayer and Jürgen Matthäus took the train to downtown Wilmington and rode the elevator upstairs to the U.S. attorney's office. They were filled with excitement. Matthäus had come to think that they would never find the lost pages. When Mayer heard that Richardson had turned over handwritten pages, he immediately ran to pass along the good news to his colleague. But they wouldn't know for sure what they had until they could examine the documents.

An agent had driven to Buffalo the weekend after Richardson's lawyer called, and on April 1 he picked up several accordion files and four banker boxes and drove them to Wilmington, where the pages were secured in a vault.

Now Olexa pulled the pages out and set them up for the museum officials in a conference room.

As Matthäus pulled the pages from the files, it was instantly obvious that this was the diary. For one thing, he knew Rosenberg's handwriting. He could see that the entries matched excerpts that had been published, and the pages lined up with a description of Rosenberg's papers drafted in 1945. Matthäus and Mayer also could tell that the pages had been part of Kempner's archive at one time. There were markings on the diary in what appeared to be Kempner's handwriting, and in among the diary pages were other miscellaneous documents similar to what museum officials had found during their convoluted collection of the Kempner Papers.

After six decades, there was no question about it. The search for the diary was over.

Mayer was beyond elated. Fourteen years in pursuit and the pages had actually been found. It was the dream of any archivist to discover a lost document of such significance, and this one had few rivals. It was mind-blowing to be sitting in a conference room in Delaware sixty-eight years after the end of the Second World War, flipping through pages scratched by Rosenberg's fountain pen—pages thought to be lost to history forever.

Someone pulled out a camera, and Mayer gave a broad smile and a thumbs-up.

Two months later, Mayer returned to the U.S. attorney's office in Wilmington, where a mob of reporters from around the world convened at a press conference announcing the rediscovery.

Hall and Olexa were there, along with John Morton, director of Immigration and Customs Enforcement, and Charles Oberly, the U.S. attorney for Delaware. Although it took law enforcement to persuade him to give up the diary, Richardson was not charged with a crime. His lawyer had agreed to surrender the papers on the condition that prosecutors not use that act against Richardson. The U.S. attorney's office had no other evidence to make a case against the former professor, and the primary purpose of the investigation had been to locate the diary. Richardson remained silent about the matter, aside from a brief statement faxed to the *New York Times* that day. "When federal agents contacted me, I was glad to meet with them and cooperate with their efforts. I'm glad that I was able to help the Justice Department and the Department of Homeland Security in recovering some documents, which the authorities have now identified as the diary of Alfred Rosenberg."

As reporters scribbled and cameras clicked, Morton took the podium to make the announcement.

"One of the enduring mysteries of the Second World War is what happened to the Rosenberg diary. We have solved that mystery," he said. Inside a glass-walled conference room beside him, the pages were on display. "The Rosenberg diary is no ordinary diary of the time. It is the unvarnished account of a Nazi leader, his thoughts, his philosophies, his interactions with other Nazi leaders. Reading Rosenberg's diary is to stare into the mind of a dark soul."

These were dispatches from the front lines of the political and cultural battles that had roiled Berlin before and during the war, written in the hand of a nearly forgotten ideologue who set the stage for the worst crimes of the century. Hidden away in folders and boxes in suburban Philadelphia and upstate New York for more than six decades, Rosenberg's diary was a time capsule from a vanished age.

The time had finally come to shine a light on the secrets buried within.

LIVES

IN THE

BALANCE

1918–1939

Alfred Rosenberg *(third row, standing, third from left in fedora and trench coat)* with band of Nazis assembled in Coburg, Bavaria, for a 1922 German Day rally. Wielding their clubs in violent street fights, the Nazis drove their opponents from the streets. *(Bayerische Staatsbibliothek München/Bildarchiv)*

4

"Stepchildren of Fate"

The city was jubilant. The morning's light rain had stopped, and Berliners flooded onto Unter den Linden, the elegant tree-lined boulevard stretching from the royal palace to the Tiergarten. The women wore their brightest dresses, as if defying the wintry gloom settling over defeated Deutschland, and they stood out among the masses of men in dark suits and hats. It was December 10, 1918. An undercurrent of violence crackled in the capital city. The Great War had been lost, and the German empire had fallen. But this was a day for celebration: The soldiers were returning from the front.

Onlookers massed in Pariser Platz under the gaze of the winged goddess Victoria, riding her chariot behind four stallions atop the Brandenburg Gate. In 1806, Napoleon had triumphantly entered the city through the gate after defeating the Prussians. Today it was festooned with a banner reading PEACE AND LIBERTY.

At 1:00 p.m., the first companies arrived in their field grays and steel helmets. Flowers sprouted from gun barrels and adorned the necks of horses. The crowd waved hats and white handkerchiefs and laurels. People climbed trees and street kiosks for a better view, lined rooftops, ducked their heads out windows, crowded every balcony. "So dense were the masses that these companies at first found it impossible to make headway," one correspondent wrote. Medics were dispatched to extricate onlookers hurt in the crush. "There must have been millions of patriotic sightseers about this time."

Finally a pathway was opened to the soldiers, and they passed on foot and on horseback, behind standard-bearers alternately hoisting the black, white, and red of the fallen Reich and the black, red, and gold of the infant revolutionary state. Some officers hauled their wives and children up onto their mounts to ride with them through the scrum. The tattered troops were accompanied by their bands, playing marches, and by their smoking, horse-drawn food trains, which they had taken to calling "goulash guns." They also brought their artillery batteries and their ammunition; in the days leading up to the march, rivals of the fledgling government feared that the frontline soldiers were being called to the capital to forcibly clamp down on the opposition.

But the day passed in peace. Ecstatic Berliners handed out chrysanthemums and cigarettes. In the grandstand, Friedrich Ebert stood out in his silk hat. The bullnecked politician had risen to chancellor the month before, following the kaiser's abdication and the November revolution, and he greeted the arrivals as if they were victors.

"Comrades, companions, citizens," he declared, feeding the myth that the Germans had not lost the war, that they had been betrayed by enemies within, "your sacrifice and deeds are without equal! No enemy has conquered you!"

Over the next two weeks, soldiers continued pouring into the city, to be welcomed by cheering crowds. "A feeling of confidence, of fresh hope in the future, seems to have returned with the troops, who responded to the ovations with the buoyant seriousness of men who, after seeing death so near, are not afraid of life," a woman who witnessed the march wrote to a friend. "The streets are so crowded and overflowing with men that I am beginning to wonder how long it will be before these reserves of latent energy will break forth and find a channel for themselves if not speedily used to some good purpose."

In among the Berliners, standing at the corner of Friedrichstrasse and Unter den Linden, a sullen twenty-five-year-old immigrant seethed. He saw nothing in the scene worth celebrating.

Alfred Rosenberg had arrived in the capital by train from his homeland of Estonia just a few days earlier. Watching the brigades of returning German soldiers, he was struck by the faces of the men: They seemed frozen and blank, shell-shocked. "At that moment," Rosenberg would write years later, "the great sorrow of the German people came upon me."

It was a picture that would stick in his mind as he quickly moved south to Munich, found his way into the nation's conspiratorial nationalist underground, and discovered knots of radical anti-Semites speaking his language.

Within months, Rosenberg would enlist in the fight and never look back.

Later, when the Third Reich dawned and Germany organized itself around the idea that its citizens were a master race, people couldn't help noticing that more than a few of the nation's leading lights failed to live up to the ideal. As a standard German joke went, the typical Nazi was as slim as the rotund Göring, as athletic as clubfooted Goebbels, as blond as Hitler, and, yes, as Aryan as Rosenberg.

"He was dark, and there seemed nothing very German in his appearance," a British military officer wrote about Rosenberg after the war. "Most Nazis thought he had Jewish blood and that he must be the 'only Aryan Rosenberg in the world.'" In fact, Rosenberg was a common enough name among ethnic Germans in the Baltic states. He said his ancestors had arrived from Germany in the 1700s, first settling in Riga, Latvia, and then in the capital of Estonia, Reval, now called Tallinn. Reval was a major city in the German-dominated Hanseatic League of merchants in the fourteenth century, but in 1710, weakened by plague and war, the city surrendered to Peter the Great. It was a major port in the Russian Empire by the time Rosenberg was born, in 1893, but as a child he could still walk the city's twisting alleyways and old courtyards and admire the defensive walls and medieval architecture of its founding days.

Rosenberg's mother died of tuberculosis two months after he was born. His father, who managed the local arm of a large German firm in Estonia, died eleven years later at age forty-two, leaving Rosenberg in the care of his aunts. Raised a Protestant, he rebelled against the faith. He was not one to genuflect. "This kneeling down," he wrote about being ordered to prostrate himself before God in confirmation class, "stirred up something in me which could never afterwards be calmed."

He would fondly remember his art teacher in secondary school, a painter who sent him out into the streets to sketch Reval. The headmaster, who taught history and geography, invited him to conduct an archaeological dig in a local graveyard, where they found a stone urn, pitchers, and rings. He was not a standout student, but his teachers liked him. At seventeen, Rosenberg went off to a technical institute in Riga, where he landed in the architecture program. Outside the classroom, he read Germanic sagas and Icelandic mythology and the Indian Vedas and philosophers like Kant and Schopenhauer. A later writer would dismiss Rosenberg as "a man of profound half-culture," but among the boys in the Corps Rubonia, a student group he joined in Riga, his nickname was "the Philosopher."

One day, on the train trip between Reval and St. Petersburg, where his grandparents lived, he met a striking woman. Hilda Leesmann, daughter of a wealthy businessman, was a year older, smart, and well-read, steeped in both German and Russian traditions. She prompted Rosenberg to read Tolstoy's *War and Peace* and *Anna Karenina*. She played the piano and exposed him to great Russian nationalist composers. She gave him Nietzsche's *Thus Spake Zarathustra*. She studied dance in Paris, and when he visited her, she took him to see Cathédrale Notre Dame and the Louvre. They ate breakfast every day at the immortal Café de la Rotonde in the Montparnasse quarter, where the likes of Picasso and Modigliani dined. She was becoming a woman of the world and being courted by the Russian ballet, while back in Riga, Rosenberg was forced to don medieval garb as an extra in a children's performance.

He and Hilda married in 1915, and they spent the summer together on a country estate, Rosenberg occupying himself with his painting and reading to her aloud from a biography of Goethe. When the summer ended, the First World War uprooted both of them. Hilda and her family decamped to St. Petersburg; Rosenberg's entire institute was evacuated to Moscow, library and all. Classes in exile were scattered all over the Russian capital; some met in hallways. Rosenberg rented a room from a couple outside the downtown district, where he ate modest family dinners at a table in a space that doubled as a bedroom. Over tea, his host would sit with a left-wing newspaper on his knee and rail against "those ruling scoundrels." Once a week, Rosenberg treated himself to dinner out with pastries and 2 percent beer. His social life amounted to hanging around cheap restaurants on Tverskaya Street, the main boulevard running northwest out of Red Square.

As Rosenberg devoured Tolstoy and Dostoyevsky, the Russian Revolution erupted around him. Rosenberg was so buried in his books that he barely noticed. Early one morning, he took the train into Moscow to discover hundreds of thousands of people filling the squares and streets. "Hysterical joy reigned, people wept on the shoulders of complete strangers," he wrote afterward, "the psychosis had gripped millions."

Later in 1917, Rosenberg learned that Hilda's health had taken a turn for the worse in the harsh northern climate. Tuberculosis had set in, and her family had packed her off to the Crimea to recuperate. He broke off his studies and joined her there. A few months later, they packed up again and returned to Estonia. Hilda was confined to bed. Rosenberg read to her, and in the meantime finished his final project toward his diploma. Chillingly enough, given the path his life would take, he designed a crematorium. Despite the upheaval in Moscow, he went back to the institute in Russia for his final examination, then returned home just in time to see German troops march into the city.

He did not stay in Reval long. He taught drawing to "rather unwilling youngsters" at a school for a few months and made some money selling illustrations of the old city. But there was nothing for him in Estonia, so he joined the tens of thousands of ethnic Germans fleeing ahead of an invasion by the Russian army in November 1918.

Before leaving, he delivered his first public remarks at a meeting held in the hall of the Brotherhood of the Blackheads, a civic association of merchants and ship owners in Reval. In a preview of countless speeches to come, Rosenberg declaimed on the evil alliance of Judaism and Marxism that had laid Russia low. According to one account, a Jewish businessman noisily led his compatriots out of the hall in protest.

Then, the very same night, Rosenberg set off for Germany. He would not return to his hometown for more than two decades.

"The train left Reval. Behind me Russia fell away with all her memories, with all her unpredictable future," Rosenberg wrote. "Behind me fell away the city of my youth with her towers and old streets and all the men with whom I had once lived there. I left my homeland behind me in order to gain a fatherland for myself. . . . Thus I came to the Reich. Originally a man completely devoted to art, philosophy, and history, who never dreams of getting mixed up with politics. . . . Life pulled me, and I followed."

Rosenberg had arranged to interview with a prominent architect, Peter Behrens, in Berlin. But he was horrified by the city, which was soon to develop an international reputation for its decadent sexual and cultural life. Behrens, it turned out, was a designer with a modernist bent. This was not the kind of mentor Rosenberg sought. He skipped the meeting and quickly made his way south to Munich.

The Bavarian capital straddled the Isar River at the foot of the snowcapped Alps, which, on clear days, rose in the south like a stage backdrop painted by artists. Conservative and Catholic, it was renowned for its genial attitude and for its beers: the royal Hofbräuhaus, the monks' Augustinerbräu. The city had been ruled by the Wittelsbach family for seven centuries, and during his reign, from 1825 to 1848, King Ludwig I had embarked on an ambitious architectural reconstruction that ushered Munich into the ranks of Europe's great cities. A broad new boulevard—Ludwigstrasse, naturally—carved its way north from the medieval city center and was lined with university and library buildings in the Italianate style. A new square, Königsplatz, anchored a complex of neoclassical museums designed to show off Greek, Roman, and Egyptian sculptures and the family's magnificent collection of Old Masters.

By the turn of the century, Munich had earned a reputation

as the center of German arts and culture, a sort of "Athens on the Isar." Painters, sculptors, writers, intellectuals, and musicians flocked to the city and were lavished with money and attention by Munich's aristocracy. The city celebrated its artists with exhibits and parades and balls. Avant-garde performers challenged the stuffy status quo in a country known for its imperial authoritarianism, and a bohemian quarter sprang up in a free-spirited neighborhood called Schwabing. "True Schwabinger," historian David Clay Large would write, "preferred cafés to beer halls." Poetry, politics, and a haze of cigarette smoke could be found around the marble tables at the Café Stefanie, which was frequented by anarchists, communists, Dadaists, novelists, and the like. The place was known by the ironic nickname Café Grössenwahn—Café Megalomania. Lenin lived in Schwabing before he went off to launch his revolution in Russia; Hitler moved into a room on the edge of the neighborhood during his first stint in Munich, from the spring of 1913 to the summer of 1914. Once Rosenberg got his bearings in the Bavarian capital, he moved into a place just south of the neighborhood on Barer Strasse, a few blocks from the royal art galleries, the university, and the Academy of Fine Arts.

By the time Rosenberg arrived, Munich was in the grip of joblessness, hunger, and unfathomable turmoil. The last of the Wittelsbach family's kings had been forced into exile at the end of the First World War. Revolutionaries in the city seized control and declared the southeastern state an independent republic. Kurt Eisner, a leader of Germany's socialist party, the Social Democrats, took charge. As a Jew, a former journalist, and an opponent of the war, Eisner was the nationalists' archetypal enemy of the state.

Penniless and alone, drifting through the city, Rosenberg was destined to be swept up by the revolutionary mood. His wife had become seriously ill, and her parents took her to recuperate in Arosa, Switzerland. He was, he would write, just another of the "many stepchildren of fate" trying to make his way in postwar

Europe. He had a little money from home, and he set about trying to sell articles and paintings. But nothing came of that, and Rosenberg was forced to apply to a relief committee for housing and to rely on the soup kitchen for daily meals of cabbage soup and dumplings. He spent his days wandering through the art museums and reading at the state library on Ludwigstrasse.

Walking the streets one day, he noticed a bulletin on a pillar advertising a performance by a dancer who had known his wife before she fell ill. Rosenberg tracked the woman down, and in the course of their conversation he mentioned that he had been trying to pitch some articles about the Russian Revolution. It was all he had to sell.

The woman gave him a name that would change the course of his entire life. Dietrich Eckart was a bohemian, a playwright, a poet, and a journalist whose weekly *Auf Gut Deutsch* (*In Plain German*) was required reading among the anti-Semitic right-wing crowd coalescing in Munich. Rosenberg went to see him the next day.

"I was received by a grumpy and yet friendly man with a striking head and a face full of character," Rosenberg would write. "He shoved his glasses up on his forehead and looked at me searchingly."

"Can you use a fighter against Jerusalem?" Rosenberg asked.

"Certainly," he said with a laugh.

Rosenberg handed him his articles, and Eckart called him the next day. Over a meal at a restaurant, the two men became fast friends and collaborators.

Rosenberg began writing for Eckart's paper. Around the same time, he discovered a shadowy anti-Semitic organization called the Thule Society, which had plotted an armed overthrow of Eisner's government. "Its membership list," historian Ian Kershaw would write, "reads like a *Who's Who* of early Nazi sympathizers and leading figures in Munich." Three months after the revolution, Eisner was indeed assassinated on the street by a young right-winger; ironically, the killer had been rejected by the Thule Society because of his Jewish blood and had gunned down Eisner to prove his merits.

Demonstrations choked the streets, and the Social Democrats lost their grip on power. A group of "coffeehouse anarchists" briefly took charge and proposed that money be issued freely. Next, a Bolshevik regime came to power and began arresting the rich and attempting to form a communist army to storm Europe.

On a cool day in April 1919, Rosenberg joined knots of angry men debating the developments in the central Marien-platz, under the shadow of the enormous neo-Gothic town hall, the Rathaus, with its weathered three-hundred-foot facade of extravagantly ornamented arches, pinnacles, and columns. Rosenberg stood on a stone balustrade, waved a sign reading, LONG LIVE THE GERMAN WORKER! DOWN WITH BOLSHEVISM! and noisily denounced the new government before a few thousand people. But when he discovered that people had taken note of his strident remarks—they were stopping him on the streets to applaud his speech—he decided to make himself scarce, fearing he would be arrested.

Rosenberg and Eckart fled twenty-five miles south to the small town of Wolfratshausen. While they were away, members of the Thule Society had been taken hostage, and in the chaos, commu-nist forces lined them up in the basement of a secondary school and shot them one by one. At the beginning of May, military units enlisted by the exiled Social Democratic government retook Munich in a bloody fight punctuated by executions and massacres. At the end of the summer, the Weimar Republic was officially founded, and Bavaria was incorporated into the new state.

After a few weeks, Rosenberg and Eckart returned from their brief self-imposed exile. In May, they attended a meeting of a new right-wing group calling itself the German Workers' Party. In a small restaurant, Rosenberg and Eckart delivered their screeds against the Jews and the Bolsheviks in the Soviet Union.

Later that year, on a Friday night in September, a thirty-year-old corporal in the German army would show up at one of the meetings of the nascent party at the Sterneckerbräu, a small beer hall with dark bead-board wainscoting and arched ceilings, where the party met every week.

Not long after that, the outfit would adopt a new name: the National Socialist German Workers' Party. Its enemies would shorten it to two syllables that better captured the party's uncompromisingly hard edge: Nazi.

Rosenberg *(left)* and Hitler in Munich during the attempted coup at the Bürgerbräukeller in November 1923. *(Keystone/Getty Images)*

5

"The Most Hated Paper in the Land!"

Adolf Hitler and Alfred Rosenberg had much in common. Though they grew up outside Germany, they were equally enthralled by the country's mythically heroic past. They were both young when they lost their parents. Both were more interested in drawing, reading, and daydreaming than pursuing careers in architecture. As young men, each had found it necessary to rely on soup kitchens to fill their empty stomachs. And once they met, it didn't take long for them to discover that they were in agreement about what they considered the major problems of the day: the destructiveness of the churches, the danger of communism, and the menace of the Jews.

Born in Braunau, Austria, and raised outside Linz, Hitler was four years older than Rosenberg. His father, a career civil servant, died in 1903, and in 1907, Hitler moved to Vienna, where he tried and failed to gain admission to Vienna's Academy of Fine Arts. ("Test drawing unsatisfactory," the examiner concluded. "Few heads.") He settled into a bohemian life. By the end of 1909, Hitler was living in a homeless shelter, emaciated and dirty. With an infusion of cash from his aunt and modest proceeds from the sales of his paintings in pubs around Vienna, he managed to survive until he came into his father's inheritance in 1913, at the age of twenty-four. That spring he departed for Munich, moved into a room above a shop in the western edge of the city's artists' quarter, and began selling his paintings of the city's landmarks: the Hofbräuhaus beer hall, the Gothic Frauenkirche, the Alter Hof, where the Holy Roman Emperor lived centuries before. He fell in love with his new German home. "The city was as familiar to me," Hitler wrote later, "as if I had lived for years within its walls."

His commonplace prejudices had not yet coalesced into the ideology that would change the face of Europe. From his days in Linz, Hitler had subscribed to the anti-Semitic, anti-Catholic German nationalism of Austrian politician Georg Ritter von Schönerer. His years of impoverishment in cosmopolitan Vienna only bolstered those views. The mayor, Karl Lueger, was a virulent anti-Semite, and the kiosks were crammed with right-wing newspapers portraying Jews as corrupt and perverse. But if Hitler concurred with the anti-Jewish chorus, that did not stop him from selling his paintings to Jewish dealers, nor did it prevent him from giving a painting to the Jewish doctor who treated his mother in her last days. Reinhold Hanisch, who met Hitler at the shelter in Vienna and helped him sell his paintings on the street, wrote in a short memoir later that Hitler seemed to get along exceptionally well with the Jews in Vienna. He even praised them as a people, Hanisch recalled, and applauded their contributions to global culture.

Hitler managed to evade compulsory Austrian military service. Instead, at the outbreak of the First World War, he volunteered in the Bavarian forces; authorities did not certify his nationality in the rush leading up to the fighting. Hitler spent the war running orders between command and the front lines, where the slaughter inured him to death and human distress. He earned the Iron Cross on two occasions and was twice wounded. He loved his regiment mates, who called him "the Artist" and marveled at his eccentricities: He did not drink or smoke, seemed to receive no mail, and spent much of his time reading.

In October 1918, he was partially blinded in a mustard gas attack near Ypres, Belgium, and sent to a hospital in Pasewalk, eighty-five miles north of Berlin, for the rest of the war. Hitler returned to Munich on November 21, about two weeks before Rosenberg's arrival.

After the Bolshevik regime was crushed in May 1919 and Bavaria joined the Weimar Republic, the German military wanted to keep an eye on Bavaria's chaotic swirl of partisan activity. With dozens of political organizations trying to build support for their ideas, the military brass wanted to be sure that embittered and defeated German troops were indoctrinated with a properly nationalistic, anti-Bolshevik attitude. Hitler joined the army's propaganda outfit as an informant and an instructor. He took classes on German history and socialism, which was where he first heard economist Gottfried Feder lecture about the evils of Jewish financiers.

Once he began leading his own indoctrination sessions that summer, Hitler roused his listeners with fiery speeches.

A man who had been at one of the sessions wrote asking for clarification on the "Jewish question." How could Germany deal with the matter when the country was being governed by liberal Social Democrats? The letter was passed along to Hitler, who drafted a reply. In his first known statement about the issue that would come to consume him, Hitler wrote that emotional attacks against the Jews would merely spark a few mass killings. What the nation needed was anti-Semitism based on "reason." When confronted with hard facts, the German people would support stripping Jews of their rights and, ultimately, removing them from German life altogether.

The letter was dated September 16, 1919, four days after Hitler first attended a meeting of the group that was to become the Nazi Party.

Hitler had been sent to the Sterneckerbräu by his superior officer, Captain Karl Mayr, to observe the fledgling outfit. Hitler ended up taking the floor, and he spoke with such vehemence that Anton Drexler, the party's founder, pressed a pamphlet into Hitler's hands and urged him to return. Acting on Mayr's order, Hitler signed up. But as it happened, he would not be a mere spy. He saw immediately that this was a party in line with his views, one still small enough that he could dominate it. Before long, the Nazi Party had become his life, and Hitler had become the most charismatic new figure on the right-wing scene.

Rosenberg met the party's future leader one day in late 1919 when Hitler visited Eckart. Rosenberg and Hitler spoke about ancient Rome and communism and the rootlessness of the Germans in the wake of the defeat. "I would be lying if I said I was overwhelmed by him and forthwith became his unconditional adherent," Rosenberg wrote after the war from his cell at Nuremberg.

Kurt Lüdecke, a wealthy supporter who helped raise money for the party, went even further: Rosenberg was in fact "no great admirer of the Hitler intellect."

But, like everyone, Rosenberg would be won over soon enough, once he heard the man speak in public. "Here I saw a German frontline soldier embarking on this struggle in a manner as clear as it was convincing, counting on himself alone with the courage of a free man," Rosenberg wrote in a letter about that first speech. "That was what, already after the first fifteen minutes, drew me to Adolf Hitler."

Eventually he would come to see that first meeting with Hitler for what it was: the most important turning point in his life, a brief encounter that "changed my entire personal fate and merged it with the fate of the German nation as a whole."

· · ·

In December 1920, the emergent Nazi Party bought a small weekly newspaper and vowed "to expand it into the most ruthless weapon for Germandom against hostile, anti-German forces." Some of the funds for its purchase came from an officer in the German army, which led to speculation that the money had come from a secret military account. Donations from small backers, wealthy private benefactors, and at least one nationalist organization helped keep the paper afloat. But the newspaper was in debt even before the Nazis bought it, and in the early days there was always some uncertainty about whether or not it would actually make it to press and onto newsstands.

Hitler took to urging supporters at his speeches to buy "the most hated paper in the land!"

The *Völkischer Beobachter* was housed at Schellingstrasse 39, around the corner from where Rosenberg lived. It was a typical newsroom—"full of confusion: phones ringing, editors dictating, visitors, the hum of voices," an employee recalled—except for the fact that the building also happened to be the headquarters of Hitler's private army of storm troopers, the Sturmabteilung, whose thugs sometimes hung around the office, swapping stories while they fiddled with their guns.

Hitler often spent hours at the newspaper in the mornings, holding forth with visitors, and the restaurants and cafés on Schellingstrasse became a locus of Nazi Party activity. At the corner of the next block was one of Hitler's favorite restaurants, Schelling-Salon, with its distinctive onion-domed cupola; the place was a regular hangout for Nazis until the owner refused to continue running a tab for the party chief. Hitler was also a fixture for many years at a dimly lit Italian restaurant a few doors down, Osteria Bavaria, where natural scenes adorned the paneled walls. Hitler and his guests preferred to dine behind a drawn curtain in a recessed alcove just inside the front door. Sometimes they walked down Ludwigstrasse to Café Heck, which looked out on the graceful Renaissance royal garden, the Hofgarten. When the weather was favorable, they could sit under the trees in wrought-iron chairs set up around tables covered with checkered cloths.

During his first years in Munich, Rosenberg spent most of his waking hours at Schellingstrasse 39, at first working under Eckart's editorship at the party's official mouthpiece but over time taking on more and more responsibility until he had become, in a sense, the chief writer for the party. His prose was often awkward and needed editing, and Hitler was not immediately pleased with the paper he and Eckart put out. He wanted something for the masses, something that would grab the attention of the people and make them see the world the way the Nazis did.

"At the beginning, the *Völkischer Beobachter* sailed on so high an intellectual plane that I myself had difficulty understanding it," Hitler would say, "and I certainly know no woman who could make head or tail of it!"

But the newspaper was publishing far more than Rosenberg's opaque musings. It ran dispatches from news agencies and stories pilfered from other papers, pieces on sports and the arts, contributions from supporters, political cartoons, jokes, articles and speeches by Hitler, party announcements ("Here Is Where We Fight Tomorrow"), serialized novels, and tabloid-style coverage of bloody mayhem and crime, with a focus on lurid sexual assaults by Jews described in graphic detail.

Because it was a party newspaper, of course, every story passed through an ideological filter, becoming in the process hysterical and derisive. Reporters jumped on every Weimar scandal. They wrote so many stories about corruption involving prominent politicians and four Jewish brothers named Barmat that it became a series: "Die Barmatologie."

The paper's writers liked to insert sarcastic exclamation points into the remarks of their enemies. They quoted Bernhard Weiss, Berlin's hated deputy police chief, this way: "The babbler (!!!) Hitler and the demagogue (!!) Goebbels cannot be taken seriously (!!!)."

In the sports section, readers found coverage of activities with militaristic applications, like hiking, gymnastics, and drill. The culture pages lamented Jewish influence on the arts. The newspaper even ran the sort of pornographic anti-Semitic pieces that made Julius Streicher and *Der Stürmer* famous. Hitler loved reading them.

"I am quite sure that at the time he despaired of humanity," Hitler said later about Rosenberg's editorship, "and his contempt for mankind was only increased when he found that the more he lowered the intellectual level of the journal, the more sales increased!"

In 1923, an aristocratic supporter sold some of her holdings of foreign stock to help finance the newspaper's conversion to a daily, and Ernst Hanfstaengl, an upper middle-class Harvard graduate who had returned to his homeland and become a Hitler acolyte, loaned the party $1,000 to buy new presses so the paper could be printed in the attention-grabbing wider format of America's major newspapers. The expansion coincided with Rosenberg's official rise to the editorship. Eckart, too bohemian to keep to a daily publishing schedule, had been forced out. Flush with cash, Hitler himself accompanied the new editor to shop for a desk. Rosenberg chose a rolltop, the better to hide his typical mess. "Hitler was almost childishly pleased," Rosenberg recalled. "Another step forward!" By November, the Nazi newspaper would have thirty thousand subscribers.

Hitler's appreciation for the ponderous writer mystified other leading Nazis. "Rosenberg was such an unappetizing fellow," wrote Hanfstaengl. Putzi, as he was known, was garrulous and well-connected; he would become Hitler's foreign press secretary. Hanfstaengl had a lengthy list of complaints about Rosenberg: that he was "intrinsically illiterate," that he had an annoying habit of whistling through his teeth while Hanfstaengl spoke to him, that he had "the taste of a costermonger's donkey," that he wore the same shirt day after day; "He had some theory about it being a waste of money to wash shirts and used to throw them away when they became unwearable even by his standards."

But above all, Hanfstaengl believed Rosenberg to be a charla-
tan. If the Nazi leader continued listening to the man, the entire
movement would run aground.

For all the hours he spent with his nose buried inside dusty tomes,
Rosenberg was no visionary thinker. He lifted from writers and
thinkers who came before him and adapted their ideas for the
audience of his day. Rosenberg's real importance was as a conduit
for the eighteenth- and nineteenth-century philosophies that
would give Nazi radicals the justification they needed to try to
alter the course of European history.

The concept of an idealized, supreme "Aryan" race made up of
tall, slender, strong, blue-eyed blonds evolved, oddly enough, out
of comparative linguistics. In the eighteenth century, a British
scholar in India, Sir William Jones, had stumbled upon resem-
blances between Sanskrit, Greek, and Latin, and he gave the
people who spoke these languages a name: Arya, the Sanskrit
word for "noble." In time, other researchers had categorized these
into families containing more than forty languages that shared
these similarities, including English and German.

Over the next century, this simple revelation was twisted out of
shape by thinkers wrestling with the question of how Indians and
Europeans had come to speak in such similar tongues. One imagined that a band of Himalayan warriors had conquered its way west
to Germany. Another decided that it was the other way around—
that Aryans had spread east from their fatherland, Germany.

In the 1800s, nationalist philosophers took this highly debat-
able pseudo-scholarly notion and made it the foundation of their
case for German exceptionalism. Lost on these men, and later
generations, was the fact that what these Aryans had in common
was language, not race.

In 1853, Count Joseph Arthur de Gobineau, an aristocratic
French diplomat, published the influential four-volume *Essay on
the Inequity of the Human Races*, in which he concluded that world

history could only be fully understood through a racial lens. Whites, and above all those mythical Germanic "Aryans," as he labeled them, were superior to all other races and responsible for every great accomplishment in civilization. Only by keeping their race pure of other strains could they ensure that they would continue to thrive.

Then came Houston Stewart Chamberlain, a Brit who fell in love with Germany despite a lineage that included English admirals and generals. Mentored as a teenager by a Prussian tutor, Chamberlain became a German citizen and befriended the composer Richard Wagner and his wife, Cosima. He married their daughter Eva and struck up a spirited correspondence with Kaiser Wilhelm II, the German emperor. Chamberlain wrote that he was haunted by demons, one of which set him to work on a book, *The Foundations of the Nineteenth Century*, published in 1899 and hailed by Rosenberg's newspaper two decades later as the "gospel of the Nazi movement." In the book, Chamberlain argued that the Jews were a bastard race and that the biologically superior Teutonic people, especially the Germans, deserved to rule the world. This was a scientific fact. It was written in the blood.

Rosenberg recalled that when he read *Foundations* as a teenager, "a new world opened up for me. . . . I said yes, yes, and yes again. . . . I was in the grip of a fundamental insight into the Jewish problem and it never let me go again."

Before he wrote his own twisted Chamberlainesque history, Rosenberg would spend his days churning out more quotidian racist fare. His first four published books peddled an anti-Semitism that was delusional, obsessive, and, above all else, paranoid. "There is no record in history," one academic wrote, "of any more pronounced or more uncompromising anti-Jewish polemicist than Alfred Rosenberg."

The Jews were responsible for everything that afflicted the world, Rosenberg declared in *The Track of the Jew Through the Ages*, published in 1920. If they were persecuted, it was their own fault. As a people, they were greedy and unscrupulous. "If one reads reports on Jewish trade in the Middle Ages . . . we notice their continual astonishment over Jewish trickery," Rosenberg wrote. "They recount the constant recurrence of falsification in exchange; feigned bankruptcy; . . . promissory notes written in Hebrew and accepted in faith, notes which, when translated, turned out to contain nothing but an uncouth sentence; the switching of packages after purchase, so that the purchaser would find stones or straw instead of what he purchased."

As "born conspirators," the Jews had no internal moral compass, so their leaders instituted a complex, technical code, "a confusion of laws." Jews could not be impartial judges or public officials, because their faith required them to treat only their fellow "chosen people" as equals. They were intolerant of gentiles. "Objectively, Jews are traitors to their nation at every step they take." They should never have been emancipated by Kaiser Wilhelm, should never have been permitted to circulate in German society, should never have been allowed to run newspapers and businesses, he insisted.

"One does not allow a poison to drift about unobserved, nor grant it parity with medicine."

"The Jewish people," he wrote the following year in *The Crime of Freemasonry*, "are chosen as a plague for all other nations by Satan, the Mephisto, who sneaks everywhere after Faust in order to take advantage at once of every one of his weaknesses and to drag him down to the dirt." Jews could try to convert, they could be baptized ten times over, but they could never change the evil in their blood.

Rosenberg did his part to promote the fraudulent *Protocols of the Elders of Zion*, first published in Russia in 1903, which purported to be the minutes of a secret meeting of Jewish leaders plotting to dominate the world by engineering wars and unrest, by controlling the economy, and by spreading atheism and liberalism through the press.

The origins of the notorious hoax remain cloudy. It was long argued that the czarist secret police had pieced it together from plagiarized sources around the turn of the century. Anti-Bolshevik Russians fleeing the communist revolution brought the book out of the Soviet Union, and soon it was published around the world.

Protocols appeared in Germany in 1919. Eckart, the publisher who first hired Rosenberg, reacted with "unspeakable horror" at this shadowy Jewish conspiracy; he apparently brought it to Hitler's attention. By 1921 the *Times* of London had exposed *Protocols* as a fake, but in a commentary Rosenberg published two years later, he was still declaring the book's authenticity an open question. Either way, he argued, the book meshed with other accounts and was an accurate outline of global Jewish strategy.

Rosenberg also wrote the definitive commentary outlining and explaining the party's official twenty-five-point platform. During these years, party members could not help but regard him as an authoritative voice on National Socialist ideology and a dominant force in the development of the party's doctrines. According to several Nazis who wrote memoirs after breaking with the party and fleeing Germany in the 1930s, Rosenberg was a key influence on Hitler in the early years. One of the defectors, Otto Strasser, contended that in 1923, Rosenberg was "the undisputed brain behind Adolf Hitler."

Kurt Lüdecke, an early supporter, recalled Hitler telling him to pay particular attention to Rosenberg's views on foreign policy.

"You haven't met Rosenberg yet?" Hitler asked one day. "You must know him better, get on good terms with him. He is the only man whom I always listen to. He is a thinker."

Hitler, of course, would have denied being anyone's marionette. In *Mein Kampf*, he described a dramatic epiphany during which, as a twentysomething young man living on the streets of Vienna, he suddenly recognized the Jewish evil. Accounts of his time in Vienna would suggest that Hitler's anti-Semitic radicalization came later, after the German defeat in the First World War, but as Hitler built a movement around his charismatic personality, he needed people to believe that he was bearing witness to a revelation born from exhaustive study and personal experience. He needed to portray himself as a singular figure. This, historian Ian Kershaw wrote, was what gave him "the claim to leadership of the national movement . . . the claim to be Germany's coming 'great leader.'"

Hitler's way of speaking gave his appearances the tenor of church revival meetings, historian Richard Evans wrote. With a flair for the dramatic, he would begin quietly and build slowly and methodically toward a rousing conclusion, his voice a shout, his hair flopping on his sweaty forehead, his hands slashing the air. A politician through and through, Hitler would connect his personal history of hard times to Germany's, a note that hit home at a time of turmoil and hyperinflation. In lacerating language, he would attack the revolution and the republic and the Jews who, he said, were behind it all. "Don't think you can fight a disease without killing the virus, without annihilating the bacillus," he raged in one infamous speech, "and don't think you can fight racial tuberculosis without taking care that the people are free of the cause of racial tuberculosis."

Toward the second half of 1920, Hitler added a significant new element to his speeches. He began issuing explicit warnings that the Jews who had brought Bolshevism to the Soviet Union now wanted to impose it on Germany. The red star, a symbol of the Soviet Union, was equivalent to "the Star of David, the sign of the synagogue, the symbol of the race high over the world, a lordship that stretches from Vladivostok to the West—the lordship of Jewry. The golden star which, for the Jew, means the glittering gold." The German people had a choice: They could live under the star of the Soviets or the swastika of the nationalists.

This was Rosenberg's influence at work. Hitler had acknowledged as late as the summer of 1920 that he did not know a lot about the situation on the ground in the Soviet Union. His Russian-speaking acolyte quickly filled him in.

The moment he arrived in Munich, Rosenberg had worked to establish himself as an expert on the workings of the Soviet Union. He argued that he knew the dangers of communism as well as anyone, because he had been there in 1917, in Moscow itself, during the first stage of the uprising. Rosenberg wrote about this "Russian Jewish Revolution" in his very first published piece, which appeared in Eckart's paper in 1919.

Rosenberg linked in Hitler's mind the phony global Jewish conspiracy and the communist uprising in Russia. His formula, as one historian would put it, was "Russia = Bolshevism = Jewry." Rosenberg went beyond that: He argued that the Jews, intent on controlling not just the Soviet Union and Germany but the entire world, were controlling *both* capitalism and communism. This was the great Jewish scam. They were pulling all the strings. They were playing both sides against the middle. On the heels of the brief but bloody 1919 communist uprisings in Munich, it was not difficult for Rosenberg's readers and Hitler's listeners to envision apocalyptic consequences should the Reds rule in Germany. Had they not just seen what happened when the communists took control? There were threats to confiscate all privately held weapons. There was a general strike and a crippling food shortage. There were summary arrests and executions. Just as they had done in Moscow, just as they had tried to do in Munich, the Jews would murder anyone and everyone who opposed them, Hitler promised. "It is quite enough to have a head on your shoulders and *not to be a Jew*: That will secure the scaffold for you."

During a typical speech delivered in Munich on July 28, 1922, Hitler told his audience that "Stock Exchange Jews" in the Soviet Union were masquerading as Marxist champions of the worker. "It is a gigantic fraud: world history has seldom seen its like."

The Jews had wrecked Russia, and they would conspire "until the whole world sinks in ruins."

"The whole of present-day Russia has nothing to show beyond a ruined civilization," he said. The Jew—"all rapacity, never satisfied"—was stealing everything for himself. "He seizes to himself the treasures of the churches, but not to feed the people: oh no! Everything wanders away and leaves not a trace behind. . . . And now Germany is reaching that stage which Russia has drunk to the dregs."

The Jews wanted to make the once great German nation "defenseless in arms" and its people "defenseless in spirit." While people might think it wise to stay silent and avoid trouble, Hitler assured them that they were doomed either way. "No, my friend. The only difference will be that I may hang perhaps still talking, while you will hang—in silence. Here, too, Russia can give us countless examples, and with us it will be the same story."

There was, Hitler announced, a single logical reaction to the prospect of a Jewish-led Soviet dictatorship in Germany: The people must fight back. "On this point there should be no doubt: We will not let the Jews slit our gullets, and not defend ourselves."

A few months later on another stage, Hitler promised that this would be a fight to the death. It was us or them, he told his adherents. Jews and Nazis could not coexist in the future Germany. "We know that if they come to power, our heads will roll in the sand," he said. "But we also know that when we get our hands on power, then God have mercy on you!"

In the years after the birth of the Weimar Republic, election after election roiled the political scene. Germany would be led by twenty different cabinets as a scrum of political parties battled for control in the Reichstag: Social Democrats, the German Democratic Party, the Catholic Center Party, the Communists, the Nationalists. Military debt, the transition to a peacetime economy, industrial disruption, war reparations imposed by the Allies in the Versailles peace treaty—all of these problems would plague the German economy, and inflation would reach preposterous levels. At one point in 1923, it took more than four trillion marks to buy a dollar.

That summer, Hitler began loudly demanding the overthrow of the hated republic. Gustav Ritter von Kahr, Bavaria's general state commissioner, responded by banning a series of scheduled Nazi rallies and ordering Rosenberg's newspaper shuttered.

Frustrated, Hitler decided the time had finally come to stage a coup and take power. He had a key ally behind him, General Erich Ludendorff, who, with General Paul von Hindenburg, had led the German forces in the First World War and by 1923 was the nation's most prominent right-wing figure.

Hitler also had muscle: a coalition of nationalist paramilitary groups, among them fifteen thousand storm troopers under the command of a man who would become one of the outsize figures of the Third Reich, known the world over for his corpulence and his bluster.

Hermann Göring was a garrulous man with an insatiable appetite for luxury and a great capacity for cruelty. Part of his childhood was spent in a medieval castle owned by his mother's lover, a half-Jewish Austrian doctor. There, amid the ramparts and turrets and decorative armor, young Hermann fantasized about Germany's mythical history, when chivalrous Teutonic knights roamed about, conquering Europe.

At first a rebellious student, he flourished in a military school. He attended Germany's equivalent of West Point, the Prussian Military Academy, and during the First World War won the Iron Cross as an infantry officer in early combat.

Bad knees and good fortune sent him to flight school. As an observer on a two-man plane, he won the attention of military leaders for his ability to shoot exemplary photographs of enemy fortifications while under fire. Soon he learned to fly fighter planes fitted with machine guns, a new innovation, and by the end of the war he had twenty-two kills to his name. For a time in

1918, Göring commanded an elite squadron of German fighter pilots, the Jagdgeschwader Richthofen, the same unit the fabled Red Baron had led before his death.

Göring was outraged by the German surrender at the end of the war, and he was intent on being part of a national return to glory. "I ask everyone here tonight to cherish hatred, a deep and abiding hatred, of those swine who have outraged the German people and our traditions," he said at a protest against the revolutionaries in 1918. "But the day will come when we will drive them out of our Germany. Prepare for that day. Arm yourselves for that day. Work for that day. It will surely come."

Four years later, the embittered war hero fell in with Hitler, just in time to help the Nazis try to overthrow Bavaria.

The question was when to strike. Rosenberg and another émigré from the East, Max Erwin von Scheubner-Richter, suggested taking von Kahr hostage and forcing him to consent to a march on Berlin. The Nazis made plans to move on November 8, when von Kahr was to speak at a beer hall, the Bürgerbräukeller, alongside the army commander and police chief.

That morning, Rosenberg was at work in the Schellingstrasse office housing the newspaper and the storm troopers. The building hummed with activity. Hanfstaengl noticed that Rosenberg, dressed in his usual unwashed shirt and tie, had a pistol resting ostentatiously on the desk.

Hitler, riding whip in hand, appeared and ducked into Rosenberg's office. "Tonight, we act," he told the men. "Bring your pistols."

Rosenberg put on his tan fedora and a trench coat, and rode in a red Mercedes with Hitler and his bodyguard over the Isar River to the beer hall. Heavily armed and wearing steel helmets, Göring's storm troopers surrounded the Bürgerbräukeller a little after 8:30 p.m. A machine gun was set up in the main doorway, and the Nazis pushed their way to the front of the hall, Rosenberg, pistol in hand, by Hitler's side.

Bedlam ensued. Hitler, wearing a black morning coat and his Iron Cross, fired his weapon into the ceiling, declared that the revolution had begun, and climbed over the tables to reach the podium. The top leaders of Bavaria were escorted into a back room.

Göring worked to calm the crowd ("You've got your beer!"), while Hitler not so politely tried to persuade von Kahr and the others to join his national coup. They refused to speak to him. "No one leaves this room alive without my permission!" he cried. Soon Ludendorff materialized to join the tense negotiations, and the Bavarian leaders finally agreed to cooperate.

The coup was announced in the hall to cheers and the singing of the German national anthem, "Deutschland über Alles."

Rosenberg rushed back to the newspaper offices to oversee publication of the official announcement of the revolution. As he broke the news to his staff, the office exploded into noisy applause.

"There is only one thing for us," Rosenberg told them. "Either tomorrow we have a German national government or we are dead."

An editor dictated a lead. "Germany awakens from her wild feverish dream, a new era of greatness breaks through the clouds in streaming brilliance, the night is illuminated, it becomes day, the eagle, the symbol of German might and greatness, arises again!"

But before the newspaper hit the streets, the putsch was already doomed.

The Nazis had failed to occupy the key military barracks, and Hitler left the Bürgerbräukeller without making sure that the Bavarian leaders would be kept under guard. Ludendorff let von Kahr and the others escape, and they quickly moved to crush the revolt. The revolutionaries had not taken control of the communications lines, and loyal troops were called in as von Kahr denounced the plotters on the radio and ordered the Nazi Party dissolved.

It snowed the following morning, the fifth anniversary of the declaration of the German republic, the black day when, to the nationalists' way of thinking, the "November criminals" had betrayed Germany. Desperate to have something to show for their botched coup, the Nazis decided to march to the center of Munich in hopes of winning over the army and the police with a demonstration of their numbers.

The revolutionaries started from the beer hall, two thousand men in a column. It felt more like a funeral march at first, but when they reached the center of the city and saw that crowds were joining them, they thought for a moment that they could still carry the day. Rosenberg walked in the second row, behind Göring, Ludendorff, and Hitler, whose arm was hooked in solidarity with Scheubner-Richter's. The marchers reached Marienplatz and the Rathaus, then turned right and continued north on Residenzstrasse toward Odeonsplatz.

At the Feldherrnhalle, a monument to Bavarian generals in the square, one hundred state policemen waited.

"Surrender!" Hitler cried.

Weapons were drawn, and in the silence that followed, a shot was fired.

For barely a minute, a barrage of bullets pierced the air. Scheubner-Richter took a bullet to the head and, falling dead, pulled Hitler to the ground, dislocating the Nazi leader's shoulder. Göring was hit in the groin. Rosenberg, no First World War veteran, dropped to the street as soon as the shooting started. The man marching next to him, Oskar Körner, owner of a small toy store, was killed. Hitler and Göring fled the chaos, as did the unharmed Rosenberg. Sixteen Nazis and four policemen were killed. Ludendorff strode, somehow unscathed, all the way to the police line, where he was duly arrested.

Hitler was rushed into a waiting car by medical staff and soon turned up at Hanfstaengl's house, south of Munich, injured and gloomy, possibly suicidal. His arrest imminent, he took up a pencil and jotted down a message to his followers in which he announced an interim party leader. He wrote a special message for Rosenberg. Then he was taken into custody in a white nightgown and brought to the prison at Landsberg am Lech, cell number 7.

No one could have been more surprised than Rosenberg to learn what Hitler had decided about the immediate future of the Nazi Party.

"Dear Rosenberg," Hitler's note read. "From now on you will lead the movement."

Rosenberg quickly demonstrated that he was entirely unsuited for executive leadership. Later, some Nazis assumed that that was why Hitler chose him. Surely Hitler hoped to return to the helm after getting out of prison. He did not want to hand the party over to a potentially powerful rival. And yet at the same time, he couldn't know for sure what the future held. A lengthy prison sentence? Banishment to Austria? He was injured and distressed, and in the rush to pass on instructions, he chose his most loyal *alter Kämpfer*— "old fighter," as the Nazis referred to their earliest members.

While Hitler spent his days in prison writing *Mein Kampf* on a typewriter, the Nazi Party splintered under Rosenberg's watch. With the organization outlawed and its finances frozen, Rosenberg first informed his compatriots in a December 3 memo that they would have to operate as an underground organization. ("Secret!" the letter warned. "Burn after review.") He began using a pseudonym, Rolf Eidhalt—an anagram for "Adolf Hitler."

A contingent of Nazis who had survived the Munich firing squad assembled in Salzburg and tried to reach Rosenberg, but he was hard to locate. Fearing imminent arrest, he moved from apartment to apartment on a nightly basis.

Even Lüdecke, an ally of Rosenberg's, said the party was adrift. "He could do little to direct us."

In January 1924, Rosenberg formed the Greater German National Community, which he intended to be the successor to the banned Nazis, but even with Hitler's blessing Rosenberg could not bring together the competing factions under his banner. His strategy was to pivot from revolutionary outfit to legitimate political party. In the spring, the new party joined other far-right groups in putting up candidates for the Bavarian Parliament and the Reichstag. But when a rival nationalist faction, the German Völkisch Freedom Party, had greater success in the elections and suggested that the Nazis join a coalition, Hitler balked—and announced that he was withdrawing from political activity until his release from prison.

Without his support, attempts to unify the far right effectively ended, and so did Rosenberg's brief, scalding experience as substitute Führer. Undermined and marginalized in a nationalist movement riven with internecine rivalries, he was ousted.

On December 20, 1924, Hitler was released from prison, and he swiftly recaptured control of the party. He raged at Rosenberg for venturing into electoral politics, even though that was precisely what he himself would decide to do next. When the *Völkischer Beobachter* reappeared, Hitler wrote the lead story, faulting Ludendorff and Rosenberg for their missteps while he was away.

Rosenberg did not attend the rousing relaunch of the Nazi Party, staged in February at a packed Bürgerbräukeller in Munich. "I won't take part in that comedy," Rosenberg told Lüdecke. "I know the sort of brother-kissing Hitler intends to call for." While the other combatants of the previous year stepped onto the stage, shook hands in forgiveness, and fell in line behind Hitler, Rosenberg—unwilling to let bygones be bygones—filed libel suits against his archenemies in the party.

Hitler insisted that Rosenberg drop the cases, and in exchange he offered to let him return to the helm of the party newspaper. Rosenberg hesitated, and Hitler asked Lüdecke to intervene: "You'd better see to it that Rosenberg comes to his senses and stops playing the offended innocent."

"That's not so easy," Lüdecke replied. "That cut went deeper than you think."

"*Ja, ja*, we'll see," the Führer said with a laugh.

Hitler stitched up the wound by handing Rosenberg not just the job but also an extraordinary letter. Despite its backhandedness, the note showed how much Hitler wanted to keep Rosenberg in the fold.

Hitler noted that the party's affairs were so confused following the attempted coup that he could understand why bitter and insulting words had been spoken by Rosenberg's rivals. "When the heart is full," Hitler wrote, "the mouth overflows." But no matter what was said in the heat of the moment, he wanted his lieutenant to know he had Hitler's utmost respect. "I know you, Herr Rosenberg, and regard you . . . as one of the most valuable collaborators with our movement," he wrote. "In the difficult period in which, quite unexpectedly and without explanation, you took over leadership of the movement, you tried to advance the cause as much as possible—with me this conviction goes without saying; in the process mistakes may have crept in, as can happen with you as with everyone else. But it is not my object to give an opinion on mistakes, but solely on intention and good will. For this I must give you the highest credit in everything."

Their relationship healed, but Rosenberg would never again be as close to Hitler as he had been before the attempted Bürgerbräukeller coup.

Hitler purchased a black, six-seat Mercedes, and he loved to speed through the countryside with agreeable compatriots riding along. Rosenberg, relentlessly serious, inflexible, humorless, seemed to know that he wasn't the sort of person anyone would invite on a relaxing day trip. Talk would turn inevitably to party business and his bureaucratic feuds with other Nazi leaders. He couldn't help himself.

"He valued me very much," Rosenberg would come to conclude, "but he did not like me."

Rosenberg was probably not as reluctant to return to the trenches as he let on when Hitler offered to return him to the editorship of the newspaper. He was thirty-two years old, and he had done only one thing since his arrival in Germany: write polemics for the party.

So in 1925, as the Nazis began to rebuild their shattered party and launched a perpetual campaign for political power, Rosenberg had no choice but to return to the office on Schellingstrasse and run the *Völkischer Beobachter*. He needed the money, he told Lüdecke, and "besides, the work is my life, I cannot give up the cause."

The party mouthpiece was as sarcastic and combative as before. The newspaper declared the leaders of the Weimar government "internationalist-pacifist-effeminate." It called Yahweh "the devil, a murderer from the beginning, and the liar and father of lies." It denounced the Jewish faith as "a mask to conduct moral and economic plundering and destruction under the protection of German state law." It attacked a rival editor as a "murderer of the German soul, a betrayer of the German people, and an agent of decay of public opinion."

Not surprisingly, the newspaper's diatribes frequently landed Rosenberg and his writers in court on charges of defamation and incitement.

The Law for the Protection of the Republic allowed government officials to ban newspapers that called for a violent uprising against the government, and the paper repeatedly racked up fines and suspensions. In March 1926, Rosenberg even went to prison for a month.

"The battle for the soul of the people was waged in broad daylight," Rosenberg wrote years later. "The attacks against us were vicious, and we answered viciously." Those *Völkischer Beobachter* articles "were frequently written at seven o'clock in the morning, were based on reports that had just come in, and were thus not always considered opinions. In their attacks our opponents spared us absolutely nothing." It was a bruising period, a time of endless wars with enemies inside and outside the party.

In 1930, Rosenberg won a seat in the Reichstag, where he was a marked man for the Nazis' foes. Once, as he rose to speak in his brown Nazi uniform shirt, Social Democrats in the Parliament were ready with catcalls sure to upset the anti-Semite with the Jewish-sounding name.

"Here's a Jew!" they cried. "Look at the nose! On to Palestine!"

More damaging were insinuations about his actions during the First World War. Hanfstaengl informed Göring that Rosenberg had spent some time in France and had been in the employ of the French military intelligence bureau. Göring helped spread the rumor. "The fellow should just finally say what he was really doing in Paris during the war," he said at one point. Nazi opponents took up the attack in the press, but a police inquiry turned up no evidence to support the claims. Rosenberg—who said it was a perfectly harmless trip to Paris to visit his then-girlfriend and future wife in 1914—won damages after taking two socialist newspapers to court over the allegations.

But the slur stuck. It came up during a Reichstag debate in 1932 and set off a brief fracas. One communist politician suggested that Rosenberg had worked against Germany during the war, and the target of his attack bristled. "You want me to box your ears?" Chancellor Heinrich Brüning, in reply to sharp criticism from Rosenberg that day, dismissed the Nazi as a "so-called Balt, who at the moment that I was fighting to the last breath in the war, had not yet discovered which his real fatherland was."

If Rosenberg found solace in his personal life, he left little record of it. He and Hilda divorced in 1923, after eight years of marriage. The marriage had effectively ended in 1918 when he departed for Germany. She did not accompany him, instead traveling with her family to seek treatment for her tuberculosis at spas in the Black Forest region of Germany and in Switzerland. "She said that at first she might have been able to help me a little, but now I had found my way. She was sick, she said, and probably would have to rely on other people for the rest of her life," Rosenberg wrote later in an account that was striking for its affectless tone. "Later she joined her parents in Reval, went to France in a last attempt to find a cure, and died."

One summer day not long after the separation, Rosenberg was leaving the newspaper offices on Schellingstrasse when he spotted "a slim, beautiful lady in a dark costume and a large black hat with a tartan band." He was immediately interested. Hedwig Kramer was twenty-four, six years younger than Rosenberg. He watched her walk into a Greek restaurant where he often ate lunch and, following her inside, he struck up a conversation. He wooed her during long walks around the ponds and meadows of Munich's Englischer Garten, Europe's largest city park, where Germans could stroll for hours without retracing their steps. They married in 1925 and had two children—a son who died in infancy and a daughter, Irene, who was born in 1930. As he and Hedwig started their family, they moved into a place on Akademiestrasse, directly across the street from the lustrous white stone edifice of the Academy of Fine Arts.

But his work was his life. Years passed with Rosenberg at his desk: studying, reading, thinking, writing. What little time he was away from the office, he spent buried in books or steeped in Germanic history. One of his first trips with his new wife was to see the castle ruins at Heidelberg.

His editorial responsibilities went beyond the gutter journalism of the party newspaper. He also oversaw an anti-Semitic journal, *Der Weltkampf* (*The World Struggle*), which couched standard anti-Semitic themes in pseudo-scholarly, footnoted articles; Hitler called it "a weapon of the first rank." Later, Rosenberg took the helm of *Nationalsozialistische Monatshefte* (*National Socialist Monthly*), which expounded on the party's ideological and theoretical underpinnings. He was an extraordinarily prolific firebrand. Before he was finished, he would write more prose than all the other leading Nazis—combined.

As 1933 dawned, the work was finally paying off. Ten punishing years after their bloody defeat at Odeonsplatz—years of beer-hall electioneering and newspaper agitation and backroom maneuvering and bare-knuckle street fighting—Hitler and the Nazis were finally, astoundingly, on the brink of real power.

Rosenberg was going back to Berlin. This time he would not be a mere bystander along the Unter den Linden, not just another spectator to history.

This time, Rosenberg was arriving at the right hand of a powerful man who was resolved to *make* history.

Hitler with some of his compatriots on January 30, 1933, the day he rose to power. *From left to right:* Wilhelm Kube, Hanns Kerrl, Joseph Goebbels, Adolf Hitler, Ernst Röhm, Hermann Göring, Richard Walther Darré, Heinrich Himmler, and Rudolf Hess. Wilhelm Frick is seated.
(Universal History Archive/UIG via Getty Images)

6

Night Descends

It all happened so quickly. Hitler came to power on January 30, 1933, as part of a political compromise. The impetuous revolutionary was supposed to be hemmed in—cooled off, controlled—by a cabinet of sensible men appointed by President Paul von Hindenburg, the hulking field marshal who'd led the German armies in the First World War.

But the Nazi chancellor was moving too fast, and the cabinet could not slow his momentum.

In the hours after his swearing-in as German chancellor, Hitler demanded a new round of parliamentary elections to consolidate his power. He knew that this time, after so many years in the political wilderness, scrapping with the powers arrayed against them in the Weimar Republic, the Nazis had everything going for them. This time they couldn't lose.

They immediately took control of the civil service and put the police, the state media, and the radio to work for the party. They won pledges from wealthy business leaders to finance the campaign. They violently interrupted their opponents' campaign rallies and shuttered rival newspapers. And after years of promising that heads would roll, they quickly made good on their threats to exact harsh retribution against their enemies.

Fear, then and always, would be the main weapon in the Nazi arsenal.

The night of Hitler's ascension, his storm troopers—a paramilitary force hardened by more than a decade of street fighting—marched in endless columns through the streets of Berlin. The torchlight parade stretched on for so many hours that, to some onlookers, it seemed that Hitler already had at his command hundreds of thousands of fanatical belligerents in brown shirts and high boots, ready to terrorize anyone who stood in their way. In fact, he did, and the paramilitary army would only grow in the coming months: By the beginning of 1934, its ranks numbered nearly three million.

The Nazis had not been in power a month when a Dutch communist named Marinus van der Lubbe torched the Reichstag, the ornate hall where the German Parliament met. Rosenberg had been driving through the Tiergarten when he saw the flames. A reporter spotted him there, watching, and Rosenberg's first thought was the same as everyone else's: Nazi schemers had probably set the building afire so they could blame it on their enemies.

Who was really to blame for burning the Reichstag would be debated for decades, but the arson was put to immediate political use by Hitler's propagandists: This, they cried, was the start of a Red plot to overthrow the German government.

The following day, Hitler appealed to Hindenburg for an emergency suspension of basic civil rights. The old war hero—the man who named Hitler chancellor, and the only person in Germany who could have stopped his rise over the next year—gave the Nazis everything they wanted. Freedom of expression and assembly, press liberties, protection from warrantless search and surveillance—all of those essential rights were discarded "until further notice" in the name of state security. The communists quickly felt the brunt of Nazi aggression, as storm troopers raided party offices, making arrests and seizing coffers. In cities all across the nation, communist sympathizers were rounded up by the thousands: writers, teachers, intellectuals, lawyers, pacifists, and politicians, even elected Reichstag legislators. The prisoners were clapped into improvised concentration camps. Some were tortured; hundreds died in custody.

Ascending to power alongside Hitler was Hermann Göring, who was appointed to lead the Prussian Interior Ministry. This put him in charge of the police forces in Germany's largest state, which included the capital. Göring quickly claimed emergency powers and put his security apparatus to work, pitilessly suppressing every political organization opposed to the Nazis.

"Whoever does his duty in the service of the state, who obeys my orders and ruthlessly makes use of his revolver when attacked is assured of my protection," Göring told his men in a February 17 directive. "I know two sorts of law because I know two sorts of men: those who are with us and those who are against us." He told foreign diplomats that he was building concentration camps for enemies of the state and that they should not "be shocked by what some people call excesses. Flogging, general cruelty, even deaths . . . these are inevitable in a forceful, sweeping, young revolution." To his enemies, Göring issued bloodthirsty warnings in a speech two days before the election: "Fellow Germans, my measures will not be crippled by any judicial thinking. . . . I don't have to worry about justice. My mission is only to destroy and exterminate, nothing more!"

It was an election season like no other Germany had seen, "a farce," according to the U.S. ambassador. The Nazis promised that this would be the last round of voting Germany would ever see, or need. Win or lose, they weren't handing over the reins.

In the end, Hitler didn't need to ignore the constitution to stay in power. The ballots were counted on March 5, and the Nazis won enough seats to maintain control. "Hitler has won an unprecedented triumph," U.S. Ambassador Frederic Sackett declared. "Democracy in Germany has received a blow from which it may never recover."

When the new parliament convened on March 23, the elegant Kroll Opera House standing in for the scorched Reichstag, Hitler took to the podium and railed against the communist threat to German security. He urged lawmakers to pass an Enabling Act by which they would hand over the bulk of their powers to Hitler's cabinet. If he was to protect the homeland, he told the deputies, he would need a tighter grip on the levers of power. Mustered outside the chamber, the storm troopers took up a chant: "Full powers, or else!" Hitler's act passed by a wide margin, setting Germany on a course for dictatorship, war, and the worst horrors Europe would ever see.

The most amazing thing, American foreign correspondent William Shirer would marvel, was that, more or less, "it was all done quite legally."

In Berlin, thirty-three-year-old Robert Max Wasilii Kempner watched the Nazi rise with unease. He was in a precarious position. His parents were Jews by birth. In the interests of assimilation they'd had their children baptized into the Lutheran faith, but it was race—not religion—that determined how the Nazis classified its citizens. Kempner was also a Social Democrat, and in 1930 he had helped build a legal case for outlawing the Nazi Party and expelling Hitler to Austria.

But despite all of that, Kempner was a born networker and a crafty operator. Even with the Nazis in power, he had surprising friends in important places.

Kempner's parents were microbiologists of some note. Walter Kempner and Lydia Rabinowitsch-Kempner thought of themselves as the loyal opposition. They believed in Germany, but not its myths—not Bismarck's "blood and iron," not the monarchy, certainly not the Teutonic legends championed by Alfred Rosenberg. "I grew up in a house where skepticism played a great role," Kempner wrote years later.

Days after the start of the First World War, on August 4, 1914, Lydia went to the Reichstag to discuss the possibility that German soldiers in the field could encounter infectious diseases like the plague, and how the military should combat them. After she listened to a speech Kaiser Wilhelm II delivered in the White Room of the Royal Palace—the historic one during which he officially informed the Parliament that Germany was at war—a reporter recognized her and asked what she was doing there. "Waiting for the plague," she replied, and while it was accurate enough literally, the metaphorical significance of her words still resonated for her son when he was an old man.

Lydia Rabinowitsch was a Russian Jew born in Lithuania to a wealthy family that owned a large brewery. The Rabinowitsches became dentists, doctors, businessmen, and lawyers; Lydia, the youngest, went to college in Bern and Zurich, Switzerland, where she studied botany and zoology.

She received her doctorate in 1893 and moved to Berlin to work for the microbiologist Robert Koch. One of the most important scientists of his day, Koch conducted pioneering research on anthrax, discovered the bacteria that causes cholera and tuberculosis, and helped prove that germs cause contagious disease. His Institute for Infectious Diseases attracted the brightest minds in the field of bacteriology at the turn of the century. It was at Koch's institute that Rabinowitsch met a smart young doctor and researcher named Walter Kempner, who was head physician in the facility's hospital. He descended from a Jewish family in Poland that had made a fortune in the mortgage bond business. Lydia and Walter married in 1898, and the following year, they were in Montenegro studying malaria outbreaks in the Balkans when Rabinowitsch went into labor. They raced home so their first child could be born in Germany. They named him Robert, in honor of their hero, Koch.

The three Kempner children were immersed in their parents' work. Their father saw patients in examining rooms at the family's large house on Potsdamer Strasse in Lichterfelde, a leafy neighborhood in a southwestern section of the capital. A microscope was set up in the study, and test animals—rabbits, mice—scuttled about in cages on the porch. The family talked about the latest in bacteria research at the dinner table. Koch took the children out on Sundays and taught them how to fly kites.

On June 18, 1917, Robert Kempner enlisted in the army. Figuring he would be drafted anyway, he volunteered. Whatever his family felt about militarism in general and the kaiser in particular, he wanted to serve. He arrived on the Western Front on October 25, 1918, just in time to retreat as the German armies fell back from a major defensive position in the face of the final Allied assaults. Returning to Berlin with his unit, he was among the legions of soldiers who marched down Unter den Linden before his discharge on December 18. He was awarded an Iron Cross for his service.

When he arrived home, he hid his military-issue pistol and carbine in the attic. At nineteen, he already had seen enough to know that he might need them again.

Two months into the Weimar Republic, the new government faced an insurrection—not from nationalists on the right but from "Spartacists" on the left. On January 6, 1919, communists moved to overthrow the new government and install a Soviet-style regime. They seized control of the Social Democrats' newspaper, tried to shut down the city with a general strike, and captured key government buildings. They even managed to set up rifles atop the Brandenburg Gate.

Two days into the uprising, Friedrich Ebert, the chancellor, hunkered down in his office and considered whether to capitulate. Instead, his minister of defense, Gustav Noske, set up a war room in a girls' boarding school southwest of the city and orchestrated a counterattack. Ebert and Noske had no choice but to call up the Freikorps, remnants of military divisions that had disbanded at the end of the war. At the time, Berlin had about a dozen such quasi-independent paramilitary units led by old army officers. Their men were hardened veterans of the war who, whether out of patriotism or military habit, volunteered to beat back the communist threat.

Even for an age soaked in blood, the communist mutiny was put down in especially violent fashion. Noske's improvised army marched north and took back the city block by block. At the newspaper offices, the facade was blown apart with mortars and tanks, and the fighters inside—some of them flapping white flags, some firing pistols from behind enormous rolls of newsprint— were killed with howitzers, machine guns, and grenades. The Freikorps launched artillery shells at the Berlin police headquarters, where the communists had organized the coup; those who tried to flee the carnage were gunned down. The revolution was crushed in a matter of days.

Kempner volunteered to go to Berlin with the remnants of his unit in the midst of the fighting, much to his father's consternation. (He asked his son, "Are you crazy?") Kempner would give varying accounts of what he did during those days. In letters seeking credit for his military service, he wrote that he had participated in "street fighting," and his military records show that he spent ten days in January and the entire month of March with his unit, the Freiwilligen-Eskadron Kürassier-Regiment No. 4.

But years later, in his autobiography, Kempner downplayed his role. He had already enrolled in the university and was home on break. He had "marched out of sheer curiosity." He didn't engage in any actual fighting; he had left the carbine in the attic at home in Lichterfelde. He stayed for only two weeks. He cast himself as a student on vacation. "It was," he wrote, "an excursion to the terror."

When he reported for duty, he was dispatched to the Hotel Eden, across the street from the zoo, which had been requisitioned as the command post for a Freikorps unit called the Horse Guards Division. Kempner answered telephones, relayed messages, and eavesdropped on the lines. He heard all kinds of things, he acknowledged, but he insisted he didn't really know "what was going on." He pulled guard duty outside the hotel and on nearby Kurfürstendamm, a fashionable street of shops and cafés. Despite the pockets of intermittent street fighting and the cold, there were actually people out and about. One of Kempner's friends met a girl on the street and let her try on his uniform jacket.

History would remember those weeks at the Eden for different reasons. On January 15 at 9:00 p.m., two leaders of the revolt, Karl Liebknecht and Rosa Luxemburg, were arrested and brought to the hotel, where they were questioned and beaten and finally hustled out the back door. They were clubbed with rifles, tossed into cars, and shot to death. Luxemburg's body was dumped off a bridge into the icy canal to molder; it was not fished out until nearly five months later.

Kempner wrote that he hadn't known anything about the notorious murders: He had quit the outfit and gone home a few days beforehand. In fact, according to his military records, he was still on duty when Luxemburg and Liebknecht were dragged out and shot.

He returned to his schooling, studying political science, law, and public administration at universities in Berlin, Breslau, and Freiburg. In 1923, straight out of law school, he was hired by a prominent defense attorney named Erich Frey, who was known for his slicked-back hair and his persuasive arguments on behalf of Berlin's wealthiest, most infamous criminals. Frey was the sort of lawyer who won light sentences for gangsters by portraying them as men with their own code of justice.

After three years at the defense tables, Kempner went over to the other side. In 1926, he worked as an assistant in the state attorney's office, but that career path ended when he was caught leaking a story to a newspaper that cast the department in a negative light.

Then, despite donning a bright yellow flannel suit for his interview with the minister—his tastes in clothing always ran to the outlandish—Kempner landed a post at the Prussian Interior Ministry. He was an ambitious and hardworking hire. Between 1928 and 1933, as legal adviser to the Prussian State Police, he handled claims against the police force, helped draft a new police administrative code, taught at the state police institute, and wrote articles for legal journals.

At a time when the Nazis were building support all across the country on the strength of bombastic populist speeches calling for a violent national renewal, Kempner found common cause with left-wingers. One of them was Carl von Ossietzky, a pacifist editor imprisoned after his newspaper revealed aspects of the military's secret rearmament, which violated the terms of the Versailles peace treaty. At Ossietzky's request, Kempner did pro bono legal work on behalf of the German League for Human Rights, the most active pacifist organization in the country between the wars. Among those in its ranks was Albert Einstein.

In 1930, the Interior Ministry grew increasingly alarmed by Hitler's revolutionary rhetoric and launched a comprehensive investigation of the Nazis. The central question was whether Hitler and his allies were guilty of treason for repeatedly discussing the overthrow of the government.

Investigators from the legal, political, and police divisions of the ministry attended public Nazi rallies and examined the party's propaganda. They pored over pamphlets, newsletters, training documents, leaflets, recordings of speeches, internal memos, and the *Völkischer Beobachter*. After months of work, ministry officials produced three detailed reports outlining the Nazi threat from political, religious, and economic angles.

The report produced by Kempner's division presented a legal basis for outlawing the party and jailing its members. The Nazis had spent the past decade telling the world what they intended to do when—not if—they took power. The radicals trumpeted their plans in speech halls, in newspapers, and in their books, not least Hitler's turgid 140,000-word manifesto, *Mein Kampf*, published in 1925. (According to the calculations of the prominent novelist Lion Feuchtwanger, the book contained "139,900 mistakes.")

Relying on the party leaders' own words, the Kempner report argued that National Socialism was more than a political organization; it was a "highly centralized" radical cult. Every member was expected to be an "obedient tool" speaking with a single voice. The Nazis were intent on replacing the republic with a dictatorship. While they claimed to be working for change from within by electing representatives to national and state parliaments, in fact they were revolutionaries who had never truly renounced the idea of storming into power by force.

They practically indicted themselves with their public pronouncements.

"National Socialism openly confesses that it is a military Party, never to constitute a numerical majority of the people," Rosenberg wrote.

"We are creating a powerful group with which we can one day conquer this State, and then, with the power of the State, we shall relentlessly and brutally enforce our will and our program," Goebbels announced. "Once we have conquered the State, the State is ours."

"We are courageously and ruthlessly building our new state," Hitler cried. "We shall do what we want; we have the courage to face any power!"

There were laws against this sort of high treason, the report argued, and the government ought to enforce them—instead of treating the Nazis like a legitimate political party in the Reichstag, instead of watching impotently as the storm clouds gathered.

One high-profile prosecution implicating the Nazis did reach a courtroom in these years. The government was preoccupied with Nazi attempts to infiltrate the army. The generals had banned recruitment of Nazis, and asked soldiers to refrain from politics altogether. But many army officers were increasingly attracted to Hitler's vision of a robust military unshackled from the limitations imposed by the Versailles peace treaty.

In the spring of 1930, three young military officers were charged with disseminating Nazi propaganda and advocating that the army stand by in the event of a Nazi coup. Kempner played a role in the investigation and sat in on the lieutenants' trial for treason. Testifying in the courtroom at Leipzig, Hitler disowned the defendants and assured the court that the Nazis had no plans for armed revolt.

"Our movement has no need of force. The time will come when the German nation will get to know of our ideas; then thirty-five million Germans will stand behind me." At the same time, he promised that when the Nazis won power—by legal, constitutional means—they would rebuild the army to its past glory and avenge the Jewish traitors who had stabbed Germany in the back in 1918 and brought the nation to ruin.

"Heads will roll!" he cried, to noisy applause in the chambers.

The Interior Ministry dossiers Kempner helped prepare went to the senior prosecutor in the Justice Ministry, who ignored them. As it turned out, he was sympathetic to the Nazis, and when Hitler became chancellor, he kept the loyal official at his post.

Three years later, in 1933, the Nazis were in power, doing everything they had promised. "Hitler certainly loses no time," Bella Fromm, the well-connected diplomatic journalist for Berlin's *Vossische Zeitung* newspaper, wrote about the day the Führer took power. "It seems an ironic foreboding that the new Hitler cabinet should start off without a Minister of Justice." Frau Bella, as she was known, was the sort of woman who materialized at every tea party, formal ball, and high-society dinner, and she knew everybody when she got there. She took pride in her sophisticated sense of the political climate in Berlin. But the fast-moving developments had made her head spin. How was it that Hindenburg had allowed this madman to take charge?

"This whole business is pretty hard to believe," she wrote, "if your mind has a leaning toward sanity."

In March, the *London Herald* reported that the Nazis were planning an assault "on a scale as terrible as any instance of Jewish persecution in two thousand years." U.S. Secretary of State Henry Stimson, though skeptical of a report that sounded so hysterical, forwarded it to the embassy in Berlin for answers.

"Little self-appointed posses of Nazis are putting what they conceive to be the finishing touches on Nazi domination, each according to its lights," *New York Times* correspondent Frederick Birchall reported a few days later. Nazis ran their swastika banners up the poles at synagogues and planted stink bombs in Jewish-owned department stores. They loudly interrupted the start of a performance at the Dresden Opera House to demand the immediate removal of the renowned conductor, who was suspected, wrongly, of being a socialist and was accused of hiring too many Jewish performers.

The arrests continued. A socialist politician was dragged from his house, pummeled into unconsciousness, spat on, and blinded with mustard powder. An anonymous refugee said he had spent two weeks at Spandau, where the guards gouged out prisoners' eyes and shattered teeth with rifle butts. One writer was forced to eat his manuscript. "There is no longer any doubt that to be either of Jewish faith or of Jewish origin and to exist in Germany now constitutes a crime in the eyes of the ruling faction there," the *Times* reported on March 20. "There is no discrimination in the matter of assessing this crime of being a Jew. Neither professional eminence, capacity in business, public service nor private virtue is being counted against it. Professors are being driven from their classrooms, music conductors from their concert halls and actors from the stage." Feuchtwanger, the novelist who panned *Mein*

Kampf, fled to Switzerland. His home was raided and his manuscripts seized.

On April 1, storm troopers picketed Jewish storefronts and tried to turn away customers with admonitions to buy in German shops.

Americans returning from Germany told terrible, "almost incredible" stories, the *Times* wrote: a group of Jews hauled to a storm trooper barracks and forced to flog one another; Jewish regulars at a restaurant beaten with brass knuckles and tossed into the street; bodies discovered in the woods and listed in police reports as "unidentified suicides."

"Uniforms were everywhere," wrote Willy Brandt, an avowed Nazi enemy who would become Berlin's mayor and West Germany's chancellor in the decades after the war. "Marching Stormtrooper columns, their yelling, the shattering noise of their motorcycles filled the streets. The whole city seemed to be an army camp." The famous cafés were half empty, the prominent intellectuals, artists, and writers missing. "Those who sat here spoke only in a whisper, suspicious looks followed me. Suspicion and fear were like a poisonous fog—it depressed me, it compressed my chest, I felt that I was suffocating."

At the U.S. embassy, the diplomats were worried. The situation felt so tense that a massacre of Jews and Nazi enemies didn't seem entirely out of the question.

And yet not all of those watching the tumult day after day were quite so alarmed, not even the *Times'* Birchall, who would win a Pulitzer Prize in 1934 for his reporting from Germany. He went on the American radio that spring to tell a nationwide audience "to dismiss from their minds any thought that there would be in Germany any slaughter of the National Socialist government's enemies or racial oppression in any vital degree. . . . You may dismiss also, I feel confident, any thought that Germany or the present rulers of Germany desire to go to war with anybody."

Birchall admitted that he was an "incurable optimist." He would not be for long.

The new regime began instituting sweeping legal measures that would, as one American diplomat put it, "detach the Jew from Germany." During the first year of Nazi rule, more than three hundred new laws and regulations were passed restricting Jewish life in Germany. Jews were fired from government posts. Jewish academics were ousted from their jobs. Jewish lawyers and judges were barred from the courts. Jewish physicians were excluded from the health care system. Businesses were ordered to fire any Jews on their boards. The Berlin Stock Exchange dismissed Jewish brokers; a number reacted by committing suicide.

The idea was to do whatever it took to prod the Jews to emigrate. The Nazis welcomed Zionist plans to help Jews depart for Palestine. "There remains the question," one of them noted, "of how much in the way of property the Jews leaving Germany will be permitted to take with them."

Not much, if the extremists in the party had their way.

One of the American diplomats in Berlin, George Messersmith, was amazed that people of Jewish descent would stay in a nation working so assiduously to make their lives as miserable as possible. "One has to live in Germany and to be really a part of its life," he wrote in a State Department report in 1933, "in order to realize the mental cruelties which are being daily inflicted here, which are in many respects much more severe than the physical barbarities which marked the first days of the revolution."

Among Göring's first moves as newly appointed Prussian interior minister in 1933 was to summon Rudolf Diels, a dashing, black-haired thirty-two-year-old who had already earned a reputation as a first-class opportunist. Two years earlier, Diels had begun working in the Interior Ministry's political police division, where he reported on the activities of left-wing parties in general and communists in particular. Diels had grown close to Göring, who now was looking to sweep his department of enemies.

"I don't want to have anything to do with the scoundrels

around here," Göring told Diels. "Are there any decent men here at all?"

Diels turned over personnel files and police dossiers on officials of questionable loyalty, and within days Göring was at work ridding his bureaucratic empire of Social Democrats and other suspected nuisances. The ministry's civil servants were required to complete forms requesting information about their religion, political membership, and race. Kempner dutifully filled out the pages; in a small show of defiance, he promised to inquire about his race.

Then Göring called a meeting and informed the ministry officials that everything would now be "done in the National Socialist spirit." Anyone with objections could quit. Kempner did not volunteer—why give up his salary any sooner than necessary?—but he didn't have to wait long before learning that he was out.

Most officials were purged with a brief note. Kempner liked to tell a story about the special treatment he received. Göring, the tale went, called the lawyer into his office and fired him—in person and with extreme prejudice.

"You are lucky I am not having you flung into jail!" the fat man shouted. "Get out of my sight. I never want to see you again!"

Kempner had a reputation for being the sort of man who never let the facts get in the way of a good tale; the real story was less dramatic. In his autobiography, he wrote that the ministry's personnel officer, an old ally, informed Kempner that he had to go, but allowed him to take a leave of absence and transferred him to the Prussian Building and Finance Administration. His new job, he claimed, was to check the levels of Berlin's waterways.

In April, the Law for the Restoration of the Professional Civil Service barred Jews from government posts, which also included schoolteachers, professors, judges, and prosecutors. But at Hindenburg's urging, the law exempted those Jews whose government service had begun before 1914 and those who, like Kempner, had served at the front during the war. Still, five thousand Jews lost their jobs under the law.

Though protected at first by his war record, Kempner was officially dismissed in September 1933 on grounds of political unreliability.

Diels, meanwhile, was rewarded with an important new post. He would head a new secret political police force, whose name, Geheime Staatspolizei, was abbreviated to three syllables that would come to strike fear in the hearts of the Nazis' enemies: Gestapo.

Kempner and Diels knew each other well. Diels was an accomplished conversationalist who, like Kempner, had a way of accumulating friends and important connections. They could often be found trading gossip in the Interior Ministry cafeteria.

Many years later, Diels would say that Kempner was "a real Gestapo man. He just happened to be racially handicapped."

Diels's face was scarred from fencing duels—two slashes across the right cheek, a deeper one on the left—but women found him attractive. He could have "played the lead in an American western," one would say. Though he was married, he did not spurn the ladies' affections. In 1931, Kempner had done his colleague a crucial favor. One night, Diels left his identification in a prostitute's apartment, and soon she appeared at the ministry to complain that Diels had beaten her. Kempner intervened, giving her some money and sending her on her way.

One of Diels's romances scandalized the diplomatic community in Berlin. In 1933, he began seeing Martha Dodd, the twenty-five-year-old daughter of U.S. Ambassador William Dodd. They could be spotted strolling through the Tiergarten, going to films, drinking at nightclubs. Martha, who separated from her husband before moving to Berlin, had quickly earned a reputation for her indiscreet affairs. She called Diels "dearie" and admired his "cruel, broken beauty." He told her about the internecine warfare in the Nazi bureaucracy and his fears that he would end up on someone's hit list. Later, when he found himself hounded by enemies who questioned his loyalty to the Nazi cause, Martha Dodd would try to come to his aid.

In February 1933, not long after Kempner left the Interior Ministry but before the Reichstag fire gave Göring an excuse to round up Nazi enemies en masse, Kempner ran into the Gestapo chief at a restaurant called Kempinski & Co. on Leipziger Strasse.

"Diels, what's going on?" Kempner asked. "What are you doing now, is there a lot of work?"

"Trouble and work," Diels said. "I have to put together lists."

"Lists for what?"

"For a possible operation."

The roundup of left-wing partisans was about to begin. "There are old friends of ours on there, too," Diels told Kempner.

Thus tipped off, Kempner urged his pacifist friends to get out of the country. One of them, Kurt Grossman, left for Czechoslovakia the day Kempner called. He explained later that Kempner "had the gift for finding out things that remained closed to other people." Another acquaintance of Kempner's, Carl von Ossietzky, refused to flee, and the Gestapo arrested him in the wake of the Reichstag fire. Already in poor health, Ossietzky was sentenced to hard labor and given regular beatings.

In the meantime, the pacifist German League for Human Rights was dissolved. Kempner burned the organization's membership lists, and, leaving nothing to chance, had the ashes dumped in the Spree.

Kempner had foreseen the consequences of the Nazi takeover in 1930. Though he managed to avoid arrest in the first, terrifying months, he surely realized just how much danger he was in as a man classified as a Jew—and a Nazi opponent, no less—living in Hitler's Reich. But he did not leave Berlin. Not yet. In that way, he was like the vast majority of Jews in Germany. For each one who hurried to the visa offices, many more—the vast majority—decided to wait and see.

Largely middle-class, they were bound psychologically and materially to the land. They *felt* German. They simply were not prepared to surrender their lives in a country where they had thrived, especially over the previous two generations.

After years as second-class citizens, the Jews had been emancipated by Kaiser Wilhelm in 1871, and they enthusiastically embraced their new freedom to hold political office, become doctors and lawyers, join academia, and operate businesses in a country that was becoming an economic powerhouse in Europe. Many Jews quickly assimilated, or tried to, by giving up the faith of their ancestors in favor of Protestantism or secularism. Germany, and in particular Berlin, became a destination for Jews of every nationality. For the first time, the important names in German finance, politics, science, and culture included Jews. During the First World War, one hundred thousand of them enlisted, eight in ten of them served on the front lines, and twelve thousand were killed for the cause.

Taking power, the Nazis thundered and raged and promised to kick them out, but for Jews it was hard to know how seriously to take the threats. Surely, many thought, Hitler would have to temper his rhetoric now that he was in power. Surely they could work out a compromise that would allow them to live in peace. Jewish leaders preached patience and calm. Maybe Germany would come to its senses and toss out Hitler after a year or two of madness.

Violence against the Jews ebbed and flowed in these years, and as much as they feared that worse attacks were still to come, they also worried about the perils of emigration. Would they find themselves penniless on the streets of some foreign land, unable to speak the language, unable to find a suitable job? Many were the Jewish breadwinners who disregarded their wives' pleas to emigrate until it was too late. All things considered, the German Jews could count more reasons to stay than to go, historian John Dippel wrote. "There was too much to overcome first—rootedness, complacency, incredulity, smugness, naïveté, wishful thinking, even opportunism." Amazingly, some Jewish businesses even thrived in the first years of Nazi rule.

Even the canniest of the Jews could not have foreseen that the entire continent would fall to the Nazis, Kempner wrote years later.

So they waited. They waited "faithfully German, patriotic."

In the beginning, Kempner waited, too, hanging on amid the arrests and the regulatory discrimination and the ugly rhetoric emanating from the rabid anti-Semites in power—men like Rosenberg, who tirelessly preached his vision of a race cleansed of all impurities and a country rid of every trace of Jewish blood.

Alfred Rosenberg, chief writer of the Nazi Party.
(Bundesarchiv, Bild 146-2005-0168/Heinrich Hoffmann)

7

"Rosenberg's Path"

He had all the charm of a mortician: deep-socketed eyes rimmed with dark circles, lips pursed rigidly in a perpetual scowl, thin hair parted and slicked back from a high forehead. "Of medium height, his ashen face and rather flabby jowls give the impression of a man of precarious health who leads a sedentary life," wrote American reporter Henry C. Wolfe after meeting Rosenberg. Wolfe thought he looked like a man who was loath to smile—as if his mission was so grave that any levity would be out of place. That, Wolfe thought, or he had chronic indigestion.

"His pale, lack-lustre eyes looked toward you but not at you, as though you were not there at all," wrote Kurt Lüdecke, the fundraiser and promoter who worked closely with the Nazi writer for a time. Rosenberg fancied himself a high-minded intellectual, but the world saw a man who was cold, arrogant, detached, and relentlessly sardonic. "A block of ice!" Lüdecke wrote. "Rosenberg's aloof and chilly irony frightened people away, making them feel small and uncomfortable in his presence."

Albert Krebs, however, was not one to be cowed, not least by Rosenberg. A labor union leader in Hamburg, Krebs had served as the commander of a storm trooper unit, a regional party boss, and the editor of a newspaper aligned with the Nazis, the *Hamburger Tageblatt*. Once, in the late 1920s, during a contentious period when the party split into rival factions in Berlin and Munich, Krebs earned Rosenberg's enmity by writing an editorial questioning the party's virulent opposition to the Soviet Union, a position that was, of course, the beginning and end of every political conversation with the editor of the official party mouthpiece. Rosenberg fired off a telegram summoning Krebs to Munich. When Krebs arrived at the office on Schellingstrasse, he was greeted frostily. "Rosenberg sat behind his desk," Krebs wrote later, "but did not rise, did not look up, did not respond to my greeting with anything more than an incomprehensible growl."

Krebs pulled up a chair. "You wished to speak with me?"

"Fourteen days ago," Rosenberg replied.

"At that point I didn't have time."

"An employee of the party press *must* have time when I summon him," Rosenberg shot back.

The two writers launched into a debate about the offending article. Nothing was resolved, but Krebs did learn some things about the party's chief ideologue. Rosenberg lectured Krebs with long monologues in which he repeated the sorts of things he had written in his newspaper pieces; when Krebs raised questions, Rosenberg ignored them. "One had the impression that he was not really listening at all. Now and then, at critical remarks, he would pinch his lips together or essay a calculated smile, which naturally earned him a reputation for arrogant surliness," Krebs recalled. "He was so rigid in acting out his imaginations and his egotistic daydreams of being the Baltic nobleman, the English lord, the scientific genius of Copernican dimensions, that this ultimately caused him completely to lose his already stunted capacity to relate to and converse with other human beings. . . . He was so wrapped up in his own opinions that he simply could not understand how anyone else could have different ones."

Krebs had other conversations with Rosenberg. Once, the party thinker argued that the chancellor Heinrich Brüning, a leader in the Catholic Center Party, planned to bring communism to Germany and crush the Protestant Church, so that the Vatican could then sweep in and impose Catholicism. Krebs was astonished. Rosenberg "imposed upon political events unreal, phantasmagoric imaginings, fantasies out of detective stories or spy thrillers."

Krebs had a hard time believing this deeply confused man was the intellectual Hitler held in such high regard. Rosenberg obviously was trafficking in cloudy, scrambled ideas—pilfered ones, no less. "Though thanks to his excellent memory and prodigious energy he had acquired an astounding mass of individual facts," Krebs wrote, "he completely lacked the aptitude to integrate these facts and develop a proper understanding of the contexts and connections of historical events."

Maybe Hitler didn't see that. Or maybe he did, and realized, ingeniously, that that was exactly the sort of ideological sage he needed for his movement, Krebs thought. "As a master of propaganda, he knew, after all, that it is precisely the incomprehensible and the nonsensical that has the greatest effect on the masses."

That was the only explanation, as far as he could tell, for the grandiose title that Hitler bestowed upon Rosenberg as the Third Reich dawned.

All the while Rosenberg was putting out the *Völkischer Beobachter* in the late 1920s, he was also working on something else: a magnum opus, a work about race and art and history that spanned millennia, a book that would go beyond the pile of daily and monthly dispatches he sent out into the world. He wanted *The Myth of the Twentieth Century* to have staying power. It was supposed to be the culmination of his thinking about Germany and its place in the world, a sweeping statement of philosophy and the most complete formulation of Nazi ideology ever set down. He expected it to mark him as the party's premier thinker.

Though he wished he could have made the book his solitary focus, he was forced to work on it in fits and starts. "I was busy the whole day with my paper," he confessed years later, "and therefore I could not develop it as thoroughly as a learned man." When he did sneak out to work on it during the day, his boss was not pleased. "Look at 'im squatting there, the fool-headed, stuck-up, undergraduate ninny!" Max Amann, publisher of the newspaper, told a compatriot one day. He pointed at Rosenberg, who was sitting at a marble table before the large window at the Tambosi café on Odeonsplatz, looking out upon the twin clock towers of the palatial Theatinerkirche, where many of the royal Wittelsbachs were buried. Rosenberg was surrounded by books and papers on multiple tables, demonstrably deep in thought. "Writing 'works'—the Bohemian!" Amann cried. "Oughta be puttin' out a decent newspaper instead!"

Rosenberg managed to finish the manuscript in 1929, and he had his wife, Hedwig, type up a clean copy, which he delivered to Hitler for approval. Six months passed. The Führer said nothing. When Rosenberg finally pressed the point, Hitler told him he thought it was "clever," but he wondered who would actually read hundreds of pages of Rosenbergian ideological theorizing. For one thing, Hitler had already published the preeminent Nazi book in *Mein Kampf.* At the same time, he was a pragmatic politician bent on seizing and wielding power, and some of the ideas in *Myth* were, to say the least, incendiary.

Whatever reservations he may have had, Hitler set them aside and approved publication. In 1930, Rosenberg's book landed on shelves.

The Myth of the Twentieth Century was a convoluted, nearly impenetrable volume. Rosenberg thought of it as a treatise on his philosophy of art and religion, and on his unconventional ideas about history and race. "Every race has its soul and every soul its race—its own unique internal and external architecture, its characteristic appearance and manner of lifestyle, and a unique relationship between its forces of will and reason," one section read. "Every race cultivates its own highest ideal. If, by the massive infiltration of alien blood and alien ideas, this is changed or overthrown, the result of this inner metamorphosis is chaos and, by epochs, catastrophe."

So it went, on and on, mostly formless and interminable. One admirer tried to help readers by publishing a lengthy glossary of its most obscure terminology.

In among the book's ambiguous acres were moments of clarity, ideas that would come to permeate Nazi thinking over the next fifteen years. Rosenberg wrote that Germanic culture and national honor had been crucial to civilization's spread through the ages. Where great cultures rose, it was a sign of Aryan influence. The intermixing of races—race chaos—had led to the downfall of the great societies. By granting equal rights to "alien blood," Teutonic man had committed "a sin against his own blood." Only by a return to racial purity could Germany become strong again.

Those steeped in the literature of anti-Semitic nationalism—Gobineau and Chamberlain, among others—would notice that they had read all of this before: There were no major original ideas in Rosenberg's book. But after the Nazis rose to power in 1933, they hailed *Myth* as one of the touchstones of National Socialism and, along with *Mein Kampf*, a book loyal Nazis were expected to own. Years later, many in the Nazi hierarchy would deny reading it closely. Goebbels called it an "ideological belch." Göring praised it in a letter to Rosenberg, but behind his back he said the first chapter had practically put him to sleep. Hitler reportedly said that he had "glanced cursorily" at Rosenberg's book and found it "too abstruse." He even hated the title. The Nazis, Hitler said, were not spreading myths. They were flooding the world with a newfound knowledge. "It is tripe," Putzi Hanfstaengl told Hitler. "And tripe remains tripe. If you fold a piece of paper over an inkblot, no one is going to mistake it in fifty years for a Rembrandt. Rosenberg is a dangerous and stupid man, and the sooner you get rid of him, the better." Franz von Papen, the conservative politician appointed Hitler's vice chancellor in January 1933, recalled that Hitler privately ridiculed the book and its author.

But Hitler, always seeking a political advantage, was known to play to his audience. Another onetime Nazi, Otto Strasser, who was later ousted from the party, recalled that Hitler had strenuously endorsed Rosenberg and his radical teachings.

Once, during a meeting in Strasser's Berlin office, Strasser objected to Rosenberg's virulent opposition to the Christian churches, his "paganism."

Hitler stood up, agitated, and began pacing Strasser's large study.

"Rosenberg's ideology is an integral part of National Socialism," he told Strasser. "Rosenberg is a forerunner, a prophet. His theories are the expression of the German soul. A true German cannot condemn them."

Two years later, upon the release of *Myth*, Strasser remembered, Hitler raved about the book as "the most tremendous achievement of its kind." Every revolution in history had been fought over race, Hitler said. "If you would only read Rosenberg's new book . . . then you would understand these things."

Whatever Rosenberg's rivals in the bureaucracy thought of

Myth, the book became a standard text in Germany. The new Nazi state mandated that it be placed on school curricula and in library collections. Teachers attending indoctrination courses were asked to bring along their copies. Law students were required to be familiar with its lessons. Hitler Youth instructors used its ideas in their ideological classes.

"Rosenberg's path," said Baldur von Schirach, leader of the organization, "is the path of German youth."

The book went on to sell more than a million copies and set its author up as an important voice in the innumerable battles over religion, art, and race during the Hitler era. In bookstores throughout the country, *Myth* rested next to its only rival in the German publishing world, *Mein Kampf.* It became everything Rosenberg could have wanted, and more: He had written a bible for the Nazi movement.

"I believe," one man told Rosenberg, "that even after a thousand years have passed, your work will endure."

The streets of 1930s Berlin hummed with activity. Every morning, office workers and factory workers poured forth from train stations and subway stops in suits and dresses and overalls. Above the din of the traffic came the cries of vendors selling flowers, fruit, cigarettes, balloons, newspapers, street magic.

Visitors might have been struck most by Unter den Linden and the Brandenburg Gate and the fragrant paths of the Tiergarten, but no place captured Berlin's true nature more than Potsdamer Platz, the capital's answer to Times Square. Luxury hotels and streetside cafés shared the real estate with beer halls and shops. Haus Vaterland, its name in lights circling a domed facade, beckoned Berliners to its movie theater, its shows, and its collection of internationally themed restaurants ("The World in One House," the slogan went). Its café, which seated twenty-five hundred patrons, was touted as the largest coffeehouse anywhere. On Potsdamer Platz, traffic from eight streets poured into a chaotic intersection. Trolley cars slashed through the center, and little Opels and gleaming Mercedes-Benzes competed with double-decker buses, trucks, taxis, horse-drawn wagons, bicyclists, and apparently fearless pedestrians. One of Europe's first traffic lights went up in the center of the square in 1925, but by all accounts it did little to tame the torrent of machines and humanity pulsating past.

In January 1933, when Rosenberg finally moved north from Munich to be closer to the action, he chose for his office Margaretenstrasse 17, an ordinary house a short walk from Berlin's busiest intersection. He would have preferred Wilhelmstrasse, home of the Reich Chancellery and the locus of the most important government ministries, but Margaretenstrasse would have to be close enough for the time being.

In the new Reich, the party operated as a sort of parallel "extralegal government," and even those not leading a government ministry could wield enormous power. For the first eight years of Nazi rule, Rosenberg worked for the party, starting in April 1933 as chief of its Foreign Policy Office. The new chancellor didn't trust Germany's veteran diplomats, including Konstantin von Neurath, the foreign minister. But as long as Hindenburg was alive, Hitler could not replace Neurath and install his own man: Neurath had the president's backing. So in the beginning, Hitler intended to use Rosenberg as a kind of back-channel foreign minister to help advance his international agenda.

In some ways, it was a natural fit for Rosenberg, who wrote a book called *The Future Course of German Foreign Policy* in 1927, was a member of the Foreign Affairs Committee in the Reichstag, and in 1932 went to Rome on behalf of the party to address an international forum on the future of Europe. But at the same time, Rosenberg had little understanding of other nations and their interests, and he had none of the diplomat's polished tact and nuanced discretion.

By all accounts, a conversation with Rosenberg always went the same way. "He would willingly begin a discussion on any subject under the sun, but no matter from what starting point he began, within five minutes he would be rolling off his tongue the phrases he had worn smooth and round in constant discussion of his own theories of blood and race," one of his interlocutors would write. "Whether one began talking about history, horticulture, or a paratrooper's high boots, Rosenberg's quick switch to the subject of blood and race was so certain that one could almost plot it mathematically."

The American ambassador in Berlin, William Dodd, remembered several such conversations with Rosenberg. He hated them. He recoiled at even being photographed with the party philosopher, as he was when they encountered each other inside the Hotel Adlon, on Pariser Platz, one November night in 1934.

"It was not delightful to me," Dodd wrote in his private diary, "for there is no German official who thinks less clearly or indulges in more bunk."

Rosenberg's first trip to London in his new role devolved into just the sort of political and public relations debacle that a friend had warned him it would be. "You can't speak even a word of English!" Lüdecke, the Nazi financier, had told him before he departed. "You haven't got one decently fitting suit to wear. Your evening clothes are impossible. You can't go to London like that—go to a good tailor first." Replied Rosenberg with a chilly smile, "Hitler was right. It's a muzzle you need." The trip in May 1933—a first attempt to counter fierce British opposition to the repressive Nazi regime—sparked protests and calls in Parliament for him to be ejected from the country. British diplomat Robert Vansittart found that Rosenberg "looked like cold cod" and had the temperament to match. Rosenberg departed early, in such a rush that he left behind gloves, a tie, a handkerchief, socks, and his nailbrush.

In the meantime, he connected with a pair of Brits who turned out to be spies. One of the men, William de Ropp, was a journal-ist put on the Nazi payroll to make introductions to key figures in Britain. The other, MI6 agent Frederick Winterbotham, posed as a Nazi sympathizer inside the British Air Ministry. Unaware, Rosenberg brought the men into the Chancellery for a summit with the Führer, then invited them to a lunch with military brass at Berlin's famous Horcher restaurant. Rosenberg thought he was laying a foundation for rapprochement between the two nations. Instead, he was helping the agents collect a wealth of information about German rearmament.

Still, as the party's nominal foreign policy guru, Rosenberg did not give up his mandate. He worked whatever angles he could. He connected with Nazi sympathizers internationally, and even financed propaganda in the United States and other countries. He developed plans for breaking up the Soviet Union. And he waited for the moment to put his mark on the map of Europe.

Whether or not that moment would ever arrive, Rosenberg would always and forever be the Nazis' foremost ideologue. He was firmly established in the eyes of the rank and file as an important champion of the cause, as the man who provided the intellectual underpinnings to their radical mission. In June 1933, he was one of only sixteen men promoted to Reichsleiter, the party's top ranking, one step below the Führer. By year's end, Hitler was hailing him in one of a series of letters of appreciation to the party's most important leaders, which were then published in the *Völkischer Beobachter*.

"My dear party comrade Rosenberg!" Hitler wrote. "One of the first conditions for the victory of the National Socialist movement was the spiritual destruction of the hostile world of ideas confronting us. Not only have you . . . unflinchingly led the assault against this world of ideas, but you have also contributed in an extraordinary way . . . to ensuring the all-permeating philosophical unity of our political struggle."

At the beginning of 1934, Hitler made Rosenberg's leading status official. His loyal aide would be the Führer's "delegate for the entire intellectual and ideological indoctrination and education of the National Socialist Party."

The interminable title—Rosenberg's handiwork, naturally—was nearly as long as the vaguely worded two-sentence commissioning order Hitler signed.

The assignment grew out of a request for indoctrination training materials from Robert Ley, who in addition to leading the German Labor Front was the party's Reich organization leader. One of his responsibilities was to oversee a Main Training Office, which was tasked with educating current and future leaders of the Third Reich. The party had grown exponentially since Hitler had become chancellor: Between January 30 and May 1, 1933, when registrations were suspended, 1.6 million Germans joined the party. Ley wanted to be sure that these "March violets," as the old Nazi fighters called them, were properly schooled in National Socialism. He envisioned an advisory role for Rosenberg: The ideologue would design curriculum, produce lesson plans, and create training materials, which Ley's staff would then use in their training courses to ensure the consistent indoctrination of party officials.

Rosenberg had bigger ideas than writing textbooks. He viewed his assignment in the broadest possible terms and set about fulfilling the grand ambition of his long-winded title.

In February, Rosenberg stepped up to a microphone in Berlin's Kroll Opera House and, speaking to an audience of party dignitaries, gave a sense of his sweeping goals. He delivered his address in the rolling Baltic German accent that marked him as an outsider, a first-generation immigrant to Germany, but as his words echoed through the grand hall, Rosenberg was making a bid for the hearts and souls of the German people. "If today we were to be content with only the power of the state, the National Socialist movement would not have fulfilled its mission," he told the audience. "The political revolution in the state has indeed been completed but the intellectual and spiritual recasting of men's minds is only just beginning."

But before he could lead the charge, Rosenberg would need to win a fight closer to home.

Hitler's was a Darwinian management style. He assigned subordinates multiple titles with overlapping responsibilities, and often issued only general instructions about his wishes. He actively encouraged infighting: He pitted his functionaries against one another, and only when territorial wars or policy disagreements reached a fever pitch would the Führer step in for a ruling. Everyone knew he could be dismissed—or worse—if he fell out of Hitler's favor. Mistrust ran rampant. "There is nobody among the officials of the National Socialist party who would not cheerfully cut the throat of every other official in order to further his own advancement," wrote Bella Fromm, the diplomatic journalist. "Hitler likes it that way. Keeps them on their toes. Also, he apparently thinks that a man who has the ability to fight his way through may be of use to him."

Rosenberg's new post put him directly at odds with one of the most powerful political forces in Berlin, a devious and deadly functionary and a brilliant manipulator of the masses: Joseph Goebbels, Reich minister of public enlightenment and propaganda. Four years Rosenberg's junior, Goebbels grew up in a working-class family in the town of Rheydt, near Düsseldorf. His parents were devout Catholics, and Goebbels considered becoming a priest. Surgery to alleviate a bone marrow disease left Goebbels with a stunted, crippled leg and a lifelong limp. Ashamed of his physical condition, he threw himself into his schoolwork and became a top student. He went on to study German literature, history, and ancient philology and earned a doctorate in philosophy. From then on he would insist on being known as Herr Doktor.

Hoping to become a writer, he kept a regular diary and tried his hand at an autobiographical novel, a number of plays, and several journalistic pieces. But he could not get them published. He could not even get a newspaper job. He worked briefly at a bank, but was dismissed during the 1923 financial crisis.

He was disillusioned when, in 1924, he fell in with the Nazis. He quickly made his mark as a speaker and began working with Gregor Strasser, a pharmacist and energetic party leader in Berlin, to rally the working class in the north to the Nazi cause. Goebbels and Strasser, older brother of Otto Strasser, were socialists as much as they were nationalists, and this set them up for a confrontation with Hitler and the more conservative men around him in Munich, including Rosenberg. Goebbels didn't understand why Nazis and communists couldn't work together. "You and I, we are fighting each other but we are not really enemies," he wrote in an open letter to the communists. "By doing so we are dividing our strength, and we shall never reach our goal." Taking aim at the Munich crowd in 1926, Strasser and Goebbels drafted a new party platform advocating the seizure of aristocratic estates, and German cooperation with a Soviet Union "freed from Jewish internationalism."

Hitler would have none of this, not least because wealthy noblemen were among his most important financial backers. He called Strasser and Goebbels to task and, in humiliatingly public fashion at a party meeting in February 1926, forced them to surrender. Goebbels, who had fallen deeply for the Nazi leader, was shattered that Hitler was sticking to the Rosenberg line. "What sort of a Hitler is this? A reactionary?" he wrote in his diary. "Russian question: quite off the beam. Italy and England our natural allies! Terrible! Our task, he says, is the destruction of Bolshevism. Bolshevism is a Jewish creation. We must break

Russia. . . . I am unable to say a word. I feel as though someone had hit me over the head."

But Goebbels was ambitious and pragmatic above all else, and he quickly returned to the Nazi fold. His diaries soon filled with accolades for his hero. (One went: "Adolf Hitler, I love you because you are both great and simple at the same time. What one calls a genius.") For his part, Hitler ostentatiously wooed Goebbels, and after the would-be dissident parted with Strasser, he was sent to Berlin to lead the charge against the very communists he had so recently tried to woo. The job required an affinity for invective, and Goebbels was the man for the job. Even one of his admirers noted that his words went down like a mix of "hydrochloric acid, copper sulfate, and pepper."

A master of backroom intrigue, Goebbels expended as much energy keeping tabs on his rivals as he did running his ministry, or so it seemed. Journalists in Berlin noted his appetite for endless hours of work, his intellect—a rare commodity in a party better known for its reliance on brute force—and his willingness to say whatever was necessary to carry an argument. "Apparently frank and straightforward, with a disarming smile and ingratiating voice, he was in reality a master at hiding his real thoughts behind a mask of urbanity," wrote Louis P. Lochner, the Associated Press correspondent in Berlin. Watching him speak, Lochner saw a showman. Delivering a speech, Goebbels might look as though he were overcome by emotion, but really he was giving a performance, every movement carefully planned and executed for maximum effect.

Goebbels did a party trick that demonstrated his mastery. He would deliver four addresses defending four different forms of government—the monarchy, communism, democracy, Nazism—and leave his listeners absolutely convinced that he was a true believer in each. "Goebbels proved to be a wizard of demagoguery," Lochner decided. "His dark piercing eyes, his straight black hair brushed back, his taut skin, made one think of certain representations of Mephistopheles."

Rosenberg had problems with Goebbels, the first being that the propaganda chief took an expansive view of his job. He would have jurisdiction, according to a Hitler decree of June 30, 1933, "over the whole field of spiritual indoctrination of the nation, of propagandizing the State, of cultural and economic propaganda, of enlightenment of the public at home and abroad." That was a description that put him firmly on what Rosenberg considered his own territory.

The bruising war that broke out as a result would consume the two men for the better part of twelve years.

The first battleground was, of all things, art. The toppling of the monarchy at the end of the war had unshackled Berlin. Overnight, it became a cultural and social hub. Leggy blondes and celebrated personalities walked the city's broad avenues and sipped their drinks at sidewalk cafés. Visitors marveled at the monumental department stores, especially Wertheim's flagship store on Leipziger Strasse, which, with its soaring atrium of glass and chandeliers and towering arches, looked like nothing less than a cathedral to consumerism.

With a population of four million, the capital was suddenly the world's third-largest metropolis, behind only London and New York. Stereotypical Berliners were cosmopolitan, cynical, and probably from somewhere else. "They are," one writer would come to decide, "the New Yorkers of Central Europe." They even spoke in a dialect that, to other Germans, came across as brash and irreverent.

While the left and the right battled for control of Germany in the streets and in the Reichstag throughout the 1920s, modernism of all shades flowered in the galleries and performance spaces. Expressionist artists like Otto Dix captured battlefield chaos and urban deviance on their canvases. The Dadaists protested whatever passed for rational thought. Modernist architects like Erich Mendelsohn designed buildings with flowing, futuristic lines. Avant-garde horror films, Marlene Dietrich in *The Blue Angel*, Bertolt Brecht's gangsters, jazz, topless cabaret, a naked diva in a bathtub, Josephine Baker shimmying in nothing but a necklace and a skirt of bananas—after dark, Berliners could see all of that and more. The kaiser's conservative authoritarianism had given way to unbounded sexual energy. Nightclubs and stage productions catered to a flourishing gay subculture. Berlin between the wars was disorderly, eclectic, and proudly leftist.

Naturally, the Nazis hated everything about it. The *Völkischer Beobachter* condemned the capital as "a melting pot of everything that is evil—prostitution, drinking houses, cinemas, Marxism, Jews, strippers, negroes dancing, and all the vile offshoots of so-called 'modern art.'" The cinema, Rosenberg lamented in 1925, was "in the hands of the Jews," and because of that it had "become a means of infecting the Volk—through lascivious images; and just as clearly as in the Jewish press, there are revealed here plans for the glorification of crime."

Rosenberg grew to become the chief proponent of a *völkisch* cultural program that rejected modernism—he called it "cultural bolshevism"—in favor of what he considered traditional art rooted in Germanic history. The *völkisch* movement was a sort of romantic, racist nationalism that celebrated the German soldier, the peasant, and folk tradition. In 1929, Rosenberg founded the quasi-independent Combat League for German Culture, which staged high-profile lectures by prominent intellectuals and spread the conservative cause in its illustrated journal.

Goebbels, on the other hand, appreciated modern art in some of its guises, and supported groups who did not want to see the arts handcuffed by the ideological conservatives in Rosenberg's camp. "We guarantee the freedom in art," the propaganda minister said time and again. He lent his prestige to an exhibition of

Italian Futurist art, decorated the walls of his private residence with Expressionist watercolors by Emil Nolde, and commissioned an Impressionist portrait of himself by Leo von König, which he hung in his headquarters.

After the Nazis took power, Rosenberg saw an opportunity to press his case against modern art. But in the fall of 1933, Goebbels formed a Reich Chamber of Culture to consolidate control over the fine arts, theater, music, radio, film, the press, and literature—giving himself a clear upper hand in the war. Refusing to retire from the battlefield, Rosenberg rebranded his Combat League and incorporated it into the government's hugely popular Strength Through Joy travel and leisure program, giving him some sway over ideological and cultural programs aimed at German workers and their families.

At the same time, Rosenberg looked for high-profile avenues of attack, hoping to undermine Goebbels and eventually supplant the new cultural agency.

He led the charge against Ernst Barlach, an Expressionist sculptor whose bulky, cloaked Gothic figures earned him a number of commissions to build First World War memorials in Germany. Goebbels counted himself among Barlach's admirers and even had small pieces of his work in his house. In the *Völkischer Beobachter*, Rosenberg took aim at Barlach's sculpture in Magdeburg Cathedral, depicting a skeleton wearing a helmet, a man with a gas mask, a woman in sorrow, and three soldiers, one of whom had a bandaged head and held a large cross. To the nationalists, the German soldier was a heroic superman. Barlach's representation, Rosenberg complained, was anything but: "little half-idiotic admixtures of indefinable human types with Soviet helmets are supposed to represent German fighting men!" Barlach tried to assuage the critics, to the point of formally declaring his support of Hitler, but in the end his work was removed from the state museum, and the Magdeburg memorial came down.

Rosenberg added to the pressure by forcing the art czar to dismiss composer Richard Strauss as head of the Reich Chamber of Music. The composer's offense: his willingness to work with Jews. Strauss had produced an opera with a pair of Jewish writers, Hugo von Hofmannsthal and Stefan Zweig, published his work with a Jewish-owned house, and hired a Jewish pianist. When the Gestapo intercepted a letter from Strauss to Zweig in which Strauss expressed a sentiment bordering on disloyalty to the Nazi regime—Strauss said he had agreed to lead the music chamber only "to prevent worse misfortunes" to artists—Goebbels was forced to jettison him.

By 1935, the propaganda minister finally realized the precariousness of his position. He was not just under fire from Rosenberg. He was also out of step with Hitler, who had long opposed modernism in the arts. At a high-profile cultural speech during the party's annual rally in Nuremberg the year before, the Führer had pointedly complained about the "stuttering Cubists, Futurists, and Dadaists" who were endangering German culture. "These charlatans are mistaken if they think that the creators of the new Reich are stupid enough or insecure enough to be confused, let alone intimidated, by their twaddle."

Goebbels, as he had done a decade earlier when forced to choose between Strasser and Hitler, fell in line with his Führer. He executed an about-face on modern art.

Never one for half measures when it came to proving his faithfulness, the convert went on to plan and produce Nazi Germany's most infamous art show. "Horrible examples of art Bolshevism have been brought to my attention," Goebbels wrote in his diary. "I want to arrange an exhibit in Berlin of art from the period of degeneracy. So that people can see and learn to recognize it." The Degenerate Art show, as the Nazis billed it, opened in July 1937: a collection of more than six hundred modernist pieces by the likes of Pablo Picasso, Henri Matisse, and Vassily

Kandinsky hung poorly in bad lighting and accompanied by lurid captions proclaiming their utter depravity.

Hitler was delighted, and Goebbels relieved: Slippery as ever, he had salvaged his place at Hitler's side.

If Rosenberg could not unseat Goebbels, that did not stop him from using his position as Hitler's ideological delegate to push his agenda into the farthest reaches of Germany. Through all of the bureaucratic fighting, even into the war years, Rosenberg kept his many cultural offices and sub-offices open and hard at work.

His Office for the Protection of Art reviewed and passed judgment on the ideological merits of new music and plays and conducted ideological background checks on performing artists and speakers slated to appear before Nazi audiences. Staffers sent the Gestapo memos about artists of questionable loyalty. Rosenberg's thinking was that it made little sense to allow the indoctrination efforts of the Main Training Office to be undermined by art, literature, plays, and music that were not in keeping with the Nazi worldview. His agency also put on concerts, underwrote lectures, and produced plays, which were taken on the road to small cities.

Rosenberg's department published an extravagantly illustrated monthly art journal, *Die Kunst im Deutschen Reich*, to spread the party's conception of properly Germanic art, and a music journal aimed at eliminating any Jewish influence from the concert stage.

Rosenberg's Office for the Cultivation of Literature had a team of staffers and a small army of unpaid volunteers—fourteen hundred at its peak—who systematically examined "the entirety of the German literature that has any molding or educative significance for the German Volk whatsoever." They reviewed new books for ideological appropriateness and reported their findings in a journal, *Bücherkunde*, that went to eight thousand subscribers in the publishing industry. Approved books appeared on white pages, unfavorably reviewed books on red; often enough, a negative review was enough to prompt the Propaganda Ministry to add a book to the list of thousands banned in Germany. Rosenberg's industrious staffers also circulated an index of Jewish authors, which ultimately included eleven thousand names. At one point, under the auspices of a campaign orchestrated by Rosenberg to gather books for soldiers on the front lines, the literature team "cleansed private households of undesirable literature."

Offices spawned offices as Rosenberg's ideological monitoring administration sprawled across the cultural landscape. An Office of Science evaluated academic appointments. An Office for the Investigation of German Rural Architecture studied peasant homes to confirm that their designs had not been tainted by outside influence but were, in fact, a perfect reflection of their builders' Germanic blood. An Office for Folklore and Party Ceremonials developed Nazi birth, marriage, and death ceremonies, which were published in a party journal, complete with prescribed music and decorations. Germanic baby names were suggested: Arwed, Erdmut, Sebalt, Ulf.

One of Rosenberg's offices even reviewed sculptures and paintings of Hitler for appropriateness before they could be displayed in public.

Rosenberg traveled all over Germany, spreading his message and accepting plaudits. Outside Berlin, he could always count on major crowds and enthusiastic welcomes. Whatever his fellow party leaders felt about him, in the cities and villages he was one of the heroes of the movement.

But in the capital, the war continued with Goebbels. Privately, the propaganda minister called the party philosopher "'almost' Rosenberg." "Rosenberg was almost adequate as a scholar, a journalist, a politician, but just almost."

Rosenberg, for his part, thought the Nazi ideology ought to be immutable, and he objected to Goebbels's willingness to change course for political gain. "As the party after 1933 gorged itself on the fruits of power," a biographer would write, "Rosenberg filled the role of the Old Testament prophet, rebuking his people for whoring after strange gods." Rosenberg concluded that his rival, the master of flash and pomp, considered the Nazi message to be merely another propaganda tool, like the blood-red banners and the torchlight marches through the streets.

He wondered whether Goebbels ever really believed in the party's principles. He doubted it. The man changed positions so adeptly that Rosenberg could only assume that he would do or say anything to stay in power.

"Our revolution," he would decide a few years later, "has an abscess."

It was not only Goebbels who stood between Rosenberg and his dream of a unified party under his ideological tutelage.

Despite Rosenberg's influence over the rank-and-file Nazis, the top leaders in the Third Reich were a gang so obsessed with wielding their clout that they did not want to be handcuffed by the man they called, derisively, "the Philosopher." They were men of action, suspicious of intellectualism. Hitler wanted to calm the international community while he secretly rebuilt the military. He wanted to stay in Hindenburg's good graces, for the man was still Germany's president, its greatest national hero, and the one person who could remove Hitler from office. He needed to be flexible. He needed to be a politician.

Rosenberg had the opposite view. "I would adopt a stand-point, irrespective of whether someone was for or against it, if I felt deeply that it was right for the movement," he wrote at one point. "I would do that even if in the end I remained <u>alone</u>." He could not have been surprised that his greatest talent was cultivating enemies.

One of them was a man who wanted nothing to do with Rosenberg's relentless moralizing: Ernst Röhm, commander of the Nazi storm troopers. The thick-necked Röhm, whose face showed the scars of his service as a German military officer during the First World War, agitated for a "second revolution" in the months after Hitler's rise to the chancellorship. He wanted the old generals swept out of power, and the army replaced with his fearsome men—the flexed muscle of the Nazi Party.

One evening in 1933, Röhm and Rosenberg stumbled upon one another at a lavish party in Berlin hosted by the Turkish ambassador. Bella Fromm was in attendance, mingling with sources. "Formal soirée," she reported. "Outside, the Tiergarten was wrapped in fog. The old Renaissance Palace glowed in dazzling light. The mighty gates were flung open. An endless stream of cars rolled in. . . . The assembly was a scene of overwhelming splendor. Military uniforms, elaborate gowns, sparkling jewels."

But the boisterous Röhm and his brown-shirted storm troopers made a scene of a different sort. The men drank far too much champagne and were soon so drunk that they were asked to kindly leave. Instead they grabbed several dozen more bottles and retired to another room.

When Rosenberg walked in, wearing tails, Karl Ernst, leader of the Berlin storm troopers, was sitting on a pink sofa, rocking one of his men on his knees.

Rosenberg had always been revolted by the overt homosexuality of Röhm and some of his men. "He surrounded himself with debauchers and parasites," Rosenberg wrote later in the diary, "his officers all had young male lovers, they cut themselves off more and more from the movement, and provoked the populace with their demeanor." As far as Rosenberg was concerned, Röhm's men were an obnoxious band of "Berlin gigolos in brown shirts."

An indignant Rosenberg hissed a few words. The drunken commander roared with delighted laughter.

"Look at that Baltic pig," Röhm shouted for all to hear. "The sissy hasn't even got the guts to drink! Too snooty to wear the brown outfit, that upstart Baltic baron! Tailcoats won't do him any good. Say, baron, who the hell do you think you are?"

Steaming, Rosenberg walked off.

But schadenfreude of the blackest variety was not far off. By the summer of 1934, Rosenberg wasn't the only one fed up with Ernst Röhm.

Rosenberg's handwritten diary spans ten years and five hundred pages.
(U.S. Holocaust Memorial Museum, courtesy of Miriam Lomaskin)

8

—

The Diary

In May 1934—the month Rosenberg first began writing down his thoughts in a leather-bound private diary—anxiety over the new, muscular Germany rippled across the United States and Europe. The *New York Times* was reporting that German munitions factories were "working at capacity," that American airplane manufacturers were selling planes and aviation technology in Germany, that German firms like BMW were churning out aircraft engines, and that the Nazis would soon be equipped with a powerful air force and stout antiaircraft defenses. "By the end of next year," the newspaper reported in May, "Germany will be as nearly impregnable against air attack as it is possible for a country to be." British leaders had begun to conclude that they had no choice but to begin making preparations for another war.

Meanwhile, across the Atlantic on a Thursday night that month, twenty thousand German Americans turned out for a mass meeting at a hulking warehouse of a sports arena on Eighth Avenue in New York City. They passed under the marquee reading MADISON SQ

GARDEN and, ushered by men wearing white shirts and swastikas on their armbands, made their way to their seats. Onstage, a pair of menacing Nazi eagles glowered.

The combative crowd had come to support a pro-Hitler group called Friends of the New Germany. The organization had been founded the year before by a German immigrant named Heinz Spanknöbel in a bid to unite bickering bands of American Nazis concentrated in the German neighborhoods of cities like Detroit, Chicago, and New York. The belligerent and ambitious Spanknöbel had won the backing of Rudolf Hess, Hitler's deputy Führer in Berlin, but in the United States he quickly attracted all the wrong kinds of attention. First, he stormed the offices of the largest German-language newspaper in the United States, the *New Yorker Staats-Zeitung und Herold,* and demanded that it toe the Nazi Party line; the editor threw him out and called the police. Then Spanknöbel raised a ruckus by pushing for the swastika to fly alongside the American flag atop the Manhattan Armory—a U.S. government building—during a German Day celebration. Jewish leaders objected, and as the dispute played out, Spanknöbel's men vandalized synagogues in the city with swastikas. A speech by Spanknöbel in Newark ended in a brawl, during which one of his bodyguards began administering beatings with a lead-filled length of rubber hose.

Soon, federal authorities issued a warrant for Spanknöbel's arrest on the charge that he was an unregistered agent of the German government, and he fled back to the homeland. But his militant group lived on under new leadership. Members swore allegiance to Hitler and declared that they were of pure Aryan blood. A band of uniformed security officers kept order under the command of a former member of Röhm's storm troopers. The organization's official newspaper, the *Deutsche Zeitung,* ran propaganda imported straight from Berlin. A youth division indoctrinated the next generation at summer camps.

And just as Hitler had done in Germany, the Friends staged rallies and speeches to build support for a Nazi movement in the United States.

At the Garden, speaker after speaker took to the podium to rail against a Jewish boycott of German goods, now nearly a year old, spearheaded by a New York lawyer, Samuel Untermyer. As a thousand communists marched in protest outside—"Down with Hitler!" they shouted—inside, the Nazi supporters excoriated their enemies. "Hang him!" some in the crowd shouted at the mention of Untermyer's name.

"We cannot and we will not permit this Germany to be maligned daily by being portrayed as one great prison," said Walter Kappe, editor of the *Deutsche Zeitung*, mimicking the bellicose language Goebbels had perfected in Germany. "We cannot, we must not, and we shall not endure this any longer, but we cry, It's all lies, lies, lies!" He accused the American Jewish leaders of incitement. They had "poisoned American public opinion against Germany. We give you warning today for the last time," he said. "If you continue the battle, you shall find us fully armed, and then you will have to bear the consequences."

The communists outside were ready to fight, there and then. After marching and chanting outside the Garden, they lingered in Times Square, waiting for the meeting to break up. Police formed defensive cordons to keep them away from the approaches to the arena, clashing with protesters trying to break through the lines. As the Friends of the New Germany scurried into subway stations and ducked into taxis, one of them felt emboldened enough to shout a message into the spring New York night.

"Heil Hitler!"

Then he dashed into a shop on the corner of Broadway and Forty-fifth Street, and a patrolman came to the rescue before the angry mob could get their hands on him.

Tension gripped Berlin, too, in May 1934. A week before the Madison Square Garden rally, Goebbels took to the podium at the

Sportpalast arena, in Berlin, to deliver his own attack on the American boycott. The propaganda minister promised that the campaign would do nothing to improve the fortunes of the Jews in Germany. "If the boycott were carried to lengths actually endangering our economic situation, it would not mean that we would let the Jews go free," he assured his listeners. "No! The hatred, rage, and despair of the German people would first of all vent itself on those who can be grabbed in the homeland. If the Jews imagine that the bloodless course of the German revolution gives them the right to disport themselves again in their habitual impudence and arrogance and provoke the German people, let them be warned not to tax our patience too severely."

The Jews, he thundered, needed to understand their place in the new German order. They were guests in the country, and they should "quietly and modestly retire within their four walls."

Goebbels's speech heralded a new propaganda campaign against "grumblers and faultfinders," traitors for whom he had invented a new word: *Kritikasters*. A year after Hitler's rise to power, cracks were starting to appear in the revolution. The Nazis had not delivered on their promises of a swift national recovery. Public support for the party had begun to fall off. Critics were speaking up in the press. Jokes about the Nazi leaders were gaining wide circulation.

In response, Goebbels's newspaper, *Der Angriff (The Attack)*, warned of the consequences of disparaging the administration, just in case anyone had forgotten about the Gestapo and the concentration camps. An example had recently been made of one editor who sarcastically protested Goebbels's press censorship: He found himself behind the barbed wire at Oranienburg, a prison camp north of Berlin. Nazi propagandists were dispatched to cafés and restaurants to deliver speeches in support of the regime; storm troopers guarding the exits made sure patrons heard the message. Mass rallies were promoted with posters—DON'T WHINE, WORK!—and by bands of Nazis riding in trucks around city streets, bellowing slogans.

Loyal Germans were ordered to buy swastika badges and wear

them in public. Even minor displays of disloyalty could have consequences. A woman overheard to declare that "it would never get any better" under the Nazis was ordered to turn up at the mayor's office on a daily basis and recite the same phrase: "Every day is better already, and will still get better and better."

As Goebbels fulminated from the podiums, it was becoming obvious that the Nazis had bigger problems than waning enthusiasm among the populace. A civil war was brewing, and Hitler was about to choose sides.

By the summer of 1934, everyone in official Berlin could feel a tightening pressure of the sort that in the Third Reich would be released only by violence.

In the midst of this ferment, on May 14, Rosenberg opened a journal bound in red leather. The endpapers were decorated with a design of jagged watercolor stripes that brought to mind deckle-edged paper. He opened it to the first page and took up a fountain pen. At the top right-hand corner he wrote, "Berlin 15.5.34," then inked over the "15" to correct the date. In a messy script, he began to write.

"I haven't kept a diary for the past fifteen years," he wrote. "Many historical turns have fallen into oblivion because of it. Now we stand in the midst of a new development that will be decisive for the future, and in which I feel especially involved in two fundamental questions." One was the "the enforcement of our worldview against all opponents." Rosenberg had been denouncing the Christian churches and their teachings, hoping to sideline the clerics so that he could instill the Nazi ideology in the hearts and souls of the German people. The other matter on his mind was Great Britain, which Rosenberg, as head of the party's foreign policy operation, still hoped to win over to the Nazi cause. This despite his failed visit to London in 1933 and the Brits' unrelenting opposition to Hitler and his belligerent minions.

Rosenberg had a ringside seat to historic times, and he resolved to document them in detail. What exactly prompted him to start this new diary—the earlier journal he alludes to did not surface after the war—was not just the ego of a public figure who was sure he would be considered a great man of history. It must also have had something to do with a book that had recently appeared on German bookshelves. His nemesis Goebbels, an avid diarist for years, had edited his entries from 1932 to 1933 and published them to burnish his reputation as a central player in Hitler's sweep to power.

If Rosenberg was going to tend to a diary, he would have to fight his general lack of discipline. He had a reputation for spreading himself too thin, for being unfocused, for launching new ventures and then leaving them to others to manage—or mismanage. The diary would also have to compete for his attention with all the other material he spent his days writing: political tracts, propaganda pieces, and memo after memo after memo.

If he planned to publish the pages, he did not say. It is possible that he considered the diary a collection of private notes to be referred to one day, years later, when he had time to draft a proper memoir about his Nazi career.

Whatever his intentions, he threw himself into the task over the summer. The unlined sheets of the red notebook filled up with whatever consumed him at the moment. Rosenberg the diarist was prone to callousness, self-pity, and the same sort of narcissism he liked to criticize in his rivals. He dealt in petty slander. He was a man who was quick to anger, who lacked empathy for the human cost of his unyielding ideology, who was wrapped up almost entirely in the Nazi Party. He barely mentioned his family. He gave no intimation of a life beyond his work.

The first pages, dated the second half of May, find Rosenberg relating reports to Hitler on the state of public opinion in Britain, grumbling about Goebbels, and protesting the duplicity of diplomats in the Foreign Office.

Goebbels's attacks on the Jews at the Sportpalast earlier in the month had caused a new storm of criticism in London, according to

William de Ropp, one of the spies Rosenberg had unwittingly recruited to act as a go-between with the Brits. As much as Rosenberg hated Goebbels, he loyally pushed back: "What, then, would we say to the agitation of the *Evening Standard* against Hitler? In London, a person can insult anyone and everything, but they shrink like a mimosa when it concerns the Jews." Privately, Rosenberg knew that de Ropp was right. It would be better if Goebbels toned down his rhetoric. It won "cheap applause" in Germany but only caused trouble internationally.

Rosenberg also worried about Goebbels's massive propaganda push against the *Kritikasters*. It merely telegraphed to the world that there was "widespread discontent" among the populace. Why else would the Nazis have to go to such lengths to silence their critics? "The strongest tool of German politics, that the whole nation is standing behind the Führer, is threatening to shatter. 'You backed the wrong pony,' our opponents tell our friends, 'the people don't believe in their power anymore.'"

But what outraged Rosenberg most of all that month was a bad bit of press. On May 9, in a story about the evolving power structure of the Third Reich, the *Times* of London had reported that Rosenberg's authority as Hitler's chief ideological delegate was not nearly as sweeping as the title would suggest. "In view of recent rumours that Herr Rosenberg has been 'shelved,' it should be explained that this resounding title was from the first regarded in well-informed quarters as much more impressive than the practical authority and sphere of activity it was likely to carry with it," the correspondent reported. "This view was strengthened when, on the occasion of Herr Rosenberg's first big speech on Nazi ideology after the appointment, the Führer's attendance at which had been prominently advertised in advance, Herr Hitler sent excuses and went with Dr. Goebbels to watch an ice hockey match and a skating demonstration by Mlle. Sonja Henie," the blond Norwegian figure skater, Olympic champion, and future Hollywood film star.

Incensed, Rosenberg stomped into Hitler's office and lodged a protest. There was no question, he said: The diplomats in the Foreign Office must have been behind the report.

The Führer just shrugged off Rosenberg's pique. What could he do?

But Hitler grew angry when Rosenberg passed along a report that a former counselor in the German embassy in London, Albrecht Graf von Bernstorff, had told retired British Army officer Graham Seton Hutchison—a fascist activist, spy novelist, and enthusiastic Hitler supporter—that the Nazi regime was in danger of imminent collapse. Bernstorff was already known to be an opponent of the new order in Berlin; he had been recalled from London the previous year.

"What should we do with this pig?" Hitler asked. He told Rosenberg that he still had to treat Neurath and the diplomats delicately, out of deference to Hindenburg. "I don't want any fights with the old man to avoid embittering his final days," he said. Once the president was dead—which would be any day now; he was frail—the time for camaraderie would be over. "Then Bernstorff must be immediately arrested."

How Rosenberg longed for that day. "The sabotage of these outdated gentlemen is nothing short of grotesque!" he wrote in the diary. "Their 'awakening' will be both very sudden and bitter."

But Hitler had more immediate concerns than disloyalty in the Foreign Office. Surely Rosenberg was aware of the mounting crisis—everyone in the government was—but he did not risk making note of it explicitly in his new diary. There were matters too sensitive to write down, even in a private journal for his eyes only.

Ernst Röhm, the chief of the storm troopers, the Sturmabteilung, had been agitating for a "second revolution" since the middle of 1933. He wanted the Nazis to go after the industrialists, the big businessmen, and, above all, the Prussian generals. "There are still men in official positions today who have not the least idea of the spirit of the revolution," he said in one speech. "We shall ruthlessly get rid of them if they dare to put their reactionary ideas into prac-tice." Röhm could back up those words with power. He had nearly three million men under his command by the beginning of 1934, men who had fought in the streets for years and expected to be repaid with jobs. Röhm wanted his storm troopers to be the foun-dation of a new German army.

But Hitler would have none of it. The revolution was over. No good could come from further chaos. Hitler knew that he needed the army's backing to stay in power. The generals had only one hundred thousand men under their command—they were still hamstrung by the limits of the Treaty of Versailles—but their sol-diers were well armed and more disciplined than Röhm's rabble-rousers. The army also had President Hindenburg's unwavering support. So Hitler wisely courted the generals, not least by pushing for full rearmament in spite of the peace treaty restrictions.

In February 1934, Röhm floated a proposal to merge the storm troopers with the army under his command. Hitler instead cut a secret deal with the generals during an April conference aboard the *Deutschland* heavy cruiser. Hindenburg was dying, and Hitler still feared that the army might turn against him when the old field mar-shal was gone. He promised to slash the ranks of Röhm's storm troopers and guarantee the army's supremacy in German military affairs if the generals pledged their support for him as Hindenburg's successor.

Unaware of the pact, Röhm continued to agitate, and rumors of coups and treachery began to circulate around Berlin in the spring of 1934.

Two powerful enemies began laying the groundwork for a move against Röhm. One was Göring, who had commanded the storm troopers in 1923, before the attempted coup at the Bürger-bräukeller. The other was a man Röhm himself had recruited into the party: Heinrich Himmler. The son of a devout Catholic sec-ondary school principal, Himmler grew up steeped in Germanic history. As a boy, he memorized the particulars of the country's most famous battles. As a teenager, he could not wait to join the fighting in the First World War. But Germany surrendered before he made it to the front lines, and he spent the first years after the war attending school and working on a farm.

Röhm ushered Himmler into the Nazi fold in 1923, and six years later Himmler was appointed to lead the SS. At the time it was a small, insignificant division within the storm troopers; he set about building it into a fearsome army. While Röhm's storm troopers were an undisciplined and violent rabble, Himmler's SS—the Schutzstaffel, or Protection Squad—was to be an elite guard, composed of the cream of the Aryan racial stock, the purest of the pure, men who lived by a strict Germanic code. After Hitler rose to the chancellorship, black-uniformed men of the SS served as his private bodyguard. But Himmler had grander ambitions than that: He wanted to run Germany's entire police state, and he set about quietly and methodically gathering power.

Himmler looked unimposing, almost scrawny, with a weak chin and small eyes behind round spectacles. But he was driven and meticulous, and he had already managed to take control of political police divisions all across Germany by the time Göring handed over the Gestapo, Prussia's secret police, in April 1934. The two overambitious Nazis then joined forces to topple Röhm. Göring and Himmler saw Röhm as a rival and a threat—a man who was simply in the way, as Göring would put it years later. The SS began manufacturing evidence that the storm trooper chief was planning a coup, and passed along the bogus intelligence to Hitler.

Still other forces were working against Röhm. Conservatives, among them Vice Chancellor Franz von Papen and his protector, Hindenburg, had long worried about the destabilizing effects of the Nazi revolution. In June, Papen delivered an uncharacteristically scathing speech at the University of Marburg, criticizing the unrestrained Nazi terror and Röhm's noisy demand for a second revolution. "Germany cannot be allowed to become a train hurtling into the blue with no one knowing where it will stop," Papen declared.

"The government is well aware of the selfishness, the lack of prin-ciple, the un-chivalrous behavior, the arrogance which is on the increase under the guise of the German revolution." Papen also lashed out at Goebbels, saying that the people would not fall for his amateurish propaganda. "Clumsy attempts at deceiving them with false optimism merely make them smile," Papen said. "In the long run, no organization, no propaganda, however good, can alone retain their confidence."

Infuriated, Goebbels blocked dissemination of the speech. A few days later at another Sportpalast speech, he dismissed the con-servatives as "ridiculous twerps." "These people will not stop the progress of the century," he said. "We will trample them down as we march forward." Papen complained to Hitler about Goebbels's ban and vowed to take up the matter with Hindenburg.

Hitler beat him to it, flying to Hindenburg's estate to see the dying president on June 21. What he heard there came as a shock. The president delivered an ultimatum: Unless the chancellor could stop the calls for a second revolution and put an end to the turmoil in Berlin, Hindenburg would declare martial law and hand the nation over to the army.

The final push to act came from Göring and Himmler. Röhm had decamped to the Hotel Hanselbauer, in the spa town of Bad Wiessee, for a few weeks of sick leave and had ordered the rest of his men to plan for summer vacation. But on June 28, at a wedding in Essen, Göring's staff brought Hitler freshly manufactured reports that Röhm's men were in fact arming themselves for an uprising throughout the country.

The Führer had heard enough. He sent Göring back to Berlin and put him in charge of clamping down on their enemies around the country.

Hitler would fly south to take care of Röhm personally.

A few days later, Rosenberg would take to his diary and jot down a breathless account of what happened next.

It reads like pulp fiction.

In Rosenberg's retelling, Hitler delicately knocks on the door of a hotel room in Bad Wiessee, where Röhm is plotting to overthrow the regime, execute his enemies, and install a ruling class of homosexuals.

But the Führer, hero that he is, has uncovered the evil plot just in time. Now Röhm is done for.

"Message from Munich," Hitler says in a disguised voice as he knocks on the door.

"Come in," calls Röhm, "the door's open."

Hitler tears open the door, flies into the room and, finding Röhm still in bed, grabs him by the throat. "You're arrested, you pig!" growls Germany's superman as he delivers the traitor over to the SS. When Röhm refuses to dress himself, an SS officer slaps him in the face with his clothing.

In the room next door, Hitler finds Röhm's deputy, Edmund Heines, "involved in a homosexual act."

"These leaders want to be everything in Germany," an exasperated Hitler says, deadpan.

"My Führer," Heines blubbers as he is kissed gently on the cheek by the young man with him, "I didn't do anything to the boy." Outraged, Hitler grabs Heines's lover and tosses him against the wall.

Next, Hitler goes into the hall and sees a man wearing rouge. "Who are you?" Hitler barks.

"The chief of staff's civil servant," the man replies.

Consumed with rage, Hitler orders the storm troopers' young lovers—*Lustknaben*, Rosenberg calls them—immediately rounded up, taken to a basement, and shot.

Hitler does not want to shoot Röhm, his old friend. But Max Amann, the head of the Nazi publishing house, prevails on Hitler to do what is necessary. "The biggest pig must be done away with." Amann and Rudolf Hess, the deputy Führer, offer to shoot the traitor personally. Instead Röhm is given a gun so he will shoot himself.

He refuses, the SS do the job for him, and so ends another chapter in Hitler's fight to protect Germany from ignominy and dishonor.

What is amazing about Rosenberg's florid account of the Night of the Long Knives—as the bloodbath came to be known—is that, despite a bit of creative license, it was more or less accurate in its description of the operation, if not in its broader outline of why the purge happened. The history of the Third Reich was playing out like something out of the pages of a twisted comic book.

At dawn, Hitler's plane landed in Munich. A light rain had fallen, but the sky was bright as he strode onto the tarmac. "This is the blackest day of my life," he told two army officers who met him there. He climbed into a waiting Mercedes and departed to settle scores. Joined by an SS contingent, Hitler proceeded to the hotel where Röhm—obviously suspecting nothing—was asleep.

Pistol drawn, the Führer woke the storm trooper chief, called him a traitor, and ordered him arrested. Then he was on to the next room, where Heines was in bed with his young lover. "Heines, if you are not dressed in five minutes," Hitler screamed, "I'll have you shot on the spot!" The storm troopers went off peacefully to Munich's Stadelheim Prison, and a call was made to Göring. "*Kolibri,*" he was told.

Hummingbird: It was the code word for him to begin the executions. Röhm's storm trooper leaders in Berlin were gunned down by firing squad, but the killing went far beyond that. Political enemies past and present were also assassinated, including former chancellor Kurt von Schleicher (along with his wife) and lapsed Nazi leader Gregor Strasser. The body of Gustav Ritter von Kahr, the Bavarian politician who quashed the attempted Bürgerbräukeller coup in 1923, was discovered in a swamp—he had been hacked to pieces with axes. "Thus November 9, 1923, was avenged after all," Rosenberg wrote, "and Kahr has been overtaken by his long-deserved fate." Erich Klausener, Kempner's former boss as chief of the police section in the Prussian Interior Ministry, was gunned down as he washed his hands. Göring ordered the murder of the man who had written Papen's offending speech at Marburg, Edgar Jung. Papen, too prominent a target, was only put under house arrest.

Göring and Himmler commanded the operation from a palace in Berlin, and one eyewitness watched as the men cheerfully monitored the progress of the killing, execution lists at hand. The Reichsmarschall was in fine spirits, but at one point, learning that someone had escaped, he began to shout bloodthirsty orders. "Shoot them down! . . . Fetch a whole company! . . . Shoot them down! . . . Shoot. . . . Just shoot them down!"

After ordering the execution of a number of storm trooper leaders in Munich—though not Röhm; not yet—Hitler flew back to Berlin.

"He wore no hat; his face was pale, unshaven, sleepless, at once gaunt and puffed," a witness reported. "Under the forelock pasted against his forehead his eyes started dully. Nevertheless, he did not impress me as wretched. . . . It was clear that the murders of his friends had cost him no effort at all. He felt nothing; he had merely acted out of rage."

The precise number of victims was lost to history. Göring ordered the records destroyed after the operation. Some estimates put the number at nearly a thousand.

Röhm was one of the last. Hitler vacillated about his fate. The man had been one of his oldest friends, a loyal lieutenant from the beginning. But Göring and Himmler urged him to dispatch with the alleged traitor, and finally Hitler agreed. SS officers were sent to the prison to hand Röhm a copy of the *Völkischer Beobachter* report about his alleged planned coup, and a gun with a single bullet in the chamber.

Ten minutes later, when they returned, they found him still alive. He had stripped off his shirt and was standing at attention.

As they shot him down, he uttered two final words: "My Führer, my Führer."

The purge made Himmler more powerful than ever. Hitler promoted the SS out from under the storm troopers, who, though hobbled and chastened, continued under new leadership to inflict violence on the Nazis' adversaries. Himmler now reported directly to the Führer, and his empire was expanding. He oversaw not just his beloved SS, the Gestapo, and the political police all over Germany but also a growing concentration camp network in which to imprison enemies of the state. Before long, Himmler would win full control of the Nazi security apparatus, and he would use it mercilessly to impose his will.

A month later, at 9:00 a.m. on August 2, Hindenburg passed away. Hitler's cabinet agreed to combine the offices of chancellor and president, and the army swore an oath of unconditional obedience to the Führer. Hitler crowned himself Germany's dictator, and no one objected. At least no one in a position to stop him.

Rosenberg met with Hitler that day, and he took the opportunity to agitate anew against the diplomats. Hitler told Rosenberg he had finally had enough of the holdovers foisted on him by the late president. "Over in the Foreign Office they will hang their heads today, for I have Hindenburg's authority," he said. "Now, the fun has ended." Hitler vowed to identify the traitors among the diplomats and haul them before the People's Court, one of the soon-to-be notorious special tribunals that handled cases against the party's political enemies. "No one," he told Rosenberg, "will want to make acquaintance with *that*."

Rosenberg noted Hindenburg's passing only briefly in his diary. "A deep sadness settles over Germany," he wrote. "A great one is lost."

Then his mourning quickly gave way to joy. Hitler finally had free rein to do as he wished. "Now," Rosenberg exulted, "the Führer is the *solitary* man atop Germany."

Now they could do whatever they wanted.

Robert Kempner's identification card, issued by the Prussian Interior Ministry in 1929. *(U.S. Holocaust Memorial Museum, courtesy of Robert Kempner)*

9

"Clever Workings and Lucky Coincidences"

While his friends fled into exile, Robert Kempner opened a business in Berlin and set about making money. After he was drummed out of the civil service in Berlin, he set up what he called a "transfer office" at Meineckestrasse 9, half a block off bustling Kurfürstendamm, southwest of the Tiergarten. Working with Ernst Aschner, a Jewish judge removed from the bench by the Nazis, Kempner helped emigrants navigate the bureaucratic maze required to escape Germany: dealing with the tax implications, transferring as many of their assets as possible, obtaining all the necessary paperwork.

The partners had a perfect location. The building next door housed a number of organizations promoting Jewish emigration to the Holy Land, including a major Zionist newspaper, the Zionist Federation of Germany, and the Palestine Office of the Jewish Agency. Kempner and Aschner promised "a smooth, favorable, and speedy settlement" to get clients on their way— not just to Palestine but to South America, Italy, or whatever distant land they had chosen. The lawyers worked on a contingency basis, charging only if their efforts were successful.

Business boomed. Though the majority of Jews stayed put after the Nazi rise to power, some eighty-one thousand of them fled Germany between 1933 and 1935, most to other countries in Europe or to Palestine. An initial wave departed following the violent boycott of Jewish stores in April 1933 and the laws passed that month forcing Jews out of many professions. A steady stream followed throughout the rest of the decade.

The Nazis welcomed the exodus. They favored any policy that would get the Jews out of the country. At the same time, they made it expensive and difficult. Their repressive policies were already forcing the Jews to surrender jobs and businesses. Now, to flee the country, emigrants often had to leave behind much of their property as well. The Reich Flight Tax was implemented in 1931 as a way of keeping capital in the country. The Nazis turned it against the Jews and increased it to such a level that some people had to sell everything just to pay it.

Bank accounts were blocked, and emigrants could get their money only by exchanging it for foreign currencies at extortionate rates. (Zionists pushing for emigration to the Holy Land, however, cut a deal with the Nazis in 1933 so that Palestine-bound Jews could keep a greater share of their assets.) Beyond that, emigrants had to produce documents and file applications and seek official permissions. At every step, they might be asked for bribes, gifts, even sex. Men from the Gestapo might knock on the door and look around for a table or a rug or a nice painting.

Meanwhile, there were waiting lists for foreign visas, and other countries often required proof that refugees would not burden the public welfare system once they arrived. The United

States required an affidavit from a sponsor who promised to step in if the immigrant fell into financial difficulty.

Confounded by the mind-numbing complexity of the process, emigrant after emigrant flocked to the offices of Kempner and Aschner. Kempner shrugged when he was asked, years later, about having made a living on the backs of Jews fleeing for their lives. He was living in a dictatorship. The rule of law did not apply. If you knew how to get around the regulations, there was a great deal of money to be made.

He could not be sure how long it would last. Kempner had less confidence than others that Nazism would turn out to be a short-term affair. Ominously, Nazi inspectors hovered about his affairs. They pored over his books, looking for evidence that he was helping Jews illegally smuggle currency out of the country.

One false move, he knew, and he would find himself behind bars. Or dead.

But it seemed worth the risk. He was doing so well financially that he could almost not afford to leave. Later, he would estimate his annual earnings in these years at $8,000, or at $138,000 in today's dollars.

He had another reason to put off emigration: He wanted to keep watch over his mother, Lydia, who had suffered under Nazism but was in no condition to flee. She was sixty-three in 1934, and her health was precarious. Her daughter had died the year before of tuberculosis—the same disease that had taken her husband, Walter, in 1920. As the Nazis consolidated their power, Lydia was forced to retire as head of the bacteriological laboratory at Berlin's Moabit Hospital and surrender her post as managing editor of a leading German tuberculosis journal, *Zeitschrift für Tuberkulose*.

Robert Kempner did send his child out of the country, to the relative safety of a Jewish boarding school in Florence, Italy.

Lucian was the product of Kempner's marriage to a woman named Helene Wehringer, which ended in 1932 after nine years. It had been an ugly separation. She accused him of beating her and violently pushing her out of their apartment, which he did not contest in court. But Kempner won custody of the boy, and a decade later, Kempner's attorney stated in an affidavit that his wife, "influenced by certain political doctrines, became heavily biased against her husband and his family because of their Jewish stock."

In 1933, Kempner still lived in the family home with his mother, and before she lost her job, he would drive her to work at the hospital. The day the Nazi banners went up along their route, she started to cry.

"Mother," he asked, "what is the matter?"

Having grown up in Kaunas, Lithuania, she knew all about the violent attacks against Jewish communities in Russia over the previous fifty years, and it seemed obvious to her that the German Jews were in for the same treatment.

"Now," she told her son, "the pogroms will start."

One day in March 1935, it looked as though Kempner had waited a beat too long to make his getaway.

The Gestapo had launched an elaborate plan to arrest a left-wing German journalist named Berthold Jacob. During the Weimar years, Jacob, a pacifist, had been fined and imprisoned for writing stories about Germany's secret rearmament. When the Nazis came to power, the Jewish writer fled to Strasbourg, France, launched a news service, and continued his investigative reporting on German military plans. He was lured to Basel, Switzerland, by agents offering to sell him a fake German passport; the Nazis had stripped Jacob of his citizenship. After drinking glass after glass of wine and liquor during a convivial dinner at a restaurant called Schiefen Eck—the Crooked

Corner—Jacob agreed to accompany his contacts to an apartment to finish the transaction. But when he climbed into their car, the driver raced north, past the Swiss guards at the border and into Germany. The journalist was taken to Berlin the same night.

Gestapo agents began poring over the address book confiscated from their prisoner. Its pages listed the reporter's military contacts and other possible informants. Two of the names were Robert Kempner and Ernst Aschner.

On March 12, the Gestapo stepped through the iron gate outside the Kempner house in Lichterfelde and knocked on the door. Narrow and tall, the elegant stone house rose three stories to a half-timbered gable and a tile roof. A trio of arches and a stone balustrade framed a veranda on the left. From the second floor, balconies looked out onto the street.

"*Mitkommen!*" the officers told Kempner when he came to the door. "Come with us!"

This was the moment that Germans, especially Jews and political opponents of the Nazis, had come to fear: the random summons to the Gestapo headquarters on Prinz-Albrecht-Strasse. Sometimes it came in the form of a postcard, and sometimes the officers arrived in person, unannounced, to force the issue. It could be that the police had some questions or wanted some information, and would quickly send you on your way. Or it could be that you were headed to what they called "protective custody" in one of Himmler's new concentration camps.

Kempner got "protective custody." He was imprisoned in Berlin's notorious, dilapidated Columbia-Haus, a former military prison known for its brutality and lawlessness.

As he arrived, he had one thought: "This is the end."

What frightened Kempner most during his nine days of solitary confinement was that he did not know exactly *why* he had been arrested. Was it related to his emigration office? His short novel about the Nazi menace, published under a pen name? His alliance with Ossietzky and the German League for Human Rights? He would not breathe a word about that, he recalled later, "for Ossietzky was not exactly a first reference during a Gestapo interrogation."

Only when he was returned to Prinz-Albrecht-Strasse and interrogated did he discover that his arrest had to do with Berthold Jacob. The Gestapo suspected Kempner of slipping him information about Nazi activities in Berlin. He denied it. "Why he had my name in his address book," he said years later, "I do not know."

After his mother, Lydia, heard the news of the arrest, she suffered a heart attack. Kempner's relatives immediately set about trying to free him, because, as he wrote later, when people you loved were arrested by the Nazis, you did not wait for justice to run its course. You did everything you could to get them out. Immediately.

Before leaving the house in Lichterfelde with the Gestapo, Kempner had called his lawyer, Sidney Mendel, who lodged a formal protest. Ferdinand Sauerbruch, a notable surgeon who knew Kempner's mother, was dispatched to speak with Oskar von Hindenburg, the son of the late president, and ask him to intervene. It is unknown whether Hindenburg tried to help, but a woman whom Kempner had been dating, Ruth Hahn—a social worker and, like himself, a Lutheran—reached out to another old contact with potential sway: Rudolf Diels.

Diels was no longer the Gestapo chief. He had made powerful enemies, and in 1934, caught in a power struggle between Göring and Himmler, he was relieved of his command and replaced by Reinhard Heydrich, Himmler's acolyte. With the Reichsmarschall as his protector, Diels escaped the Nazi purge on the Night of the Long Knives, was appointed district president in Cologne, and eventually given a post in Göring's business empire. He even married a relative of Göring's.

Surely Diels remembered how Kempner had helped him out of the compromising situation with the prostitute. Whether he returned the favor in 1935 and stepped in to help his old colleague, neither man would say.

In any case, Kempner was freed within two weeks. In a letter to a friend a few years later, Kempner said only that he made it out of Columbia-Haus in one piece thanks to Ruth's "clever workings coupled with lucky coincidences."

As for Berthold Jacob, the newspapers got wind of the story. An international outcry ensued. The Swiss protested the Gestapo's crossing the border to arrest the journalist without their knowledge and permission, and the matter went before an international tribunal. Hitler, still sensitive to diplomatic pressure in the early years of his dictatorship, ordered the journalist freed after six months.

For Kempner, there was no question now. He knew he needed to get out of the country. In August 1935, his mother died, and he finally began making the necessary arrangements. Traveling abroad on behalf of his clients, he quietly researched the best place to land with Ruth, whom he had married on May 25, 1935, soon after his release from prison. The Netherlands was too close, Britain a long shot for all but the most prominent emigrants, France inhospitable for the long term. Palestine still seemed tenuous.

One day, Kempner met an old colleague for coffee on Potsdamer Platz amid the din of the streetcars and pedestrians and circling automobiles. Thin and bespectacled, Werner Peiser, a Jew, had worked as a press secretary to the Prussian prime minister, then moved to the Prussian Historical Institute in Rome before being dismissed upon the Nazi rise to power.

Casting about for work, Peiser landed on the idea of starting a school for Jewish children whose parents wanted to send them ahead to safety. He brought in a financial partner, lined up the necessary official approvals, and placed ads in German newspapers. Opened in the fall of 1933 with a handful of children, Peiser's Istituto Fiorenza soon was a going concern with about thirty students. His school had one irresistible selling point: its location. "Landschulheim Florenz," the pitch went. "Set in the Tuscan countryside." As one alumnus noted later, "It is not difficult to advertise a boarding school located in Tuscany." When Kempner decided it was time to get his son, Lucian, out of Nazi Germany, he sent him to Peiser's school. Now Peiser suggested Kempner come to Florence, too, and help run the institution.

The more Kempner thought about it, the more Italy seemed like the perfect place to wait out Nazism.

While Hitler greatly admired Benito Mussolini, the Fascist leader who came to power in Rome in 1922, the Italian dictator had not been won over yet. In particular, he was suspicious of Hitler's designs on Austria. After German-backed Nazis in Vienna assassinated Austrian chancellor Engelbert Dollfuss and tried to overthrow the government in the summer of 1934, Mussolini infuriated Hitler by massing his armies at the border and vowing to come to the aid of the Austrian government if need be.

Kempner knew that Germans had long been welcomed in Italy; they didn't even need a visa.

Crucially, he wrote later, in Italy "there was no Jewish question." At least not yet.

So he sold the family home in Lichterfelde and his mother's library of books. The Kempner grand piano went to the Haus Vaterland, on Potsdamer Platz, for five hundred marks. His passport had expired, but the police chief in his district owed him a favor and quickly secured him a new one. Kempner presented Ruth with a ring to commemorate their emigration.

Then he set about packing a suitcase. A small one. He did not want it to look like he was fleeing for good.

He could not afford to raise suspicions.

Rosenberg spreading the Nazi philosophy to the German people, 1933. *(Bundesarchiv, Bild 102-14594/Georg Pahl)*

10

"The Time Isn't Ripe for Me Yet"

In a gun caisson pulled by six black horses, the flag-draped coffin of Paul von Hindenburg rolled across the Prussian plains. The funeral cortege seemed to stretch on forever: trumpeters, flag bearers, infantry, cavalry, artillery, high-ranking generals, relatives, servants. The wheels of Hindenburg's carriage crushed flowers and pine twigs tossed before the procession. Torches flickered in the gloom for mile after mile.

The president's remains were bound for the Tannenberg Memorial, in East Prussia, site of his great military triumph over the Russians in August 1914, where he would be laid to rest alongside twenty unknown fallen soldiers. At five o'clock the following morning, August 7, 1934, the procession arrived at the colossal memorial. It was a fortress, a martial Stonehenge, with eight soaring battlements jutting above the fields and stone walls enclosing an octagonal courtyard. On this somber day of mourning, the towers were shrouded in black, and the smoke pouring from their summits "converted them into so many sacrificial altars," one attendee thought. Seven planes, black streamers flapping from their wingtips, circled overhead as SS and storm trooper units stood in regimented formation.

The foreign dignitaries and party officials took their seats, and the Führer ascended the small platform above the casket to commit the field marshal to the hereafter.

"Departed General!" Germany's freshly minted dictator commanded. "Enter now into Valhalla!"

In the audience, Rosenberg silently rejoiced at Hitler's words. For years Rosenberg had been lashing out against Christianity, earning himself international infamy as figurehead of the Nazi Party's radical anti–church faction. During the funeral he had listened with annoyance and disgust as a military chaplain proclaimed that Hindenburg had stayed "true unto death to the living god." Rosenberg complained in his diary later that the chaplain had "assailed us with Bible quotes." He could not understand why any German worth his blood would fall for this sort of magical mumbo jumbo. "The church demonstrated again that it speaks a Chinese language in German words," Rosenberg wrote in his diary later in the day. "The nation no longer wants to hear this gibberish from Psalms, 'prophets,' etc."

But Rosenberg could always count on Hitler to set things straight, and he glowed after the Führer sent Hindenburg off to an afterlife not in the Christians' heaven but in the palace of the mythical Norse god Odin. Anyone listening closely, Rosenberg was sure, could only hear that as a shot across the bow of Christianity.

He prayed that it would be the first of many. He had had so many conversations with Hitler about the treachery of the churches. If only he could persuade him to go public with their ideas about wresting the German people away from their clerics.

For all his public rants against Jews, Rosenberg rarely dwelled on that central Nazi obsession when he picked up his fountain pen and added to his growing private diary. It was as though he considered it a topic barely worth considering, a battle all but won with the Nazi takeover. Rosenberg was looking ahead to the next war.

In the Christian churches, the Nazis were taking on an institution that had stood its ground for centuries. They were at the beginning of a fight that would span ages, Rosenberg realized, but still he proselytized with the fervor of a man who hoped to win in his own lifetime.

"The holy ground may not be Palestine," he crowed in one speech, "but Germany."

He cheered any and every incremental report of progress. In Oldenburg, he was told that "in a parish of four thousand people, the sermon would have to be canceled thirty-one Sundays a year because of a complete absence of visitors." To break the churches, Rosenberg believed, the Nazis needed to undermine Germans' core beliefs, to peel away the faith of their fathers and then replace it with something new. "When we put on our brown shirts," he told a crowd in Hanover in 1934, "then we cease to be Catholics or Protestants. We are only Germans."

He laid this out in *Myth*, which included a vicious attack on modern Christianity. He argued that Jews of antiquity, chief among them Saint Paul, had undermined the true message of Jesus, had infiltrated Christianity and taken charge, had spread a false message of submission and suffering, humility and universal love. It was a ploy to subjugate the faithful, to make them weak and pliable. By Rosenberg's way of thinking, Saint Paul's message of equality before God—"There is neither Jew nor Greek, there is neither slave nor free, there is no male and female, for you are all one in Christ Jesus"—amounted to "nihilism." He rejected the idea of one religion for all people. The Germans could not submit to a faith that expected them to sit down at the same table with inferior races. He rejected the idea of original sin, for the Nordic man was a hero. He ridiculed central Catholic concepts: a fiery hell, a virgin birth, the resurrection on the third day. All of these teachings were charlatanisms, "magic . . . one superstition after another."

In *Myth*, Rosenberg laboriously cataloged the sins of Christianity through the ages: how the churches relied on "systematically falsified history," how the Vatican ruthlessly persecuted, hunted down, and exterminated as heretics anyone who questioned official Church policy, how clerics defended their authority with the sword and the Inquisition. The teachings of the Church, he wrote, were "inwardly false and dead."

Germans—free, powerful, hardened—needed a new, muscular faith, a "religion of the blood" that would bind them together in a common, heroic fight for national honor. They were a race of supermen who would return Germany to glory after decades of suffering and ignominy. Rosenberg envisioned a new German church, a national popular faith. The Old Testament would be abolished, the New Testament expurgated of supposed Jewish messages, and a "fifth gospel" written to reflect the authentic teachings of Jesus. All the "horrible crucifixes" would come down, for the church would focus not on Christ's suffering but on his heroic life. The Germanic Jesus was "the powerful preacher and the angry man in the temple," and he would be portrayed as "slim, tall, blond, high-browed," because he was most likely Aryan, not Jewish. Hosannas to Jehovah would be swept from the hymnals. Instead of following the Bible, with its stories of "pimps and livestock dealers," the faithful would turn to Germanic myths for inspiration. "Today a new faith is awakening—the myth of the blood; the belief that to defend the blood is also to defend the divine nature of man in general," the prophet of this new national faith declared. "It is a belief, embodied with the brightest knowledge, that Nordic blood represents that *Mysterium* which has overcome and replaced the older sacraments."

In his diary, too, Rosenberg longed for some great charismatic reformer to sweep away the denominations and their outrageous hypocrisies and their miserable religious art. The "often horrible, distorted Late Gothic carvings" should be moved out of the sanctuaries and consigned to the museum. The "disgusting Baroque emblems" should be torn down. Statues of the saints should be replaced with busts of great Germanic heroes. Then and only then would the Nazis own the German soul. The gospel of "blood and soil," the message that the Aryan race and Deutschland must prevail over all, would be preached from the pulpits in place of Deuteronomy and Leviticus, and inside the churches, "no Jewish 'prophetic words' will resound anymore."

At the end of 1934, Rosenberg told an audience in Stuttgart that the Nazis intended to convene "a social order with all the holy mysticisms of the Medieval age" in the Nazi headquarters in the Bavarian capital. "You all know that there is a senatorial hall with sixty-one seats in the Brown House in Munich which has never yet been in use," he said. "We only await the signal of the Führer to lay the foundations of this holy order of Germany in this hall."

Rosenberg, who officially left the church in 1933, thought he had the Führer on his side. A number of times over the years, he would engage Hitler in far-reaching philosophical discussions about the Christians and their two thousand years of treachery.

Once, Rosenberg told Hitler of his shock when he visited Ettal Abbey, a Benedictine monastery south of Munich, as an eighteen-year-old and saw, under the central dome in the church, that "the skeletons of the saints lay in glass cases with gold rings on their bones and gold crowns on their skulls." This, he sputtered, was something out of Africa. This was the sort of thing an "Ashanti religion" did. In Russia, going to church was just something people did, "a non-mandatory oriental custom with beautiful singing." But in Germany, congregants were expected to actually *believe* the Bible stories.

"Whatever the <u>meaning</u> life or the world had, we would never fathom," Hitler told Rosenberg during one of their conversations.

"All the microscopes didn't bring us any solutions, only expanded our insights by a bit. But if there is a god, we have the duty to develop the skills we were given. One could be wrong about this, but not pretend, or lie."

On another occasion, he told Rosenberg how he wished they could return to the age before Jesus, to the glory days of Greece and Rome. Hitler vowed never to bomb Athens; he cherished Rome. "Even in its decline, it was still magnificent, and one could understand how young Teutons had been overwhelmed by the sight," Hitler said. Just look at the difference between "the regal head of Zeus" and "the agonized Christ" and you could appreciate the difference between the cultures. "How free and cheerful the ancient world seemed in comparison to the Inquisition, the burning of witches and heretics."

The way Hitler saw it, he told Rosenberg once, the ancients were blessedly unfamiliar with two evils: syphilis and Christianity.

But Hitler could not risk saying these things in public. "More than once he emphasized, laughing, that he had always been a heathen, and now the time has arrived for the Christian poison to face its end," Rosenberg wrote in his diary, but "these performances have remained strictly secret." The chancellor had to worry about practical considerations. As he wrote in *Mein Kampf,* even a politician who despised the churches needed to recognize that religion was the key to maintaining civic order. "For the political man, the value of a religion must be estimated less by its deficiencies than by the virtue of a visible better substitute. As long as this appears to be lacking, what is present can be demolished only by fools or by criminals." He could not openly offend Germany's forty million Protestants and twenty million Catholics if he expected to keep the people on his side.

In the years leading up to 1933, the Nazis had cloaked themselves in Germany's Protestant tradition to win the votes of the faithful. After Hitler came to power, a faction of German nationalists and Nazi sympathizers unified the many scattered Protestant congregations under a Reich Church. With Hitler's backing, a Nazi named Ludwig Müller became Reich Bishop, charged with overseeing the Protestant faith and spreading the Nazi gospel. This was not an official state church—not yet, at least—but it fit with the broader Nazification happening in every corner of German life. The nationalists who dominated the new church were more than happy to fight the Jewish threat and promote a racially "pure" form of Christianity. Some pastors even took to leading services in their SS uniforms.

Catholics, meanwhile, had a more complicated relationship with the Nazi Party. They did agree on some points. Like the Protestants, the Catholics deplored the rise of atheistic communism and welcomed Hitler's anti-Bolshevik drive. The German bishops condemned the cultural liberalism of the Weimar Republic. Most significant, a strain of anti-Semitism had run through Catholic thought for centuries: Theologians traced Jewish corruption all the way back to Calvary. But for the Catholics, this was a matter of religion, not race. A Jew could convert and be saved by Jesus. The Nazis, of course, did not recognize this distinction. On the official rolls, a Christian Jew still counted as a Jew.

The Catholic antagonism toward the Nazis was mainly a matter of politics. The bishops had supported their own political organization, the Catholic Center Party, in the years before the Nazis came to power. And they could never fully embrace a party that espoused blasphemies like Rosenberg's. The clerics had read his *Myth* closely and feared that his threatening ideas about men of the cloth would become state policy. "Rosenberg's outlook on life," one theologian who fled Germany concluded in 1937, "is stark dementia and his mental disease is likely to infect more and more of his fellow countrymen if the present conditions continue." If this was what Hitler and the Nazis really had in mind, they decided, the churches were doomed.

At the end of 1930, soon after *Myth* appeared, Cardinal Adolf Bertram, archbishop of Breslau, spoke out against the Nazis and their worship of a superior Aryan race. "Here we are no longer dealing with political questions," he wrote in a piece that appeared in *Germania*, a Center Party newspaper, "but with a religious delusion which has to be fought with all possible vigor."

In 1931, the Bavarian bishops decreed that Catholic priests could not join the Nazi Party because of its hostility to the faith, and ruled that Nazis could be refused the sacraments. Bishops in other dioceses issued instructions barring the faithful from enlisting with the party.

Once in office, Hitler did what came naturally: He told the churches what they wanted to hear, and then he did whatever he wanted—often the opposite of what he had promised. In his first radio speech to the nation, on February 1, 1933, Hitler expressly declared Christianity "the foundation of our national morality." That March, as Hitler lobbied the Reichstag to pass the Enabling Act and give him broad new powers, he promised several concessions to the Catholic politicians. In his speech on the day of the vote, he said the churches' "rights are not to be infringed."

In response, the German bishops lifted their restrictions on Nazi membership in the Church. The bishops and the major Catholic labor, youth, and fraternal organizations urged the flock to obey the new national government and work with Hitler to renew Germany's honor.

The Catholics were eager to cut a formal deal to ensure their place in the new German order. The bishops worried that their freedom to preach would be curtailed and that Catholic schools would be shuttered. Catholic Center Party civil servants were being fired, and many Catholic organizations were being threatened and intimidated. Priests were being arrested, and Catholic offices raided. The bishops were worried, first and foremost, about protecting the institution. They raised no objections to the new regime's withering assault on communists. They did denounce the Nazi idea of elevating one race above all others; the Catholics invited people of all races to worship in their cathedrals. And they did vocally protest the persecution of Jews who had converted to Christianity. But they did not speak out explicitly against the broader implications of Nazi anti-Semitism on Germany's Jewish community at large.

Over the spring and summer, Hitler's deputies negotiated a formal treaty with the Vatican. Under the terms of the deal, reached in early July 1933, the Vatican agreed to stay out of German politics, and the Nazis guaranteed Catholics religious independence. But the provisions of this Concordat were open to interpretation, and Hitler was not one to be hemmed in by diplomatic promises.

Nazi harassment of the churches continued virtually unabated. On the very same day the cabinet ratified the deal with the Vatican, it approved a law ordering the sterilization of the diseased and disabled, a law the Catholics vociferously opposed.

It seemed that Catholic leaders were operating on a fundamental misunderstanding. They believed that if they showed patriotic fervor and agreed to stay out of affairs of state—as they did in other countries—they would be left alone. They would cooperate with the regime if only the Nazis would stop bullying them. What they did not see, at least not at first, was that the Nazi ethos required that the party have a controlling say in every aspect of German life. They did not realize that the Nazis viewed them as competition. "The bishops," wrote historian Guenter Lewy, "failed to grasp the basic fact that it was of the essence of Nazi totalitarianism to eliminate from public life entirely the influence of the churches." The regime would not share the loyalty of the populace with any other institution.

In December 1933, a throng of parishioners crowded into St. Michael's Church in Munich for Advent Masses. On their way inside the sixteenth-century Renaissance cathedral, they passed beneath an enormous bronze of a winged Saint Michael the Archangel, defender of the faith, wielding his long staff against the neck of an anguished Satan, portrayed as half human, half beast. They took their places in the pews under vaulted ceilings that glowed a luminous white and listened as Cardinal Michael Faulhaber took to the pulpit and lashed out against Rosenberg's apostasy.

Faulhaber, as archbishop of Munich and Freising, led the country's largest Catholic community. He had opposed Hitler's attempted coup in 1923, and in reply to attacks from the Nazis that winter, he declared that every life was precious—pointedly including the Jews'. But like other clerics in Germany, he took a more practical approach after Hitler became chancellor. After the Nazi boycott of Jewish shops in April 1933, Faulhaber wrote privately to Cardinal Eugenio Pacelli, the Vatican secretary of state—and future Pope Pius XII—that it made no practical sense for Catholics to publicly object: Protesting would have merely prompted Hitler to retaliate against the Catholics. The archbishop noted that an outcry from international Jewish supporters had prompted Nazis to swiftly suspend the boycott. "The Jews," he argued, "can help themselves."

After the Vatican signed the Concordat, Faulhaber congratulated Hitler and wrote, "May God preserve the Reich Chancellor for our people."

But that morning at the pulpit of St. Michael's, Faulhaber had more celestial arguments on his mind. He attacked those who, like Rosenberg, declared the Old Testament a Jewish book that poisoned Christianity. He criticized those who denied the Judaism of Jesus and "tried to save Him with a forged birth certificate, and have said that he was not a Jew at all but an Aryan.

"When such voices are raised, when such movements are afoot, the bishop cannot remain silent," Faulhaber said. Inside the cavernous cathedral, the rapt audience listened noiselessly. Outside, loudspeakers broadcast his disembodied voice to crowds who had been turned away from the packed church. "When racial research, in itself not a religious matter, makes war upon religion and attacks the foundations of Christianity, when antagonism to the Jews of the present day is extended to the sacred books of the Old Testament . . . then the bishop cannot remain silent."

The archbishop did not need to name names. His target was clear to everyone listening.

The following month, when Hitler named Rosenberg his ideological deputy, the churches reacted with grave alarm. Though Hitler insisted that Rosenberg clarify that his *Myth* was an outline of personal beliefs—not official Nazi dogma—few in Germany believed that the party philosopher had written what he did without at least the Führer's tacit approval. Hitler never had the firebrand silenced, nor blocked him from writing, nor punished him.

Two weeks after Rosenberg's appointment, the Vatican placed *Myth* on its index of banned books. "The book scorns all dogmas of the Catholic Church, indeed the very fundamentals of Christian religion, and rejects them completely," read the official explanation of the decision by the Sanctum Officium. Rosenberg was thrilled. "This feeble protest will contribute its share to the wider dissemination of this work," he wrote. "I am in the best of company on the Index."

On the day of the Vatican's announcement, Cardinal Karl Joseph Schulte, Cologne's bishop, was dispatched to the Reich Chancellery to lodge a formal objection to the promotion of this known heretic and chief enemy of the churches. Hitler interrupted Schulte's complaints. "I have no use for that book," he said. "Rosenberg knows it. I told him that myself. I do not want to know about heathen things, like the cult of Wotan and so on."

Schulte wasn't swayed. "You cannot talk like that about Rosenberg and his book anymore, Herr Reichskanzler."

"And tell me why not?"

"Because a few days ago you officially appointed this same Herr Rosenberg as ideological instructor of the Nazi Party, and thereby as instructor to a large portion of the German people. Henceforth, whether you like it or not, you will be identified with Herr Rosenberg."

"That's right," Hitler answered, "I identify myself with Herr Rosenberg but not with the author of the book *Myth*." If Rosenberg's writing upset the Vatican so, Hitler warned, it should not protest too loudly. That would only drive more Germans to read the book, or at least try to. After all, he told Schulte, it was the bishops who had made *Myth* so widely known by speaking out against it.

The Church decided it had no choice but to attack Rosenberg, in print and from the pulpit. The clerics could not censure Hitler; the Concordat had outlawed that. (Notably, *Mein Kampf* was never placed on the Vatican's Index.) But they could go after Rosenberg if his statements did not count as official dogma. They were making a fine distinction: They would be loyal to the regime without tolerating heresies from its leaders.

"There are heathens again in Germany," intoned Clemens von Galen, the bishop of Münster, criticizing Rosenberg for ranking the Aryans above all others. "The so-called eternal racial soul is in reality a nullity." The priests protested Rosenberg's endorsement of eugenics to end "the breeding of sub-humanity" and his support for polygamy to promote the "upbreeding" of the Aryan race. Rosenberg had argued in *Myth* that every German woman must do her patriotic duty and produce children. Simple arithmetic justified extreme measures: women outnumbered men. Besides, he asked, "should these millions of women be regarded with a pitying smile as old maids who have been robbed of their vital right?"

Catholic scholars drafted a pamphlet outlining the factual errors, historical inaccuracies, and theological misstatements in *Myth*. There were a lot of them: The publication ran to 144 pages. It was issued in five cities at the same time, the better to prevent the Gestapo from seizing all of the copies, and von Galen had it published in his name to protect the anonymous critics who had penned the arguments. The precautions were necessary. Nazis were conducting surveillance and keeping Rosenberg informed with intelligence reports on the doings of the Church.

Faulhaber, too, kept up his attacks. When he denounced Rosenberg anew from the pulpit in February 1935, Rosenberg wanted to have him arrested.

"As one doesn't yet dare touch the Führer, one intends to run down his most dangerous colleague," he wrote. "The answer to the man will not fail to materialize. According to the new law, I could charge him and jail him." Special courts had been prosecuting Germans under the recently enacted Law Against Malicious Attacks on State and Party. But even Rosenberg could see that arresting a man of Faulhaber's stature would set off a firestorm of criticism.

One way or another, "the wicked cardinal"—as Rosenberg called him—would have to pay.

That's what Alban Schachleiter told Rosenberg a short while later, "practically on his deathbed." An ally of the Nazis, the Roman Catholic abbot wrote a piece in the *Völkischer Beobachter* in early 1933 urging Catholics to fall in line behind Hitler. This article appeared before the bishops had lifted their restrictions on Nazi membership in the church, and Faulhaber responded by censuring Schachleiter and barring him from performing masses in the archdiocese. In the early years of the Third Reich, the abbot, trying to make peace between the Nazis and the Church, pressed Hitler to publicly disavow Rosenberg's *Myth*. Despite that, Schachleiter maintained cordial relations with the book's author, and never let go of his bitterness toward Cardinal Faulhaber. Speaking to Rosenberg that day, his raspy voice "aglow with hatred," the dying abbot said that "material justice cannot reach the cardinal anymore, but I hope celestial justice will pay him back."

Hitler was right about one thing. Rome's declaration of war only raised the profile of Rosenberg's book. Flipping through letter after letter from readers, Rosenberg began to think that he had reawakened millions of Germans who had been hypnotized by the priests and their Bibles. "My *Myth* now has a printing of 250,000 copies, a once-in-a-century success," he wrote in his diary the day after Christmas in 1934. He relished the attacks and vowed to engage the Vatican in a fight to the death. "Rome's counterattack should have its answer. They've realized that everything's now at stake. . . . Rome's Christianity is founded on <u>fear</u> and humility, National Socialism on courage and pride. . . . The great upheaval has begun."

While the Catholics battled Rosenberg, Ludwig Müller, the Nazi-appointed Protestant Reich Bishop, saw his campaign to unify his church splinter and fall apart. Nazi supporters in the congregations demanded that disloyal pastors be removed and that all Jewish employees, even the Christian converts, be fired. Some, following Rosenberg's reasoning, pushed for the church to renounce the Old Testament and tear down the crucifixes. This was too much for other Protestants, and dissidents began to declare their independence. A rival Confessing Church formed, repudiating Müller's leadership.

In 1935, Hitler set up a Ministry for Church Affairs and installed Hanns Kerrl to crack down on the rebellion among the clerics. Over the coming years, the new church czar tried everything. A key Protestant publisher was seized. A church in Munich was crushed. Dissident ministers were silenced; seven hundred were jailed.

One, Berlin's Martin Niemöller, was an early Nazi supporter, had even voted for Hitler in 1933. Although he was acquitted of charges and released—he insisted he had raised only religious complaints—the Führer personally ordered his immediate rearrest. Niemöller was incarcerated in the Sachsenhausen concentration camp, outside Berlin, where he was put in solitary confinement. Famously, Niemöller spoke with regret in speeches after the war about how he had done nothing when the Nazis arrested the communists and the socialists and the Jews, and how there was no one to stand up for him when the Gestapo came to take him away.

From the start, Rosenberg looked on Kerrl's new Ministry of Church Affairs with a jaundiced eye. He considered Kerrl out of his depth. His philosophical views were "quite primitive. . . . Personally he can do as he pleases, but officially he has no right to make this the creed of the movement." The whole project seemed wrongheaded, he believed; they should not be working with the churches but preparing to crush them.

"The entire healthy party is following me in this," Rosenberg wrote in his diary, "and considers the church ministry as what it is—a necessary evil, while the conviction of its necessity is lessening consistently." At the same time, Rosenberg welcomed whatever controversy Kerrl stirred up as he tried to promote the Reich Church. "Everything that happens will finally lead to the bed that I, first and foremost, have prepared," Rosenberg wrote.

He added: "Kerrl naturally doesn't love me."

Kerrl wanted to do whatever it took to get the churches aligned with the Nazis. But everywhere, Nazi firebrands were fomenting unrest.

One of them was a Rosenberg ally, Carl Röver, the governor in heavily Catholic Oldenburg. On November 4, 1936, he decreed that neither the crucifix nor portraits of Martin Luther could be hung in public buildings, including schools. Instead, images of the Führer were to be prominently displayed. "This news swept through the land like wildfire," the rural area's Catholic leader wrote in a letter to parishioners. "For us, any attack on the Cross is necessarily an attack on Christianity."

Catholics protested as never before, turning out by the hundreds to demonstrate in the streets. One priest vowed to fight the order to the death if necessary. Parishioners left the party en masse, and several mayors threatened to resign. Parishes rung their bells continuously. So many dissenters drove to Oldenburg to deliver petitions one day that the little main square was gridlocked with cars. Von Galen, the bishop of Münster, wrote in his pastoral letter that month that "a chill of horror" had gone through his heart when he heard of the decree. "Was it to be here . . . that the first fatal step was to be taken along the path of Rosenberg?"

In the face of this unusual public uprising, the Nazis did something unexpected: They backed down. Before a crowd of seven thousand, Röver said that a "wise government" admitted its errors. "The crosses shall remain in the schools."

Von Galen applauded the faithful for battling this offense against Catholic religious freedom. "From nearly every parish your representatives, brave German men, tried and tested in both war and peace, have journeyed to Oldenburg and, casting aside the fear of men, have given witness for you and for your loyalty to Christ, the Crucified One. Thank God for this manly Christian courage."

Whenever he was in Berlin, Hitler hosted a standing lunch at the Reich Chancellery on Wilhelmstrasse. These meals started late and ran very long, in keeping with the Führer's eccentric schedule. He would wake up late and read newspapers and reports in his bedroom, then finally emerge from his private quarters around noon for briefings in the Wintergarten, overlooking the courtyard gardens behind the Chancellery building. Only then would he find his way to the dining room and take a seat at the large round table that gave him a view of a Kaulbach painting called *Entry of the Sun Goddess*.

Before twenty or thirty guests—Rosenberg, Goebbels, and Göring were regulars—Hitler would deliver long monologues, or listen and pass judgment as the others debated some question of the day. Goebbels entertained people with jokes and caricatures of Nazi critics. Once, Hitler held forth on dietary matters: vegetarians like himself versus, as he called them, "corpse eaters." "He is of the conviction that plant eaters are the <u>persevering</u> forces of life," Rosenberg wrote in his diary. "Meat eaters like the lion had sudden, enormous power, but no perseverance. Elephants, steer, camels, and buffaloes, on the other hand, were counterexamples that spoke for themselves. That the plant is agreeable to us could be seen in the treatment of the sick. Children and sick people are nowadays given fruit and vegetable juices, not meat." Hitler assured his guests that once scientists understood "the science of vitamins," then man could live to be 250 years old.

The lunches could be unbearable for anyone who had real work to do.

One day in January 1937, two months after the fight over the crucifixes, Rosenberg was at the Führer's table when Kerrl began to complain about the fallout from the episode. How was he to make peace with the churches if Nazi leaders in the field sparked unrest?

Hitler waved his hand and waxed philosophical. So a few "tactical mistakes" were made. This was only natural in war. The controversies would blow over, and in any case, the priests' complaints were of no great consequence.

"The big battle for the absolute supremacy of the state over the church will continue," Rosenberg wrote later in his diary, recounting Hitler's argument. "We must carry on the battle of the great Kaisers against the popes, and we will end it. If the church was unwilling, then only the tactics . . . need to be considered: whether to cut one vein after another, or to fight an open war. The church is losing its power all over the world, after all."

"Have we come to power with or without the churches?" Hitler asked. "And what do you think, Kerrl, do more people stand behind us today than before?"

"More before."

"Well," Hitler replied, "don't go insane, Kerrl."

Kerrl sat "entirely crumpled up" in the face of the Führer's lecture, Rosenberg wrote. Kerrl's job wasn't to gain the cooperation of the clerics; it was to establish the Nazi Party as "the master of the church." The way Rosenberg saw it, the churches weren't even interested in religion anymore. They just wanted political power.

They had to be stopped. Kerrl, the fool, didn't see that. He never understood the task he had been chosen to complete. "This just goes to show," Rosenberg wrote in the diary, "that it has consequences when a person who is <u>so</u> ideologically incompetent thrusts himself into an office to which he cannot measure up."

Rosenberg had no doubt about his mission. At every opportunity, he spoke out against the churches.

"By a lengthy struggle we have managed to acquire this gem of inner wisdom," he said in one typical speech. "If there is a heaven . . . then the man who fights with honor and makes sacrifices for his race and its highest values will more surely get there than the man who with prayers in his mouth betrays alike his people and his country."

As the political and cultural fights raged inside Germany, the Nazis rebuilt their army and prepared to take the battle outside their borders.

At the end of the First World War, the Saarland had been excised from Germany's western flank and delivered to France, on the condition that in fifteen years its population would be allowed to vote on whether the region should be reunited with Germany. In January 1935, the largely German-speaking population voted overwhelmingly to rejoin their fatherland. "In the end," Hitler said on Reunification Day, March 1, 1935, "blood is stronger than any documents of mere paper."

Two weeks later, he told the world that Germany was building an air force, Göring's Luftwaffe, and had begun drafting an army of a half million men, thus violating the terms of Versailles and challenging his European neighbors to do something about it.

At the beginning of 1936, Hitler decided to push the German border still farther west by sending troops to reoccupy the Rhineland. The hill country, carved by the Rhine, Ruhr, and Moselle Rivers, extended from the Netherlands to Switzerland and included the cities of Düsseldorf, Cologne, Bonn, and Mannheim.

Though it remained part of Germany after the war, it was a demilitarized zone. Hitler's generals warned that the army was not prepared to fight if the French tried to stop the incursion. By the time Hitler announced the move, a contingent of three thousand German troops had secretly slipped into position, and France did not try to dislodge them. They thought the occupation force was far larger, and did not want to risk a war over what was already German territory. The risk paid off.

Hitler immediately called for new Reichstag elections and a referendum on the reoccupation of the Rhineland. On March 29, the Nazis carried the election with 98.9 percent of the vote.

That night, Rosenberg found Hitler on the steps of the Führer's apartment inside the Reich Chancellery. "Well, Rosenberg," Hitler called out, "what do you have to say to this? Didn't I pick a great election slogan? Even the bishops had to make room for the mood on the Rhine and ring the bells!" He laughed, then added what other observers took to be a jab at the writer: "The result would not have been the same if we had voted on *Myth*."

"No," Rosenberg answered. "That will only be possible a hundred years from now."

Rosenberg took pride in being a man who was considered so dangerous, so controversial, so unbending that he had to be kept under control lest he wreck the entire Nazi revolution. But still, he told Hitler once, it was difficult to be considered only a man of ideas. Rosenberg recounted in the diary that, in reply, Hitler assured him that he told everyone and anyone that Rosenberg was the deepest thinker in the party, that he was "the church father of National Socialism."

Reflecting on the exchange, Rosenberg was realistic. "I am quite aware," he wrote, "that the time isn't ripe for me yet."

Kempner's wife, Ruth *(left)*, fled Germany with him in 1936, and they helped run a boarding school for Jewish students in Florence. *(U.S. Holocaust Memorial Museum, courtesy of Robert Kempner)*

Margot Lipton *(right)*, his secretary at the school, became his mistress. *(U.S. Holocaust Memorial Museum, courtesy of Robert Kempner)*

11

Exile in Tuscany

Kempner took a simple precaution as he fled Nazi Germany: He and his wife traveled separately. "If one of us should be arrested," he decided, "the other must be on the outside." A year after his arrest and interrogation, he was still rattled. He packed his suitcase, took the train to Tempelhof Airport, and asked the ticket agent what time the next flight left for Italy. Directed to the gate, he discovered that, as fate would have it, he would be tagging along on a private plane chartered by Fritz Hess, father of Rudolf Hess, Hitler's deputy Führer. It was headed to Cairo, with a stop in Venice. No one recognized Kempner as he boarded and found a seat.

As Kempner looked out the window as the plane lifted off the tarmac and Berlin fell away, his departure seemed final. It crossed his mind that he would never again return to his birthplace.

Arriving in Venice, Kempner bought a rail ticket to Florence, where the following day he met his wife and her mother at the train station.

After all the worry—years of anxiety—the trip had been perfectly uneventful.

The Kempners were part of a small but steady stream of Jews entering Fascist Italy. Two years after the attempted Nazi coup in Austria that had alarmed the Italians, tensions between Hitler and Mussolini were beginning to ease: When the League of Nations threatened economic sanctions after Italy invaded Abyssinia—modern-day Ethiopia—in a bid for a new African colony, Germany stayed neutral, much to Mussolini's relief.

But the country was still seen as a refuge from the Nazi terrors back home. The Italian Foreign Ministry allowed Jewish immigration "to the extent that it does not involve persons who were active in political parties directed against fascism." Even stateless immigrants did not need visas, and there were few work restrictions. Crucially, following a 1934 German-Italian trade agreement, refugees were able to transfer sizable amounts of foreign currency into Italy for investment, at least for the time being. So artists, writers, politicians, doctors, and academics fled south, attracted by the favorable conditions and low cost of living.

Kempner had accepted Werner Peiser's offer to take charge of administrative affairs at the boarding school in the hills outside the city. Peiser's Istituto Fiorenza was a refuge for Jewish children, mostly teenagers, forced out of the public schools by the Nazis. Citing overcrowding, Germany in 1933 capped the non-Aryan population in its secondary schools and universities at one and a half percent. The Jewish kids who were still enrolled were tormented by hostile teachers and students. In some classes, they were segregated onto "Jewish benches" and taught that Jews were inherently dishonest and racially inferior. Outside the classroom, they were bullied by newly minted members of the Hitler Youth. One student remembered seeing Streicher's notoriously anti-Semitic *Der Stürmer* tabloid tacked up on the walls at his Jesuit school in Munich. "You smell like a Jew," a classmate told him. The Nazis, wrote another schoolchild who ended up in Florence, "left us in no doubt that they wanted to see the last of us, and sent the message either politely through their headmasters, or more peremptorily through the local chiefs of police."

Some of the parents who sent their children to Peiser's school had already fled Germany and needed a place for their children to continue their schooling. Most of them had hustled out their children while they made the necessary emigration arrangements for themselves. Those children had been sent ahead, Kempner said, as "pioneers."

Sometimes it seemed to him that whenever Goebbels opened his mouth, applications to the school spiked. Kempner was amazed that the Nazis even let the newspapers print their notices. "More or less we advertised: If you do not send us your children . . . then they will be killed."

The drive to the school from Florence twisted along narrow, cobblestoned roads that would suddenly open up onto lovely vistas of olive orchards and vineyards. "The Tuscan landscape is like a beautiful woman: constantly changing," wrote one of the students who made the trip.

The school occupied several villas in the town of Arcetri, including Il Gioiello, or the Jewel, where the astronomer Galileo had spent the final years of his life under house arrest after running afoul of the Inquisition. The headquarters of the Istituto were in a mansion situated at the highest point in the village. It looked like a palace to the arriving students, with its wrought-iron front gate, cypress-lined drive, and tower dating to the twelfth century. Inside, they ate and studied in rooms with red-tiled floors and high ceilings. French doors in the dining room opened up onto a terraced garden with lemon trees, flower beds, and a tennis court. Rolling hills and the peaks of the Apennine Mountains rose in the distance. The building was known as the Villa Pazzi, and though it was named after a famous Florentine family, the boarders joked that it could be translated as "the Madhouse." In fact, their temporary home was a quiet enclave, a country estate hemmed in by thick, ancient walls draped with wisteria. One student recalled sitting on a balcony one day overlooking the fields. "There was a little mist, the sky had a few clouds, but the sun broke through off and on. It was so calm and peaceful—the cocks were crowing in the distance, and the birds were singing. The air was balmy and the church bells were just beginning to ring." The Istituto Fiorenza felt like a hideout from a world gone crazy.

The children studied a standard classical curriculum. They recited Plato and read *Commentarii de Bello Gallico*, Julius Caeser's commentary on the Gallic Wars. They staged plays and recitals and poetry readings. They took day trips to Florence, where the students gazed at the massive, architecturally ingenious dome of the Santa Maria del Fiore cathedral, stood before Michelangelo's *David*, and examined the Medici masterpieces in the famed Uffizi Gallery. The school was small enough that teachers could give the children individual attention, and they built a close-knit community.

Peiser attracted an impressive faculty, though few were professional teachers. Among them were renowned linguists, a journalist, an actress, and a future authority on Renaissance philosophy. They earned little or nothing; some worked for room and board. Their living quarters were tiny. "The singular beauty of the landscape represented the main part of our subsistence," one of the teachers recalled. Tuition was not cheap, and the school tended to attract the children of the upper middle class and the wealthy, or, as one teacher complained, "the spoiled brats of the bourgeoisie."

Kempner's arrival brought changes to the school. He worked to recruit more students, and soon nearly a hundred children were enrolled. Mostly Jews, the students hailed not just from Germany but also Austria, Hungary, Romania, and Poland. With the crisis escalating in Europe, the curriculum no longer focused only on the humanities and preparation for tests that would qualify the students to go on to higher education. The students now spent their days on more practical lessons to prepare them for work in exile. The children studied foreign languages—Italian, Hebrew, Polish, but above all English—and learned skills required to become woodworkers, metalworkers, bookbinders, stenographers, pharmacy assistants, and medical technicians. Not everyone welcomed the addition of this abrasive and confrontational lawyer to their warm academic community in 1936. Some teachers were upset that Kempner, so focused on permanent emigration, was changing their "small redoubt of humanistic cultivation" into a "transit facility."

"He liked to approach human relations like a detective," wrote Ernst Moritz Manasse, a teacher who clashed with Kempner. He would regale them with amusing stories about prying sensitive information out of people. But, Manasse wrote, without elaborating, he couldn't help but feel disturbed by the "morally troubling methods" Kempner described in these tales.

As time went on, another teacher found that Kempner was bringing the same sort of tactics to bear on the faculty and staff at the Istituto Fiorenza. Wolfgang Wasow wrote in his memoir that Kempner was one of the few people he had met in his life "whom I thoroughly detested." The man hardly bothered to learn any Italian; trying to angrily wave someone out of his office, he would confuse *venga* ("come") with *vada* ("go.") "His mannerisms combined a brusque insensitivity, even rudeness, with an obviously faked solicitude when he felt that was called for," Wasow wrote. "Beyond that, I am convinced that he was . . . a crook. I would not be able to prove that claim in a court of law, but the indications are so numerous that most of my fellow teachers strongly agreed with me."

One day he accused Kempner of spying on the staff by steaming open outgoing letters and reading them. Wasow was fired on the spot.

But the teenagers loved their time in Italy. "We were carefree, happy, concerned only with our own affairs," one recalled.

They gossiped. They pulled pranks. They debated Zionism. They stole cherries from the fields. They slept with the windows open and shrieked when bats flew inside. They mocked the booming speeches of the Führer, using a comb for a mustache. They fell in love.

For three months every summer, the entire school decamped to the Hotel Continentale in Bordighera, on the Italian Riviera, for a sort of working vacation away from the Tuscan heat. At the time, tourists stayed away from the resort town during the hot summer months, so the hotel owner was happy to rent the place to the boarding school. Amid tropical blue skies and palm trees, they would hike and swim and stage cabarets. Some of them took day trips to Monte Carlo. "How wonderfully beautiful it is here," Kempner wrote, "every day with carnival, cake, and sport."

Looking from the hotel balconies out onto the Mediterranean, the exiles could see ocean liners steaming west to America, and dream of being aboard.

They felt so far from the dark realities of Nazi Germany. "We were relieved to have escaped," Manasse wrote, "and allowed ourselves to be seduced by the beauty of Florence and its surroundings, the friendliness shown us by our Italian neighbors, and by the camaraderie among us, students and teachers whom fate had thrown together."

All of that was about to change. In the spring of 1938, the tenuousness of their situation became impossible to ignore.

Kempner's younger brother, Walter, had moved to the United States in 1934 for a job on the medical school research faculty at Duke University, in North Carolina. He hated Hitler and did what it took to put an ocean between himself and the Führer. In 1938, Robert Kempner would have to wonder whether he had made a life-altering mistake by not doing the same.

On September 15, 1935, during the party's annual rally, Hitler announced sweeping new restrictions against the Jews. Approved immediately by the Reichstag, the first of Germany's Nuremberg Laws officially made second-class subjects of the Jews and prohibited them from flying the German flag, which would in any case bear the swastika. The second regulation, based on the principle that "the purity of German blood is essential to the further existence of the German people," barred mixed marriages, outlawed sex between Jews and Aryans, and made it illegal for Jews to hire Aryan women under age forty-five as domestic servants.

Tourists and foreign businessmen did not necessarily notice this mistreatment, or else they did not consider it terribly alarming that Jews were being excluded from virtually every aspect of German life. Many returned home highly impressed with the country's swift rejuvenation under Hitler's rule.

The Nazis were capable of putting on a gracious face, never more so than during the 1936 Olympics, when Goebbels advised his countrymen to "be more charming than the Parisians." The signs that read JUDEN UNERWÜNSCHT!—"Jews unwelcome!"—were removed from storefronts and restaurants. Newspapers took a break from the denunciations. The violent mobs were nowhere to be seen. Tolerance was the order of the day.

The visitors "were duly impressed by the might of the regime, by the enthusiasm of the youth, by the propaganda of Goebbels," wrote Willy Brandt. "It was difficult not to be overwhelmed by it, for wherever you looked you saw the successes of Nazism confirmed in the smiling faces of the young people, in the new monumental buildings, in the economic boom. Berlin offered magnificent scenery for a spectacle that took the breath of the world away."

But it was only that: scenery and spectacle. Once the Olympics ended and the crowds departed, the persecution began anew. "Not a single dissenting voice disturbed the jubilation," Brandt continued, "for the cries from the concentration camps and the death rattle of the tortured victims did not reach the stadium."

Two days after the closing ceremonies, Wolfgang Fürstner, a

German military officer who oversaw the construction of Olympic Village, shot himself with his service pistol. Officials had discovered his Jewish ancestry, and he was demoted and told he would be dismissed from the army. Rosenberg had little sympathy. Instead he applauded Fürstner for dealing appropriately with his tragically mixed blood. "My deep regards for his deed," Rosenberg wrote in the diary.

Over the next two years, any illusions the Jews still had about Hitler and the Nazis would fade away.

In the summer of 1938, a friend wrote Kempner about conditions inside Germany: Everyone who could possibly get out, he reported, was preparing for departure.

The Florence exiles thought they had escaped persecution. The Italian Fascists were not strident anti-Semites of the Nazi sort. Privately, Mussolini had even dismissed the racial foundations of the Third Reich and said that Hitler's head seemed to be crammed with muddled ideologies and incoherent philosophies.

By 1936, rapprochement between the two nations was at hand. Allying with Mussolini to support General Francisco Franco and the Nationalists in the Spanish Civil War, Hitler dispatched artillery and aircraft and thousands of soldiers. On April 26, 1937, in the most infamous assault of the war, German and Italian planes bombed and strafed the village of Guernica, killing more than 1,600 people and inspiring the famous Picasso mural. The war put Germany and Italy in opposition to France and Britain and smoothed the way for an alliance of convenience between the two dictators. They soon worked out a secret accord forming a Fascist-Nazi Axis, and in September 1937 Germany welcomed Mussolini with military pomp and enormous flag-waving crowds.

The next year, Mussolini returned the favor. Hitler arrived in Rome on May 3, 1938, and, accompanied by the king of Italy in a horse-drawn carriage, rode through St. Paul's Gate, past the Pyramid of Caius Cestius, and into the city center. Dramatically lit to lend the scene an air of religious ceremony, Rome was "transformed into a vast operatic stage," an Italian journalist wrote. It was "a spectacle worthy of Nero: the Coliseum launched flames from its falling arches, the pines radiated green and yellow lights which made them appear crystalline, the Arch of Constantine appeared phosphorous, and ruins of the Forum emanated reflections of silver."

Over the coming week, Hitler would revel in Italy's historic architecture, watch carefully choreographed military exercises, and spend hours in museums and galleries. "Rome," he would say later, "captivated me."

On his last day in the country, Hitler stopped in Florence for a whirlwind visit. The dictators wound through the streets in a black convertible at the head of a twenty-car motorcade flanked by a motorcycle guard. Bells rang, and the Italian air force flew tight formations overhead. The city was mobbed by cheering Italians and bedecked with banners bearing swastikas. The two visited the Basilica of Santa Croce, where Michelangelo, Machiavelli, and Galileo were buried. Heralded by Florentine trumpeters, they stepped onto a balcony outside the Palazzo Vecchio and, beaming, greeted enormous crowds of well-wishers in the square below. They wandered through the Uffizi galleries, dined at the Palazzo Medici, and took in a Verdi performance.

En route to the train station, the two dictators were toasted with fireworks spelling out "Führer" and, for Mussolini, its Italian equivalent, "Duce."

Then it was over. Hitler stepped into his bulletproof train and bade Mussolini and Italy farewell.

Hitler was in Florence for all of ten hours. But the Jewish teachers at the boarding school, along with their wives, twenty-one male students, and Kempner's elderly mother-in-law, spent three weeks in prison. "Our imprisonment was part of the festivities," one of the students wrote. "We were hostages, and thus put in the weird position of being obliged to hope that the Visitor would return home without a scratch."

In 1936, police in both countries had begun sharing information and documents about potential "subversive elements" within their borders. In preparation for Hitler's visit in 1938, the Gestapo worked closely with the Italian police to systematically identify and investigate German, Austrian, and Polish exiles living in the fascist state. Nazi security officials were stationed in nearly two dozen Italian police departments, and they compiled detailed lists that classified the immigrants as "dangerous," "suspicious," or trustworthy.

Then, in April, the month before Hitler's planned arrival, SS and Gestapo officers flooded Italy to conduct interrogations and search houses. On April 20 and May 1, Jewish émigrés were arrested en masse.

Men and women went to separate jails. It took some time before the guards could be convinced that the émigrés were not the usual thieves and prostitutes who populated the cells. The men had to surrender their belts, in case they had ideas of suicide. But at a time when prison in Germany meant the concentration camp, the conditions during their detention were mild. A friendly priest helped smuggle news in and letters out under his cassock, the inmates were allowed to roam around the jail during the day, and after Hitler was safely through the Brenner Pass and onto German soil, everyone was released.

As if by osmosis, anti-Semitism seeped across the border into Italy. The Nazi-led incarceration of the immigrants seemed to make Mussolini believe that his country, like Germany, had a Jewish problem. A few months after Hitler's visit, in the summer of 1938, Il Duce was mimicking his ally to the north. "Without a clear, certain, and omnipresent racial consciousness, empires cannot be held," he wrote in an Italian newspaper piece. Mussolini announced that his ancestors were Nordics through and through, and in July his government issued a "Manifesto of Racial Scientists," laying the groundwork for sweeping measures to exclude Jews from Italian life.

The first of those laws, approved in September 1938, left no wiggle room for the boarding school. Jews were no longer permitted to attend, teach at, or work for Italian schools— kindergarten through university, public or private.

In addition, Jews who had arrived in Italy after 1919 were ordered to leave the country within six months.

Kempner had seen it coming, and this time he did not delay. He had known for months that his time in Italy was up. The warning signs had been there all summer. German officials in Berlin began to question whether the school was anti-Nazi and cut off tuition transfers from parents. Italian authorities made threatening visits. On August 22, the administrators were asked to report on the racial lineage of the teachers and students. "A sense of fear and foreboding permeated the school," a student wrote, "and we knew that our carefree existence was coming to an end."

One day, an Italian official appeared and demanded that Peiser sign a document "confessing" that his Istituto Fiorenza was a liberal, Social Democratic institution. Peiser asked whether he would be arrested if he signed it. Yes, came the reply.

Peiser and Kempner wanted no part of being returned to an Italian prison or, worse, being extradited to Germany. "We were told confidentially," Kempner wrote a friend later, "that it would be better to leave the country immediately and not wait until the last minute."

Finally, on September 3, they received the inevitable news: The Italians had ordered the institution shut down on the grounds that it was "inspired by political and ideological ideas contrary to Fascist doctrine."

At the time, the teachers and students were in Bordighera for their summer break. Kempner and Peiser rushed to make overnight arrangements to return the children to their families "through suitable persons." Then they fled to Nice, just across the border in France, with their wives, some of the teachers, and the ten students who had valid visas.

On the morning of September 4, Gabriele Schöpflich, who taught at the school, arrived in the dining room of the hotel in Bordighera to the news that Kempner and Peiser were gone, along with "all those children whose fees were paid in foreign currency."

The dozen students left behind were "thunder-struck." Schöpflich and a colleague were left to clean up the mess. The hotel staff had not been paid in a week, and they quit en masse. Storekeepers confronted them with enormous bills they could not pay—among them the butcher, the milk dealer, the grocer, and the hardware dealer. Over the next ten days, Schöpflich and a colleague reunited the remaining students with their guardians. "Neither of us got much sleep during those ten days," she wrote. She personally accompanied two children to Florence to meet their mother at the train station for the trip back to Vienna.

Rumors spread about the messy departure. Kempner's secretary, Margot Lipton, a twenty-four-year-old Jewish woman from Frankfurt, received a letter not long after from her sister in Rome, Beate Davidson.

Davidson wrote that the reports of the school's dissolution had made her nauseous. How was it even possible to shut down overnight? Was it true that some children had been left behind to be cared for by people in the community? "The school is responsible for these underage children, after all," she wrote. "To leave children behind in a foreign country, penniless, under the current conditions, is simply outrageous." She had heard that Kempner told the children not to discuss the circumstances of the school's closing with their parents. She had heard that Kempner insisted on keeping his destination a secret. She had heard that he had taken someone's passport as collateral. She had heard that the school left behind debts. These things were criminal, Davidson said. Did Lipton not know anything about any of it?

Davidson quickly received a letter from Kempner and Peiser.

They told her they were greatly offended that someone who knew them both would accuse them of outright fraud. They dismissed the allegations as the gossip of bitter and spiteful *"Judenweiber"*— Jewish broads.

An Italian lawyer had been hired to settle their liabilities. They had left behind debts because some parents had not paid all of their tuition bills. (In another notice sent to parents to explain the circumstances of the closure, Kempner and Peiser listed the "bad debtors" who owed the school more than three thousand lire.) Besides, wasn't the Italian government to blame for their default? And hadn't they been forced by circumstances to leave behind all of their furniture? How could they be "chided as swindlers" in the Jewish community? How dare anyone criticize them for fleeing before the Italians could throw them in prison again? "Do you think that we wanted to let them lock us up again after the experiences in April and May, when we and our women had to share our quarters with whores and criminals for three weeks? . . . No, dear honorable madam, we had not yet become so lethargic or masochistic as to let them take our freedom or life, aside from the loss of lots of money and valuable items."

As for the students, Kempner and Peiser said they had told the parents for months that the school was in trouble and the children needed to find new homes. They rescued those whom they could.

In many cases, the administrators wrote in other letters to friends, the students did not want to—or could not safely—go back to their parents in Poland or Hungary or Germany. "If we had been alone, we would have never been arrested . . . because we could have driven off," Kempner wrote to a friend in Paris. "But we could not leave the children alone. At the same time, we could not have taken one hundred children with us because that would have cost a lot of money, and their parents . . . would have written that it was not necessary and would not pay for it, because children are never arrested."

Kempner's life had become unimaginably complicated. He had little reason to believe that France would be "the last station of our earthly pilgrimage," he wrote to a friend, for the Western democracies seemed to be "in complete ignorance of the methods of the Third Reich and its Axis friends."

He had ten schoolchildren in his care, plus his wife, his mother-in-law, and his secretary, Margot Lipton.

And at some point, he had to share with his wife three inconvenient facts: that he had been carrying on an affair with Lipton; that she was pregnant; and that the child was his.

Kempner's fifteen-year-old son, Lucian, did not make it to France with his father. The boy had spent two years at the Istituto Fiorenza. Lucian's mother, Helene, who was not Jewish, had unsuccessfully contested the boy's departure in court, complaining that Kempner had taken Lucian out of the country without her permission.

At the end of 1937, Kempner made arrangements for his ex-wife to spend two weeks with Lucian "at a small Italian mountain resort or at a similar place." Kempner bought her a round-trip train ticket, third-class. Day after day, Helene and Lucian went on long walks until one night, to Kempner's horror, they did not return. On New Year's Eve, Helene told Lucian that his father had given them permission to go skiing elsewhere in Italy, but instead took the boy back to Germany with her. Lucian said later that he was abducted, and that Nazi and Fascist authorities had assisted his mother in the plot. He did not even have a valid passport at the time.

As the son of a Jewish father, Lucian counted as *Mischling*, mixed race, and the Nazis were still debating which of them would be subject to discriminatory treatment as Jews. Kempner could not risk returning to Germany to fight for the boy, but he appealed to the courts, challenging Helene's fitness to be a parent. He produced letters showing that she had a history of alcoholism and addiction to painkillers, that she had considered suicide by overdose, that she had venereal disease, that a doctor had told her she needed to turn her life around. Unlike his ex-wife, Kempner argued, he had a stable financial situation, and he ran a school where Lucian could study. Helene countered that the school operated "in a Marxian–Bolshevistic spirit and under Jewish influence," and that students were taught "an anti-German attitude."

The courts ruled in Kempner's favor, but still Lucian was prevented from leaving. He could not get a passport, he said later, and the authorities ensured that his mother kept physical custody of him. She enrolled the boy at Zinzendorfschulen, a Moravian boarding school for boys in Königsfeld im Schwarzwald.

"My mother has subjected me to much suffering," he would write, "and the Germans only made it worse."

There was little that Kempner could do but write letters to his son and send them off to Nazi Germany. "I thought you might have forgotten completely that you still have a dad," he wrote shortly after fleeing to Nice. He assured Lucian that things had "settled down here today," and said nothing of his chaotic departure and the shuttering of the school. "We are still in beautiful Nice, which you still know from our trips there last year," he wrote a week later. "It is still wonderfully warm and we have beautiful weather. . . . Did you speak Italian with the Italian workers or have you forgotten it all? What about your other foreign language skills in general—French, English? You know that you need to cultivate these, a boy like you with a Jewish father and Aryan mother in particular needs foreign languages; you are old enough to know this and to keep this in mind."

He included stamps and asked Lucian to send photographs. "Please write me again very soon."

Rosenberg at Hitler's side in the front row of Nuremberg's Apollo Theater during a 1934 cultural meeting of the Nazi Party. *(SZ Photo/Scherl/The Image Works)*

12

"I Had Won Over the
Old Party's Heart"

In Nuremberg, "the most German of all German cities," as the mayor called it, the church bells rang for half an hour straight on September 6, 1937, to mark Hitler's arrival for the opening of the annual Nazi Party rally. By the hundreds of thousands, the party faithful convened for what promised to be the biggest rally to date—eight days of speeches and spectacle, regimented marching, and fearsome demonstrations of military might.

In vast acres of tents and makeshift barracks, the rank and file would get three and a half million mess kits and a dose of campground camaraderie, assuming the weather held. Proper lodging was so difficult to find that delegates from the United States and Britain would stay on the special train that had brought them south from Berlin. Nazis of higher stature would stay in hotel rooms and dine at Nuremberg's more notable restaurants, like the Goldenes Posthorn bratwurst house on Glöckleinsgasse, which dated to 1498 and had been a favorite of Nuremberg's famous painter Albrecht Dürer. More than a few visitors would take the opportunity to find Nuremberg's red-light district and try to slip past an SS cordon to visit one of the hundred or so prostitutes who all, conveniently, lived in close proximity.

That week, Rosenberg was not just another speaker at the rallies. He was a guest of honor. Eighteen years after first turning up at a regular meeting of a tiny band of beer-hall anti-Semites in Munich, he was being hailed as the man who'd laid the ideological foundations of National Socialism. His masterwork, *The Myth of the Twentieth Century*, already rested beside *Mein Kampf* in the cornerstone of Nuremberg's Congress Hall, the monumental arena rising in the middle of the rally grounds. When finished, it would be larger than the Colosseum in Rome.

Rosenberg couldn't know it, of course, but the lavish attention he would receive in Nuremberg this week would turn out to be the high-water mark of his life.

Hitler had chosen Nuremberg as the regular site of the party rallies for reasons of symbolism: He wanted to tap into the country's glorious past. Six hundred years earlier, the medieval stronghold had ranked as one of the wealthiest and most important cities in Europe. Behind a thick defensive wall and a moat three miles around lay an old town still arrayed with properly Germanic architecture: a wonderland of Gothic gables and intricate carved doorways, a traditional market square, extravagant churches, and, at the top of a rise, an impregnable castle that once hosted Holy Roman emperors. For a party that invoked mythical folk traditions, Nuremberg was the perfect backdrop. "In few cities," Rosenberg's *Völkischer Beobachter* declared, "does the contrast between past and present find so precise an expression as in Nuremberg—turrets, mighty walls, and towers give testimony of manly power and fighting spirit."

The party rallies at Nuremberg were more than political conventions. They were mystical ceremonies designed to demonstrate the strength of the Nazi mass movement and feed the Führer cult.

Over the coming days, Goebbels would attack Bolshevism, the diplomats would have tea with Hitler at his hotel, and the leader of the National Socialist Women's League would train the wives of Germany how to run a household the Nazi way. The Blood Banner, a flag carried through the streets of Munich during the failed Bürgerbräukeller coup in 1923, would be used to consecrate new Nazi standards. The SS and the storm troopers would march through Nuremberg, formation after tight formation passing through the narrow cobblestoned streets, below spectators hanging out open windows. Hitler would stand on the balcony at his hotel, the Deutscher Hof, above a sign reading HEIL HITLER in lights on the facade, and salute crowds of Germans who, one reporter recalled, "looked up at him as if he were a Messiah." In an awe-inspiring demonstration at a time when fears of war preoccupied the world, the German military would show off its newest machinery: motorized artillery, armored cars, motorcycles, tanks, spotter planes, bombers. New fighters would dive the field at 370 miles per hour while anti-aircraft guns rushed forward as if to challenge them.

And in what would be the most striking image from the rallies, hundreds of thousands of Nazi men would assemble on Zeppelin Field and stand at attention in disciplined order. The scene reinforced their absolute insignificance as individuals. Hitler would stand at the center of an imposing grandstand punctuated by 170 pillars of white stone. At night, when hundreds of spotlights flooded the scene, some of them pointing skyward to create Nazi architect Albert Speer's famous "cathedral of light," the glow would be seen more than one hundred miles west in Frankfurt.

"Heil, my men!" Hitler would cry.

"Heil, my Führer!" the masses would reply.

It rained off and on all week, mostly on. The afternoon following his fanfare arrival in Nuremberg, Hitler and his entourage made their way east in a convoy of black Mercedes-Benzes, through streets mobbed with supporters, to the Luitpoldhalle, where the opening ceremonies were held. "The cheers heralding his coming could be heard half a mile away," *New York Times* correspondent Frederick Birchall wrote. "They grew louder until at his entry the throng inside the hall took them up in a frenzied chorus of Heils." The delegation marched through the entrance, a monolithic block of white stone flanked by twenty towering red Nazi standards, and into the hall. It was fashioned after a cathedral, with a central aisle leading to a high stage. An enormous swastika hung like a crooked cross behind the speaker's platform. Flags were marched to the fore. The room quickly grew humid; speakers sweated in the klieg lights.

The pageantry of these opening ceremonies was stirring enough to move even the cynical observers in the Western press. William Shirer, the foreign correspondent, wrote in his diary that it was "more than a gorgeous show; it also had something of the mysticism and religious fervor of an Easter or Christmas Mass in a great Gothic cathedral." Was it any wonder, he asked, that Germans treated Hitler's every word as something akin to gospel?

Later that evening, Hitler and Rosenberg proceeded to the Opera House, where they entered to the strains of Wagner's "Entry of the Gods into Valhalla." Rosenberg delivered an address "containing copious extracts from his books," as Birchall would write in the *Times,* and then Goebbels rose to make the announcement that the Nazi Party's ideological chief had been anticipating with great relish: Alfred Rosenberg would be one of the inaugural recipients of the German National Prize for Art and Science.

A "tangible jolt" rippled through the space, Rosenberg wrote in his diary, and the applause seemed to go on and on "with unanimous force."

The prize was newly created, a protest against the Nobel Committee's decision in 1936 to award the Peace Prize to Carl von Ossietzky, Kempner's pacifist friend, locked up by the Gestapo three years earlier. The committee lauded Ossietzky as "a citizen of the world whose cause is freedom of thought, freedom of speech, and free competition in the realm of ideas." The Nazis were outraged. "It is preposterous and fatal," one of them told the *Times*. Hitler responded by barring Germans from accepting any future Nobels, and creating his own rival honor. The German National Prize came with an award of one hundred thousand marks and a lavish pin studded with diamonds, decorated along the edges with Nazi eagles, and featuring a golden bas-relief of a helmeted Athena. "I am almost embarrassed," Rosenberg wrote, "to wear such a precious star."

"In his works, Alfred Rosenberg has distinguished himself because he fought untiringly to maintain the purity of the National Socialist worldview," went the citation Goebbels read for the audience. "Only future generations will be able to assess accurately just how deeply this man influenced the spiritual shape and worldview of the National Socialist state. The National Socialist movement, and with it all the German people, rejoice with deep satisfaction that the Führer awarded this prize to one of his oldest and closest comrades."

Everyone could see, Rosenberg wrote in his diary, that the award was no mere "academic matter," given his "bitter battle against Rome." He had been told that the Vatican viewed it as a blow to the Holy Father himself. "I have stood by my work, and even if the Führer had to hold back officially, he has always let me lead the battle," Rosenberg wrote, his delusional ego swelling with every sentence. It was clear to him now that his positions—those radical statements in *Myth* that Hitler had assured everyone were Rosenberg's personal opinions—were now one and the same with Reich policy. They were nothing less than the "foundation for the Führer's entire revolution."

Everyone, too, was moved by this recognition of Rosenberg's work, or so it seemed to the honoree. Hitler himself had fought back tears when he broke the news beforehand. "Only you can receive the first prize of the Reich. You are the man, after all. . . ." At the Opera House, friends wept. Carl Röver, the governor of Oldenburg and a close Rosenberg ally, walked over to Hitler and told him that it was the greatest day of *his* life. "And now I knew that I had won over the old party's heart," Rosenberg wrote, "which was now as if liberated by the Führer's grand gesture."

Above all, he took great pleasure from the fact that it was Goebbels himself who had to recite the proclamation. "This after doing his utmost to push me aside with all kinds of chicanery, for which he had all means at his disposal given his executive control over all the news media." This after telling people that Rosenberg's *Myth* was doomed to vanish into obscurity in the face of the Church's protests. "This gentleman was mistaken here, just as in all deeper questions," Rosenberg boasted to his diary. "Now he had to read out aloud that only a future age would grasp in full what AR meant for the formation of the National Socialist Reich."

He reveled in his fame. The month after the award announcement, he arrived for a speech in Freiburg to the sight of garlands and flags and cheering crowds on the Münsterplatz before the towering spire of the centuries-old Catholic cathedral. Surely, he wrote later in his diary, the city had never seen anything like it: a "radical anti-Roman heretic being received like a king by the people" in the archbishop's own city.

On his forty-fifth birthday, in January 1938, Rosenberg welcomed Hitler to his new home in the wealthy Dahlem neighborhood of Berlin, which he, like the rest of the Nazi hierarchy, had appropriated from Jewish owners. The Führer brought along a bust of Dietrich Eckart, the man who had first brought Rosenberg and Hitler together back in 1919. He also handed Rosenberg a photograph of himself in a silver frame with an inscription that moved its recipient like nothing else. "For my old, most faithful fellow combatant Alfred Rosenberg," it read, "with the best wishes for his 45th birthday, in cordial friendship, Adolf Hitler."

Goebbels may have handed him the award, but Rosenberg's war with the propaganda minister would not let up. Since 1933, Goebbels had grown ever more affluent: His suits were custom-made, his parties lavish. He had moved into a palace near the Brandenburg Gate and bought a summer home and a yacht on an exclusive lake north of the capital. He had also amassed power in spades. He controlled the press, the radio, the theater, and—his favorite by far—the film industry. Fancying himself a sort of studio head, Goebbels took to ordering script changes, reviewing raw footage, mingling with screen stars, and romancing pretty actresses. During the Olympics in 1936, he threw an enormously expensive party for three thousand people on an island that had been decorated for the occasion like something out of the movies. Entertained by musicians from the Berlin Philharmonic, arriving guests made their way over a pontoon bridge strung with lanterns. The long night of drinking and dancing was punctuated by a spectacular fireworks display.

Goebbels held sway over thousands of jobs, so many that even those who hated him were afraid to challenge him. They did not want to suffer his wrath. "They watch," Rosenberg complained, "while I fight the battle."

Nor did Hitler move against Goebbels, however much Rosenberg protested the man's "flagrant failures" as Germany's culture czar. Rosenberg could find fault in every Goebbels production. The minister's Reich Chamber of Culture arranged for dance performances during a three-day celebration of the 650th anniversary of the University of Heidelberg, a propaganda affair staged to beat back allegations that the Nazis were hostile to academia. To Rosenberg's outrage, the event featured Hungarian *czárdás* and Polish dances, and, as Rosenberg put it in the diary, "Niggerstep!" "We've been fighting the nigger ways for years—and now they show up as <u>our</u> celebratory dances!"

Why, Rosenberg asked in his diary on another occasion, was Goebbels doing nothing to educate the German people about the underpinnings of the Nazis' theories about the Jews? Nobody seemed to know anything anymore about the key texts, like Theodor Fritsch's *Handbook of the Jewish Question*. Rosenberg agreed with what one of his compatriots told him: "If this continues this way, our children will declare us dumb for having been so worried about the Jews!" Future generations, he worried, would not realize that the Nazis had thwarted a Jewish plan to destroy Germany and control the world.

The problem with Goebbels, Rosenberg thought, was that he was too wrapped up in his own personality, too narcissistic, too busy having pictures taken of himself. He was an actor, "a man who <u>plays a minister</u>." Hitler might not see it, but the rank-and-file Nazis surely did.

When Rosenberg and Goebbels appeared at a party conference at around this time, the audience greeted Goebbels with "repeated hissing" and "icy silence," Rosenberg claimed in his diary. "This was a moral annihilation. . . . Party and population will simply not put up with the scandalous abuse of the executive for the purpose of disgusting self-adulation." Meanwhile, the preening Rosenberg wrote, his own remarks were met with an "incessant ovation." They saw him as Goebbels's opposite.

"I have won the heart of the movement, which is a great joy considering what sometimes seemed to be a hopeless battle against the poisoning of the party by the vanity of Dr. G."

Much to Rosenberg's glee, Goebbels's career would soon be in grave danger. It had nothing to do with Rosenberg's multitudinous accusations. It had to do with Goebbels's marriage.

He had a weakness for women, and he begged his wife, Magda, to consent to an open marriage. She refused, but in 1936 he learned that she was sleeping with another Nazi official. Goebbels was livid—doubly so because he had found it out from Rosenberg. Later that year, Goebbels fell for a twenty-two-year-old Czech film actress, Lída Baarová, and they began a public affair. Her husband caught them in the act and left her; Magda pushed Goebbels into their guesthouse.

Two years into the affair, when Goebbels suggested that a ménage à trois would solve their marital woes, Magda ran to Emmy Göring complaining about "that devil in human form." Hermann Göring arranged a meeting for Magda with Hitler himself, who had been the best man at the Goebbelses' wedding and had grown close to the couple in the early years of their marriage. Magda told the Führer that she wanted a divorce. Hitler refused to allow it, then called in Goebbels and demanded that he end the affair or lose his ministry. Hitler did not want a scandal at the highest ranks, but neither could he afford to lose his deviously talented propaganda minister. Goebbels reluctantly agreed to break it off with Baarová. "Life is so hard and cruel," Goebbels complained in his diary. "But duty comes before everything."

Magda was not mollified. In October 1938, she again pleaded for permission to leave Goebbels, and Hitler again negotiated a cease-fire.

In Berlin, Goebbels's enemies sensed that he might be doomed. Himmler, the SS chief, came to see Rosenberg at the end of 1938, and reported that the Gestapo had received "dozens" of sexual assault complaints against Goebbels. He had forwarded some of them to Hitler and lobbied for the propaganda minister to be fired. "He's now the most hated man in Germany," Himmler said he told the Führer. "Earlier, we railed against the Jewish managers who sexually harassed their employees. Now Dr. G. does it." Rosenberg gleefully spread these rumors and allegations far and wide.

He could not understand why Hitler would not simply jettison the man. The minister belonged in jail, not in a leading position in the government. "Dr. G.," Rosenberg wrote in his diary, "is morally isolated within the party, despised."

And yet Rosenberg could sense what Goebbels was thinking: that he would dodge the consequences, that he would "survive everything and still prevail over all that is wholesome."

Much as he hated to admit it, he also knew Goebbels was probably right.

Two months later, at a reception for the diplomatic corps, Goebbels was heard to declare that if Hitler didn't approve of his lifestyle, he should not have brought him into his inner circle back in the fighting days. Everyone needed to let him live his private life the way he wanted. "Despite my knowledge of the seediness of Dr. G," Rosenberg wrote of this bit of gossip, "I was still astounded by his forthrightness."

If only Hitler had banished Goebbels in 1924, Rosenberg wrote, when the young writer had briefly rebelled against the Führer's leadership. The Nazis would have been saved from his destructive ways. He had made a career of spraying "pus" on their enemies; now he was bespattering the party faithful as well.

"With the perpetual tolerance of this character," Rosenberg complained, "the degradation of our revolution began."

The Goebbels affair was a sideshow in a momentous year that saw Hitler point Germany finally and decisively toward world war.

At the end of 1937, he ordered his generals to prepare for invasions of Czechoslovakia and Austria. Having already brought the Saarland and the Rhineland back under his control, he now wanted the German-speaking lands in the East. They would form a strategic buffer and be a source of manpower and raw material for the Reich. Hitler told the nation's military and foreign policy leaders at a meeting in November that "the aim of German policy was to make secure and to preserve the racial stock and to enlarge it. It was therefore a question of space." This meant going on the attack—perhaps as early as the following year.

The military chiefs balked: Surely an attempt to annex their neighbors by force would mean war with France and England. Though Germany had been rearming for years, it was not yet ready for another war against the great powers of the West.

But as it happened, Hitler soon had no need to worry about such internal objections. When Foreign Minister Konstantin von Neurath, the Hindenburg-era holdover, issued frantic warnings, Hitler finally replaced him—though not with Rosenberg but with the more pliable Joachim von Ribbentrop.

Then Hitler took advantage of a pair of scandals to sweep out the top military leadership.

At the beginning of January 1938, Field Marshal Werner von Blomberg, minister of war and commander of the armed forces, had married his secretary, Margarethe Gruhn. He was a widower; she was thirty-five years younger. While the newlyweds jetted off to Capri for their honeymoon, anonymous callers prompted an investigation of Gruhn's background: It turned out that she had been a prostitute and had posed for pornographic photographs. Göring brought the files to Hitler, who exploded with rage and, even after he calmed down, fired the field marshal.

At the same time, Hitler recalled being shown documents smearing General Werner von Fritsch, the army commander in chief and the man most likely to succeed Blomberg. Fritsch, according to the dossier compiled by Himmler's secret police and brought back to the Führer, had been caught engaging in homosexual acts and for several years had paid blackmail to keep the matter private. "A lot of stinking lies!" Fritsch cried when told of the charges, but he, too, was forced out.

Riding the momentum, Hitler removed twelve other generals, reassigned another fifty-one, then personally assumed command of the German armed forces.

He quickly put the military to use as an instrument of diplomatic intimidation. On February 12, 1938, Hitler summoned Austrian chancellor Kurt von Schuschnigg to the Berghof, the Führer's mountain retreat near the southern Bavarian town of Berchtesgaden. Schuschnigg found the German dictator bristling with manic energy. Hitler threatened to invade if the Austrian leader did not sign an agreement handing the Nazis all but complete control. Schuschnigg initially capitulated, but on March 9 he called for an up-or-down vote on Austria's continued independence from Germany. A furious Hitler sent German troops to the border, Schuschnigg's government collapsed, and on March 12 the Führer rode into the land of his birth as a conquering hero.

In April, votes were held in both countries on Austria's annexation. In Austria, those who refused to vote or cast a "no" vote were harassed, beaten, paraded around wearing a sign announcing their treasonous behavior, even thrown into asylums. Following the intimidation campaign and the manipulation of the ballots, it could be reported that 99.75 percent of Austrians wanted their country to become a part of Germany.

Encouraged by this bloodless occupation, Hitler turned his attention to Czechoslovakia, where three million ethnic Germans lived in a western region known as the Sudetenland. Egged on by the Nazis in Germany, the leader of the Sudeten German Party began agitating for concessions from the Czech government; in early 1938, he was demanding nothing less than secession. In the meantime, Hitler, who wanted all of Czechoslovakia, had his generals prepare for an invasion while he searched for a defensible pretext to set the army loose without sparking international outrage.

Privately, he told his generals in May that "it is my unshakable will that Czechoslovakia shall be wiped off the map!"

Publicly, he said he simply wanted to bring the Sudeten people—who, he insisted, were being terrorized by the Czechs—to safety in the Third Reich. Britain and France did not object. They were more interested in staving off war than standing up to the dictator, and in Munich in late September, after tense weeks of negotiations with an increasingly unhinged Hitler, they conceded to the Nazi occupation of the Sudetenland.

"I believe," British prime minister Neville Chamberlain declared from the window of 10 Downing Street, "it is peace for our time."

Five weeks later, liberated from the whims of international public opinion, the Nazis lashed out at their great internal enemy.

Up to this point, the campaign against the Jews had generally relied less on physical attacks than on legal maneuvers. In 1938, a series of new discriminatory measures further isolated the Jews from Germany's economic life. They were required to register their assets; later, they would be permitted to withdraw only limited amounts from their bank accounts, and only with bureaucratic permission. They were required to publicly identify their storefronts as Jewish-owned. They were required to have "recognizable" Jewish first names, or else to add "Sara," for women, and "Israel," for men, to their legal names.

Regulatory measures finally gave way to open violence after a Pole named Herschel Grynszpan walked into the German embassy in Paris on November 7, 1938, and shot a diplomat. He was outraged that his parents had been deported from Germany. Two days later, when the diplomat died, Goebbels, Hitler, and the rest of the Nazi leadership were in Munich for their annual celebration of the 1923 Beer Hall Putsch. They did not want to let the opportunity pass.

The Führer ordered an immediate retaliation against the Jews of Germany: Burn down their synagogues, destroy their property, arrest as many of their men as logistically possible. But—and this was important—make it appear like a spontaneous uprising against the Jews by an angry populace.

Goebbels assembled the party leaders and informed them of the diplomat's death.

"Comrades," he cried, "we cannot allow this attack by international Jewry to go unchallenged. It must be repudiated."

Instantly, the directive spread by telephone all across the country, from the party leaders to regional headquarters to local storm trooper units and party offices.

At 11:55 p.m. on November 9, a telex went out to police commanders around Germany with orders from Hitler. Attacks on Jewish property would be breaking out shortly. The violence was not to be stopped unless it involved looting or "other special excesses."

Nazis poured into the streets, generally in civilian clothing, and began attacking more than a thousand synagogues throughout the country. They did not stop there. They walked about, smashing the windows of Jewish-owned shops and destroying whatever was inside. Jewish houses got the same treatment. In some places, Jewish cemeteries were desecrated. A Jewish orphanage was ransacked and the kids left to fend for themselves. Jews were ordered to dance outside a house of worship in their pajamas while the Nazis hosed them down. Hundreds of Jews were murdered.

In Oberlustadt—the town from which the grandfather of Holocaust museum archivist Henry Mayer had fled in 1937—the Nazis used a potato hoe to smash through the front door of the synagogue. A crowd armed with axes charged inside. They began pulling the Torah scrolls from the ark, tossing them in the court-yard, and setting them ablaze, along with pews that had been hacked apart. A few unrolled the parchments and pretended to recite the Hebrew while their compatriots danced around the raging bonfire chanting, "Hokuspokus." A police officer in the village poured gasoline under the stairway leading to the choir, and soon the synagogue was fully aflame. Then the mob marched through the town and set upon the small community of Jews.

Villagers, including children from the Hitler Youth and the League of German Girls, stood outside the home of Heinrich's cousins, Salomon and Elise Frank, breaking open the shutters and smashing the windows. Nazis rampaged through their house with their axes. They destroyed the furniture and the dishes and shoved the family out onto the street, where they beat Salomon, who was disabled, with clubs.

Salomon's brother, Jacob Frank, was supposed to be at his home celebrating his wife's birthday that day with their daugh-ters, Irma and Martha. But the police came for Jacob in the morning, and the women were left behind to defend the home. Martha tried to shut the gate against the invaders, but the crowd forced it open. The blow knocked several of her teeth out, and she fled inside just ahead of the marauding villagers.

Breaking through the door, the Nazis chopped at the legs of the couch, gashed the upholstery, and hacked apart tables and chairs. They ripped out the lights, threw the bedsheets outside, emptied the pantry of fruits and vegetables. The women bolted from room to room, hiding in terror, before they were finally forced to flee. They made it to Salomon's barn, where they found a carriage. They piled Salomon inside, pushed him to the train station, and fled to the city of Karlsruhe.

The men of Oberlustadt had been arrested that morning, and all but the elderly were dispatched to Dachau, the concentration camp near Munich. They were among thirty thousand sent to concentration camps that week. At Dachau, the new prisoners were forced to stand in the cold, stock-still. Anyone who stepped out of line received a savage beating. Their new accommodations had no beds, just floors covered with straw.

Back in Munich, Goebbels celebrated the event that would come to be known as Kristallnacht, the Night of Broken Glass. "As I drive to the hotel," Goebbels wrote in his diary, "windows shatter. Bravo! Bravo!" Days later he told the world that this had been a spontaneous anti-Semitic uprising, that authorities had done everything they could to stop the violence that night.

In a typically cruel Nazi twist, Jews were blocked from receiving any insurance payments for the damages, and as punishment for the murder of the diplomat in Paris, they were ordered to pay a collective fine, which Göring set at one billion reichsmarks. As the man assigned to keep Germany's economy on track, he was upset to learn that the rampaging Nazis had destroyed millions of reichsmarks' worth of goods in Jewish shops.

"I would have preferred it," he said, "if you had beaten two hundred Jews to death and hadn't destroyed such valuable property."

Rosenberg had much the same complaint about Kristallnacht. He had no sympathy for the Jews who had lost their homes and synagogues, their freedom and their lives, but he thought the pogrom was an excessive and unnecessary emotional outburst that had done little to help the Nazis accomplish their goal of ridding Germany of the Jews. He also worried about the financial costs of the destruction wrought by the rampaging mobs, and laid the blame on his usual scapegoat.

"Damage to public property: almost 2 Winterhilfswerk: 600 million!" he wrote in his diary. The Winterhilfswerk was an annual fund drive to supply food and clothing to the poor. "For everything G. does, we must pay. It is horrible."

For Jews in the Reich, Kristallnacht was the event that finally extinguished any hope that they could stay put in Germany. The time for patience had passed. Their countrymen were not going to overthrow Hitler and bring back the age of tolerance. Rosenberg's diatribes and Goebbels's speeches could no longer be dismissed as empty words. The Nazis wanted the Jews gone, and if they were not willing to leave on their own, they would be run out of their homes by force.

Over the next ten months, more than one hundred thousand Jews would flee the country.

Twice as many would be left behind.

A snapshot of the Hudson River and the Empire State Building taken by the Kempners upon their arrival in the United States aboard the SS *Nieuw Amsterdam* on September 1, 1939. *(U.S. Holocaust Memorial Museum, courtesy of Robert Kempner)*

13

Escape

The refugees from Kempner's Istituto Fiorenza spent the days in Nice searching for ways out. It was an intensely dispiriting time for all of them. As one put it, a realistic attitude, helpful friends, and luck were the necessities of the time. "Each one of them waits, watch in hand, until he or she can go to another country," wrote Walter Hirsch, a teacher who found himself out of work after the school disbanded, in a letter to a friend. His situation was, for the moment, "bearable." Tutoring paid for cigarettes, and new soles for his shoes. But he feared the future.

"Recently I have endured so many disappointments," he wrote, "so many signs of disregard, meanness, misunderstanding, and rejection when I wanted to be understood, that I have turned bitter and distraught."

On October 21, 1938, seven weeks after arriving in France with their temporary visas, Robert and Ruth Kempner were formally stripped of their German citizenship. They could not go back to Berlin, and they could not stay in Nice permanently. Instead they hunted for jobs that would get them to the United States. Kempner made contact with colleagues overseas about university positions and rounded up letters of recommendation from friends and allies. He pitched himself as an expert in police management, a college-level lecturer in administrative law, and a writer. One of the recommendations he had received from former colleagues lauded Kempner's "courage in meeting the challenge of National Socialism."

Among the people Kempner wrote to was the dean of the Women's Medical College of Pennsylvania, where his mother had taught briefly decades earlier before returning to Berlin to get married and work for Robert Koch; her portrait still hung in the Department of Bacteriology. The dean connected him with Stephen Sweeney, director of the Institute of Local and State Government at the University of Pennsylvania. Sweeney wrote to say that he would happily have Kempner at the institute, but only if he was "willing to come to this country without any commitment on our part" and would accept an "honorarium" of just a few hundred dollars.

Kempner wrote back in December to accept the offer. The actual salary was "not of great importance," he wrote, because he had the means to support himself for the time being. He told another correspondent around this time that he had "several hundred thousand francs," the equivalent of perhaps $100,000 today. What he needed was a letter confirming that the institute would pay him. That way he could apply for a visa that was not subject to the U.S. immigration quota, which limited the number of Germans who could be admitted each year. "Without this non-quota visa I would have to wait some years until I could go to America because the German quota is very overcrowded," Kempner wrote. "I do hope you will give me a chance . . . awaiting your answer with great impatience."

In the meantime, the Kempners enlisted the help of a family

friend in Philadelphia, Otto Reinemann, who had immigrated from Germany in 1934 and landed a post in the city's municipal court system. Reinemann promised to press Kempner's case in Philadelphia.

While Kempner waited, he hedged his bets. All things being equal, he wanted to stay on the Côte d'Azur rather than uproot his life and move to the United States. He and Peiser spent the fall and winter of 1938–1939 working to reestablish their school in Nice. They asked for financial aid from the American Jewish Joint Distribution Committee—"the Joint"—which raised money to assist beleaguered Jews in Europe. With help from Kurt Grossman, the journalist who had been general secretary of the pacifist German League for Human Rights, in Berlin, before the Nazi takeover, the school received twenty-one thousand francs. That helped them support the ten students who'd fled with them from Italy.

They could still find scores of Jewish parents in Germany, Poland, Czechoslovakia, Austria, and Italy who would gratefully send their endangered children to Nice, whatever the cost. The trouble was that students could not get visas; in France, the paperwork took months. Kempner wrote to the Human Rights League, in Paris, for help getting visas for "these unfortunate children, whose parents are in concentration camps in many cases, or are being tortured in the most horrible ways."

Once it became obvious that securing visas would be difficult or impossible, Kempner and Peiser looked to recruit refugee children already in France. They advertised for students in the French and Swiss newspapers, and when Foreign Minister Georges Bonnet proposed in December 1938 that France set up an organization to care for the orphaned children of German Jews, Kempner urged Grossman to be ready to pitch the school to the new group. "Get moving," he wrote, "and the reward will not fail to appear!" Kempner asked for leads from a pacifist professor named Emil Gumbel, the pacifist mathematics professor forced out of the University of Heidelberg, who had emigrated to Lyon, France, and now ran a refugee aid committee. Gumbel warned that nobody would pay Kempner to teach and shelter children. Undeterred, Kempner wrote to British and French refugee committees, offering the school's services for six hundred francs per month, the equivalent of $350 today. To a refugee committee based in Nice, Kempner explained that he knew of wealthy Jews in the city— some of them émigrés, some of them visitors from the United States and England—who could perhaps be encouraged to donate large sums to educate refugee children.

The administrators were canvassing for students at the same time activists in Britain were working to organize Kindertransports to rescue young people from the Nazi peril on the Continent. But the tone of Kempner's letters suggested that he was more interested in earning a living than helping to solve a looming humanitarian crisis, and once job prospects abroad showed some promise in early 1939, Kempner quickly abandoned his campaign to reconstruct the boarding school. Instead he began searching for someone to take responsibility for the students who had fled with him from Bordighera. "Do you have any interest in taking over the leadership of a small home with ten Jewish children from different countries, which at the present offers a favorable existence and is probably very expandable?" he wrote one former colleague in Paris. "Dr. Peiser and I await contracts from America."

As Kempner looked for a way out in the spring of 1939, Germany's neighbors fell one after the other, and war loomed on the horizon.

First, Nazi-led machinations prompted the Slovaks to break away from Czechoslovakia and submit to German protection. Then the Czechs themselves knuckled under after a dark-of-night meeting between Hitler and President Emil Hácha, during which the German leader reported that the army had already begun the invasion and the Luftwaffe would take the Czech airfields in a few short hours. The dictator gave Hácha two options: surrender or face the bloody consequences. The Czech leader fainted under the strain, recovered after Hitler's doctor administered pharmaceutical injections, then signed away his nation to the Germans. By the end of the day, on March 15, 1939, Hitler was sleeping in Prague's ancient Hradčany Castle, from which kings and emperors and national presidents had ruled.

Next, Hitler began agitating against Poland. His grand goal was to carve out *Lebensraum*, or "living space," for Germans, and his eastern neighbor would have to give way. Once again, he found a pretext for invasion. Poland had received a "corridor" to the Baltic Sea after the First World War, cutting the German state of Prussia in half. East Prussia was now an island surrounded by Poland, Lithuania, the Baltic Sea, and the heavily German port city of Danzig—now called Gdansk, Poland—which had been declared a "free city" under the protection of the League of Nations.

The Nazis considered this entire arrangement unacceptable and demanded that Poland hand over Danzig and permit the Germans to build a highway and railroad to East Prussia. The Poles declined, and when Chamberlain announced on March 31 that the British would guarantee Polish sovereignty, Hitler exploded in anger. "I'll cook them a stew they'll choke on!" he snarled in the privacy of his office in the Reich Chancellery. Within days, he had approved a war plan to crush Poland.

Three weeks later, on April 28, 1939, Hitler appeared before the Reichstag to deliver a reply to a telegram from Franklin D. Roosevelt in which the president asked Hitler to assure Germany's neighbors that he would not attack them. In a speech to a worldwide audience, the Führer insisted on Germany's peaceful intentions. He had no war plans against any nation. "I have brought back to the Reich provinces stolen from us in 1919," Hitler thundered. "I have led back to their native country millions of Germans who were torn away from us and were in misery . . . and, Mr. Roosevelt, without spilling blood and without bringing to my people, and consequently to others, the misery of war."

So he said. But that was about to change. Hitler's army spent the summer of 1939 preparing to unleash a new innovation in warfare: the Blitzkrieg.

Kempner's university job in the United States still hadn't come together by the late spring of 1939. In May, Kempner wrote to Sweeney at the University of Pennsylvania and told him he was getting desperate: His transit visa in France was about to expire. "I shall have the greatest difficulties if I cannot get to the United States within a short time." Sweeney also received letters on Kempner's behalf from Peiser, who had left Europe in May after landing a teaching post in Atlanta, and from Kempner's brother, Walter, at Duke University.

Robert Kempner wrote repeatedly to Reinemann, as well, pressing for more help. They could not wait much longer. Authorities had given Kempner a hard time about a short extension of their transit visas, and they received that leeway only because Ruth had had an operation to remove her appendix and needed to stay in the hospital for twelve weeks.

The trouble was that Sweeney was offering Kempner very little money, just a few hundred dollars in all. To qualify for a non-quota visa, Kempner needed to show that the institute would pay him a living wage, at least $200 per month, for two years.

To skirt this requirement, Kempner resorted to some financial trickery. If the institute could bump up its salary offer on paper, he wrote Sweeney in May, "friends of mine" could then "deposit the difference" to reimburse the university. In fact, Kempner planned to pay most of his "salary" up front by transferring his own funds to a third party, who would then donate them to the university. Sweeney expressed willingness to accept the unorthodox arrangement, and Kempner canvassed for a "trustee" to handle the transaction. Reinemann, his friend, asked the dean of the Women's Medical College, but she balked. If she was going to do someone a favor, she would prefer it be for a woman.

Instead they turned to Wilbur Thomas, whose Carl Schurz Memorial Foundation worked to foster better relations between Germans and Americans. He agreed to help, and on June 9, with all parties in agreement, Reinemann cabled Kempner in Nice to tell him to wire the cash.

The next morning, Kempner dispatched a telegram to Philadelphia: BANK TRANSFER INITIATED THOUSAND THANKS.

Reinemann wrote back that the contract was on the way. "We thus receive the opportunity to begin a new epoch in our lives," Kempner replied, thanking his friend for lobbying so fiercely on his behalf. The contract arrived on June 21. The next day, the Kempners filled out paperwork at the consulate. To make sure everything went smoothly, Kempner carried a slip of paper bearing typewritten talking points. "How do you do," they read. "I have received an appointment at the University of Philadelphia and I beg you to give me a non quota visa. I have all my papers with me and I think that everything is alright."

Five days later, they had papers for themselves, for Ruth's mother, and for Margot Lipton, Kempner's mistress. The letters to their friend in America soon brimmed with jittery elation as the existential questions gave way to practical ones.

Could a European radio be used in the United States? Could he recommend a hotel for them until they found an apartment?

How much would a two- or three-bedroom apartment cost in a nice Philadelphia neighborhood? Would it have a balcony?

They had to abandon their furniture in Florence; could they rent some?

Could they bring Reinemann anything from Europe?

But it was not a time of unalloyed joy. A bitterness crept in to temper the celebration. Over the course of the twisting journey from Berlin to Philadelphia, Kempner was undergoing a transfiguration: from a prosperous, well-connected senior government official into a struggling, unknown immigrant research associate. Already, he had lost his occupation, his family home, his furniture, and much of his savings. The Nazis had taken virtually everything from him, short of his life.

Now, as he made his final escape, Kempner was leaving behind still more: his sons.

In March, Lipton had given birth to André. Unable to secure a visa for the infant in time, they decided to put him in the care of a children's home in Nice and hope for the best. Meanwhile, Lucian was still stuck in Germany and still, his father knew, in grave danger. *Mischlinge*, mixed-race Jews, had been exempted from the provisions of the discriminatory Nuremberg Laws, but as a friend wrote to Kempner in 1938, "for the half-Jew, there will be no future in the Third Reich in the long term."

In July 1939, not long after he received the visas, Kempner mailed a resigned note to his son in Germany.

"Dear Lucian," it began. "You are turning 16 years old now and I want to wish you all the best for your birthday—above all that you will once again have the fortune to live in a free country as a free, equal person where you can work wherever you want without being subjected to limitations because of race or religion. This, my wish, I am certain will one day come to fulfillment, and I will be happy to have you back as my son. The fulfillment of this wish will be more important for your entire life than the small material wishes that I, much as I would like, cannot fulfill right now since, as you know, the Third Reich has plundered me as it has done with other non-Aryans or political personae non gratae. I don't know where you will be celebrating your birthday this year, nor do I know whether this letter will be intercepted by criminals, but none of that matters. I am still with you in spirit, with my thoughts and feelings for you that are still the same today despite everything that has been done to me. Don't forget that I am only fighting this battle out of love for you, not for egotistical motives, but because I as your dad know—better than all of those who decided to let you vegetate in the Third Reich—what it means to be a Jew, a non-Aryan, a *Mischling*."

Toward the end of August, Kempner and his entourage made their way to the port city of Boulogne-sur-Mer, on the English Channel in northern France, and stepped aboard the flagship of the Holland America Line, the SS *Nieuw Amsterdam*, a fast, luxurious cruiser commissioned the year before. As the 758-foot ocean liner set off for America, dark steam pouring from twin stacks striped green and gold, Kempner could have no idea when—or even if—he would see his boys again.

A week later, the ship eased into New York Harbor and snugged up to the pier at the end of Fifth Street in Hoboken. The terminal was crowded with Americans waving and cheering and greeting friends and family. The Kempners collected their bags, stepped off the boat, and caught a bus across the Hudson River and into Manhattan. Three years after leaving Berlin, they had made it to safety.

The date was September 1, 1939. That very morning, Adolf Hitler had unleashed his armies in Europe and set off the deadliest war the world would ever see.

AT WAR

1939–1946

Rosenberg, on his forty-fifth birthday, welcoming Hitler
to his home in Berlin's Dahlem neighborhood. *(SZ Photo/
Scherl/The Image Works)*

14

"The Burden of What's to Come"

He did not see it coming. Alfred Rosenberg heard the earth-shattering news on the radio at the same moment as everyone else in Germany, just before midnight on August 21, 1939: His beloved Führer was making peace with Rosenberg's most hated enemy, the Soviet Union. Hitler was dispatching a delegation led by Foreign Minister Joachim von Ribbentrop to Moscow to finalize a nonaggression pact.

Just the idea of it—the odious Ribbentrop hoisting glasses of vodka in the Kremlin with Joseph Stalin—was too much for Rosenberg to stomach.

No one in the Third Reich could possibly have been more shattered to hear of the pact than Rosenberg. Twenty years he had spent sounding the alarm about communists and their "Jewish criminality." It had been his life's work. It was and would always be the centerpiece of his entire political worldview. Now what was he supposed to do? Swallow hard and fall in line?

Surely this was not the Hitler of *Mein Kampf*, who had written that living space for the Germans could only come at the cost of the Soviet Union and its territories, and who had ridiculed the idea of an alliance with the Bolsheviks. "Never forget that the rulers of present-day Russia are common bloodstained criminals; that they are the scum of humanity which, favored by circumstances, overran a great state in a tragic hour." Surely this was not the man who had issued this dire warning: "The fight against Jewish world Bolshevization requires a clear attitude toward Soviet Russia. You cannot drive out the Devil with Beelzebub." Surely this was not the Führer who had told Rosenberg, a few short years back, that the Nazis could never find common cause with the Soviet Union, that nest of bandits, "because it wasn't possible to forbid the German people from stealing, and to simultaneously remain friends with thieves."

By sending Ribbentrop to cut a deal with Moscow, the Nazis were suffering "a moral loss of face in light of our twenty-year fight," Rosenberg wrote in his diary, seething. "History will perhaps one day clarify if the situation that arose must have arisen." He could only hope that it was another of the Führer's strokes of strategic brilliance, a momentary alliance of convenience before Germany returned to the long-term plan Rosenberg had envisioned all along, which was not to befriend the communists but to annihilate them.

He needed to see Hitler. He needed to understand what had happened.

The pact had grown out of Hitler's plans for the invasion of Poland. While his generals put together the military plans, the Führer began to smooth the diplomatic path. He did not want war with Britain in the West—not yet—and he could not afford a confrontation with the Soviet Union in the East.

Mulling over his geopolitical predicament, the German dictator consulted a foreign minister who, in the opinion of nearly everyone *but* Hitler, lacked the diplomatic acumen and political judgment to handle the questions at hand. Even Rosenberg, no master of tact himself, could see that. "That he is his own worst enemy with his vanity and arrogance . . . is not a secret," he wrote in 1936. "I have put this down in letters to him—the way he conducted himself from the moment the sun began to shine on him."

Ribbentrop's was a cultured upbringing. After his mother died, his father married the daughter of an aristocrat. He was no nobleman himself; as an adult, he would earn the right to use "von" in his name only by paying a distant relative to adopt him. Ribbentrop grew up playing tennis and the violin, lived for a time as a teenager in the Swiss Alps, studied in London for a year, and at seventeen sailed with friends to Canada, where he spent the next four years falling in love with a woman and building a wine import business.

The First World War brought him back to Germany. Starting over after the armistice, he built a successful wine and liquor business and became a wealthy man. In 1932, he joined the Nazi Party, and early the next year he found himself in a position to help midwife the deal that handed Hitler the reins of power. Ribbentrop had served in Constantinople during the war with Franz von Papen, who rose to the chancellorship in 1932 and who, during those fateful weeks in January 1933, had Hindenburg's ear. Ribbentrop spent that month shuttling between Papen and Hitler as the two men negotiated a division of power. Pivotal secret meetings took place in Ribbentrop's villa in the wealthy Berlin neighborhood of Dahlem, with Papen arriving in Ribbentrop's limousine and Hitler sneaking in quietly through the garden. "His acting as an intermediary in 1932 was very important to the Führer," Rosenberg wrote later in the diary, "and he feels extraordinarily indebted to Ribbentrop."

The first time Ribbentrop spoke with the future Führer, at a 1932 party Ribbentrop hosted, the men talked at length about Britain. Ribbentrop had lived in London only briefly, but the conversation must have stuck in Hitler's memory, because from then on he—quite wrongly—considered the wine dealer an expert on the empire. "It was the harmony of our views about England," Ribbentrop recalled, "which on this first evening spent together created the seed of confidence between Hitler and myself."

In the early days of the Third Reich, Ribbentrop used his status in the Nazi ranks to secure meetings with British and French officials. Unbeknownst to Hitler, the international diplomats considered him a lightweight. He was unschooled in foreign policy protocol, he was a clumsy and duplicitous negotiator, and he managed to be both ignorant and arrogant. None of this stopped Hitler from giving the diplomat his own foreign affairs task force, the Büro Ribbentrop, and sending him to London to negotiate an important naval agreement with the Brits. To the amazement of his many enemies, including Rosenberg, Ribbentrop succeeded, and in 1936 Hitler named him ambassador to England. But as he worked to mend fences, the Brits repeatedly rebuffed his unsophisticated approaches, and began referring to him as "Herr von Brickendrop" and "von Ribbensnob." Hitler was impressed that Ribbentrop seemed to know all the key figures in British politics, to which Göring replied: "Yes—but the trouble is, they know Ribbentrop." Failing to win over the British, Ribbentrop instead turned resolutely against them.

Hitler named Ribbentrop foreign minister in 1938, and a year later Ribbentrop told the Führer not to worry about Britain's reaction to the planned invasion. Just as they had looked the other way on Czechoslovakia, Ribbentrop promised, the Brits would not go to war over Poland.

Hitler accepted that dangerously misguided counsel, and looked east for an alliance.

By the spring of 1939, it was public knowledge that Britain and France were negotiating a coalition with the Soviets to block Nazi aggression in Poland. Hitler may have fulminated against the Soviets for years, but now, facing powerful enemies in the West just as the shooting was about to start, he decided to do whatever it took to get Stalin on his side. So as Hitler's invasion deadline approached—September 1, the better to avoid the mud come autumn—the Nazis worked against the clock to cut a deal.

Stalin, suspicious of the Western democracies and as coldly practical as Hitler himself, was already open to the idea of joining hands with the Nazis. He feared that all he would get from an alliance with Britain and France was a world war, the costs of which would fall disproportionately on his nation as the sole bulwark along the lengthy front in the East.

Months of talks and telegrams between Germany and the Soviet Union came to a head on August 20, when Hitler wrote Stalin to say he wanted to finalize the pact "as soon as possible," for the "crisis" in Poland could erupt at any time. "The tension between Germany and Poland," he wrote, "has become intolerable."

At 9:35 p.m. the next day, Stalin cabled his agreement. "The assent of the German Government to the conclusion of a nonaggression pact," he wrote, "provides the foundation for eliminating the political tension and for the establishment of peace and collaboration between our countries."

The news was immediately broadcast on German radio, and two days later Ribbentrop flew to Moscow to discuss the particulars.

He met for three hours in the afternoon with the Soviets and then returned in the evening, but there were no real disagreements, even when it came to a secret codicil carving up the lands between the two countries. The Soviets would get the Baltics to the north of Lithuania, and the two nations would split Poland along its major rivers. Most of the night, in fact, was spent not hammering out technical details but swapping opinions about international affairs and saluting each other with warm—and repeated—toasts. "I know how much the German nation loves its Führer," Stalin said when it was his turn. "I should therefore like to drink to his health." Then the men drank to Stalin's health, and to Ribbentrop's, and to the Reich, and to their new relationship.

In the early-morning hours, before the meeting broke up, Stalin pulled Ribbentrop aside to tell him how seriously he would take their new pact. He guaranteed on his honor that he would not be the one to break it.

Rosenberg, as the Third Reich's most committed anti-communist, had been necessarily left out of the loop during the negotiations leading up to the deal. All along, he had been hoping that Germany could come to a power-sharing agreement with Britain. These were two Aryan nations that should work with each other, not steel themselves for war. They should stand together to rule as masters over the world. But this wasn't going to happen, and he bitterly blamed Ribbentrop—this "joke of world history," Rosenberg called him—for mishandling affairs in Britain. Ribbentrop had done nothing to foster goodwill; he had done the opposite. "In London itself, v. R., who after all had been sent there on account of his alleged 'connections,' put everybody's nose out of joint," Rosenberg wrote in the diary. "Undoubtedly, much was due to <u>his</u> individual personality." Rosenberg had apparently forgotten his own disastrous goodwill mission to England years before.

"I'm of the conviction that he's conducted himself with England just as stupidly and arrogantly as he has here," Rosenberg remembered telling Göring earlier in the year, "and therefore has been just as personally rejected."

The foreign minister really had only one friend in Germany, Göring replied, and that was Hitler. "Is von Ribbentrop a clown or an idiot?"

"A really stupid individual," Rosenberg muttered, "with the usual arrogance."

"He'd bluffed us with his 'connections.' When you looked closer at the French counts and English aristocrats [he knew], they were owners of champagne, whiskey, and cognac factories," Göring said. "Today the idiot believes he has to play the 'Iron Chancellor' everywhere," he said. "However: Such an imbecile takes care of himself, bit by bit; only he *can* bring about terrible calamity."

Now, with the Moscow pact, that calamity had arrived. Rosenberg's loyalty to Hitler was suddenly in conflict with his certainty that the Führer had made an error of disastrous proportions. Rosenberg could understand a temporary alliance; he claimed he had even spoken about such a duplicitous arrangement with Göring once. This did not sound temporary. The newspapers were declaring Germans and Russians to be traditional friends and allies. "As if our fight against Moscow had been a misunderstanding, and the Bolsheviks were the true Russians, with all the Soviet Jews at the top! This little embrace is more than embarrassing."

Rosenberg, always willing to bow to his hero's wisdom, tried to convince himself that Hitler had had no choice but to reach an accord with the Soviets before Britain and France did. It had been a matter of self-preservation. "The Führer's change of direction," he acknowledged in the diary, "was probably a necessity in light of the given situation." And yet he could not shake the sense that Hitler was taking a major gamble.

"I have the feeling that this Moscow pact will eventually have dire consequences for National Socialism," he wrote in the diary. "It was not a step taken freely, but rather an action from a forced position—a supplication on behalf of one revolution to the head of another. . . . How can we speak of the rescue and reshaping of Europe when we must ask the destroyer of Europe for help?

"And now the question arises once more: Did this situation have to arise? Did the Polish question have to be solved now and in this form?"

No one, he thought, had answers to any of those questions.

"Close your hearts to pity!" Hitler told his military commanders ten days before sending his armies off to war against Poland. "Act brutally! . . . Be harsh and remorseless! Be steeled against all signs of compassion!" He did not want the army to simply defeat the Polish forces; he wanted "the physical annihilation of the enemy. . . . I have put my Death's Head formations at the lead with the command to send man, woman, and child of Polish descent and language to their deaths, pitilessly and remorselessly."

Hitler's savagery was, as ever, rooted in racial bias: All Germans learned at an early age that the Poles were a disorderly, primitive people who deserved to be ruled by strong masters. At the same time, geographic realities were at play: Poland stood in the way of Germany's eastward expansion, and the leaders in Warsaw had enraged Hitler by rejecting his boisterous demand for territorial concessions.

So on the first of September, the Germans roared across the border from the north, south, and west: one and a half million men, three hundred thousand horses pulling artillery and matériel, fifteen hundred tanks, hundreds of the Luftwaffe's new planes. Against this Blitzkrieg—literally, "lightning war"—the Poles stood no chance. Their lines were strafed by fighters and broken by armored tank divisions. Their air force was destroyed. Their cities were leveled. Civilians fled by the thousands, in cars and wagons, on bicycles and on foot. They headed east, where their escape was cut off by the Soviets. One hundred and twenty thousand Polish soldiers were killed in the fighting—ten for every German dead. A million men were taken prisoner.

Two decades after the surrender that gave birth to the Nazis, the Germans had built the world's most feared war-making machine. "The army standing today is incomparably superior to the one of 1914," Rosenberg wrote in the glow of victory, "a completely different bond between the leadership and the troops: the generals eating in the same kitchen with the men, the generals at the head of the front. When he sees the whole battalion pull ahead . . . [he thinks:] Such humanity will never exist again."

Rosenberg himself was out of commission—literally—the day the Second World War dawned: He was laid up with a chronic ankle ailment for most of August and September. Rosenberg had long been plagued by poor health. In 1935, 1936, and 1938, he spent months in an SS medical facility in Hohenlychen, north of Berlin, receiving treatment for a joint inflammation so painful he could barely move. "The old, intense arthritis in my foot is back with the same old pain, and the back muscle is rebelling again," he wrote in his diary in 1936. The medical superintendent, Karl Gebhardt, determined that Rosenberg was highly susceptible to weather changes and that a sedentary lifestyle had caused him to become excessively overweight. The doctor also blamed "psychic isolation," for Rosenberg had few friends with whom he could have open and honest conversations.

Even if he had not been all but confined to his home, he wrote bitterly in his diary in 1939, Hitler still would not have called on him during the momentous first days of the invasion. The Führer had no need for an ideologue who had made his mark as the chief agitator against Germany's newest ally.

"Other men, different than those from the years of struggle, decisively make up the Führer's circle."

On the day the war started, Rosenberg hobbled into the Reichstag to hear Hitler lay out his case. The Poles were to blame, Hitler insisted. They had ignored his perfectly sensible offers.

They had refused a peaceful settlement. He had had no choice but to attack. "I am wrongly judged if my love of peace and my patience are mistaken for weakness or even cowardice," he said. "I have therefore resolved to speak to Poland in the same language that Poland for months past has used toward us." The Poles had fired on German soldiers, he claimed—it wasn't true—and the army had merely retaliated. "From now on," he said, "bombs will be met with bombs."

Before the speech, Rosenberg ran into Göring, and the two men spoke in the atrium while they waited for Hitler to arrive. "I just have the feeling," Rosenberg said, "that England has been deliberately underestimated."

He was right. In the days before the invasion, Britain's leaders had worked to bring the Germans and the Poles to the negotiating table. Hitler assured the nation's ambassador in Berlin, Nevile Henderson, that he only wanted peace with Britain. His argument was with the intransigent Poles. Just as soon as he settled matters with Poland, he would be done with war—forever. But at this late date, after Austria, after Munich, after Czechoslovakia, London finally knew better than to accept Hitler's promises. On August 25, Britain signed a mutual assistance pact with Poland. Ribbentrop had been wrong: They would not sit idly by.

Hours before the invasion, after days of fruitless diplomacy, Henderson found himself at tea with Göring, who was in a typically expansive mood. If the Poles did not give in, he explained to the ambassador, Germany would "crush them like lice," and it would be "most imprudent" of the Brits to intervene.

On the morning of September 3, Henderson arrived at the German Foreign Office to deliver Britain's official declaration of war. Ribbentrop did not receive the ambassador on this momentous day. Instead his interpreter accepted the brief communication, then rushed over to Hitler's office, where he found the Führer at his desk and Ribbentrop standing at a window. The men listened silently, then, after a long moment—it "seemed an age," the interpreter wrote later—Hitler, wearing a "savage look," turned to his foreign minister. "What now?"

William Shirer, at this point CBS Radio's Berlin correspondent, stood on the plaza outside the Chancellery, listening with a crowd of Germans as word came over loudspeakers that Hitler had led the nation into another world war. "It has been a lovely September day, the sun shining, the air balmy, the sort of day the Berliner loves to spend in the woods or on the lakes nearby," he wrote in his diary. When the announcement was over, "there was not a murmur. They just stood there as they were before. Stunned."

The French declared war the same day as the British, but neither country was prepared for a fight, and they did nothing to stop Germany from overrunning Poland. Over the coming weeks, overtures by the Nazis failed to bring Britain and France to peace talks. Rosenberg could not understand Britain's bullheadedness. Even after six years of listening to the country's leaders, Rosenberg was as confused as everyone else in Berlin about what they wanted. "We've done just about everything," he wrote in his diary, "but an insane, Jewish-led minority reigns. Chamberlain is a weak-willed old man. It seems they won't easily see until something has been horribly hammered in."

In the Reich Chancellery, Hitler was coming to the realization that the Nazis could do nothing to persuade the British to stand down. The time had come to pound them into submission, he told Rosenberg.

"If the English don't want peace," Rosenberg wrote a month into the war, "he will assail and ruin them by all available means."

In the meantime, the Nazis unleashed their radical worldview on the people of Poland. Heinrich Himmler led the way.

On the Night of the Long Knives, in 1934, it was Himmler who had passed along manufactured evidence that Röhm was plotting a putsch, and it was Himmler's SS that did much of the killing when Hitler ordered the great purge. In the years since, the SS had grown into a fearsome force. Officers wore black uniforms bearing a logo on the collar that resembled ancient runic bolts of lightning. The caps bore a silver "death's head" skull-and-crossbones insignia. "I know there are many people who fall ill when they see this black uniform," Himmler said once. "We understand that, and don't expect that we will be loved by many people." He envisioned the SS as a sort of religious order and instituted pagan rites and rituals handed down by Teutons and Vikings, whom the Nazis considered to be their Aryan forebears. Rosenberg was not the only apostate in the hierarchy. Himmler, too, believed that "the final confrontation with Christianity" was upon them. His SS did not celebrate the birth of Christ; they celebrated the summer solstice.

After the annexation of Austria, Himmler's men followed in the army's wake, arresting tens of thousands, then subjecting the Jews to cruel humiliations. When Shirer traveled to Vienna to report on the scene, he was shocked to see Jews scrubbing graffiti off the sidewalks and cleaning toilets while mobs jeered. "Many Jews killing themselves," the journalist wrote. "All sorts of reports of Nazi sadism."

Immediately after the invasion of Poland, Himmler consolidated his sweeping, all-powerful police operation into a Reich Security Main Office managed by Reinhard Heydrich. Ruthless, amoral, and cynically efficient, Heydrich was loathed and dreaded in equal parts. Raised by a father in the opera and a mother in the theater, Heydrich mastered the violin; he also became an expert fencer. He rose to lieutenant in the navy, but his military career ended when he impregnated the daughter of an important industrialist. Himmler brought him into the SS, where he was put in charge of gathering intelligence on political adversaries and fellow Nazis. He quickly became a favorite of Himmler's, and by 1936 he ran both the Gestapo and the criminal police. Three years later, everything was placed under a single umbrella.

After the army blasted through the Polish defenses, Heydrich dispatched five special killing units called Einsatzgruppen to sweep through the defeated country, shooting and hanging anyone who might one day try to organize a resistance, including intellectuals, aristocrats, leading businessmen, and priests.

When the fighting was over, Poland was divided into three parts. The eastern lands became part of the Soviet Union. The western lands were annexed by Germany, to be "depopulated and resettled with Germans," as Hitler had announced to his generals in the days before the assault. The central lands, which included the cities of Warsaw, Krakow, and Lublin, became a German colony known as the General Government. Run by a ruthless Nazi administrator, Hans Frank, this land of eleven million people would become a vast dumping ground for everyone deemed undesirable by the Nazis.

In October, Hitler added a new position to Himmler's portfolio: Reichskommissar for the strengthening of the German race. He would coordinate the complex resettlement of ethnic Germans in the new colonies and oversee the elimination of "the harmful influence of such alien parts of the population as constitute a danger to the Reich."

Over the coming year, Himmler managed the brutal deportation of more than one million Poles and Jews into the forsaken General Government. They were taken from their homes, herded into unheated railway cars, and dropped off with no provisions for their care. Once they arrived at their destination—if they arrived alive; many died en route—Frank implemented harsh measures: ghettos, forced labor, and deprivation of food. "I'm not remotely interested in the Jews," he said in the spring of 1940. "Whether they have something to eat or not is the last thing on earth I care about."

Other Poles were shipped to Germany, where they worked for slave wages in often miserable conditions. They were housed in overcrowded camp barracks. Tags reading OST—"East"—were stitched onto their clothes to discourage Germans from defiling themselves by fraternizing with them. Children from Polish orphanages, many of whom were left alone because the Nazis had sent their parents away, were delivered to German foster parents in the Reich.

In the meantime, ethnic Germans from Estonia, Latvia, Romania, and elsewhere were repatriated and moved into the newly cleansed western portions of Poland annexed to the Reich, which included the cities of Poznan and Lodz.

During a brief visit to the newly conquered land, Hitler's dark view of the populace was only confirmed, Rosenberg reported. "The Poles: a thin German layer and underneath it, a horrible substance," he wrote in his diary after a meeting with the Führer at the end of that fateful month of September 1939. "The Jews are of the most horrific sort. The cities are coated in dirt. He's learnt a lot in these past few weeks. Above all: If Poland had ruled over the old parts of the Reich for another few decades, everything would be louse-ridden and depraved; here, only the unerring hand of a master can rule."

Amid the great upheaval in Europe, Rosenberg looked for distractions. "Painted today after a long time," he wrote one day in the diary. "Studies that I painted 21 years ago have arrived from Reval. With further painting, they haven't become any better." On his birthday, he was cheered by the letters that arrived. "It is a strange feeling to know that, bit by bit, hundreds of thousands have been inwardly revolutionized by my work. Many have found inner peace and relief through it; a new <u>meaning</u>, since the old one had been lost. So write men and women, girls and schoolboys. Some write poems, many describe their progress."

He thought about the war under way, and the wars to come, and about the people he had been writing for since 1919, the people of Germany. He wondered if they really knew what was ahead.

He wondered, he wrote, whether they would have the strength to "bear the burden of what's to come."

Kempner spent his first years in America working from an
office at the University of Pennsylvania's Blanchard Hall on
Walnut Street in Philadelphia. *(University of Pennsylvania)*

15

On the Make

Arriving in New York after the weeklong trip from Boulogne-sur-Mer, Robert and Ruth Kempner settled into Room 1063 of the Hotel Pennsylvania, on Seventh Avenue, right across the street from the Beaux Arts facade of Penn Station. On a picture postcard of the hotel, Ruth jotted off a note to Otto Reinemann, the man who had helped make their emigration possible. She was overwhelmed by the trip, by Manhattan, and most of all by their good fortune.

The newspapers reported that if they had sailed just one week later, their captain would have been forced to extinguish the ship's lights in the dark, for fear of U-boats. The Holland America Line decided to lay up the vessel that brought the Kempners to America, the *Nieuw Amsterdam*, rather than risk more North Atlantic runs at a time of war. Other friends and allies of the Kempners were still stuck back in Germany and France; soon their frantic appeals would begin arriving in the mail.

Ruth's elderly mother had made the journey, as had Margot Lipton. Whatever strains Kempner's dalliance with Lipton had put on his marriage, Ruth must have come to terms with the arrangement: Lipton would move into the Kempner home. She had left her parents behind in Frankfurt. They would be deported to Theresienstadt concentration camp, in what had been Czechoslovakia, and would not survive; her siblings made it out of Germany and settled in England, America, and Israel. In time, Lipton came to see the Kempners as family, too, and the feeling was obviously mutual.

The Kempners had spent the months before the trip furiously studying English. Beyond the native language, they knew next to nothing about the country. What mattered, Kempner said later, was that they were in "a vast, a rich, and a politically free country."

Kempner knew that the immigrant life would not be easy. He would never get back what he had left behind in Berlin. His elevated rank before his dismissal from the Prussian Interior Ministry—Oberregierungsrat, senior government official— meant nothing to Americans. His knowledge of the ins and outs of German law and police administration did not help him understand the U.S. system. Surely, it did not help his prospects that he could give off an eccentric first impression. One person who interviewed him for a study of displaced scholars in the 1940s noted that he "was rather carelessly dressed" and "sat slumped in his chair." He fixed his questioner with an unblinking gaze. "Some of the facts he gave and the very nature of his responses did not seem to ring true," the interviewer wrote, "and I got the impression of a mentally disturbed individual."

At least he had lined up a job, tenuous and modest as it was, as a research associate at the Institute of Local and State Government at the University of Pennsylvania. He knew judges and businessmen and professors of some prominence who had arrived and started out as dishwashers or bookkeepers. Not every immigrant

was an Albert Einstein. Not everyone made it to a place like the
University in Exile at the New School for Social Research in
New York, which had been established for displaced scholars.
Reputations and degrees did not always translate. Many new
immigrants had to survive and retool, all the while watching for
job listings in the refugee newspapers.

Kempner being Kempner, it was not enough to merely read
the papers seeking an opportunity; he set about getting his own
name in the press so that opportunities might call on him.
Amazingly—perhaps with help again from Reinemann, who
worked in Philadelphia government and likely knew a few
reporters—Kempner managed to have a story written about his
arrival before September was out.

"Ex-Advisor to Germany's Police Comes Here to Begin
New Life," the headline in Philadelphia's *Evening Public Ledger*
announced on September 29. The brief feature recounted his
mother's work at the Women's Medical College of Pennsylvania
and his flight from the Nazis. He told the paper that he was in
the United States to stay, that there was nothing for him back in
Europe; he said nothing about Lucian and André. "It is better,"
he explained, "to begin a new life in this country."

He made a point of telling the reporter that his police work in
Berlin had had nothing to do with the Gestapo. He merely had
been a legal and administrative bureaucrat before the Nazis took
over.

"Please say that I am just at the university as a student," he
concluded, "and please say that I am not a political man and cannot discuss politics."

He had a reason to be defensive, Kempner explained later in
his autobiography. During the war years, Americans had a simple
formula: "German is German." Fearing Nazi saboteurs and spies,
they believed that all immigrants had been cut from the same
untrustworthy cloth, whether or not they were Jewish, whether

or not they had been disenfranchised by Hitler, whether or not they had fought the Nazis.

So the clip from the *Public Ledger* gave Kempner a calling card, a tiny shred of credibility as he began making his way in a strange land.

The Kempner entourage moved first into a redbrick row house on a stretch of Osage Avenue in Philadelphia, not far from the campus of the University of Pennsylvania. His office was on the top floor of Blanchard Hall, a quaint three-story house on Walnut Street with a stone Gothic facade crawling with ivy, a mansard roof, and notably heavy walnut doors.

In his new post, he wrote reports, delivered lectures, and published articles in academic journals. He also took courses in political science, interviewed German refugees for a weekly anti-Nazi broadcast on Philadelphia radio, and drummed up invitations to speak in public. He pitched himself as a survivor of the Führer's goons. So close had he come to death, Kempner claimed, that a number of European newspapers had falsely reported his execution by firing squad following his 1935 arrest by the Gestapo. The talks, which he gave at local clubs, high schools, and colleges, had eye-catching titles: "I Know These Men: Hitler, Göring, Himmler, Goebbels," "Love in Dictatorships," and, naturally, "My Scrapbook Begins with My Death."

After paying his own salary to get hired in 1939, Kempner received grants in later years, including a stipend from the Emergency Committee in Aid of Displaced Foreign Scholars. He also won a $1,000 grant from the Carnegie Corporation of New York to study police and administrative methods in the Third Reich. Ordering research material from Nazi Germany required some subterfuge, he explained. "Since my name is on all Nazi blacklists as expatriated enemy of the regime and my own books were burnt by the Nazis I gave names such as Cemper or Cempen."

His studies sometimes took him in unusual directions. Once, he wrote to a professor at Washington University inquiring about "the problem of the new Nazi physiognomy" of Hitler Youth and SS officers. "The new Nazi generation," Kempner wrote, "has 'frozen' faces, created by certain administrative devices. With respect to this fact, I should like to ask your advice as to whether or not there exist studies in the same or similar lines, e.g. about the changed faces of longtime prisoners, of immigrant groups, etc."

Much of Kempner's library had made the convoluted journey out of Nazi Germany and across the ocean with him, and he put it to productive use. He self-published the report he had helped draft in 1930 to establish the party's criminal nature, which he repackaged as *Blueprint for the Nazi Underground as Revealed in Confidential Police Reports.*

He also tried to interest publishers in an annotated English translation of *The Myth of the Twentieth Century*, "the prophecies of this 'Nostradamus—Rosenberg.'" The English-speaking world needed to read "the only existing and official basic work of Nazi philosophy, new religion, and political theory," Kempner wrote in pitch letters to Knopf, Oxford University Press, Macmillan, and other publishers.

He was certain it would be a bestseller, and he suggested that they could take the proceeds and give them to dispossessed German exiles.

One after the other, the publishers politely declined. "I am just afraid that that turgid performance would never get anywhere in the American market," one editor replied, "nor would it mean anything to ninety-nine out of a hundred American readers."

Amid all of this studying and writing and speaking, Kempner was angling for something bigger. He wanted to work for the world's most celebrated law enforcement agency.

Kempner had first written to J. Edgar Hoover, director of the FBI, in December 1938, while he was still in Nice. Though the refugee's command of the English language was not yet fluid—he had studied more Greek than English in school—he got his point across.

He introduced himself as an "expert criminalist," a former police instructor, and "First Secretary in the Police Department of the German Home Office in Berlin." Asking if the Bureau might have a place for him, Kempner assured Hoover that he would "be able to render very good services to your country, knowing numerous branches of the criminalistics subjects which are of greatest importance for the United States at present."

The recipient of his letter had become famous, thanks to Hollywood's portrayal of his furious pursuit of notorious bank robbers and murderers. Hoover's career had begun at the Justice Department three months into the First World War, when hysteria about enemy spies and saboteurs swept the country. The day the United States entered the war, nearly a hundred Germans were rounded up and arrested; some twelve hundred others were monitored. The Espionage Act of 1917 outlawed all acts of disloyalty. Even speaking out against the war was a crime. The Bureau hunted for German spies, cracked down on the antiwar Industrial Workers of the World labor movement, arrested tens of thousands of suspected draft dodgers.

After the war, Hoover was chosen to lead the Justice Department's new Radical Division, and with nearly sixty-one agents from the Bureau at his command, he quickly built up dossiers on thousands of people who might be working for the overthrow of the American government. The agents infiltrated America's communist organizations, arrested their members, and drove the movement into hiding. Critics began to worry that civil liberties were being trampled, and when it came to light that agents had spied on members of Congress, President Calvin Coolidge moved to rein them in. "A secret police system may become a menace to free government and free institutions," Coolidge's new attorney general, Harlan Fiske Stone, said, "because it carries with it the possibility of abuses of power which are not always quickly comprehended or understood." He fired the Bureau's director and gave the job to Hoover, on one condition: The surveillance had to end. Hoover consented—then found a way to continue in secret.

In 1938, on the cusp of a new war, American fears had to do with Nazis and Fascists. The German-American Bund trumpeted a pro-Nazi message in magazines and in the streets. Father Charles Coughlin, a Catholic priest in Royal Oak, Michigan, who built a radio audience of forty million in the years before the war, agitated against "Jewish conspirators" and the communists. "When we get through with the Jews," he cried at a speech in the Bronx, "they'll think the treatment they received in Germany was nothing." Sinclair Lewis stoked paranoia with his bestselling novel, *It Can't Happen Here*, which envisioned a duly elected U.S. president declaring a dictatorship.

Amid this drumbeat of anxiety and panic about spies and saboteurs, a new president turned to Hoover.

In an order so secret he did not have it written down, Roosevelt on August 25, 1936, directed the Bureau's chief to gather intelligence about Nazis and communists in America. Hoover took things a step further. He passed along intelligence not just about foreign agents and infiltrators but also about Roosevelt's political enemies, including aviator Charles Lindbergh, whose visits to Germany had left him impressed with Hitler and the Third Reich. "I am absolutely convinced that Lindbergh is a Nazi," Roosevelt told a member of his cabinet.

In February 1938, agents uncovered a ring of German spies who had infiltrated U.S. military and defense contractors. At work for a decade, the criminals managed to swipe blueprints for new planes and warships. The case planted a chilling idea in the public consciousness: Nazis really were here, at work on this side of the Atlantic.

Hoover soon persuaded Roosevelt to give him sweeping control over America's intelligence and counterespionage operations. The president secretly authorized wiretaps against potential spies and subversives, flouting a Supreme Court decision barring them. The Bureau compiled lists of potential traitors who should be arrested or monitored if the United States went to war.

Civil libertarians—among them Attorney General Robert H. Jackson, the future chief U.S. prosecutor at the Nuremberg trials—fretted about Hoover's aggressive tactics. When Eleanor Roosevelt discovered that agents were digging into the background of her secretary, she wrote Hoover a personal letter. "This type of investigation seems to me to smack too much of the Gestapo methods."

This was the man and the agency that Robert Kempner wanted to work for in the summer of 1938.

Kempner's letter to Hoover, however, did not clear the way for a personal meeting with the FBI director. Hoover's office replied with a brief note and a booklet outlining how to become a special agent. But the director offered this unknown German refugee no words of encouragement.

Undeterred, Kempner wrote in July to report that he had lined up work in the United States. Could he call on Hoover when he made it to Washington? He wanted to deliver "information especially interesting for your branch at the present time." Hoover replied that Kempner could surely come and be "conducted on a detailed tour of our facilities and exhibits."

Even this brush-off did not discourage Kempner. On September 25, 1939, the exiled lawyer drafted a letter to inform Hoover that he had arrived. "I consider it a special privilege to live and work in the USA, and to contribute my modest share of knowledge along these lines which I collected during many years of service in Berlin and other places. I hope that there will be an opportunity for me soon to come to Washington for a visit. I shall be delighted to call on you and to discuss matters of common interest with you."

Kempner seemed to know one thing about his new country: It took a hustler to make it in America.

Looted treasures stacked high in a church in Ellingen, Bavaria.
(National Archives)

16

Thieves in Paris

Secret plots against Hitler's life swirled about the Third Reich. One group of conspirators formed in the army among generals who were alarmed that, after crushing Poland, the Führer planned to turn west and immediately attack France. The army was not ready, they insisted. Outraged, Hitler declared them weak-willed and dropped hints that he might suspect their treachery. The plotters scattered.

On November 8, 1939, the sixteenth anniversary of the failed Munich putsch, Hitler stood at a podium in the Bürgerbräukeller, the same beer hall where he had fired his pistol into the ceiling and held the leaders of Bavaria hostage so long ago. Each year the old fighters descended on Munich and marched down the streets as they had back in 1923, only this time they were the victors, hailed as conquering heroes by the crowds. Hitler loved the spectacle. One year, he turned to Rosenberg walking in the second line and said, beaming, "You can't reach this with your old saints." Rosenberg took to calling it a "Germanic Corpus Christi procession"—the Nazi answer to the pope's procession through the streets of Rome with the Blessed Sacrament.

Hitler's commemorative speech at the beer hall was an annual tradition, and he usually addressed the crowd in the evening between eight thirty and about ten o'clock. This year, a time bomb ticked away in the pillar behind the podium, set to explode at nine twenty, halfway through the speech.

But Hitler broke from routine. A little after nine o'clock, he ended the address and, rather than mingle with the crowd as he usually did, hopped into a car and sped over to the train station.

"He told me that he absolutely had to go back to Berlin," Rosenberg noted three days later in his diary. He had an important meeting in Berlin about the invasion of France; it had been planned for November 7, but bad weather forced a postponement. "After his abbreviated speech he had been asked to join the old fighters in the gallery of the Bürgerbräu. He asked what time it was. 9:10. . . . Out of consideration for the train schedule, he didn't want to be late, . . . so he departed quickly. Had he not done that, we'd all be buried in ruins."

The bomb went off on time, tearing apart the pillar and the roof above. Sixty-three were maimed, eight killed. The next day, Rosenberg's paper, the *Völkischer Beobachter*, hailed "the miraculous salvation of the Führer."

Like Hitler, who suspected a British Secret Service plot, Rosenberg wrote in his diary that foreign saboteurs were "working to dispose of us." The assassination attempt prompted Rosenberg to inspect his house. "It is a trifle to throw a bomb into my bedroom, at me, in the deserted space at night." At the same time, he was philosophical. Great men took great risks. Hadn't that been the message of the attempted coup in Munich in 1923? "Ultimately: without carelessness we never would have been able to begin."

The near miss also made him think about the state of public opinion in Germany. Here, as usual, Rosenberg found Goebbels to blame. The propaganda minister had destroyed the trust of the people, Rosenberg wrote, and he carried the blame for the "rancor in the country. . . . The amount of trust destroyed by Dr. Goebbels's arrogance and others' showing off cannot be estimated. We all pay . . . for what individuals destroyed with their vanity and Levantine pretensions."

Rosenberg didn't know it, but he was onto something. The time bomb at the Bürgerbräukeller had been set by a carpenter, Georg Elser, working alone. He had spent months hiding out after hours, whittling away at the pillar and installing the explosives.

By the time the bomb went off, he was already under arrest. He had been picked up trying to cross into Switzerland illegally.

Under interrogation, he said he had been upset about the direction Hitler was taking Germany, fearful of another war, and alarmed by the Nazis' clampdown on civil liberties. He had decided that Hitler needed to go, and Goebbels and Göring as well.

Britain and France spent late 1939 and early 1940 ramping up their war production and preparing for the fight ahead. In the meantime, the Nazis turned their sights on Denmark and Norway.

Two strategic factors drove Berlin's decision to move against neutral Scandinavia. German naval officers did not want their access to the ocean blocked by a British cordon across the North Sea, as had happened during the First World War. At the same time, they warned Hitler—correctly, it turned out—that the Brits wanted to occupy Scandinavia and cut off Germany's source of iron ore in Sweden. During the winter months, the passage from Sweden to Germany was choked with ice, and the ore had to be shipped via a Norwegian port.

Rosenberg found a role to play in this chapter of the war. Since 1933, he had cultivated an alliance in Norway with a right-wing politician named Vidkun Quisling, whose National Unity Party aimed to bring Nazism to his homeland. In August 1939, Rosenberg arranged for a small band of Quisling's followers to train in Germany, and later that year, with talk of a Scandinavian operation percolating in Berlin, he passed along word to the German navy that Quisling was plotting a coup. Perhaps, Rosenberg suggested, the Norwegian conspirator and the Germans could work together?

In December 1939, Quisling met with Hitler three times, outlining his plans for a coup and promising that he had support within the Norwegian military. Hitler was reluctant to intervene. He told Quisling he preferred a neutral Norway, but he would not stand by if the British moved to take the country's ports and block German imports. For the time being, he promised only financial support for Quisling's movement.

Before leaving Berlin, Quisling visited Rosenberg and thanked him warmly for his help.

Rosenberg replied that he looked forward to visiting Scandinavia as a welcome guest. "We gave each other a squeeze of the hand and will probably not see each other again," Rosenberg wrote in his diary, "until the action has succeeded and Norway's prime minister is named Quisling."

Over the coming months, Hitler warmed to the idea of a Scandinavian occupation, and on April 9, 1940, German armies charged into Denmark and Norway. The Danes surrendered immediately, but the Germans met fierce resistance from the British navy and from the Norwegian army.

On the day of the invasion, Quisling took to the radio, announced that he was the new leader of Norway, and urged his countrymen to end their resistance to the Germans. "Today is a great day in German history," Rosenberg wrote in the diary. "Denmark and Norway occupied. I congratulate the Führer for this work, which I also helped prepare."

The king and the ministers of the legitimate government fled north, and the next day they sent the Nazis a different message. They would not back Quisling. They would fight. But their resistance made little difference, nor did the help from the British. The Germans quickly occupied Oslo and the other major cities.

Rosenberg crowed about his bit part in the invasion. It could not be denied that his Foreign Policy Office had "fulfilled a historic task" by laying the groundwork for the operation, he wrote in the diary at the end of April. "The occupation of Norway is perhaps decisive for the war."

It wasn't, but the German victory in Scandinavia did have one significant outcome. It led to a backlash against Prime Minister Neville Chamberlain in the British Parliament. The fall of Norway, coming after the annexation of Austria and the loss of Czechoslovakia and the demise of Poland, doomed his administration.

On May 10, he stepped down, and a man who had built a reputation as an unyielding enemy of the Third Reich rose to power: Winston Churchill.

In April 1940, Rosenberg went on a speaking tour in western Germany, and he took a side trip to see Saarbrücken and the fortifications on the heights south of the city. Along the border, the Germans had their Westwall and the French their Maginot Line, massive networks of impenetrable defenses: heavy antitank posts sunk in the earth, row upon row of barbed wire, subterranean bunkers, armored turrets. France had officially been at war with Germany since September 1939, but neither side had been prepared to go on the offensive. By the spring of 1940, however, the "phony war" was giving way to real fighting. In the weeks before Rosenberg's reconnaissance trip, the French and German armies traded heavy artillery blows, and the skies were punctured by dogfights between the air forces. Skirmishes broke out as German patrols probed Allied fortifications. Tension was mounting.

Rosenberg wandered through the desolate landscape and jotted down impressions in his diary. "Villages shot to pieces in no man's land. Abandoned old French trenches [littered] with mattresses and blankets. A French café enlarged as a small concrete blockhouse. Uninterrupted bunker construction." The German officers and soldiers he met seemed to be in good spirits. But in Saarbrücken, the houses had been reduced to piles of rubble.

"If the entire west should appear like <u>this</u> someday," Rosenberg wrote, "it would be nightmarish."

May 10, 1940: "The final battle begins," Rosenberg wrote, "and decides the fate of Germany. Arguably forever, for centuries at any rate."

The Allies had had years to prepare, and still they were not ready for the war plan the Nazis drew up for the invasion of the West. They had expected a German dash through the Netherlands and the heart of Belgium. Instead, Hitler backed a daring plan for a massive force of tanks and armor to push through the Ardennes farther south. A bleak, inhospitable, frequently foggy stretch of thick woods and hills, the Ardennes would be lightly defended; the Allies thought it far too rugged for an armored assault.

The plan worked to perfection. In the north, the Dutch quickly surrendered after the Germans bombed Rotterdam on May 14. In Belgium, the Allies held the line at first in the north, where they had concentrated their armies to counter what they believed to be the main invasion force.

Meanwhile, in the Ardennes to the south, German tanks and armored vehicles slowly ground their way west in four lines stretching more than a hundred miles. The Germans made it to the Meuse River unscathed, and after breaking through the Allied front on May 14, they sprinted across the open country unchecked. By May 20, they had reached the English Channel, and they swiftly encircled French and British forces at Dunkirk. Though 340,000 Allied soldiers managed to escape to safety across the Channel, the first round of fighting was all but over. The Germans swept south in a great wave, entering Paris unchallenged on June 14.

French leaders asked for an armistice. A week later, they were summoned to the woods of Compiègne, the very place where Germany had surrendered to the Allies in November 1918. Hitler led a delegation to the clearing to open the talks, and when he arrived he made a point of walking over to a monument commemorating the end of the First World War and the fall of Germany. It read: HERE ON THE ELEVENTH OF NOVEMBER 1918 SUCCUMBED THE CRIMINAL PRIDE OF THE GERMAN EMPIRE—VANQUISHED BY THE FREE PEOPLES WHICH IT TRIED TO ENSLAVE. He read the inscription with visible contempt. William Shirer, the foreign correspondent, there to witness and report on the historic moment, watched the Führer closely. "I have seen that face many times at the great moments of his life," Shirer wrote in his diary later. "But today! It is afire with scorn, anger, hate, revenge, triumph."

The French signed a crippling armistice the following day. Two days after that, the Germans demolished the monument.

In the six years since Hitler named him indoctrination chief, Rosenberg had seen his teachings seep into every corner of German life. *Gleichschaltung*, or "coordination," put the Nazis in control of labor unions, business chambers, teachers' leagues, student societies, youth associations, and practically every other social and community group down to the local level: shooting clubs, singing clubs, sports clubs.

Subject to ideological education at all hours of the day, every German citizen, inevitably, was introduced to Rosenberg's radical ideas.

Rosenberg regularly lectured before the leaders of the Hitler Youth, which by 1939 had 8.7 million children on its rolls. Hitler viewed the organization as a training ground for future soldiers and party loyalists. To go along with the continuous physical education, hiking, camping, and sports—plus, as the war went on, more soldierly activities like Morse code, orientation, and marching— the children received a dose of ideology. They sang songs, read books, and sat for carefully packaged lessons about the Führer, Germanic myths, and racial purity. Among the materials that Hitler Youth instructors were required to study and teach was *Myth*.

The book seemed ubiquitous in the Third Reich. Secondary school teachers were required to take accreditation tests that required knowledge of the theories it put forth. A publication of the National Socialist Teachers League declared in 1935 that "every German fighting for freedom of mind and soul" had a duty to read it. "Rosenberg has, in his *Myth of the Twentieth Century*, put into the hands of Germans a weapon with which to regain their honor and spiritual self-determination." Educators, university students, civil servants, even businessmen were subjected to Nazi indoctrination camps where *Mein Kampf* and *Myth* were used to teach the importance of racial purity. "National Socialism is an ideology, and that ideology is to be found in Rosenberg's *Myth of the Twentieth Century*," a party training official said at an indoctrination session for university students in September 1935. "People who do not possess our faith, or cannot possess it on account of their racial inferiority, must be eliminated."

Himmler's men received Rosenberg's message through the official SS newspaper, *Das Schwarze Korps*; his articles were reprinted in *SS-Leitheft*, the ideological training bulletin for the SS leadership that arrived in striking covers bearing the lightning-bolt SS logo on a black or red background.

And yet, even as Rosenberg saw his philosophies percolate through the culture, he argued again and again for Hitler to further expand his authority over German hearts and minds. Rosenberg wanted a bigger podium from which to preach to the people. With the nation at war, he argued that Hitler needed Rosenberg's singular voice to keep the party and the populace faithful to Nazi doctrines.

It was no coincidence that Rosenberg's scheme would in the process diminish the enormous influence of his archrival Joseph Goebbels.

"The people are now looking for the party," he wrote in the diary one day in September 1939, recounting an argument he'd made to Rudolf Hess, Hitler's deputy Führer. They had given the Nazis their vote of confidence, and leaders had abused that trust. Goebbels's Reich Chamber of Culture had become corrupt. Robert Ley, after arranging for Rosenberg to prepare indoctrination materials for the party, then tried to "defraud me of my life's work behind my back," Rosenberg complained. "Thus the party loses its shape: the ostentatious behavior of the parvenus in some places, the uncomradely obstructing of others out of peacock-like vanity, and then petit-bourgeois weakness and indecisiveness. So many thousands of sensible National Socialists continue to ask: 'Will the Führer not intervene? Can he continue to force Dr. G upon us? Will no organization ever come?' They continue to work faithfully, as always—because they <u>struggled</u> and this struggle cannot be abandoned—but no longer with <u>that</u>, our inner faith, as we all once had."

Rosenberg saw the party splintering without his forceful guidance on ideological matters. The only thing holding the Third Reich together was Hitler's unimpeachable authority. Once the Führer died, his acolytes would go to war against one another, like the generals of Alexander the Great fighting over the spoils he left behind in ancient Greece. The time had come for a "reformation," and he was the man to lead it.

Later in 1939, Rosenberg took up his case with Hitler. The war was not just about territory, he told Hitler. It was also a war for souls. He worried that the people were being seduced by new leaders and "art nouveau philosophers." The churches were strengthening their subversive activities, and the Nazis could not let up in the fight against them. The clergy still clung to the idea that they—not the Nazi Party, not Rosenberg—were responsible for Germans' spiritual well-being. One theologian even had the gall to suggest that the party's ideological training belonged in the hands of the churches. "This unabashed memorandum teems with naive, narrow-minded arrogance, but it shows how utterly uncomprehending a bombastic, Old-Testament-filled Christian mind is, when confronted with German life," Rosenberg wrote. "This backwardness incarnate doesn't once <u>suspect how</u> outdated it is." In some regions, priests had proclaimed the war a punishment from God. They were corroding the souls of the men, and

Goebbels's tactics—"fairy tales and lying propaganda and vaude-ville performances"—would not win the day against these enemies.

"During this time, I believe I have fought faithfully for the party's trust," he argued, "and if we're not strict, our struggle will be lost in the future."

Rosenberg put his idea in writing and shepherded it through the Nazi policy-making machinery, negotiating and compromis-ing to make it palatable to his rivals. But in the spring of 1940, Hitler suddenly vetoed the idea, blaming, of all people, Benito Mussolini. The Italian dictator worried about the repercussions in Catholic Rome if Hitler gave the heretic Rosenberg a new high-profile posting. Hitler told Rosenberg he understood Mussolini's concerns. The move would "strike like a bomb now, in the moment before the beginning of the great offensive." Later, the Nazis could do whatever they wanted, but now was not the time to deal with a fresh rebellion from the clerics. "The church still has something like hope that it will be able to perpetuate itself," Hitler explained. "With your appointment they'll finally bury all such hopes, allow all inhibitions to fall away."

But the Führer soon had other ideas for his loyal lieutenant.

Over the coming five years, Rosenberg's boundless ambition and indefatigable pursuit of personal power would land him lead-ing roles in some of Nazi Germany's most infamous crimes.

The new chapter in Rosenberg's life started, innocuously enough, with plans for a new library. On Hitler's instructions, Rosenberg was designing a Nazi Hohe Schule—"High School"—an institu-tion that, they hoped, would ensure that the party's teachings were carried on generation after generation. The main campus was to be built on Lake Chiemsee, a scenic stretch of freshwater, sur-rounded by mountains, in southern Bavaria. The architect envi-sioned an imposing slab of a main building, 262 feet tall, with austere lines in the Nazi style, capped with monumental pillars and watched over by a pair of stone eagles high above.

The Hohe Schule would be the pinnacle of an elite ideological educational system. German teenagers who hoped to take leadership positions in the party in the future would be required to attend one of the newly built Adolf Hitler Schools. Run by the Hitler Youth, the schools would emphasize military and physical preparation. The top graduates could then go on to the Order Castles—three of these were built, at great expense, in the Rhineland, Bavaria, and Pomerania—where the chosen few would be steeped in racial biology, advanced athletics, and ideological training. The Order Castles would also be places where current party leaders went for training and continuing education. The Hohe Schule would train the instructors for the Adolf Hitler Schools and the Order Castles, giving Rosenberg sway over the entire party educational system.

Beyond that, Rosenberg's institution would instruct the party's indoctrination personnel and become a center for Nazi research. Outposts would be established all around the country to study communism, theology, "racial hygiene," Germanic folklore, art, and more. The first institute opened in Frankfurt, and there Nazi scholars studied the most pressing matter of the day: the Jewish question.

Institutions need libraries, and libraries need books. In January 1940, Hitler ordered party and government officials to assist Rosenberg's effort to build collections for the Hohe Schule. Rosenberg persuaded the city of Frankfurt to share its collection of Jewish materials, and began to purchase other libraries.

But at the dawn of the war, Rosenberg saw a new opening. On June 18, four days after the fall of Paris, one of Rosenberg's staffers discovered that major Jewish and Masonic institutions in the French capital had been abandoned; their archives would be a gold mine for Rosenberg's research institute.

Making the most of this opportunity, Rosenberg asked for Hitler's formal permission to launch a task force to gather up material abandoned by fleeing Jews so that future scholars could study it. Hitler quickly agreed, and the soon-to-be infamous Einsatzstab Reichsleiter Rosenberg, the Reichsleiter Rosenberg Task Force, was born. Before long his men—with help from the Gestapo, the SS Security Service, and the secret military police, the Geheime Feldpolizei—were ransacking libraries, archives, and private collections all across Holland, Belgium, and France.

They went after the collections of two major Jewish institutions in Paris, seizing fifty thousand books from the Alliance Israélite Universelle and the École Rabbinique. They confiscated twenty thousand books from Lipschutz, a major Jewish bookstore in Paris. They plundered the large private collections held by the Rothschilds. They occupied major Masonic lodges; these were actually "fighting organizations," to Rosenberg's mind. Since this was a Rosenberg production, they also zeroed in on Russian and Ukrainian libraries in the occupied West. The Einsatzstab had fierce competition, especially from Himmler's Reich Security Main Office, which was creating a large, secret research library of its own to aid its investigations of Nazi enemies. But Rosenberg quickly managed to sweep up hundreds of thousands of books. One shipment of 1,224 cases of books in August 1940 filled eleven railcars.

"The things my Einsatzstab confiscated in Paris," Rosenberg noted in his diary, "are doubtlessly unique."

At his new Institute for the Research of the Jewish Question in Frankfurt, Rosenberg was compiling the world's greatest library of Judaica; it would have hundreds of thousands of pilfered volumes. He wanted to give scholars the material they would need to study Germany's great enemy in granular detail. "Whoever in the future will want to study the Jewish question," he wrote in his diary, "will <u>have</u> to go to Frankfurt."

But before long, the mission of Rosenberg's Einsatzstab would undergo a radical expansion. As they surveyed the landscape of their freshly conquered territory, the leaders of the Third Reich had their eyes on objects far more valuable than dusty piles of library books.

· · ·

Hitler envisioned a grand museum complex in Linz, Austria, the city where he grew up. His whirlwind 1938 tour of Florence's Uffizi and Borghese galleries had convinced him that his nation did not have anything like the sort of world-class pieces his museum would require. That was about to change. Inside Germany, the Gestapo was confiscating art and other valuables from Jews—for "safekeeping." The best pieces were to be earmarked for Linz or other German museums, and the rest sold or destroyed.

In 1939, with artwork flooding into his storerooms, Hitler named an art historian, Hans Posse, to sort through the mass of confiscated art and choose what would go in the Führermuseum. Backed by a practically unlimited budget and empowered to drive the hardest of bargains, Posse also began acquiring new pieces on the open market.

He had competition from Hermann Göring, who as a plunderer had no equal in Nazi Germany. Göring imagined himself to be a Renaissance man. He furnished his Berlin residence with paintings on loan from German museums; an enormous Rubens hid a movie screen. He had begun building his massive art collection soon after the Nazis took power. In 1936, when Hitler put him in charge of the German economy, government funds flowed into Göring's coffers, and those with business interests showered him with lavish private gifts. Fifty miles north of Berlin in the Schorfheide Forest, the Reichsmarschall built an extravagant estate called Carinhall, which foreign visitors found notable not only for its immense size but also for its ostentatiousness. Paintings confronted visitors by the hundreds, alongside giant taxidermied lions and bison. Göring kept a bowl of diamonds on his desk to give himself something to fiddle with during meetings.

After the annexation of Austria, the Germans pillaged Vienna. Prominent families lost their collections; some Jews surrendered their possessions in exchange for permission to emigrate. The crown jewels of the Holy Roman Empire—scepters, orbs, Charlemagne's prayer book, everything studded with gems—were seized by Nuremberg's mayor on the grounds that, after four centuries in his city, they had been removed to Vienna in 1794 for safekeeping and never returned.

Following the invasion of Poland the next year, the Nazis took the world's largest Gothic altarpiece, carved by German sculptor Veit Stoss, from the Church of Our Lady, in Krakow, and made off with famous paintings by Rembrandt, Raphael, and Leonardo.

In the Netherlands, Göring's agents made arrangements to snap up loot even as the Allied armies were being encircled at Dunkirk. The Nazi dragnet seemed to capture everything: the property of those who had been arrested and of those who fled before the invasion and those who left their artwork with galleries and those who tried to ship their valuables out of the country.

Not everything was stolen outright. The Nazis gave the operation a veneer of legality by buying collections. But these were forced sales at discount prices under threat of confiscation. "Should you this time again not be able to decide," Göring warned one hesitant Belgian dealer, "then I should be compelled to withdraw my offer and then things would go their normal way, without my being able to do anything to impede it."

Sometimes an exit visa was part of the deal for the desperate seller. One dealer traded four panels by Brueghel to win the freedom of two Jewish employees. Another managed to get visas for twenty-five relatives in exchange for Rembrandt's 1634 *Portrait of a Man of the Raman Family*. One of the most significant transactions involved the collection left behind by Jacques Goudstikker, a Jew who was a major dealer in Old Masters. Fleeing the Nazis by sea in May 1940, he fell through an uncovered hatch into the hold of the ship and broke his neck. Two of his employees managed to convince Goudstikker's widow that if they did not sell the collection at a steep discount, everything would be confiscated. Göring walked away from the transaction with six hundred paintings, including nine by Rubens.

In the summer of 1940, the Nazis turned their attention to defeated France. Hitler ordered the art "safeguarded," and Ribbentrop's ambassador, Otto Abetz, immediately took it upon himself to do the work. His men raided bank vaults, art galleries, and the private homes of Jews. Loot piled up in the embassy. But military officers—believing that they, not the ambassador, had been given the responsibility for the art treasures—objected to Abetz's aggressiveness and tried to block him from shipping the material out of the country. Other players were also competing for the spoils, among them Goebbels, in his role as leader of the Reich Chamber of Culture.

But this time, Rosenberg beat out his rivals. Hitler handed the job of securing "ownerless Jewish possessions," as the order put it, to the Einsatzstab. Unlike Göring, Rosenberg had no private art collection to build. He could be counted on to scrupulously and slavishly secure the loot for the Führer.

Göring's agents were already at work in France, of course, so Rosenberg immediately wrote to say he hoped for full cooperation. The Reichsmarschall wrote back enthusiastically. He offered to solve one of Rosenberg's problems: how to get the artwork back to Germany. Railcars could be difficult to come by, but Göring put the Luftwaffe at Rosenberg's disposal to help pack, prepare, safeguard, and transport the art shipments.

The two Nazi leaders had a complicated relationship. During Rosenberg's brief tenure as head of the party in 1923–1924, when Göring was in exile, recuperating from the gunshot wound he suffered during the failed coup, Rosenberg had Göring's name stricken from the Nazi rolls, and Göring never forgot it. A decade later, at the same time that Gestapo chief Rudolf Diels was feeding Göring dossiers on potentially disloyal Prussian Interior Ministry officials, he was also handing over intelligence on other Nazis. In his memoir, Diels claimed that Rosenberg's file included love letters to a Jewish woman, Lisette Kohlrausch, who had been arrested by the Gestapo. He wrote that Rosenberg had managed to get her released, but the affair put him in a compromising position. In the space of a moment, Göring could reveal the episode to Hitler and destroy Rosenberg's career. (The letters Diels mentions are lost to history, if they ever existed.)

But in the middle of 1940, Göring's support seemed like a blessing to Rosenberg. Rivals quickly deferred to the Einsatzstab's authority. Göring's Devisenschutzkommando, a currency control unit, helped conduct raids and even turned over to Rosenberg's agency art it discovered on its own. The Nazis seemed to know without asking where to find the most important galleries and museums and banks and warehouses and private residences. Huge moving vans had appeared before the homes of wealthy Jews, a witness wrote in her diary. "Beautiful tapestries, carpets, busts, masterpieces, china, furniture, blankets, sheets, all were taken away to Germany."

A central storehouse was established at the Jeu de Paume, a small museum on the Place de la Concorde, and soon art was pouring into the offices so swiftly that Rosenberg's art historians could barely keep up with it. "By using all possible ways and means we discovered and seized all Jewish art collections that were hidden either in Jewish homes in Paris, in castles in the provinces, or in warehouses and other storage places," Rosenberg reported to Hitler. "The escaped Jews knew how to camouflage the hiding places of these objects of art." The famous French Rothschild collections had been scattered throughout Paris, Bordeaux, and the Loire region.

At lunch with Hitler in early September, Rosenberg excitedly reported about what had been found in a Rothschild palace in Paris. Under a trapdoor in a secret cellar lay sixty-two boxes full of documents and books, and a little chest holding porcelain buttons once worn by Frederick the Great himself.

After the war, when asked under interrogation about seizing the art and antiquities without compensation, Rosenberg would offer a simple justification:

"The owners were all away."

•   •   •

It quickly became clear to Rosenberg that the collaboration with Göring would come at a cost.

Göring struck up a close relationship with the Einsatzstab men in Paris, especially Kurt von Behr—the same von Behr who, five years later, would lead the Allied armies to the papers Rosenberg had hidden in Schloss Banz. Imperious and vain, von Behr was born into an aristocratic family and once led the German Red Cross. Though he had not been in the army since the First World War, he arranged to be named a lieutenant colonel by the Paris military government. He spoke French, strode around wearing flamboyant uniforms, cultivated contacts in high places, and threw lavish parties. His wife was British but hated her native country. Other Einsatzstab men complained that von Behr was "an unscrupulous egomaniac" who knew nothing about art and carried himself like a gangster. Even in a regime that took rapaciousness to historic levels, the von Behrs stood out.

The Einsatzstab office in Paris was unlike any other in the Rosenberg empire, according to an investigation compiled by the U.S. Office of Strategic Services at the end of the war. The men in charge carried on open affairs with the secretaries. One woman "appropriated objects of value for herself such as furs, jewelry and silver," and engaged in a bitter feud with a colleague that led to "hysterical slander and counter-accusations." Another employee was suspected of spying on the staff for her boss. The military administration came to detest von Behr and his entire operation.

At the beginning of November, Göring came to Paris to shop. His agents had scouted private collections before they were confiscated and ensured that the best works were sent to the Jeu de Paume.

At the gallery, von Behr staged an elaborate private showing for the Reichsmarschall. Champagne was popped, and the museum was decorated with palms, elegant furniture, and fine rugs. The guest of honor wandered among the art all day, returning two days later to consider the relative merit of still more works. He reserved some two dozen pieces for himself—a Rembrandt, a van Dyck, a set of stained-glass windows, a few tapestries—and strategically earmarked others for Hitler's Führermuseum, notably Vermeer's masterpiece *The Astronomer.*

At the end of this visit, Göring presumptuously issued an order delineating how the spoils would be divided—this despite having no formal authority over the Einsatzstab and the art seizures in Paris.

First, Göring decreed, Hitler's representatives would reserve what they wanted for Linz. Then Göring would take what he needed "to complete the collections of the Reichsmarschall." Next in line, Rosenberg could take what he wanted for his Hohe Schule. Finally, German and French museums could pick over the haul. In an empty demonstration of benevolence, Göring declared that whatever art was left—if anything was left—could be auctioned off, with the proceeds going to widows and war orphans.

Three weeks after Göring's shopping spree, Rosenberg arrived in Paris, a city that even the Nazis could not bring themselves to bomb.

"I have no intention of attacking the beautiful capital of France," Hitler said as the army ripped through France in the summer of 1940. Part of his reasoning was strategic. The Nazis knew that destroying Paris—as they had Rotterdam, for example—would antagonize the British, whom they hoped to bring to peace negotiations in the wake of the French defeat. But Hitler also admired the city for its beauty and style. He called it "one of the jewels of Europe" and vowed to protect it.

Two weeks after the Germans rolled into Paris without a fight, the Führer climbed into a Mercedes convertible and toured the city. The streets were surreally empty—nearly four million people had fled. He stopped at the Opéra to marvel at its architecture, and the Hôtel National des Invalides to see Napoleon's tomb. He posed for the snapshot that every tourist must get in Paris: standing before the Eiffel Tower.

If the Nazis did not destroy Paris, they did make their presence felt. When Parisians returned to the city after the surrender, they found a city overrun with young soldiers in uniform. The swastika seemed to flutter from every balcony. Freshly painted signs had bloomed on major intersections, directing traffic in German. The streets honoring famous Jews had new names. The empty Grand Palais on the Champs-Élysées had been pressed into service as a military truck depot, and the Nazi administration had taken up occupancy in most of the famously opulent hotels and palaces around the city; a survey of addresses they commandeered would run to six hundred pages.

The Nazis luxuriated in the city's pleasures: the restaurants and cafés, the nightclubs, the Casino de Paris, the Folies Bergère. Laden down with francs exchanged at favorable rates, they flocked to the city's chic shops and sidewalk markets. They were happy to "keep Paris Paris," as the Propaganda Ministry had ordered. Many of the soldiers, whether stationed in Paris or visiting on leave, relied on a slim new German travel guide issued a month after the occupation. "For the majority of us, Paris is an unknown land. We approach her with mixed feelings: superiority, curiosity and nervous anticipation. The name of Paris evokes something special." When their grandfathers spoke of it, the ones who had fought in France in 1870, the name sounded "mysterious, extraordinary. Now we are there and we can enjoy it at our liberty."

Rosenberg went to Paris to deliver a speech at the Palais Bourbon, former home to the lower house of the French Parliament, now the seat of the Nazi occupation. Luftwaffe field marshal Hugo Sperrle and other military commanders were among the six hundred people who assembled in the palace's grand semicircular chamber to listen to Rosenberg's address.

"A strange feeling to speak at this spot, from where Clemenceau and Poincaré thundered against the Reich; from where the worldwide agitation against Germany again and again had their source," Rosenberg reflected later in his diary. "I was the first to speak for the National Socialist revolution at the grave, so to speak, of the French revolution." Rosenberg's remarks, titled "Blood and Gold," received a great deal of press in Paris. "From what I heard, the speech was the topic of the day among all the French," Rosenberg wrote later in the diary. "Wedged between church and democracy, they saw a new spiritual path here. For now, however, an inner change of France is not to be expected. . . . The Frenchman has not yet understood the magnitude of his collapse."

Rosenberg attended a party at the Hôtel Ritz that night, then visited Sperrle's opulent, newly renovated quarters in the Palais du Luxembourg. Soon after the victory in France, the Luftwaffe had begun bombing British airfields, infrastructure, and cities to prepare for a planned amphibious invasion across the English Channel. In months of dogfights, British Spitfires and Hurricanes won the battle for air supremacy against the German Messerschmitts, and by September 1940 Hitler had scrapped the plans for the assault. But the Blitz continued: nightly bombing raids of London, Liverpool, and other British cities that sent the Brits scurrying for cover. In Paris, Sperrle showed Rosenberg aerial images of the devastation his pilots were inflicting.

While he was in Paris, Rosenberg also visited the Einsatzstab staff, hard at work inside the Jeu de Paume. The museum was decorated with chrysanthemums in his honor. "There were many precious things to see," he noted in his diary. "Rothschild, Weill, Seligmann, etc. had to hand over the result of one hundred years of stock profits: Rembrandt, Rubens, Vermeer, Boucher, Fragonard, Goya, etc. etc. were there in high numbers, [alongside] ancient carvings, Gobelin tapestries, etc. The art appraisers estimate the value at almost one billion marks!"

But Rosenberg had reason for concern. Göring was already claiming some of the art as his own.

Rosenberg could have been killed returning from Paris. After taking in a production at the theater, he dashed to the airfield and climbed aboard Field Marshal Gerd von Rundstedt's plane for the six-hundred-mile journey back to Berlin. When the pilot returned to Paris, the gauges froze, and the pilot was forced to turn back. He landed in such a hurry that one of the plane's wings slammed into the ground. "When he heard about it," Rosenberg recounted, "Sperrle almost lifted the poor captain into the air by his buttons."

Back in Berlin, Rosenberg set about trying to keep Göring from wresting away control of the art-looting operation in France.

A letter had arrived from the Reichsmarschall, in which he told Rosenberg he fully backed the Einsatzstab's authority. But he noted, accurately, that his own men and intelligence sources had helped track down much of the treasure, and explained that he would be keeping a few items for himself—"a small percentage," he wrote—which he promised to leave to the Reich at the end of his life.

Rosenberg dispatched his Berlin-based art adviser, Robert Scholz, to Paris to visit the Einsatzstab. He reported back that, in fact, Göring planned "a wholesale movement" of artwork to Carinhall. This set off alarm bells. Wasn't Hitler supposed to be the man to decide what happened with the seized art? Rosenberg sought the Führer's intervention. He had Scholz write Hitler's aide in the Chancellery office and suggest that fifteen freight-car loads of the most valuable pieces be moved out of France immediately so that they could be unpacked, inventoried, and turned over to Hitler.

On December 31, Hitler ruled on which pieces he wanted for the museum from the French stocks, claiming forty-five paintings, along with a number of tapestries and several pieces of eighteenth-century French furniture. Most of the objects had been confiscated from the Rothschilds: Vermeer's *Astronomer*, a Rembrandt, a pair of Goyas, a trio of Rubens, three works by Boucher. The art was transported to Munich in February on the Reichsmarschall's special train and stashed away in air raid shelters in the Führerbau. Göring, for his part, would get fifty-nine pieces for himself.

But the Nazis were only getting started.

By the time they were finished, they would take an estimated one-third of all privately owned art in France.

The Einsatzstab, for its part, took nearly twenty-two thousand objects from more than two hundred private Jewish collections in France: oil paintings, watercolors, drawings, bronze sculptures, tapestries, coins, porcelain, jewelry, antique vases. Between 1941 and 1944, twenty-nine shipments went to storage depots in six German castles, including the storybook Neuschwanstein Castle, in the rugged mountains southwest of Munich. The Nazis took Boucher's *Portrait of Madame Pompadour* and Panini's *Christ at the Pool of Bethesda*. They took a painting of a woman by Frans Hals, a harbor landscape by Vernet, and a river scene by Berchem.

The French protested, to no avail. Rosenberg's staff reminded them that the Germans were putting down a global Jewish conspiracy. By confiscating the priceless treasures of France, they were merely compensating themselves "for the great sacrifices of the Reich made for the people of Europe."

Göring visited the Jeu de Paume at least twenty times and kept upwards of six hundred pieces of art. On one visit, he was shown twenty-two chests of jewelry pilfered from the Rothschilds' homes in the countryside. Looking over the pieces, which included pendants dating to the sixteenth century, the Reichsmarschall chose six of the finest and dropped them in his pocket.

Rosenberg resented Göring's muscling into his operations. Ever the loyal Nazi, Rosenberg believed that the treasures belonged not to one man but to the entire party, which had "paid for the struggle against the Jews for twenty years."

Later, Rosenberg would insist that he "forbade, in a very strict manner, all of my collaborators to appropriate even a trifle object as a souvenir." But he was never in a position to prevent Göring from taking what he wanted. It would come out later that Rosenberg was not immune to temptation. He had furnished his own home in Berlin with three valuable paintings taken from the Netherlands, one of them by the Dutch portrait artist Frans Hals.

In the end, both men got what they wanted: Göring his share of the looted art, and Rosenberg control of an operation that would be recognized as one of history's most sweeping art confiscations.

Rosenberg's Einsatzstab produced leather-bound volumes of photographs to document the treasure now in Germany's possession. One April, Rosenberg sent a few of them to Hitler "in my desire to give you, my Führer, some joy for your birthday." He had even more, he explained, and he offered to deliver them personally "with the hope that this short occupation with the beautiful things of art which are nearest to your heart will send a ray of beauty and joy into your revered life."

As for the "degenerate" paintings, the French Impressionist works and other modern fare so offensive to Nazi sensibilities, they were exchanged for Old Masters. In one transaction, American investigators found, Göring had approved a trade with a German art dealer in Paris named Gustav Rochlitz, who selected eleven paintings by Degas, Matisse, Picasso, Renoir, and Cézanne, among others, in exchange for "a highly questionable Titian portrait and a pedestrian work by Jan Weenix."

Later, other modern pieces—by Picasso, by Miró, by Dalí—were kicked from their frames, taken to the garden at the Jeu de Paume, and burned with the trash. On the Einsatzstab's meticulous lists, names of the condemned artwork were crossed out and marked with a single word.

Vernichtet. Destroyed.

In the spring of 1941, Rosenberg's attention would shift to destruction of a darker sort. Not art, but lives.

An assault gun with the SS Division Totenkopf—the "Death's Head" Division—speeds through the Soviet Union at the start of Operation Barbarossa in the summer of 1941. *(Bundesarchiv, Bild 101I-136-0882-12/ Albert Cursian)*

17

"Rosenberg, Your Great Hour Has Now Arrived"

Tuning in on their radios at the end of March 1941, Germans heard the voice of Hitler's ideological czar booming out across the airwaves. Rosenberg was talking about the Jews, and though his delivery was formal and stilted, to anyone listening with even half an ear, his words were unmistakably murderous.

"We are of the belief that this great war constitutes a cleansing biological world revolution," the Reichsleiter was saying. "Today we consider the Jewish question one of the most important political problems facing us in Europe, a problem which must be solved, and will be solved. And we hope, yes, we know already today, that all nations of Europe will march behind this cleansing in the end."

In Frankfurt, Nazi dignitaries were gathered in the medieval city hall that weekend to dedicate Rosenberg's new Institute for Research on the Jewish Question. A crowd of anti-Semitic reporters, writers, and minor officials from ten European nations had descended on the city to discuss how to eliminate the Jews from the Continent. The timing was right, everyone knew: With the Nazis now in control of an enormous swath of Europe, the enemies of the Jewish people finally had the power to turn their words into deadly action. Rosenberg had attended the first part of the conference, but after Hitler summoned him to the capital on urgent business, he could not make it back to Frankfurt in time, so he read his keynote address from Berlin and broadcast it to all of Germany.

This war would exterminate "all those racially infecting germs of Jewry and its bastards," he told the radio audience. "All the nations are interested in the solution to this question, and here we must declare with the utmost passion: We will and can no longer endure to see the greasy fingers of Jewish high finance meddle once again in the *völkisch* interests of Germany or other peoples of Europe. Nor are we any longer willing to put up with seeing Jewish and Negro bastards, instead of German children, running around in German towns and villages."

The only question was "where to put the Jews." The idea of an independent Jewish state was dead; it had only been a Zionist ploy to create a center from which Jews could continue their insidious control of the globe. Rosenberg suggested deporting them to a reservation, where they would be held "under experienced police supervision."

Whatever the logistics, "we, as National Socialists, have only one categorical answer to give here to all the questions: For Germany, the Jewish question will only be solved when the last Jew has left the Greater German space," he said. "For Europe, the Jewish question will only be solved when the last Jew has left the European continent."

As he spoke those words, Rosenberg already knew that, for the first time in his life, he would have a chance to put his rhetoric to practical effect.

Finally, Hitler was giving Rosenberg the power to shape world history.

By July 1940, Hitler had already turned his attention to his ultimate target: the Soviet Union. Rosenberg had been right all along. Despite the historic pact with Moscow, Hitler was still secretly committed to its destruction—the sooner, the better.

He didn't trust Stalin to stay true to their deal. Taking advantage of Germany's invasion of the West in May and June 1940, the ruthless Soviet leader had grabbed new territory of his own. First, Stalin engineered the occupation of Estonia, Latvia, and Lithuania, then successfully demanded that Romania surrender two eastern provinces to the Soviets. Once Stalin began bargaining with Germany for even more concessions in Eastern Europe—control of Finland, a pact with Bulgaria allowing for Soviet military bases on the key Dardanelles and Bosporus straits—Hitler set his war plans in motion.

A blueprint was drawn up, code-named Operation Barbarossa. Germany would crush the Soviet armies and occupy a territory stretching to the Ural Mountains, far to the east of Moscow. When the German armies poured across the border, Hitler crowed, "the world will hold its breath." Remarkably, Stalin, normally suspicious to the point of paranoia, did not believe reports he received about Hitler's imminent treachery.

Rosenberg's Foreign Policy Office had been working on the Russian question intensively for nearly a decade. He first mentioned the work in his diary in August 1936: "Twice now, the Führer has asked me to prepare explanatory papers in case of a Russian attack." His men were eastern experts. They paid close attention to developments in the East, prepared ethnic and political breakdowns of the population, and stayed in close contact with anti-communist leaders. They studied how the country could be carved up when the time came. Throughout the fall of

1940, they produced a biweekly newsletter for party officials on internal affairs in the Soviet Union.

They were well aware of the suffering endured by the people of Ukraine, Belarus, and western Russia in the years since their incorporation into the Soviet Union.

In the early 1930s, peasant farms all across the Soviet Union had been confiscated, collectivized, and transformed into sprawling agricultural zones. The idea was to make the country's farms more efficient so surplus grain could be sold, thereby financing modernization throughout the nation.

The first step was to crack down on affluent farmers, the kulaks. The Soviets took aim at them with propaganda that would sound familiar in Nazi Germany: These men were rapacious apes, not humans. Nearly two million kulaks were arrested and deported to gulags. The brunt of this harsh Soviet agricultural policy fell disproportionately on the Ukrainians. Collectivization failed miserably; the anticipated grain surpluses did not materialize. Stalin stuck to the program even as five million peasants starved to death.

City dwellers waiting in breadlines were beset by begging children with swollen bellies—children who, paradoxically, had not been able to survive in the farmlands. Guards kept watch over the fields in towers to prevent theft. Anything grown on the collective fields was state property now, and harvesting a bit of it to feed yourself or your family amounted to a crime. When quotas were not met, authorities accused the peasants of sabotage, raided their homes, and seized all of their food. In many places, the populace resorted to cannibalism.

Ostentatiously ignoring the famine in the summer of 1932, Stalin traveled south by luxury train to a vacation in Sochi.

Five years later, during the Great Terror, the region suffered new shocks. Stalin ordered another vicious persecution of the kulaks, and this time targeted Poles and other ethnic minorities living in Soviet Ukraine and Belarus. These people were foreign spies intent on overthrowing the communist state, the dictator cried. "To the complete destruction of all our enemies, themselves and their kin!"

More than seventy thousand Ukrainians were executed in the kulak action, often by a bullet to the back of the head following secret hearings by troikas working at a feverish pace. Ethnic Poles in Ukraine and Belarus were picked up in black trucks and taken away by the tens of thousands. They ended up in the gulags, or the cemetery. Wives were exiled and children taken to orphanages to ensure that they were not brought up as Poles.

Amazingly, the killings prompted no international outcry. They were hardly noticed.

Now, in 1940, Hitler looked to the east and plotted yet another round of horrors for the people. Studying the maps, he saw a tabula rasa on which to construct a utopian thousand-year plan. Vast regions would be emptied of undesirables, by deporting them or shooting them or starving them or, it later turned out, by gassing them. Then loyal and pure Aryan Germans would resettle the land. The Reich would have access to all the grain and oil it needed for self-sufficiency. "The German colonist ought to live on handsome, spacious farms. The German services will be lodged in marvelous buildings, the governors in palaces," Hitler proclaimed. "What India was for England, the territories of Russia will be for us."

By March 1941, when Hitler called for Rosenberg, he had decided that after the armies pushed into the Soviet Union and decimated the forces in their way, authority would quickly be handed over to a new German political administration. The Führer gave Rosenberg the great responsibility of planning the political reconstruction of the occupied East. But Rosenberg arrived on the scene relatively late. Many important decisions already had been made, and from the very start his political plans took a backseat to the military and economic goals that had been under discussion for months.

Göring was to oversee the work of stripping the region of the raw materials needed to run war factories and, just as important, seizing food the Germans at home needed. Even in peacetime, the nation had to rely on food imports. Now the British Navy was stopping and searching ships bound for the Reich and aggressively confiscating essential supplies, raw materials, and foodstuffs—a blockade that threatened to cause debilitating shortages in Germany. Hitler feared becoming dependent on Stalin for food. What if the Soviets used that as leverage? What if they threatened the Germans with starvation, as they had the Ukrainians in 1932? Already, Germany was suffering shortages of bread, fruits, and vegetables, and meat rationing was on the horizon. Göring feared losing the home front on account of empty German stomachs.

This was the backdrop of a plan developed in the winter of 1940–1941 by Herbert Backe, state secretary in the Reich Ministry for Food and Agriculture, and seconded by General Georg Thomas, chief of the military's War Economy and Armaments Office. Germany's grain deficit could be solved, Thomas argued in a report shared with Hitler in February 1941, by taking it from Ukraine, the breadbasket of the Soviet Union.

Theoretically, according to his calculations, a small reduction in Soviet consumption would free up millions of tons of grain for the Germans. There was no reason to worry about the people who would be placed on thin rations, Backe wrote in a directive to his staff at the dawn of the invasion. They were "inferior," he argued, and in any case, "the Russian has stood poverty, hunger, and austerity for centuries. His stomach is flexible; hence, no false pity!"

A summary of the hunger plan drafted by Göring's economic planners in May made no such rationalizations. The people of the

Soviet Union would "face the most terrible famine" during the war. The Nazis would cordon off Moscow, Leningrad, and the other cities of the North from the food supply in the South. The invading armies would get first dibs on this nutrition. Whatever remained would be transported west to feed the people of Germany and occupied Europe. "Many tens of millions of people in this territory will become superfluous and will die or must emigrate to Siberia," read the report. Given the German food shortage, this was what it would take to win the war. "With regard to this, absolute clarity must reign."

The plan met no resistance from the military brass, who saw it as a key to their war strategy. They could move faster if they fed men off the land and freed up the rail lines to ship ammunition, fuel, and other supplies. As in Poland, speed was the key.

The Germans expected to be finished with the Red Army within ten weeks.

When he joined the planning team, Rosenberg—"this Nazi dolt with a positive genius for misunderstanding history," as foreign correspondent William Shirer would put it—began doing what he did best: writing memos.

He brought the first document to a private dinner with Hitler on April 2. The Führer wanted to talk away from the bustle of the office, so they ate in Hitler's dining room in the old Chancellery on Wilhelmstrasse, where he kept his personal residence. Then the two men retired next door to the conservatory, the Wintergarten, where the windows overlooked a grassy courtyard lined with trees.

In the plan he presented to Hitler, Rosenberg argued for ruthless treatment of greater Russia. The Nazis should destroy the "Jewish Bolshevik" government in Moscow and prevent a legitimate replacement. They should dismantle the nation's industry and tear up its transportation networks. They should lay waste to the land and use it "as a dumping ground for undesirable elements of the population."

Rosenberg had different ideas about how to handle the Baltics, Belarus, and Ukraine. He argued that here they needed to be smart. They had to think about the political considerations. After the war, they would need these allies to form a defensive cordon around Moscow.

Rosenberg suggested that the three Baltic states be incorporated into Germany after the "necessary removal" of the Latvian intelligentsia and the deportation of "racially inferior sections" of the Lithuanian people—a quarter of a million Jews lived there in 1941.

For Ukraine, Rosenberg supported cultural and political independence, but at the same time he argued that the region should be expected to provide all the raw materials and grain the Germans needed during and after the war.

Belarus was a hopeless case. Backward and populated by Jews, it could never be independent.

After Rosenberg outlined his thinking, Hitler took the memo to read later that night. "I want to set up an office for the entire Russian question, and you will be in charge," Hitler said. "Draw up comprehensive guidelines. Whatever money you need is at your disposal. Rosenberg, your great hour has now arrived."

The two men watched a newsreel together, then returned to the Wintergarten and spoke into the night about the psychology of the Russians and the role of the Jews in the Soviet Union. "There is no need for me to express my feelings at greater length," the starstruck Rosenberg wrote in his diary that evening when he returned home. "Twenty years of anti-Bolshevist work will now have their <u>political</u>, world-historical consequence. Millions . . . and their fate will be placed in my hands. Germany will be delivered for centuries from a burden that always, in various forms, weighed upon her. What does it matter if millions of <u>others</u> will curse the enforcement of this necessity, if only a future great <u>Germany</u> blesses these deeds in the future!"

Rosenberg also made one other enigmatic note about his evening in the Wintergarten. Hitler, he wrote, had spoken in great detail about his own vision for the East. Exactly what the Führer told him was sensitive enough that Rosenberg was loath to write about it, even in his private diary.

"I don't want to record [it] today," he wrote. "But I will never forget it."

One thing Hitler didn't tell Rosenberg, apparently, was that he had no intention of following his advice about the eastern territories.

"Greedily, childishly," one historian would write about Rosenberg during these years, "he stretched out his hands for power."

As the date of the invasion approached, it became clear that Rosenberg was not simply planning a civilian administration overseeing the East. Hitler had decided that, once the war began and the Germans had occupied the Soviet territories, the loyal Reichsleiter was going to run the new ministry. No one else seemed to think it was a good idea to hand Rosenberg the keys to the organization, particularly one that, on paper, looked omnipotent. As Goebbels wrote, Rosenberg could "only theorize . . . not organize."

Almost immediately, rivals threw up obstacles to Rosenberg's rule. None were as powerful and ruthless as Himmler, who had spent the previous year and a half brutalizing the Polish population. Hitler wanted to send the SS chief east behind the army to clear the newly conquered lands of Jews, communist leaders, partisans, and any other enemies, real or imagined. "The Reichsführer-SS is, on behalf of the Führer, entrusted with special tasks for the preparation of the political administration, tasks which result from the struggle which has to be carried out between two opposing political systems," read a military directive dated March 13, 1941. "Within the framework of these tasks, the Reichsführer-SS shall act independently and on his own authority."

On the strength of that directive, Himmler refused to put his police forces in the East under the authority of Rosenberg's new civilian ministry.

Rosenberg balked. "Then I cannot take over this assignment," he told Hans Lammers in April. Lammers, a bald lawyer with a wandering right eye, was the conduit for all official orders out of Hitler's Chancellery office. Already, Rosenberg complained, he had to share power with the military and with Göring's economic division. If Himmler had free rein as well, Rosenberg's ministry would be left with virtually no power.

"The police cannot possibly form a parallel government," Rosenberg raged to Lammers. "Their measures could possibly impede the political goals we seek to achieve."

Lammers agreed to talk it over with the SS chief the next morning. When the meeting dragged on and on, Rosenberg knew that Himmler had dug in and could not be moved. At a quarter after twelve, Lammers finally returned.

"Hopeless," Rosenberg wrote. "H. claimed that Göring would do everything, he had the free executive authority, and I would be involved in an advisory function. I did not work on a problem for twenty years in order to 'advise' Herr Himmler, who has never had a single idea about this matter, and who only through my work in the past fifteen years even knows anything about the Ukraine, etc. What his young people have bungled so far has certainly not been a glorious chapter."

Rosenberg stormed off to stew. At the beginning of 1941, he had purchased a small farm in Mondsee, Austria, "a glorious place in the middle of paradise," a country house with an orchard, livestock, some woods, and half a mile of waterfront on a picturesque lake just outside Salzburg. There he pondered his predicament. Once again, Himmler was "trying to seize things away." Himmler didn't want to work for anything; he just wanted to grab at more power. "In principle, he has enough big tasks, worthy of a life's work."

Rosenberg could see it play out before his eyes like a film: On the precipice of greatness, he could see himself falling short.

"I hope," he wrote, "this will end differently."

On May 2, Rosenberg hosted a key meeting with the high-level leaders in charge of the coming economic exploitation in the East. They discussed the consequences of the German plan in brutal detail: If the army took what it needed from the invaded territories, "undoubtedly x million people" would starve. These millions would include captured Soviet soldiers, for no provisions were made for them.

After the meeting broke up, Rosenberg wrote in his diary that it had been "good general staff work."

That day, he briefed Hitler, and the conversation spooled into a longer discussion about Rosenberg's mission. He thanked the Führer for his trust. Over the past month he had begun to feel alternately overwhelmed by and excited about the job. He was to oversee a region stretching from the Baltic to the Caspian Seas. Looking over the military maps, he was awed by the vast spaces that were to fall under his administration. The possibility for chaos was enormous. "The longer I think about the problems," Rosenberg said, "the bigger the task in front of me seems."

"But it is a great positive assignment that you are receiving," Hitler said. And in any case, he continued, "I must take responsibility for the step." As he said this, Hitler had tears in his eyes, Rosenberg recorded later in the diary.

On June 20, two days before Operation Barbarossa began, Rosenberg spoke to key government colleagues about the plan to break away the western reaches of the Soviet Union from Moscow and create territories allied with Germany. It would be important to create goodwill in the East and win over the people. "There is a difference as to whether after a few years I have won forty million people to voluntary cooperation, or whether I must place a soldier behind every peasant." At the same time, paradoxically, he endorsed the starvation policy: Feeding Germans would be the top priority during the war, Rosenberg said, and there would be no obligation to also feed the eastern people.

"We know that this is a harsh reality, bare of any feelings. A very extensive evacuation will be necessary without any doubt," he said, "and very hard years will certainly be in store for the Russian people."

Rosenberg was scheduled to meet with Rudolf Hess, Hitler's deputy Führer, on the evening of Saturday, May 10, 1941, to brief him about his new assignment. But the day before, a call came in from Hess's assistant. The meeting would have to be moved up to Saturday morning. The deputy Führer had to leave for something urgent.

The aide didn't elaborate, and Rosenberg didn't pick up the clues, but he would soon find out that this would be a momentous day in the life of Rudolf Hess. Rosenberg was about to be one of the last Nazi leaders to see Hess before the war was over.

It was too late for Rosenberg to take the train from Berlin, so instead Hess sent a plane to rush him to Munich for the meeting. When Hess greeted him at half past eleven in the morning, he looked "pale and sickly," though that was nothing out of the ordinary. Hess had been a slavish follower of Hitler from the start. For many years Hess held great sway in the party, but after the war began he could hardly get in to see Hitler. More and more, Hess's chief of staff, Martin Bormann, won the Führer's attention.

Rosenberg and Hess settled in to discuss personnel in the planned Eastern Ministry. But when Rosenberg tried to drill down into the details, Hess waved him off. He only wanted to talk about the most important things. His mind was too preoccupied to deal with anything minor.

Before lunch, Hess's three-year-old son came downstairs and they chatted a bit.

"Later it seemed obvious to me," Rosenberg would write, "he wanted to say farewell to his 'butz' who would henceforth and for the rest of his life have to carry the consequences of his father's deed."

Hess apparently didn't tell Rosenberg what was troubling him, but it seems he was terrified of the imminent two-front war. Like Rosenberg, he thought that Britain belonged in the Nazi camp. If he could make peace with Britain, then Hitler and Germany would be free to throw everything they had against the Soviets.

That evening, a few hours after his lunch with Rosenberg, the deputy Führer flew off from an airfield just outside Munich. He jumped out near Glasgow around 10:00 p.m., parachuting into a field while his Messerschmitt crashed in flames.

Encountering a farmhand on the ground, Hess demanded an audience with the Duke of Hamilton, a wing commander in the Royal Air Force, whom Hess claimed to have met during the 1936 Olympics. Hess told Hamilton that he had come to deliver a peace offer to the British. After further interrogation by other officials, the British realized that Hess had come without Hitler's knowledge, to urge them to lay down their arms before it was too late.

The man sounded delusional. They decided to hold him as a prisoner for the duration of the war.

The day after the flight, Hitler received a letter Hess had left behind. It outlined his plans and suggested that if the Führer objected to his wild gambit, he should dismiss Hess as an imbalanced lunatic. Hitler—who, according to Rosenberg, "felt nauseous" upon reading the letter from Hess—did just that.

On a Sunday night radio broadcast, the Nazis broke the news of the flight to the world, reporting that Hess suffered from a mental illness.

Rosenberg was as stunned as anyone in the party. He had not seen it coming, even over lunch with the man on the very day of his incredible journey. "It was _so_ fantastic, so far outside the realm of political possibilities, that we were speechless at first,"

Rosenberg wrote in his diary. "But I thought Hess had been suffering from depression. He practically had had nothing to do, the party had slipped from his leadership, he had felt that he was not able to measure up to his position. . . . The depression about not accomplishing anything had manifested itself in an utterly unexpected fashion. . . . Hess had been living in an unreal world. His love for pendulum dowsers, astrologists, healers, etc., apparently was rooted so deeply already that they had been determining his <u>actions</u>. . . . This otherworldly fantasy of Rudolf Hess will someday be the basis for a future playwright's historical tragicomedy."

He thought there was a bit of good news in the disappearance of Hess from the scene. No longer would the Third Reich face the unpleasant prospect of being led in the future by "a deeply sickened man."

But Rosenberg did not foresee the trouble ahead. Replacing Hess was his hated chief of staff, the bullnecked "Machiavelli of the office desk," Martin Bormann. He had been seen as the real power in the party even before his nominal boss flew off. Quiet and serious, the archetypal behind-the-scenes operator, Bormann seemed to be always by Hitler's side. "Hess had obviously gotten on the Führer's nerves, and so Bormann took care of requests and assignments," Rosenberg would write in his prison memoir after the war. "Here is where he began to make himself indispensable. If, during our dinner conversation, some incident was mentioned, Bormann would pull out his notebook and make an entry. Or else, if the Führer expressed displeasure over some remark, some measure, some film, Bormann would make a note. If something seemed unclear, Bormann would get up, leave the room, but return almost immediately—after having given orders to his office staff to investigate forthwith, and to telephone, wire, or teletype. Then it might happen that before dinner was over Bormann had an explanation at hand."

In time, Bormann would become the chief obstacle to Rosenberg's advancement.

Plans for the occupation of the Soviet Union continued apace. Rosenberg, Goebbels wrote in his diary, was already acting as if he were "the Czar of Russia; always the same thing: spheres of authority." Himmler was still doing everything he could to keep Rosenberg at bay, but on Göring's explicit orders, Heydrich, the chief of Himmler's security apparatus and the man delegated to find a final solution to the Jewish question, had been instructed to involve Rosenberg's ministry when necessary.

In the months before Operation Barbarossa, Heydrich tried to work out an arrangement between Himmler and Rosenberg. Why not recommend that Hitler appoint Himmler's higher SS and police leaders to be the Reichskommissars leading Rosenberg's civilian administrations in each of the occupied territories? Such "personal unions" were common in the Third Reich. An official held positions in two agencies, which could foster cooperation or could just as easily lead to intractable conflicts of interest. In this case, it would make Himmler the de facto leader of Rosenberg's ministry.

"It would mean political leadership by police officers!" Rosenberg cried, turning him down. He countered with a suggestion that Himmler appoint an SS-Führer in Rosenberg's office, subordinate to the minister. The matter was still unresolved a few days later, when he wrote to Himmler to see if they could work together. "I am keen on his reaction."

His letter did not change Himmler's mind. Rosenberg was asking him to submit reports about his preparations for the work in the East. He also wanted to approve personnel that Himmler planned to appoint in the occupied territories. To the Reichsführer-SS, this was all too much. Himmler urged Bormann to put a stop to Rosenberg's interference. "The Führer told me . . .

that in my tasks I am not to be subordinate to Rosenberg," he wrote to Bormann. "The manner in which Rosenberg approaches this question once again makes it endlessly difficult to work with him, man to man. . . . To work with, let alone under, Rosenberg is surely the most difficult thing in the Nazi Party." In June, Bormann pressed Himmler's argument with Lammers: "Especially in the first weeks and months, in the carrying out of their really difficult task, the police must under all circumstances be kept free of all obstacles that could arise out of disputes over jurisdiction."

But the dispute raged on. Himmler even began arguing that he shouldn't just have police power—he ought to be in charge of political affairs in the occupied territories as well.

This, Rosenberg said, would be "completely unbearable," a recipe for "unparalleled chaos."

The matter remained unresolved when the Germans began their assault on the Soviet Union in the early-morning hours of June 22, 1941.

The Soviets were taken entirely by surprise. Stalin didn't believe the first reports of artillery fire across the thousand-mile front stretching from Finland to the Black Sea. It was the biggest invasion army in history: three and a half million soldiers in more than half a million trucks and tanks, supported by seven hundred thousand artillery guns and nearly three thousand planes. The Germans raced across the Baltic states and Ukraine, the Red Army disintegrating before their very eyes. Soldiers died in head-on clashes or retreated or deserted into the woods or surrendered en masse. Within days, the German generals were already declaring victory. In Moscow, Stalin was not in a position to disagree. At the end of June, he left the Kremlin for his dacha in Kuntsevo, just outside the city, telling his aides, "Everything's lost."

Hundreds of thousands of soldiers—eventually it would be

millions—were taken prisoner by German forces who had no plan for interning them, and in fact no intention of trying to keep them alive. Commissars of the Communist Party were shot on Hitler's orders. Surrendering Soviet troops were marched in ragged processions, beaten with clubs, and forced to scrap for food on their way to German prisoner-of-war camps, which, in the fall of 1941, were often merely open fields encircled by barbed wire. "They looked like starved animals, not like people," one witness wrote in a diary published after the war. If the railways were used, the Soviets were crammed inside open cattle cars until there was standing room only.

In many camps, soldiers had no choice but to relieve themselves in the huddled crowd. At one, the headquarters caught fire, and those who were not immolated were shot trying to flee. At another, inmates asked to be put out of their misery. German guards reported cannibalism. By the end of the year, the death toll in the camps stood at three hundred thousand. More than three million Soviet prisoners would perish before the war ended.

History was cruel, Rosenberg wrote as the war progressed. The Russians had killed and banished ethnic Germans by the hundreds of thousands, he argued, and "for these murders, the Russian nation as a whole will thus have to pay." The people were to blame, he rationalized: They should never have allowed the communists to take power.

The Russian people, in other words, were like inmates who had made peace with the guards—and instead fought the very people who would liberate them.

Three weeks after the invasion, in the middle of July, the bureaucratic battle for control over the newly occupied territories came to a head. Hitler was triumphant. Germany was on its way to taking an enormous chunk of the Soviet Union, and now it was time to discuss how to implement the sweeping reconstruction of the region. After a small lunch and beers, the top men in the Third Reich convened for a long meeting at Wolfsschanze, Hitler's "Wolf's Lair" in East Prussia. Rosenberg was there, along with Göring, Bormann, Lammers, and Wilhelm Keitel, chief of the armed forces.

The Germans, Hitler declared, were entering the Soviet Union as liberators. Or at least that was what they should tell the people. As for Germany's real plans, the Führer ordered strict secrecy. Nobody could see—yet—that they were preparing "a final settlement." What really mattered was that the German leaders were all in agreement about the necessary measures: "shooting, resettlement, etc." Everyone needed to understand something, Hitler said: "We shall never leave these regions."

"We now have to face the task," Hitler told them, "of cutting up the cake according to our needs, in order to be able: first, to dominate it, second, to administer it, and third, to exploit it."

The men looked at maps as Hitler carved up the new territory. Leningrad would be "razed to the ground." What was left would go to the Finns, who, upset at losing part of their land in a brief, bloody war with the Soviets in 1939–1940, had sided with Germany during Operation Barbarossa to get it back. East Prussia would get Bialystok. The Baltic states would become a part of the Reich. The Crimea would be cleared and resettled with ethnic Germans.

Hitler was receiving reports that ununiformed Soviet partisans were already beginning to fight the Germans behind the front lines, but he was not alarmed. These pitiful attempts at resistance would give the Nazis the perfect cover, Hitler said. "It enables us to eradicate everyone who opposes us."

The Führer also wondered: Should the Germans have armored cars?

Unnecessary, Göring replied. If the people were so foolish as to riot, the Luftwaffe could simply bomb them into submission.

"Naturally," read the minutes of the meeting, which were drafted by Bormann, "this giant area would have to be pacified as quickly as possible; the best solution was to shoot anybody who looked sideways."

In the midst of this, Rosenberg continued his twisted argument for trying to win over the hearts and minds of at least some of the conquered people, but Göring interrupted Rosenberg's monologue. The war machine needed raw materials and the German people needed food. He didn't have time to worry about building future alliances.

It got worse for Rosenberg as the men began to discuss the practical matters at hand: the appointment of the Reichskommissars, Rosenberg's deputies in the East. Rosenberg wanted an ally in the all-important Ukraine. Instead, Hitler overruled him and appointed a party leader named Erich Koch. Rosenberg protested the decision. He feared that Koch, whose brutal, unvarnished pragmatism had led his supporters in Berlin to label him a "second Stalin," would never follow orders. But Hitler waved him off. "All decrees are just theory," he said. "If they don't conform to the necessities, they need to be changed." Hitler did accept Rosenberg's recommendation of Hinrich Lohse to lead the Baltic states and Belarus.

When the meeting ended, Rosenberg shook Göring's hand. "Here's to good cooperation," the Reichsmarschall said.

But Rosenberg could see looming battles ahead.

Himmler did not attend the meeting. He had already worked out his powers in the eastern territories.

In June, Himmler had argued that because Hitler had put him in charge of resettling ethnic Germans in the newly occupied territories, he should be given expansive authority "pacifying and consolidating the political situation" in the East. Two days after the invasion, Himmler even asked an aide to draw up his own general plan for the reconstruction of the East.

Rosenberg vociferously objected to this blatant trampling on his territory, and he seemed to win the fight—but only on paper. Himmler did not secure explicit political authority over the territories, but he did get the freedom to operate independently on Rosenberg's turf. The Reichskommissars would take orders not only from Rosenberg, their nominal superior, but also, when police matters were involved, from Himmler. If there was an emergency, Himmler didn't even need to inform Rosenberg of these orders to his Reichskommissars. SS and police leaders were assigned to the civilian administrators at all levels, but they, too, took orders from Himmler, not ministry officials.

Geography also amplified Himmler's power: Rosenberg decided to work not out in the field but in Berlin, while the Reichsführer-SS roamed about the occupied territories, monitoring developments and issuing orders. On the ground, he would have all the leeway he could possibly want.

For the new Reich minister, it was not the victory he had hoped for. How was it that, three and a half months after his triumphant meeting with Hitler, he had been left with a department primed for disaster? What had Hitler been thinking? Did he consider the ministry a massive cover for the exploitation and murder that would go on behind the scenes, a fig leaf of German regulatory order? Historians would grapple with those questions for decades and never come up with a satisfactory answer. Hitler's bureaucratic decision making did not always make sense.

Backroom intrigue may have played a part in the appointment. Rosenberg, surprisingly, had won Bormann's support. Bormann loathed Rosenberg, but at the dawn of the occupation, he saw in him a minister he could control, or at least ignore. He quietly and forcefully pushed Rosenberg for the position, though not for the full and unhindered powers Rosenberg wanted.

"I had been assigned a gigantic task," Rosenberg wrote in his diary three days after Hitler signed the order appointing him to lead the Ostministerium—the ministry for the occupied eastern territories—"possibly the greatest the Reich could ever assign, the protection of European independence for centuries." Rosenberg wished Hitler had given him "full authority for this task," but he did not intend to simply surrender to his internal enemies.

He had a central government ministry at his command, and he planned to make the most of it.

Over the next three years, as the Nazis began to deliver on the anti-Semitic threats that had, in large part, grown out of his angry screeds—threats that he himself had given chilling clarity to in his radio speech that March when he called for a "cleansing biological world revolution"—Rosenberg would make sure that his ministry had the chance to do its part.

A man from one of the Einsatzgruppen killing units prepares to shoot a Ukrainian Jew at the edge of a pit in Vinnitsa, Ukraine. *(U.S. Holocaust Memorial Museum, courtesy of Sharon Paquette)*

18

"Special Tasks"

Everybody at the tables in the Reich Chancellery dining room for Hitler's standing lunch seemed to be in the most cheerful of spirits. Rosenberg was there, alongside Bormann, Hess, and Lammers. It was January 1940, a year and a half before Operation Barbarossa, and the Nazi leaders discussed the usual weighty matters: the war with England and the progress of the racial cleansing in Poland. But eventually the conversation devolved into black humor.

Talk turned to the Jews, and Rosenberg prophesied "a terrible Jewish pogrom" if the people of the Soviet Union were to awake and unleash their anti-Semitic fury.

At this, Hitler chimed in.

If massacres did break out in the Soviet Union, the Führer said with a smile, maybe Europe would ask *him* to sweep in and protect the eastern Jews.

The assembled Nazis roared with laughter.

And, Hitler continued over the hooting—*and* perhaps he and Rosenberg could organize a special congress to discuss the burning question of the times: the "humane treatment of the Jews."

During the radio address at the opening of the Institute for Research on the Jewish Question in March, Rosenberg said that the Jewish question would not be solved until the last Jew had left Europe. It would fall to Himmler and Heydrich, the chief of Himmler's Reich Security Main Office, to turn those words into practical action.

At the beginning of 1941, the prevailing thinking among Nazi planners was that the Jews would be deported to some distant and desolate land. Madagascar, the French colony five thousand miles away off the coast of Africa, had been considered and rejected as logistically impractical. Operation Barbarossa seemed to offer a more viable location for this Jewish reservation: in the territories of a soon-to-be-defeated Soviet Union. But before the end of the year, the invasion had stalled, and Nazi thinking on the Jewish question had taken a radical turn. Complete extermination would be in the works.

The Jews of the Baltics, Belarus, and Ukraine would be the first victims of this deadly shift in Nazi policy, and Rosenberg and his civil administration would play an important supporting role in the killings.

During Operation Barbarossa, a fundamental misunderstanding of Rosenberg's now became an essential part of the German strategy in the East. All the way back in 1919, he had argued that the Jews were behind the communist movements in the Soviet Union and elsewhere, an idea exaggerated and twisted out of shape until it came to be understood that, in fact, *all* Jews were communists—that to defeat the Red menace, the Germans needed to eliminate the Jews.

Hitler bought into that wrongheaded conclusion, and in the run-up to the invasion, it became an essential part of the basic instructions handed down to the Germans storming into the East. They were told that this would be no ordinary war. This would be a clash of two irreconcilable worldviews, between Nazism and Bolshevism, between the Aryans and the Jews. In speeches to military commanders before the invasion, Hitler urged them to use "force of the most brutal kind" in this "battle of annihilation." Guidelines issued to the German soldiers declared the Soviets to be nothing less than mortal enemies. "This fight requires ruthless and energetic measures against Bolshevist agitators, irregulars, saboteurs, Jews and the total elimination of all forms of resistance, active and passive."

Much the same message was delivered to the SS, police units, and Einsatzgruppen under Himmler, who would sweep in behind the army and "pacify" the territories. These were, in the cold, coded language of the 1941 military directive, the "special tasks" that Hitler had given the Reichsführer-SS.

In the early days of the war, as the Einsatzgruppen were let loose in the East, Heydrich issued instructions that gave his men great latitude in deciding who should be executed: communists, Jews in the party or the government, and "other radical elements (saboteurs, propagandists, snipers, assassins, agitators, etc.)." Himmler told a band of SS soldiers departing for the front lines that they would be dealing with "a population of 180 million, a mixture of races, whose very names are unpronounceable, and whose physique is such that one can shoot them down without pity and compassion. . . . These people have been welded by the Jews into one religion, one ideology, that is called Bolshevism."

At first, the victims of Himmler's Einsatzgruppen and security forces were men. The pretense was that the Nazis were shooting Resistance fighters and Soviet agents and communist agitators and the Jewish intelligentsia. The victims were accused of looting or sabotage or spreading propaganda or carrying the plague.

But almost immediately, the Nazis expanded their killing

operations to include women and children and began systematically murdering civilians by the hundreds of thousands in the
newly occupied territories.

Typically, the Jews would be gathered in a central square and
marched to some isolated location outside town. If mass graves
had not yet been excavated, the first to arrive would be ordered
to dig them. The victims would be shot at the lip of the pit, or
as they lay on the bodies of those murdered before them. Some
would still be breathing when their bodies were covered with
dirt.

The largest killing operation took place in the outskirts of
Kiev, Ukraine, in late September 1941, after bombs and mines set
by the Russian Resistance had destroyed the headquarters of the
German occupation authorities. Furious, the Nazis blamed the
Soviet secret police and, by extension, Kiev's Jews. Posters
appeared all around the city ordering them to turn out at a specific
intersection on September 29. They were to bring their papers and
their money, their luggage and their jewelry, because they were to
be resettled. The following day was Yom Kippur, the Jewish Day
of Atonement.

Arriving, the Jews found no resettlement train. Instead they
were marched toward a checkpoint outside the Jewish cemetery.
Before long, those in line knew what was happening. They could
hear gunshots in the distance.

At the checkpoint, they handed over their belongings, down to
their wedding rings and their clothing. In groups of ten they were
harried and pummeled as they made their way to a ravine by the
name of Babi Yar. In all, 33,761 people were shot over the coming
days. "Since the bodies were later exhumed and burned on pyres,
and the bones that did not burn crushed and mixed with sand,"
historian Timothy Snyder wrote, "the count is what remains."

Babi Yar was only one in a series of mass killings in the second
half of 1941. In August, more than twenty-three thousand foreign Jews deported from Hungary—mostly Russians and Poles—

were massacred in Kamenets-Podolsk, a city in western Ukraine. In October, another ten thousand were shot dead in Dnipropetrovsk. In the meantime, Jews disappeared in smaller actions in towns and villages from the Baltics to the Black Sea.

Back in Berlin, Rosenberg received regular reports about which cities in his vast territory had been declared *Judenfrei*, "free of Jews."

Not only cities but entire countries: Rosenberg's homeland, Estonia, was the first. All fifteen hundred of its Jews were eliminated. In September, Rosenberg welcomed reports from a pair of ministry officials returning from a tour of Latvia and Estonia. They told him that the people there—those who had survived the Nazi onslaught—were happy to have been liberated following the brutal Soviet occupation of the Baltic states in 1940–1941, during which thousands of Estonians, Latvians, and Lithuanians were executed or deported.

"Not only were the Jews poisoning their minds, they themselves were divided," he wrote in his diary after the discussion. "They had experienced such horrible things that the German master was a salvation for them. Now that both the Jews and communists have been eradicated, the people are coming alive again."

In many places, the Nazi killing operations were complicated by the fact that the Germans wanted to employ Jews as forced laborers in factories, shops, and construction projects. Those Jews "fit to work" found themselves temporarily spared, living in horrific limbo while they watched the police drag their neighbors away to their deaths.

Minsk, the capital of Belarus, was a case in point. The city fell six days into the war. In early July, all men younger than forty-five were rounded up and taken to a camp established in an open field. More than 140,000 prisoners of war and civilians were crammed into an area the size of a city square. Food and water were limited. The men were beaten with rubber truncheons and shot on the slimmest of pretexts. Rosenberg received a dispatch about the camp conditions in July. "The limited guard force, which bears the burden of guarding without being replaced for days, turns to the prisoners in the only possible language, and that is the language of weapons, and they do this mercilessly." After a while they were separated by nationality and race, and the Russians and Poles were released. The Jews were not.

One morning, the guards asked all educated Jews—engineers, doctors, accountants—to register for work. Two days later, they were pulled out of the camp and shot. The men left behind were marched back to the city, moved into a ghetto along with the rest of the city's Jews, and put to work for the occupation. With a population of at least seventy thousand, the Minsk ghetto was the largest in the occupied Soviet Union.

The Jews starved on nettles and potato peels, and lived in terror. "Suddenly, the Gestapo swoop down on the ghetto in trucks and begin seizing men," wrote Mikhail Grichanik, a tailor who worked at a garment factory in Minsk and spent several months in the ghetto before escaping; the Nazis executed his mother, his wife, his three children, and three other relatives. "They go into apartments, beat people with rubber truncheons and lead them out under the guise of sending them off to work: to the peat bogs and such places. No one ever saw any of those taken away alive again." Einsatzgruppen reports documented this phenomenon with precise statistical accuracy: August 16—615 executions. August 31 and September 1—1,914. September 4—214. September 23—2,278.

In September, the patriarch of the Kovarsky family reportedly watched, hidden with one of his sons, while the police stormed into his home and murdered his other two boys, both of his daughters, and their grandmother. The oldest girl was first ordered to take off her clothes and dance for them on a table.

Black vans, their windows covered, began patrolling the streets at night, picking up Jews, partisans, stray children. Those in the ghetto discovered, to their horror, that the vehicles were an experiment in gassing victims: They were outfitted so that the engine exhaust was redirected into the locked rear cargo area, asphyxiating the passengers. The Jews called them "soul destroyers."

On November 7, 1941, the police rousted the entire population of the Minsk ghetto out onto the street. "The howls of mortal fear and horror, the cries of desperation, the weeping of children, and the sobbing of women . . . could be heard throughout the city," recalled a teacher who survived the bloodshed, Sofia Ozerskaya. The date was symbolic: It was the day the Soviets celebrated the communist revolution. Staging a derisively festive mock celebration, the Nazis ordered some of the Jews to don their finest clothes and then, led by a man hoisting a red banner, march through the streets singing patriotic songs. When the parade was over, all the Jews were pushed into trucks and driven off to a nearby camp, where they were herded into granaries to await the end. Over the next few days, they were dragged out to trenches and, one by one by one, shot down. The operation killed twelve thousand people.

Two weeks later, another seven thousand were rounded up and shot. A Jewish barber named Levin, known to some of the Nazi officers and protected as a skilled laborer, frantically begged the commander to also spare his wife and daughter. Instead the German agreed to save one or the other; the man would have to choose.

"Levin took his daughter," reported Grichanik, the tailor. "When the workers were brought to the factory, they were as white as paper and could not say anything."

The Germans would rule Minsk for nearly three more years.

Amid the ongoing massacres by Himmler's men, two of Rosenberg's planned seven civil administrations set up operations in newly occupied territories: Ukraine under Erich Koch, and the Ostland, encompassing the Baltic states and part of Belarus, under Hinrich Lohse.

At the end of July 1941, Lohse was dispatched to Kaunas, Lithuania, following conversations with officials in Berlin, including Hitler himself. There, Rosenberg's man met twice with Himmler and was briefed on the decimation of the Jews, already well under way. In July, fifteen thousand Jews around the country were arrested, driven to the outskirts of town, gunned down, and then buried in mass graves. The Einsatzgruppen were assisted by thousands of Lithuanian volunteers. On August 1, Lohse returned to Berlin and reported his findings to Rosenberg and other high-level leaders in the eastern ministry. Describing the massacres of the Jews in Lithuania—he put the number at ten thousand, and said the victims perished at the hands of "the Lithuanian population"—Lohse said the killings went on night after night. "According to the decision of the Führer," he said, "the Jews should be totally removed from this area."

The day after the meeting, Lohse moved to coordinate Jewish policy with the SS leader in his territory. He followed guidelines Rosenberg had issued while mapping out the political administration of the East in the spring: "forced labor for the Jews, creation of ghettos, etc.," as "a temporary solution" to the Jewish question. Under Lohse's more detailed regulations, Jews would be "cleansed" from the countryside. They were not allowed to move without permission; they could be arrested at any time, "in case of necessity"; they were to wear the yellow star; they were barred from using sidewalks, cars, or public transportation; they could not go to theaters, libraries, museums, pools, playgrounds, or athletic fields; their property was to be seized.

Harsh as these steps sounded, they were not quite severe enough for the SS, who bristled at this encroachment onto their turf.

Franz Walter Stahlecker, the commander of the Einsatzgruppen A killing unit in the Ostland, pushed back. Lohse was ignoring the fact that, for the very first time, a "radical treatment of the Jewish question" was now possible, Stahlecker wrote. He called for a meeting to talk about the matter further, because Lohse's guidelines involved "general orders from a higher authority . . . which cannot be discussed in writing."

In reply, Lohse revised the order to stress that the restrictions he'd outlined were only "provisional . . . minimum measures," and that civil administrators were not to interfere with the work of Himmler's security forces. After the edict was issued, Stahlecker wrote to his Einsatzgruppen officers and reassured them that the SS had Lohse's full support as they pursued their deadly solution to the Jewish question.

Stahlecker was right. This dispute, like many others that would erupt between the SS and the eastern ministry throughout 1941 and 1942, was largely over jurisdiction. The issue was whether Jewish policy in the eastern territories ought to be a police matter handled by the Reichsführer-SS or a political affair overseen by the Reich minister. Rosenberg had not given up in his fight to make his ministry the ultimate authority in the East. One of his aides, Otto Bräutigam, thought that unwise. When it came to the Jewish question, he said, he "did not regard it as undesirable to emphasize the jurisdiction of the SS and Police Leaders."

But in 1941, as Himmler's forces murdered the Jews in his empire, Rosenberg did not want to be cut out of the action.

In September 1941, Rosenberg set in motion a fateful step. Berlin learned that Stalin had uprooted six hundred thousand ethnic Germans living along the Volga River and shipped them in cattle wagons to Siberia and Kazakhstan. "Hatred of Moscow surged again in all of us, more than ever," Rosenberg wrote in his diary. Deportation, he wrote, meant murder. "I gave instructions for a very sharp statement and sent the wording of the draft to the Führer. Who gave it an even sharper edge. Yesterday I had someone prepare a proposal for broadcasting a radio message to Russia, England, and the USA, stating that if this mass murder were to be carried out, Germany would make the Jews of central Europe suffer for it." In his memorandum, Rosenberg recommended that Hitler retaliate by immediately deporting "all the Jews of central Europe" to the East.

Hitler had resisted calls to begin the expulsion of the Jews. He had planned to do it following the victory over the Soviets in what he expected to be a brief and lopsided war. But Stalin's armies had survived the shock of the early blows, and three months after the invasion it had become clear in Berlin that Moscow was not going to simply collapse and surrender anytime soon.

After a round of discussions with Ribbentrop and Himmler, Hitler decided that Germany could no longer wait, and on September 17, he ordered the SS chief to set the deportations of German, Austrian, and Czech Jews into motion.

Goebbels was thrilled: In the East, he had written in his diary a month earlier, the Jews would be "dealt with under harsh circumstances."

When officials in the Ostland learned that thousands of Jews were to be deported to their territory and that new concentration camps were to be constructed in Riga and Minsk, they were not pleased. Word eventually came back from Rosenberg's ministry not to worry—it would be a temporary affair, and then the Jews would be gone. Rosenberg's adviser on race matters, Erhard Wetzel, drafted a reply to Lohse in which he raised the idea of building a "gassing apparatus" in Riga, Latvia, to deal with those deportees who were "not fit for work." Viktor Brack had helped run a program in which tens of thousands of mentally ill Germans were euthanized, many of them with lethal gas. Brack was more than happy to send his technicians to Riga to develop a facility to deal with Lohse's Jews.

There is no evidence the letter went out, and nothing came of the proposal—the death camps were built in occupied Poland—but what is notable is the admission that Rosenberg's ministry had "no objection if those Jews who are not fit for work were removed with Brack's aids."

.   .   .

On October 4, Heydrich met with leaders of Rosenberg's ministry and pressed for cooperation. He didn't want to argue, he told them, and in any case, "the implementation of the treatment of the Jews lies in every respect in the hands of the Security Police." But in the fall of 1941, civil administrators under Lohse began to raise objections to some of the killings by Himmler's rampaging security forces.

The major point of contention was not the murders themselves. No Nazi wanted to appear soft on the Jews. Rather, civilian officials objected because they had not been consulted ahead of time, or because massacres conducted in broad daylight destabilized their cities, or because they wanted some of the Jews exempted for forced labor.

One of Lohse's district leaders, Heinrich Carl, reported that at eight in the morning on October 27, an officer with a police battalion had appeared in Slutsk, Belarus, and announced that his unit was ordered to liquidate every Jew in the city. In a memo that made its way up the chain of command to Lohse, Carl protested that he had received no notice, and besides, some of the Jews were craftsmen: tanners, carpenters, blacksmiths. If the Jews were executed, the factories in the city would have to be shut down immediately. But the police commander told Carl that he had orders "to clear the whole town of Jews without exception."

The gunmen went to work with an "indescribable brutality" bordering on "sadism." They began dragging Jews out of their workplaces, putting them on trucks, and shooting them outside the city. People were beaten with rubber clubs and rifle butts. "Everywhere in the town shots were to be heard," Carl wrote in the memo, "and in different streets the corpses of shot Jews accumulated."

Some Jews were buried alive. One girl dashed about town, trying to raise money to save her father's life.

The police stripped the watches and rings off the victims and looted homes for boots, leather, gold, and whatever else they could carry. The non-Jews in the town were "dumbfounded," he wrote. "It will take a long time until we shall regain the confidence of the population which we have lost."

Around the same time, another district leader reported that killings in Liepaja, a city on the Baltic Sea in Latvia, had caused major disturbances. "Even the officers ask me if it was necessary to liquidate children." Lohse moved to block further executions in the city. He also objected to a plan to liquidate the ghetto in Riga, after which Himmler quickly sent a messenger to tell him not to interfere: "Tell Lohse it is my order, which also reflects the Führer's wish."

The SS lodged a protest with Rosenberg's ministry, which asked Lohse to explain his actions.

"I have forbidden the wild executions of Jews in Liepaja because the manner in which they were carried out was not justifiable," Lohse replied. "I should like to be informed whether your inquiry of 31 October is to be regarded as a directive to liquidate all Jews in the East?" Lohse had no particular qualms about killing Jews, but he needed these particular Jews. "Of course the cleansing of the East of Jews is a necessary task; its solution, however, must be harmonized with the necessities of war production." The Reichskommissar did not want to lose a valuable source of labor until replacements could be trained.

Rosenberg's ministry sent a cryptic reply in December. Discussions in Berlin had settled the matter. "Clarification of the Jewish question has most likely been achieved by now through verbal discussions," the letter read. "Economic considerations should fundamentally remain unconsidered in the settlement of the problem." Lohse could consult the SS if he had questions.

Apparently, he didn't. He dropped the matter.

Those discussions in Berlin clarifying the Jewish question came in mid-November 1941 with a meeting between Rosenberg and

Himmler. On November 15, a Saturday, the two leaders ate lunch together at 2:00 p.m. and afterward spoke for four hours about the disputes between Rosenberg's political leaders and Himmler's security forces.

It is unknown whether Himmler spoke to Rosenberg in detail about his increasingly radical plans to escalate the liquidation of the Jews in Europe. Himmler had been casting about for more efficient methods of murder since witnessing a massacre in Minsk in August. Shaken, he decided that shooting Jews by the thousands was too difficult on the killers' psyches. Even as he met with Rosenberg in November, construction was under way on the first full-fledged gas chamber, at a camp in Belzec, southeastern Poland.

The best measure of what Himmler told Rosenberg is that, three days after the meeting, Rosenberg gave an address in which he spoke of the "biological eradication" of the Jews.

On Tuesday, November 18, representatives of the German press were invited to an afternoon news conference at the headquarters of Rosenberg's eastern ministry, a large limestone-clad building located on the southwest edge of Berlin's Tiergarten. This was Rosenberg's official introduction as minister for the occupied eastern territories. His appointment had just been announced publicly, because Hitler had thought it wise to keep the planned occupation authority a closely held secret during the early months of Operation Barbarossa.

Wearing a striped suit with a Nazi Party pin on the lapel, Rosenberg told the assembled loyal German journalists, who in the Third Reich operated under the purview of the propaganda minister, that he had called the meeting because he wanted them to understand what was happening in the East. But they could not write about it, at least not explicitly. It was merely a background briefing; everything he was about to say was strictly confidential.

His remarks were not reported in the press, but a copy of the speech was found among his papers after the war. After speaking about the plans to break up the Soviet Union forever and exploit its natural resources, Rosenberg turned to the Jewish question.

"In the east," Rosenberg told them, "some six million Jews still live, and this question can only be solved in a biological eradication of the entire Jewry of Europe. The Jewish question is solved for Germany only when the last Jew has left German territory, and for Europe when not a single Jew lives on the European continent up to the Urals. This is the task that fate has assigned us." He remembered Germany's surrender on November 9, 1918, as "a day of fate and decision. At that time, Jewry showed it was intent on the destruction of Germany. Thanks only to the Führer and the strength of character of the German nation, they did not succeed." But as long as Jews lived on the continent, the danger remained that sympathetic Europeans would allow them to thrive again. That was why it was necessary to banish them all. That was why it was necessary "to expel them over the Urals or eradicate them in some other way."

He couldn't have been more clear. Deportation to the East had become a euphemism. By the end of 1941, it meant death.

The technical objections that Lohse and other civil administrators raised in October and November were exceptions to the rule. From Rosenberg on down, the administrators in the eastern ministry endorsed the killings, cooperated with Himmler's police forces, and smoothed the path to murder.

They drew up lists of Jewish properties. They helped round up the victims. They went along to witness the carnage; some of them actually took part in the shootings.

At the end of November, after being told that Himmler, and by extension, the Führer, had ordered the liquidation of the Riga ghetto, Lohse watched without objection while Himmler's men and Latvian police marched fourteen thousand people into Rumbula Forest six miles outside town. There they were joined by the surviving passengers from one of the first transports of Berlin Jews to the East; many of the deportees had frozen to death en route. The victims took off their clothes, lay down in trenches, and were shot. The graves were covered with dirt and the earth tamped down with a steamroller.

In December 1941, Karl Jäger, Himmler's Einsatzcommando leader in Lithuania, wrote a blunt accounting of his work in the territory since the summer. "There are no longer any Jews in Lithuania," he reported, "except the working Jews and their families," those who had been saved as forced laborers. Jäger counted about 35,000 survivors out of a pre-occupation population of more than 250,000.

If not for the petty economic objections, he added, he would have happily killed them, too.

By the end of the year, 70 percent of Lithuania's Jews—177,000 people—were dead. Almost all of them had been killed *after* Lohse arrived. In Latvia, about 90 percent of the country's 75,000 Jews had perished. Across the entire East, as many as 800,000 Jewish civilians were already dead.

In the meantime, Catholic priests were attacking the Nazis anew in speeches and in print in the second half of 1941, and Hitler was not pleased. "It appears," he told Rosenberg, "that some of the shavelings"—a term of disparagement, referring to clergymen who shaved their heads in an outward display of religious devotion—"seem to have a headache. They can only be relieved of it by having their heads removed."

"Apparently," Rosenberg added in his diary, "these gentlemen still didn't know him well."

The priestly protests had to do with a different sort of mass killing operation than the one under way in the East: a secret Nazi program to euthanize disabled children and adults, known as T4 after the address of its Berlin headquarters, Tiergartenstrasse 4. Hitler launched the program in 1939 as part of the Nazi effort to engineer a pure Aryan race. Word of the program spread after institutions were asked to fill out questionnaires about their patients. Many victims were in the care of church-run organizations, and though religious leaders were alarmed and quietly lobbied against the killings, they did not publicly campaign for the end of the program, fearing that the Nazis would retaliate against them.

But on August 3, 1941, the bishop of Münster, Clemens von Galen, finally decided to denounce the killings from the pulpit. "I am reliably informed," he told the parishioners at St. Lambert's Church, "that in hospitals and homes in the province of Westphalia, lists are being prepared of inmates who are classified as 'unproductive members of the national community,' and are to be removed from these establishments and shortly thereafter killed. The first party of patients left the mental hospital at Marienthal, near Münster, in the course of this week." Soon, he said, the victims' ashes would be sent back to the next of kin with word that their loved ones had died of natural causes.

This was murder, von Galen said. Human beings were dying because they were no longer "productive" in the opinion of the Nazi hierarchy. If such a twisted principle was to stand, "then woe betide all of us when we become aged and infirm . . . woe betide the disabled . . . woe betide our brave soldiers who return home with major disabilities, as cripples, as invalids!" Under such a policy, the bishop continued, "no man will be safe: some committee or other will be able to put him on the list of 'unproductive' persons, who in their judgment have become 'unworthy to live.' And there will be no police to protect him, no court to avenge his murder and bring his murderers to justice."

His remarks set off a firestorm, and on August 24 Hitler suspended the euthanasia program as secretly as he had launched it. There may have been reasons beyond public opinion. T4 had already reached a quota Hitler had set: seventy thousand victims. And—as Wetzel, in Rosenberg's office, had hinted in the infamous letter he drafted to inform Reichskommissar Lohse about "Brack's aids"—the euthanasia personnel were about to be dispatched to the East, where gassings on a far greater scale were planned.

Four months later, in December 1941, Rosenberg and Hitler were still talking about the uprising. Hitler couldn't understand it. "If the churches were so adamant about keeping the idiots," Rosenberg wrote in his diary, "he'd let them have all the imbeciles to use as priests, and their followers." The sermons had been broadcast on the BBC. They were translated into other languages, reprinted as pamphlets, and air-dropped by the British over Germany, France, Holland, Poland, and the rest of occupied Europe. Other clerics had taken up the cause, writing letters and speaking out.

"The Führer said these gentlemen wanted to be 'martyrs,' hoping for honorable captivity," Rosenberg wrote, and in some cases they got their wish. The Gestapo rounded up the people who spread von Galen's sermon and sent them to concentration camps. But not the bishop himself. While leading Nazis demanded that von Galen hang, Hitler feared the internal political ramifications and did not want to turn him into a martyr. Instead, he decided he would wait until after the war to settle the score. One way or another, Rosenberg wrote in his diary, "the Bishop of Münster will one day be facing rifles."

Despite the cancellation of T4, the gassing of disabled children in Germany continued.

And so did the murder of Jews. When the deportations from Germany began, von Galen said nothing, at least not in public.

On December 12, 1941—five days after the Japanese bombed Pearl Harbor and one day after Germany declared war on the United States—Hitler invited the party's top leaders to his private quarters in Berlin and told them that it was time to deal with the Jews once and for all. "The Führer is determined to clear the table," Goebbels wrote in his diary about the secret speech. "He warned the Jews that if they were to cause another world war, it would lead to their own destruction. Now the world war has come. . . . Those responsible for this bloody conflict will have to pay for it with their lives."

Later that month, Rosenberg was due to deliver a speech at Berlin's Sportspalast arena to threaten new reprisals against the Jews as a result of the ongoing Allied naval blockade of German shipping. He had planned to say that the "world-wide agitation against Germany" engineered by "New York Jews" would be met with "corresponding German measures against the Jews living in the East." Six million Jews lived under Nazi control in the eastern territories, and they were the "source and spring of Jewish power throughout the world." Germany needed to begin "destroying the springs from which the New York Jews had drawn their powers" by setting in motion "a negative elimination of these parasitic elements." It was to be a speech not unlike the off-the-record remarks he had made a month earlier before the German press.

But in the wake of America's declaration of war, it seemed to Rosenberg that the timing was not right for such combustible comments. One of the Nazi rationales for issuing threats against the Jews was to discourage the United States from entering the fight. Now events had overtaken him.

He met with Hitler on December 14 to discuss what to do. "With regard to the Jewish question," Rosenberg wrote in a memo about the meeting, "I said that my remarks about the New York Jews would perhaps have to be changed now, after the decision." Presumably, he meant the U.S. decision to enter the war. "My position was that the extermination of the Jews should not be mentioned." Hitler agreed, then added a sentiment that didn't need saying in present company, for above all else it had been the driving impulse of Rosenberg's entire political life: The Jews had brought on this war and destruction, and they would be the first to feel its bitter effects.

On that same day, Hitler hosted a separate meeting with

Rosenberg, Himmler, and Philipp Bouhler, one of the top administrators of the T4 euthanasia program.

If the Nazis were not ready to talk about extermination publicly, it had become a central topic among party leaders in the days
following Hitler's secret remarks to party leaders. The governor-
general in Poland, Hans Frank, was a case in point. He had been
there to hear what Hitler said, and he returned to his kingdom in
an apocalyptic frame of mind. "As for the Jews, well, I can tell
you quite frankly that one way or another we have to put an end
to them . . . they are going to disappear," he told a gathering of
Nazi officials in his territory. "They have to be gotten rid of."

Five weeks later, on a Tuesday in January 1942, fifteen Nazi
bureaucrats stepped out of their cars in front of an SS guesthouse
in the fashionable Berlin suburb of Wannsee. The town had a
pretty waterfront and a beach, and in the summer it was a getaway
for the wealthy and prominent. But on this morning, snow was
falling on the lake outside the windows. Settling into their seats,
the men warmed themselves with cognac.

Among the officials around the table were state secretaries and
undersecretaries of the Foreign Office, the ministries of the Interior, Justice, and Economics, and the General Government in
occupied Poland. Seven were SS officers who dealt with the Jewish question. Robert Kempner would later describe the assembled
group this way: "Those were the gentlemen who knew the things
you had to know." Like the other ministers, Rosenberg did not
attend the meeting personally. He instead sent two important
members of his eastern ministry: Alfred Meyer, his deputy minister, and Georg Leibbrandt, director of the ministry's political
division. They undoubtedly briefed Rosenberg on the discussion
later.

Reinhard Heydrich had called the bureaucrats together,
though the invitation was characteristically circumspect about the

matter to be discussed. Adolf Eichmann, who organized and managed the deportation of the Jews from all around Europe as head of the Jewish section of the Reich Security Main Office under Heydrich, drafted a summary afterward to distribute to attendees and other officials. Eichmann's Protocol was incriminating enough that all but one of its thirty recipients destroyed it; the surviving copy ensured that the hour-and-a-half discussion would go down in history as a watershed moment in the Nazi planning for the final solution.

Heydrich wanted to line up the various ministries behind his blueprint for the final solution. He reminded the bureaucrats that he had been tasked with the responsibility of ridding Europe of the Jews and explained that previous measures to encourage Jewish emigration—a decade of attacks, arrests, and discrimination—had not resolved the issue. Instead Hitler had approved a new solution: "evacuating Jews to the east."

Heydrich outlined the general plan. Europe would be "combed" of Jews from west to east, and those Jews strong enough for hard labor would be worked literally to death. "In large, single-sex labor columns, Jews fit to work will work their way eastwards constructing roads. Doubtless the large majority will be eliminated by natural causes," Eichmann's summary read. "And doubtless any final remnant that survives will consist of the most resistant elements. They will have to be dealt with appropriately, because otherwise, by natural selection, they would form the germ cell of a new Jewish revival. (See the experience of history.)"

Despite that blunt description of a policy that would, one way or another, sentence all of Europe's Jews to death, the men in attendance that day would later deny that Heydrich spoke of genocide. But Eichmann would testify that the minutes had been necessarily written in euphemisms, a code language to obscure what the fifteen men in the Wannsee villa were really talking about: not evacuating the Jews, but exterminating them.

It was a meeting that came to symbolize the puzzling horror of the Holocaust: how an enlightened and advanced nation like Germany could devolve into the worst kind of barbarism. "Here was the distinguished ambience of an elegant villa, in a cultivated suburb, in one of Europe's most sophisticated capitals," historian Mark Roseman wrote. "Here were fifteen educated, civilized bureaucrats, from an educated, civilized society, observing all due decorum. And here was genocide, going through, on the nod."

A few months before the meeting at Wannsee, Hitler had mused about all that he had already done to isolate Germany's Jews. A grim analogy popped into his head—one that linked a vile campaign slogan from the 1920s to the accomplishments of the famous bacteriologist who was Robert Kempner's namesake and godfather.

"I feel like the Robert Koch of politics," the Führer told a compatriot. They were speaking before dawn, and the sky had just begun to lighten in the east. Hitler explained himself: "He found the bacillus of tuberculosis and through that showed medical scholarship new ways. I discovered the Jews as the bacillus and ferment of all social decomposition. Their ferment.

"And I have proved one thing: that a state can live without Jews."

Max and Frieda Reinach with their daughter, Trude, in happier times.
(U.S. Holocaust Memorial Museum, courtesy of Ilana Schwartz)

19

"Our Own Tragic Special Destiny"

The day the Second World War began, a Jewish couple in Berlin named Frieda and Max Reinach opened a small black notebook of graph paper and began keeping a diary for their grown children, who had managed to escape from Germany. A half century later, the little diary, its black cover repaired with Scotch tape, would find its way to a distant relative two generations down the line—Henry Mayer, chief archivist at the Holocaust museum in Washington, D.C.

"When I attempt in this small booklet to keep track of the days and weeks to follow, I do this for you, beloved children, so you shall one day understand and come to know the time in which we live, what we suffer," wrote Max. "Your parents trust in God who was our protector in difficult times before and who will remain so. Thus it is written: 'You are the children of the Eternal God. If a father is angry with his children, he will nevertheless not expose them to total destruction.' Our conscience is clean and pure and the only thing we fear is God."

Before the war, Frieda had been a schoolteacher, while Max sold cigars. When they lost their jobs, they both volunteered at the Jewish Community Center soup kitchen. But day by day, as the war went on and the offenses piled up, Frieda grew increasingly depressed. The family had not been particularly religious, but Max turned back to his faith and became resolute and philosophical about the trials of living in Germany during the Third Reich. He vowed that he and Frieda would not cease fighting for their lives. They would not weaken like others who lost faith. "Suffering and sorrow, such as cannot be put into words, has overwhelmed all of us and we need a rock-like belief and faith in God in order to survive these trials of the present time," he told his children. "Your parents have the firm willpower to survive this time full of horror and to find in a different future, perhaps, some years of peace."

"We have to wear, according to law, the star of David . . . and underneath the star it says: *Jude*," Max wrote in September 1941. The regulations required that it be sewn onto the clothing on the left side of the chest. Almost a million were produced on rolls of cloth, then clipped and sold to the Jews for ten pfennigs apiece. Wearing the star marked a Jew for questioning by the Gestapo. Not wearing it put a Jew at risk of arrest. Max was horrified: "I would never have thought something like this could happen."

Year by year, restrictions grew ever more harsh. Jews were prohibited from going into the train station without a permit. They were barred from Berlin's central government district. They were not permitted to drive cars. "Jews," a Nazi pamphlet read, "no longer have any business behind the wheel of a vehicle in Germany!" They were ordered to obey an 8:00 p.m. evening curfew—9:00 p.m. on weekends. They were required to surrender their company stock, their jewelry, their art. They lost their phone service. They lost their radios, which they were ordered to turn in on the holiest day of the year, Yom Kippur. They were placed on rations even thinner than those of their Aryan neighbors and were allowed to shop for just an hour, late in the day when the store-fronts were practically bare.

"For sixty years," Max lamented, "we have lived always with the idea not to appear or be different from others, and now, the kids in the street mirthfully count Jews. Our equality as citizens has gone."

The Propaganda Ministry tacked up posters bearing Hitler's "prophecy" from a January 30, 1939, speech before the Reichstag: "If the international Jewish financiers inside and outside Europe should succeed once more in plunging nations into another world war, the consequence will not be the Bolshevization of the earth and thereby the victory of Jewry, but the annihilation of the Jewish race in Europe!"

In May 1942, Max meditated on the Jewish people and "our own tragic special destiny." The deportations had begun.

The first trains had rolled out of Berlin on October 18, 1941, and from then on, the Jews were no longer allowed to emigrate.

Max noted in the diary that his and his wife's sisters and brothers had been "evacuated"—Max and Jule and Moritz and Martha and Liane and Adele and Bernhard. "Most of our friends here have also been taken away and life has become very lonesome." And yet he still believed he would see his children again. If he was wrong, he wrote, no one should mourn. "You will remain our sunshine till our evening comes and until dark night surrounds us," he wrote. "Your childhood was happy and delightful for you and for us and memories will remain."

Frieda picked up the notebook a few days later, and she could not hide her anger. "How many thousands of Jews, since October 1941, have been 'evacuated'?" she wrote. "'Evacuated,' as they call it, from Germany. 'Evacuated,' as they call it euphemistically. . . . I am terrified at the thought of 'evacuation,' and this horrible possibility hangs over our heads every moment, with good reason.

Whenever I think of it, I am utterly in a panic and I know: If we have to go this road, I shall never again see you, beloved children."

For a time, they had sent food and money to some of their relatives in the ghetto in Lodz, Poland, even though they had little to eat themselves and had lost a great deal of weight. As time went on, they were not allowed to buy meat, fish, butter, eggs, fruit, coffee, alcohol, or tobacco with their ration cards. They could not buy shoes or soap or firewood.

In the parks, they were permitted to sit only on benches reserved for Jews. "They were painted yellow," Frieda wrote. "We refused to use them." Then they were barred from the parks altogether.

Soon after that, the Jews were ordered to turn in their pets. "Violation of this regulation," read the official notice, "will result in police measures."

On May 24, 1942, one of the women sharing their apartment was ordered to surrender her room. "This," Max wrote, "is always the first step for being sent away."

In June, they wrestled with whether Max should register to work for the Nazis. They didn't need the money; they could hardly spend it on anything. But working might keep them safe from "evacuation." Their jobs at the Jewish Community Center gave them protection for the time being, but they would be even more secure if Max worked in a munitions factory contributing to the war effort. On the other hand, by registering to work, Max might prompt the Nazis to move against him and his wife. "The decision is so difficult and complicated," Frieda wrote, "because whatever one may decide, it might turn out to be just the wrong thing."

They had not heard from their relatives out east. "Where are they," she wrote, "and how are they?"

They had to turn in their electric appliances—vacuum, iron, heating pad, stoves. They were banished from the barbers. They were forced to hand in their typewriters and bicycles and cameras and telescopes. "Lovely, no?" Frieda wrote. "This also, however, is not really bad. What happens daily are: arrests, shootings of people, executions. Is it surprising that I am scared? . . . Only a miracle could save us, and that miracle has to come soon. Otherwise, we are all lost." They tried to hope that Germany would lose the war, but it seemed like wishful thinking. "This is not the time to dream."

It was summer, but it was rainy and cold. At the beginning of the year, they had been ordered to give up their fur and wool clothes.

On June 29, Max registered for work. They sent him away to await a decision. One week later, word came back: They were being "evacuated" and were ordered to report to the authorities in four months. They were filled with dread, and yet Max still had moments in which he felt "strangely more quiet inside."

"My going to register for work, as you see, was the wrong thing to do," he wrote. "But each human being has his own destiny. My protector shall not leave us in this fear and torment, for HE has always been with us."

Three and a half months later, on October 20, Frieda and Max were summoned to the Jewish Community Center offices at Oranienburger Strasse at seven in the morning. There, alongside the rest of the organization's fifteen hundred employees, they waited in terror for the men from the Gestapo to appear.

A year before, Jewish leaders in Berlin had been coerced into helping the Nazis organize the transports to the East. A former synagogue in the Tiergarten district was converted into an "assembly camp," where staff from the Jewish center helped process the people selected to go east. Jewish leaders cooperated "despite grave misgivings," according to one of those who survived the war. They did not yet realize that deportation meant death. They wanted to make sure that the passengers on the trains had proper clothing and provisions for the journey. They believed the operation would be less brutal if they did not leave everything in the Gestapo's hands.

But now the Gestapo was coming for them as well.

The staff waited for several hours in the community center's meeting rooms and hallways and offices. The police arrived and announced that five hundred staffers would lose their jobs immediately, and those selected were to report to the assembly camp in two days. For every individual who did not appear, the Nazis promised to shoot one Jewish leader.

A transport list was drawn up. The Reinachs were on it.

They returned home at three that afternoon in shock.

Frieda took up the pen at midnight and wrote a few final words to the children, hoping that someday the diary would find its way to them. "We are victims of our Jewish destiny, and we lose our country, our home, our possessions. Everything . . . A few more days in our beloved home, and then—nothingness." She wished her children and grandchildren a happy life. "I know that you will never forget us but here is a wish: Do not let your life be overshadowed by our destiny."

Two days later, Max left his own final testament. He promised to go without fear. Whatever happened was meant to happen. "Our material possessions have gone, and almost naked do we leave the country in which we have lived for more than four hundred years," he wrote. "We do not know as yet where we have to go, but God is everywhere, and wherever we call for him, we shall find him."

The deportations had become routine. On October 22, Frieda and Max arrived at the assembly camp. They registered their remaining assets, which were then confiscated. Their bags were searched for stray valuables. Early in the morning four days later, they walked from the camp to the freight depot two miles north. Along with nearly eight hundred others, including eighty-eight children under fifteen years old, they boarded third-class passenger cars and set off for the East.

Their luggage did not make the trip. Back in Berlin, their apartments were in demand.

On October 29, Frieda and Max and the rest of the Jews condemned to death arrived at a station on the outskirts of Riga, Latvia, more than seven hundred miles away from Berlin. After they disembarked, they were taken into the forest and shot.

A little while later, their daughter Trude, in Israel, received a message from her parents, sent from Berlin through the German Red Cross a few days before their deportation. "From a deeply moved heart we send you our profound farewell. May God protect you."

It was signed simply, "Your sad parents."

A month later, Nazis began sending the trains from Berlin directly to Auschwitz. In all, fifty thousand Jews were deported from the city before the end of the war. Only eight thousand Berlin Jews survived.

What the Nazis attempted, one historian would write, was the "careful erasure of the complete social existence of the deportees."

But before the Reinachs left, a woman living in their apartment building agreed to keep the diary and try to get it to their children. So committed was this woman to her mission that she wore the diary in a belt around her waist. After the war, she gave it to an American soldier, along with an address of relatives in the United States. When he returned home, he delivered it to the Reinachs' daughter Lillian, outside Boston.

Years later, Trude translated the pages for her English-speaking grandchildren. It was not only that she wanted them to read it, she said; she had a "deeper motive." Passing along the diary to another generation was an act of faithfulness to the memory of her parents, and of her husband's parents and the millions of others who lost their lives at the hands of the Nazis.

She closed her letter with a bit of verse that she attributed to a German Jewish writer named Alfred Kerr:

> Dead are only those
> Who are forgotten.

As a lawyer, Kempner was infamous for his aggressive interrogations. *(U.S. Holocaust Memorial Museum, courtesy of Robert Kempner)*

20

Nazis Next Door

Half the German immigrants who arrived in New York decided to stay there, as far as Robert Kemper could tell. So many ended up in Washington Heights that the neighborhood came to be known as the Fourth Reich. Kempner wound up in Philadelphia, but he wanted no part of city life, and as soon as he got his financial affairs in order, he left for Lansdowne, a one-square-mile suburb filled with old-growth trees and large Victorians. It reminded him of the Lichterfelde neighborhood back in Berlin. He bought a house in a quiet subdivision and invited city friends to come down and sit on his veranda, which overlooked a small creek running through a park.

Idyllic as his little oasis felt, life had become more complicated for the recently arrived Germans now that the United

States was at war with the Nazis. "The question of whether I am really an enemy alien is not yet finally settled," Kempner wrote in a letter protesting a decision by authorities that had required him to disable his short-wave radio so he could not listen to German stations in Europe. "I am expatriated by special decree of the Hitler Regime and therefore not a German national but stateless. I owe no allegiance to a foreign power, but only to the U.S." Though he won the argument over the radio, it was emblematic of the uphill battle he and his fellow émigrés faced in their new home.

"The immigrants all had a serious fault," Kempner wrote: "they spoke with a heavy accent." That made people wonder. "Is that a German? Should we not have the man watched, because he was an agent of Hitler's, or still could be?"

Those were questions Kempner could help answer. The answers to those questions, in fact, were precisely what he had to sell when he arrived in New York in the fall of 1939: He could help identify agents dispatched by the Nazis to secretly push their cause in America.

Hoarder that he was, he had managed to bring seven boxes of original German government documents with him across the Atlantic. He called them *Handwerkszeug*: his tools. He did not intend to give them away for free.

Years later, Kempner told a story about how he had come to work with the U.S. Justice Department. One day, two young federal prosecutors came to visit him at Penn, perhaps prompted by the letters he had been sending officials in Washington offering his services. In 1940, a Special Defense Unit had been established in the Justice Department to gather intelligence on Nazi propaganda in the United States and build cases for criminal prosecution. The division would be "a control tower in the government's fight to eliminate subversive activity," largely by monitoring and clamping down on fascist-friendly press. By the summer of 1941, Kempner had made contact with the division.

According to Kempner's account, the visiting prosecutors, who casually called him Bob, asked what he could do for them. "Can you get documents for us?"

Direct as ever, he asked, "How is it then with the pay?"

"That is somewhat difficult," one of them replied. "You are still actually an enemy alien."

"Listen," Kempner said with a shrug. "If your organization is such that it does not have funds for such cases, then the whole matter is not worth anything."

The men smiled.

Of course, one of them said. "There are funds for everything."

With that out of the way, Kempner gave them a sampling of his files. He showed them documents involving the Nazi Party's Foreign Organization, under Ernst Wilhelm Bohle. The agency, which tried to coordinate the activities of party members living abroad, was suspected of leading a fifth column of informants and saboteurs, and Kempner showed the lawyers documents outlining its mission and tactics.

Bohle initially supported the Friends of the New Germany, the band of anti-Semites that had raised the uproar at Madison Square Garden in 1934. But the Friends were inept, and soon became an embarrassment. The Nazi Party in Berlin, fearing that the blunt rhetoric of its unofficial American satellite would exacerbate already tense relations with Washington, publicly distanced itself from the group, which promptly disbanded. A successor, the German-American Bund, rose in its place, but its leader, Fritz Kuhn, was jailed for embezzlement and forgery soon after Kempner arrived in 1939.

Still, there were plenty of other Nazi sympathizers carrying the flag for Hitler in the United States. Prosecutors and policymakers in Washington feared that a dangerous national fascist conspiracy was at work—one aimed at overthrowing democracy by inciting racial hatred. Given the success of Hitler's propaganda machine, it did not seem out of the question that these Nazified psychological warriors could, like the best advertisers, infiltrate the American subconscious and wreak havoc.

Later, Kempner would ridicule the German efforts to foment trouble in the United States. "The Nazis managed it very foolishly, and unattractively, very wild," he would say. "I mean, separate little groups undertook sabotage efforts, Nazi propaganda, espionage. . . . What the fifth column was supposed to do for Germany was laughable. They had actually convinced themselves in Berlin that one could set up a German front in America, which would in any event keep America from entering the war."

But during the war, the stateside agitators did not seem quite so comical, and Kempner was among those warning that they were a grave threat to U.S. security.

The Justice Department set about monitoring, silencing, and arresting the German propagandists. Federal prosecutors under Attorney General Robert Jackson and his successor, Francis Biddle, put dozens of Nazi supporters on trial for violating a newly passed sedition law, the Smith Act, and for the more pedestrian crime of failing to register with the U.S. government as an agent of a foreign power, which was the equivalent of prosecuting a gangland mobster for income tax evasion.

Kempner soon became one of the regular paid independent experts in these cases. Prosecutors appreciated his assistance, because he had personally witnessed the rise of the Nazis and could help delineate the parallels between the Nazi and American propagandists. The only problem, it seems, was his style of dress. He favored colorful jackets and pants. They told him they would prefer he adopt the style of the American man of business and government: dark suit, white shirt, silk power tie in a solid color.

Among those Kempner helped prosecute were employees of Germany's Transocean News Service, a pro-Nazi outfit with ties to the Foreign Office and the propaganda ministry in Berlin; Friedrich Ernst Auhagen, a former professor at Columbia University who ran a pro-Nazi group called the American Fellowship Forum; and Carl Günther Orgell, whose Volksbund für das Deutschtum im Ausland had been financed by Rosenberg's party Foreign Policy Office to spread the Nazi gospel far and wide.

During the biggest sedition trial in American history, *United States v. McWilliams*, in 1944, Kempner "helped work out the theory of a very difficult case," wrote prosecutor O. John Rogge. Twenty-nine vociferous pro-German propagandists in America had been rounded up and put on trial en masse. They were a rambunctious cast, and on many days the trial veered toward farce. "Seldom," wrote one reporter who sat through the proceedings in Washington, "have so many wild-eyed, jumpy lunatic fringe characters been assembled in one spot."

The prosecution argued that the defendants were part of a Nazi conspiracy to overthrow democratic governments the world over. They had violated the Smith Act of 1940 by working with German government and party officials—and with one another—to print and distribute books, newspapers, and pamphlets that effectively encouraged "insubordination and disloyalty among members of our armed forces." Their propaganda aimed to convince the troops that America's democratic system was "neither worth defending nor fighting for."

The conspirators, Rogge told the jury, planned to follow the whole Nazi playbook. They wanted a homegrown Hitler. They wanted to move against the Jews. They spoke of violent revolutions, of bloodbaths, of "hanging people from lamp posts." They envisioned pogroms that would "make Hitler's look like a Sunday-school picnic." Just as the Nazis had, the American fascists would first win the propaganda war in America, then undermine democratic institutions, then seize power with help from disloyal members of the military. The defense denied being part of any such conspiracy—"I'm a Republican, not a Nazi!" one cried—and raised such a ruckus in the courtroom that the trial stretched on for months and months. It was nowhere near ending when the judge had a heart attack and a mistrial was declared.

Rogge and Kempner tried to resuscitate the case, but the matter was dismissed after the end of the war.

Civil libertarians in America worried about the implications of the prosecutions, but Kempner's own recent dispossession from his homeland as a subversive gave him no pause as he helped Americans root out and silence their potential enemies. What mattered was that he was fighting the Nazis again—and making a name for himself. Just a few short years after stepping off the ship in Hoboken, Kempner was circulating among key American political figures.

As fate would have it, the prosecutors running the cases against the Nazi provocateurs were going places.

Soon they would pull Kempner along for the opportunity of a lifetime.

At the same time he was helping the prosecutors in the Justice Department, Kempner continued writing his obsequious dispatches to Hoover, still hoping to catch the eye of the FBI director, whose campaign against potential subversives went far beyond the efforts of the Special Defense Unit. By May 1941 the Bureau's "suspect enemies" list—compiled using intelligence gathered via the sweeping domestic surveillance program Roosevelt had secretly authorized five years earlier—had eighteen thousand names on it.

Kempner sent Hoover a note suggesting that the FBI prepare for postwar Europe by studying basic police questions: "personnel, areas, location of present headquarters, character of local forces, etcetera. . . . I would be glad to prepare a memorandum on the main problems involved; maybe it could be useful for different purposes."

He offered to share what he knew about Kurt Daluege, the Nazi police official and "dangerous fellow" elevated to deputy protector in the former Czechoslovakia.

He sent gifts. For Christmas in 1942, he presented the director with a copy of his book about the Nazis, *Twilight of Justice*, published under the pen name Eike von Repkow in 1932. Only two copies survived, he claimed. All the rest had been burned on Hitler's orders. On another occasion, Kempner offered Hoover the original report on the Nazis he had helped draft for the Prussian Interior Ministry in 1930. The "historical and prophetic" document "was brought out of Germany by me under personal risk," and, he assured Hoover, it would surely be a fine addition to the FBI museum.

Kempner had come to learn that he could always count on short, polite, impersonal replies to his letters. Though the correspondence did not lead to the private audience he sought with America's most famous lawman, Hoover did forward one of the letters to the special agent in charge of the FBI's Philadelphia office with instructions to follow up, and in 1942 Kempner was hired as a researcher and confidential informant. He was only a "special employee," essentially a freelancer billing the Bureau $14 a day plus expenses, but he considered it "a great privilege" to work for the FBI in any capacity, and given the amount of time he put in, the work provided a tidy monthly paycheck. At the end of the year, Kempner thanked Hoover for letting him make "some small contribution in our fight against Hitler; this time on the winner side, and not, as between 1928 and 1932 on the side of the losers." In another typically terse reply, Hoover replied that Kempner's help had been "most encouraging."

At the time, working as a special employee for the Bureau primarily meant fighting communists. Hoover's Cold War began before the Second World War even ended. He was convinced that the Kremlin was already working with stateside communists to spy on the United States.

Kempner led a small team of German-speaking researchers and translators compiling biographical records of German communist leaders, monitoring communist groups in Philadelphia, and reporting on potential communist front organizations. He provided intel on the German Society of Pennsylvania and on ship movements along the Delaware. His team translated stories from newspapers published by German communists in London, Mexico City, Buenos Aires, and New York. He traveled to Manhattan on a monthly basis to buy communist literature for FBI analysis.

In February 1943, he even offered to spy on "Central European Communist Party–related persons" in New York, who were already making preparations to return and take control of the postwar government, Kempner reported to the special agent in charge. "This writer would have such conversations under the 'headline' that he has to work on a scientific study on postwar planning."

He also collected and passed along intelligence on a smattering of individuals, from the notable to the unknown, in the United States and in Germany: Harry Eisenbrown, an American professor who moved back to Germany in 1937 to teach; Ezra Pound, the American poet who spoke out in support of Hitler; Fred Kaltenbach, a native of Dubuque, Iowa, who spent the war in Germany delivering pro-Nazi radio broadcasts aimed at the U.S. heartland; and Ruth Domino, a German writer who the FBI thought, erroneously, was married to an important Comintern operator in America, Gerhart Eisler.

It seemed Rudolf Diels had been on to something when he described Kempner as "a real Gestapo man."

The FBI was assembling a massive library of secret dossiers documenting the activities of millions of Americans, and Kempner was doing his small part to contribute to the cause.

Rosenberg at an airfield in Kiev during a 1942 visit to Ukraine. His Reich Ministry for the Occupied Eastern Territories never found its footing. *(Yad Vashem)*

21

The Chaostministerium

Bitter disappointment met Ukrainian nationalists who believed that the German invasion in 1941 heralded the establishment of a new, independent state. In July, a round of arrests by Reinhard Heydrich's security forces immediately stamped out a brief flickering of nationhood in Lviv, and before the summer was out, Hitler was already busy dismantling Ukraine.

Whatever the propaganda leaflets fluttering over the conquered territories said, the Nazis had no intention of truly liberating the people of the East.

On August 1, Hitler decided that a western region of the country, Galicia, ought to be added to Hans Frank's General Government in Poland. The next month, discussions were under way to hand over to the Romanians a strip of southwestern Ukraine, including the key port of Odessa on the Black Sea. General Ion Antonescu, the Romanian prime minister, had allied his nation with Germany, and sent his soldiers to fight alongside the Nazis during Operation Barbarossa in the summer of 1941. They would be among the most enthusiastic perpetrators of the final solution: In the first year of the war, Antonescu's men would massacre 380,000 Jews—gunning some of them down, burning others alive, starving the rest to death.

"The Führer," Rosenberg noted in his diary on September 1, "literally loves Antonescu, who has truly behaved exceptionally both militarily and personally."

When Hitler offered Odessa, Antonescu demurred: He could not defend such a crucial port. But Rosenberg figured the general would change his mind. The Romanians had besieged the city in August; 17,000 of their soldiers would be killed and 74,000 wounded before Odessa surrendered in the middle of October. "The Romanian troops have surrounded Odessa and are letting a lot of blood in this battle," Rosenberg wrote in his diary. "Antonescu supplies fifteen divisions. Appetite comes with eating."

Ukraine's "dismemberment" was a terrible idea, Rosenberg complained. "Apparently reason and foolishness are engaged in a battle that's undecided. . . . The concept of winning over the Ukrainians to mobilize politically against Moscow could be completely crushed, possibly, if we gave in."

But it was clear that Hitler, contrary to what he had told Rosenberg and others before the war, would not allow self-determination for the peoples of the East. A free, resurgent Ukraine might become a formidable future adversary. Likewise, Hitler opposed Rosenberg's idea of a new university in Kiev to spark a reflowering of Slavic culture and pride. "It would be a mistake to claim to educate the native," Hitler told confidants during one of his private wartime monologues over dinner, which were documented by Bormann and published after the war. "All that we could give him would be a half knowledge—just what's needed to conduct a revolution!" He did not even want to teach them to read.

The Ukrainians would get nothing from the Nazis.

Less than nothing, in fact: Over Rosenberg's vociferous objections, Hitler did indeed give Antonescu the chunk of Ukrainian territory he wanted, the region between the Dniester and Bug Rivers known as Transnistria.

In September 1941, Rosenberg finally realized that he had lost the battle. "The Führer is of the opinion that if a people of such proportions allows itself constantly be oppressed, it isn't worth being regarded as independent by others," he wrote in his diary. He couldn't mask his confusion. Had he been misled by his hero? "This stance . . . is quite different from my own, and—as I had reason to assume—different from the one with which he used to agree."

But as always, Rosenberg tacked to follow his Führer. Hitler visited the cities of Berdychiv and Zhytomyr, and left even more convinced of the population's depravity. "Which isn't terribly surprising," Rosenberg wrote in his diary, "as both of these are mostly Jewish cities." Perhaps Hitler was right, he decided. Perhaps there was no point in trying to inspire the Ukrainians culturally. Perhaps it would be better to leave them as they were, "i.e. the current primitiveness." "The fertile grounds, the riches of natural resources, and finally, the German sacrifice of blood have caused a change in the Führer's attitude, and concern about supplying all of Europe with food has prompted him to take the protection of these resources under his direct management. After all, he was the one who conquered the Ukraine."

Still, Rosenberg worried. Soon his administrators would face both "passive resistance" and assassination attempts. A million soldiers might be needed to keep a lid on the angry populace. The Ukrainians might ally with the Russians to "create a pan-Slavic front, exactly what I had wanted to avoid with my original plan." Left unchecked, the situation on the ground could easily spiral into a full-on revolution against the Nazis.

Already the Ukrainians were waking up to the fact that they had simply swapped oppressors.

Hitler's grand idea for the East was to treat it as a colony. The Germans would govern like the masters they were born to be.

"Out of the newly won eastern territories," he said, "we must make a Garden of Eden." The "living space" he had been talking about all these years was finally within reach.

But as the Nazis arrived in their new empire, confusion reigned. The men Rosenberg commanded were hundreds of miles away from his Berlin headquarters. By the time his orders reached the hinterlands, they were more or less outdated. Phone connections were lousy and mail service slow, making it impossible for Rosenberg to take charge of matters. So from the Reichskommissars to the lowliest district leaders, everyone had great latitude to interpret and ignore commands emanating from Rosenberg's distant Ostministerium. In the East, Goebbels noted, "everybody does as he likes."

So sprawling and disjointed was Rosenberg's operation that Goebbels took to calling it the Chaostministerium. "In that ministry plans are being hatched for future decades, when in reality the problems of the day are so urgent that they cannot be postponed," Goebbels wrote in his diary. "The ineptitude of the ministry is owing to the fact that there are too many theoreticians there and too few practical men." Another term was bandied about for Rosenberg's administrators: *Ostnieten*—"Eastern nobodies."

Rosenberg had no authority over Himmler's SS, and he was duty-bound to support Göring's efforts to confiscate food and raw materials from the Ukrainians.

Worse still, his nominal underling in Ukraine, Erich Koch, had turned out to be the uncontrollable despot Rosenberg had expected when Hitler appointed him in July. A forty-five-year-old former railroad official, Koch once said that if not for Hitler, he would have become "a fanatic communist." He had written a favorable book about the Soviet Union, and in years past had even supported a closer alliance between the Nazis and the Bolsheviks—itself a major character flaw in Rosenberg's eyes. In 1928, Koch became leader of the largely rural state of East Prussia, where he was known for his arrogance and his love of a good conspiracy, remembered one acquaintance, Hans Bernd Gisevius, a German intelligence officer during the war. "A first-rate demagogue, a bold adventurer, at home in the highest and lowest walks of life, he towered above his fellow leaders. He had a vigorous imagination and was always ready to pass on—in whispers and under the seal of absolute secrecy—utterly fantastic stories." In East Prussia, his Erich Koch Institute grew into a sprawling, corrupt business empire with holdings in a variety of companies; sometimes owners were forced to sell out to it, under threat of arrest. The revenues from his conglomerate financed a lavish lifestyle.

In another country, Koch "might have done a great deal of good," Gisevius wrote. "But the inevitable result of his being able to do as he pleased was that he devoted his versatile talents to swindling. By the time he was assigned to the Ukraine in 1941, he had become a megalomaniac." Koch lived like a king—aptly enough, in the East Prussian city of Königsberg.

Koch and Rosenberg could not have held more diametrically opposed views on the problem in the East. Koch followed Hitler's line to a fault: Germans as masters, Ukrainians as slaves. Nothing should stop the Nazis from exploiting them brutally. "I have not come here to spread bliss," he said in one speech. "I have come to help the Führer. The people must work, work, and work."

Koch, who wore a Hitler mustache, his hair swept back from a high forehead, did nothing to hide these extreme views, even from those he was oppressing. "If I find a Ukrainian who is worthy of sitting at the same table with me, I must have him shot!" he said at one point. "We are a master race," he said on another occasion, "that must remember that the lowliest German worker is racially and biologically a thousand times more valuable than the population here." They were dealing with *Untermenschen*, subhumans. Contact between the races should be limited; sex was out of the question. "This people must be governed by iron force, so as to help us to win the war now," he said. "We have not liberated it to bring blessings on the Ukraine, but to secure for Germany the necessary living space and a source of food."

During his tenure, Koch ruled by terror. His measures were "hard and uncompromising." Insubordination was met with the severest of punishments, up to and including death. Koch wanted the population to feel under "constant threat," even when they were doing nothing to provoke the Nazis.

In short, the Ukrainians were to be treated "like the Negroes," as Koch put it. Like something out of the antebellum American South, they would work vast plantations to feed the German people. Ukraine would be a land of public floggings. When Rosenberg wrote to protest this treatment and call for the end of the whippings, Koch shrugged. "True enough," he wrote about one incident, "about twenty Ukrainians were whipped by the police because they sabotaged important bridge construction across the Dnieper. I knew nothing of this measure. Had I known what a chain of reproaches this act would unleash, I probably would have had those Ukrainians shot for sabotage."

Rosenberg made it plain that his disagreements with Koch had more to do with pragmatism than with any moral qualms. Yes, the Nazis needed to pacify the region so they could get what they needed from it, but Koch's blend of "moody improvisation and loud provocative behavior" were simply counterproductive, he wrote in a letter reprimanding the Reichskommissar. Koch's public statements did nothing but antagonize the people and encourage them to join the Resistance fighters. Surely it would be better to keep silent about what the Nazis really thought about the Slavs. The consequence of Koch's violence would be "acts of sabotage and the formation of partisan behavior." As Rosenberg wrote later in his diary, "a people in war can endure everything, but not open contempt."

Rosenberg complained to Hitler, but Koch had the Führer on his side. And he had better access: Hitler's military headquarters, the "Wolf's Lair," lay in East Prussia, right in the middle of Koch's domain, while Rosenberg's office was four hundred miles away in Berlin.

With help from his friend and ally Martin Bormann, Koch was

reporting directly to the Führer on a regular basis, while Rosenberg fired off memos from afar.

Word filtered back to Rosenberg that, at headquarters, his enemies denigrated him as "*schlapp*"—weak.

The disagreement might not have mattered had the war ended within a few weeks or months. But by the end of 1941, the Soviets finally had stiffened their defenses and halted the Nazi advance. More than 300,000 German soldiers in the East had been killed or wounded. Then the first units retreated, snow began to fall, and the Soviets assaulted the German armies on the outskirts of Moscow. Everything—all the brutal plans and blueprints and utopian designs—had been built upon the idea of a swift end to the fighting in the East.

Now the Germans were in for a long war.

"Some still haven't yet understood," Rosenberg wrote in his diary, "that things have to be calculated differently now."

While Rosenberg argued about the treatment of the Ukrainians, his civil administrators worked with Himmler's SS on a renewed campaign to massacre the Jews in the eastern territories. In April 1942, Heydrich visited Minsk, and over five days in the middle of May, sixteen thousand Jews from the ghetto were executed in the region. After a new wave of shootings throughout the spring and summer, Lohse, Rosenberg's Reichskommissar in the Ostland, was informed by Wilhelm Kube, the chief civilian administrator in Belarus, that "in the last ten weeks we have liquidated about fifty-five thousand Jews." The same story unfolded in Ukraine, where only a few thousand Jews were saved for forced labor. On December 26, 1942, Himmler received a report that in the last four months of the year, 363,211 Jews had been killed in Ukraine and the Polish city of Bialystok.

In the midst of this orchestrated bloodshed, one of its masterminds lost his own life.

In September, Hitler appointed Heydrich to the top post in the

Protectorate of Bohemia and Moravia, part of the dismembered Czechoslovakia. Heydrich crushed the opposition, and in response, exiled Czech leaders in London devised a plot with the British to kill him. On May 27, 1942, two assassins attacked Heydrich's car with guns and grenades; he succumbed to his wounds a week later. The Nazis responded to Heydrich's assassination with a wave of killings. The village of Lidice, accused of harboring the assassins, was burned to the ground after its men were murdered and its women sent to a concentration camp. The children of Lidice were separated into racial categories: Those deemed suitable were put up for adoption by German families; the rest were executed.

Heydrich's death, of course, did nothing to slow the progress of the extermination of the Jews.

The first killing center opened in Chelmno, Poland, where, beginning in December 1941, Jews were locked fifty at a time into the back of gas vans like the ones the people of the Minsk ghetto had grown to fear. The first gas chamber was constructed at a camp in Belzec, in eastern Poland, and went into operation in March 1942. This space was built to look like a decontamination shower; instead a piping system directed car exhaust inside.

To the north, similar camps opened in Sobibor and Treblinka that spring and summer, and gas chambers were installed at an existing concentration camp, Majdanek. As time went on, the victims were not fooled by the ruse of the showers. At Treblinka, the naked Jews were beaten and harassed as they made their way, terrified, through a chute leading to the gas chambers. "Roadway to Heaven," the SS called the walk.

The largest of the killing centers, Auschwitz-Birkenau, a few hundred miles to the west along the Vistula River, began operation in February 1942 and became the final destination of the Jews of Germany, France, Belgium, Holland, Italy, Serbia, Slovakia, Romania, Croatia, Poland, Denmark, Finland, Norway, Bulgaria, Hungary, and Greece. There, the Germans constructed a killing system so efficient that its designer patented it. Victims were locked into the underground chambers. Containers of Zyklon B, cyanide pesticide pellets, were lowered through the ceiling. After everyone was dead, other camp prisoners removed their gold fillings, prosthetics, and hair, put the bodies in elevators, and sent them upstairs to the ovens to be burned.

All told, the Nazis put to death more than three million people, most of them Jews, in the six camps—about half of the overall Jewish death toll during the war.

One night amid all this bloodshed, at a hall in the Polish city of Poznan, Himmler spoke frankly to a group of SS leaders about the work they had been doing. "Most of you will know what it means when a hundred corpses are lying side by side, or five hundred or a thousand are lying there. To have stuck it out . . . this is what has made us tough. This is a glorious page in our history and one that has never been written and can never be written."

A series of successful military campaigns in the Soviet Union gave Germans hope in 1942. The Nazis swept into the Crimea and the Caucasus, and on September 12, following weeks of carpet bombing by the Luftwaffe, the German Sixth Army under General Friedrich Paulus entered the city of Stalingrad.

It was a key city on the Volga River between Moscow and the Caspian Sea. Hitler desperately wanted to claim the prize, and he vowed to kill its entire male population and deport every woman and child. Stalin, aware of the strategic and symbolic importance of a city that bore his name, threw everything into its defense. The Red Army refused to surrender, firing on the Nazis from the ruins and setting booby traps everywhere. The harried Germans were caught unaware when the Soviets sprang a massive counterattack in November and surrounded 250,000 German soldiers. A Nazi airlift and a rescue mission failed to relieve the men, who were soon starving, freezing, riddled with lice, and short on ammunition. Millions of letters mailed home by the besieged soldiers made the German people aware of the crisis.

Hitler refused to give General Paulus permission to try to break out of Stalingrad, for it would have meant retreating in the face of the enemy. Nor would he allow him to give up the fight. But on January 31, 1943, Paulus, recognizing the utter futility of his situation, finally surrendered his forces to the Soviets.

The defeat stunned the nation. Gloom settled in all across the Reich. In some circles Stalingrad was viewed, even in the moment, for what it would turn out to be: the beginning of the end.

In the meantime, in the occupied territories, Rosenberg's fears had come to pass. Fed by the escalating brutality of the German occupation, fierce resistance had sprung up. The Germans faced sabotage, assassination, and defiance as dissidents joined organized partisan movements. In May 1942, Rosenberg was fortunate to have cut short a visit to the Ostland; the train he had been scheduled to ride derailed after saboteurs severed the tracks. Later that year, a Soviet spy captured in Kiev confessed to plans to assassinate Rosenberg during a visit to Ukraine. One operation involved blowing up the opera, but on the day in question, the hall was filled with Ukrainian civilians. Schedule changes foiled other attempts.

Back in the Soviet Union, Rosenberg recounted in his diary, it was said that after being shot at by partisans during the trip, Rosenberg had "barricaded himself at home: double iron shutters, reinforced walls, concealed machine guns at all windows." Rumor had it he was wearing a bulletproof vest and traveling with a major security contingent. All of it was false. Rosenberg couldn't help but laugh. "I don't have a single male person in the house with me at the moment, have never driven with SS protection." The radio report concluded with what sounded to Rosenberg like a call for communists in Germany to take action against him, "i.e., a fresh incitement to commit murder."

Fueling the resistance was a brutal campaign by the Nazis to find forced laborers. With millions of Germans on the front lines, the country's factories and farms and mines needed workers. At first the Nazis relied on propaganda pamphlets and posters in the occupied eastern territories. One newsreel, *Come to Lovely Germany*, played at the movie theaters. The Germans promised good wages, free housing and health care, even personal savings accounts.

Optimistic Ukrainians volunteered in the beginning, but soon ugly rumors filtered back: Workers were being transported in railcars with no food or toilets; those who tried to leave were sent to concentration camps. By the middle of 1942, nobody was volunteering anymore. Some feared that the Nazis would treat them the way they had the Jews; one story circulated that the people who got on the labor trains were shot and turned into soap.

Authorities in Berlin set higher and higher labor quotas. Aided by local leaders in Ukraine, the Nazis rounded up people at city markets and movie theaters. They raided villages at midnight. If residents fled to avoid the roundups, their homes were burned and their livestock confiscated. Violence broke out at the train stations as families were forcibly separated. There were reports that the Nazis forced pregnant women to have abortions rather than let them be exempt from the labor drive.

Eventually, entire age groups were enlisted. "Ukraine," victims of the impressment campaign said, "is being liberated from the Ukrainians."

More than three million people would be shipped west from the occupied Soviet territories during the war; a million and a half came from Ukraine.

Back in Berlin, Rosenberg was troubled by the labor drive. The men behind the program thought only of expediency and meeting quotas. They thought nothing of the fallout from the escalating violence. "The demand for two million eastern workers is necessary for the Reich," he wrote. "For the east, however, it is the hardest blow to the buildup work. . . . If one surrounds villages from the outset, it only reinforces the fear of earlier Bolshevist deportations and makes the situation more difficult for everyone in the end."

The labor roundups were accomplishing one thing: They were turning the country against the Nazi rule.

•   •   •

Rosenberg's ministry had another problem. His men in the East desperately needed furnishings for their quarters.

To deal with these "terrible conditions," the minister wrote in a request to Hitler, he proposed seizing the "home furnishings" of Jews in the occupied West—both those who had fled and those who "will leave shortly." The Nazis had already taken every price-less piece of art they could find from the departed Jews. Now, through the Möbel Aktion, Operation Furniture, they were going to take their more quotidian possessions: their tables and chairs, their kitchenware, their blankets, their mirrors.

Operating out of a fifty-room mansion that the Germans had seized from a pair of wealthy Jews, Kurt von Behr began hiring mov-ing companies to empty the contents of the unoccupied Jewish apart-ments in France, Belgium, and the Netherlands. At least sixty-nine thousand residences would be cleared out over the course of two and a half years. To sort, repair, and repack the home furnishings, von Behr established three depots in the center of Paris and requisitioned Jewish workers from an internment camp in the northeastern suburb of Drancy. One of the camps was housed in a former furniture store. Another was in a large and elegant home in a wealthy section of the city. The third was in a warehouse by the railroad.

The crates came into the camps by the thousands every day, filled not just with furniture but also with rugs, safes, kitchenware, silver, toys, books, blankets, lamps, instruments, clothing, even nightgowns—everything, in short, that a house might contain.

The sorters found plates with uneaten food still on them.

They found half-written letters.

Sometimes, amazingly, workers would recognize something of their own. One saw a photograph of his own daughter.

Using bolts of fabric that had been seized, Jewish seamstresses at the camps manufactured clothing for Nazi officials and their fami-lies, including dresses, handbags, and shoes for von Behr's wife.

The threat of deportation hung over the camps at all times. Men and women were shipped back to Drancy not just for attempting to flee but also for such offenses as becoming infested with lice. Whenever von Behr appeared to inspect one of the depots, he insisted that workers face him at all times, a rule that would have been ridiculous had the consequences not been so deadly. In time, the Jews would learn that when laborers were sent back to the transit facility, they did not return.

The loot was shipped not only to Rosenberg's ministry officials in the East but also to the SS, to the Gestapo, to a house Göring owned in Berchtesgaden, and to other well-connected Nazis. The prisoners would polish some of the finer objects and place them on shelves, and von Behr would usher dignitaries through to select what they wanted, as if they were shopping at Wertheim's on Leipziger Strasse in Berlin. Special orders were delivered to French collaborators, Nazi generals and soldiers, German civilians who knew the von Behrs, even film stars.

Rosenberg personally ordered "an impressive quantity of sheets, towels, and other accessories," according to one prisoner. A woman claiming to be his niece visited Paris on shopping expeditions for her boss, who needed furnishings for his home in Dahlem, the wealthy Berlin suburb. The demand became so overwhelming that it even drove Operation Furniture officials in one city, Liège, Belgium, to request the arrest of more Jews so that their homes could be plundered.

Most of the loot, however, ended up in the hands of ordinary Germans. Though the operation started on the pretext of furnishing Rosenberg's ministry offices, the mission soon changed. After the Allies began bombing large German cities, the bulk of the furnishings were diverted instead to the thousands of families who had to resettle after their homes were obliterated.

In the eastern occupied territories, meanwhile, the Einsatzstab concentrated on its original mission: the plunder of art and priceless archives.

There, the task force had competition. A special army unit dismantled the Amber Room in Catherine the Great's palace in

Pushkin, south of Leningrad, packing up the legendary engraved panels—aglow with amber backed by gold leaf—and shipping them to Königsberg, where the Nazis put them on display. The soldiers also seized the czars' famous Gottorp Globe, a nine-foot planetarium in which the constellations were superimposed on elaborate paintings of their namesakes: the lion, the bear, the swan.

After the Germans had taken everything they wanted, they set about vandalizing the palaces and historic sites of special meaning to the Russian people. They pillaged the former home of poet Alexander Pushkin. They parked their motorcycles inside Tchaikovsky's old residence. They burned the rare manuscripts they found at Tolstoy's home, Yasnaya Polyana.

In the meantime, the SS looted cities like Minsk and Kiev, sending the choicest pieces to Himmler's castle in Wewelsburg, for decorating, and to the offices of his archaeological unit, the Ahnenerbe, for study.

Rosenberg's men, too, found plenty of treasures there for the taking in the occupied East. They raided palace libraries, museums, and Communist Party archives, confiscating hundreds of thousands of books. In Vilnius, Lithuania, the Einsatzstab took over the Institute for Jewish Research and set up one of many central collecting points. The Nazis ordered forty Jews from the city's ghetto to catalog material pouring in from around the region and prepare the most valuable books for shipment to Germany. Much the same thing was happening in Riga, Minsk, and Kiev.

Train cars filled with Russian art, books, furniture, and archaeological treasure—even a famous butterfly collection—clattered west through the blood and mud of wartime Europe.

Not all of the plunder survived. Books considered to be worthless were pulped by the tens of thousands. Torah scrolls swept up in the operation were of no interest to Rosenberg's office. An Einsatzstab official, in reply to a question from the field, suggested that they be taken apart for their leather, which was used to bind other books or to make belts or shoes.

One cache of books was lost when the crates were flung from

a transport train to make room for a delivery deemed more valuable: hogs.

"It is amazing the valuables from all over Europe have been secured here," he wrote in his diary one day in 1943, after visiting one of the storehouses of loot in Estonia. "The most precious works of literature, manuscripts by Diderot, letters by Verdi, Rossini, Napoleon III, etc. And of course, all the inflammatory Jewish and Jesuit literature against us." He couldn't help but be pleased. His "laughably small" unit had accomplished so much in just a few short years.

At the beginning of 1943, as his fiftieth birthday dawned, Rosenberg battled melancholia. During the war years, he had celebrated the day—which he shared with Göring, of all people—in a low-key way, but this year he would have a lavish event befitting his importance to the party. "After all," he wrote, "Göring and I have already become part of the history of the National Socialist revolution." In the morning, a choir of children from the Hitler Youth and the League of German Girls entertained him at his home. Leading Nazis greeted him at his offices, and two hundred guests shared stew and beer at a ballroom in Rosenberg's ministry building, the former Soviet embassy on Unter den Linden.

Others sent touching letters. "I was moved the most by the Führer's handwritten note," Rosenberg wrote. Hitler declared Rosenberg one of the "foremost intellectual shapers of the party," thanked him for his loyalty, and rewarded him with a gift: 250,000 reichsmarks. "We both know how different we are from each other," Rosenberg continued. "He is aware of the fact that I consider some people whom he allows to act in the foreground, presumably for reasons of state, to be vermin." At least, Rosenberg thought, he could take comfort in knowing that Hitler appreciated him. "I answered him that I now may express that, in all these years, I have never swayed in my faith in him and his work, and that it has been the greatest honor of my life to be allowed to fight at his side."

But his faith was about to be severely tested.

．　．　．

As the dispute with Koch escalated, Rosenberg discussed reorganizing of the Ostministerium leadership with a top Himmler aide, Gottlob Berger, chief of the SS Central Office. Rosenberg was making a last stand to oust the intransigent Reichskommissar in Ukraine, and he knew he needed a powerful man like Himmler on his side. He offered an alliance: He would appoint Berger his state secretary overseeing personnel and policy—if he could be assured of SS support in his fight against Koch.

In January, Rosenberg met with Himmler in Poland for three hours, and the SS chief happily agreed to the Berger appointment, pending Hitler's approval.

It was an easy decision for Himmler. With a loyal aide inside Rosenberg's ministry, he would have even greater sway in the East. As for Koch, Himmler made no promises. "H. was suddenly very lenient towards Koch, whom he appreciates as a 'driving force,'" Rosenberg wrote in his diary, "and he also didn't think that the Führer would drop him."

The deal with Himmler required Rosenberg to jettison his loyal aide Georg Leibbrandt, who had worked in Rosenberg's Foreign Policy Office from 1933 to 1941 before joining the Ostministerium. SS and Gestapo leaders had long questioned Leibbrandt's trustworthiness, ever since he spent 1931 to 1933 in Paris and the United States on a Rockefeller grant.

Leibbrandt took his firing bitterly. "If the war is lost," he predicted, "then you, Minister, will be hanged."

In the first months of 1943, the war with Koch finally came to a head. Rosenberg objected to a harsh new directive Koch had issued, and Koch replied by firing off a fifty-two-page jeremiad against his longtime antagonist, accusing Rosenberg of undermining his position and asking Hitler to rule on the question.

Rosenberg called Koch to Berlin for a meeting, at which the two combatants shouted at each other. Rosenberg, now fearing that *he* might be the one fired by the Führer, wrote a letter to the Chancellery demanding that he be allowed to remove Koch, who had "become symbolic of deliberate and ostentatious contempt for the people," who had "almost completely ruined a great political opportunity," and who had a "complex which I can define only as pathological."

While the dispute raged, Himmler stayed neutral. The tentative alliance he and Rosenberg reached in January had come to nothing. In March, Hitler blocked Berger's appointment as unnecessary; a few days later, Himmler invited Koch to visit so they could "speak at length about all things."

On May 19, Hitler finally met with the warring parties at his field headquarters, which was now in Vinnitsa, Ukraine.

Rosenberg quickly discovered that the preceding two years had done nothing to change the Führer's mind about Ukraine. In fact, Hitler had told dinner guests one recent night that "anyone who talks about cherishing the local inhabitant and civilizing him goes straight off into a concentration camp!" If he thought it would help, Hitler told his generals around the same time, he would simply lie and promise the Ukrainians liberation. But as for taking real steps to lift up the population, that would only raise hopes and lead to problems controlling the population.

After listening to Rosenberg and Koch air their grievances, the Führer ruled on the matter. Reiterating that Germany needed food and workers from the occupied East, he finally and forever denounced the approach that Rosenberg had spent years advocating. "Conditions force us to adopt such harsh measures," Hitler said, "that we can never expect the political approval of the Ukrainians for our actions."

As the meeting broke up, the minister was furious. He refused to even shake Koch's hand.

Rosenberg had been soundly defeated. He would never recover.

Rosenberg took to his diary to rant. The Führer had insulated himself behind gatekeepers, notably Bormann, and had become so focused on military and foreign policy matters that important issues were not being dealt with in Germany itself. There was no debate, no discussion. It was unclear whether Bormann even relayed Rosenberg's memos anymore or simply filed them away unread. When Bormann sent directives from Hitler, nobody could be sure whether it was an authentic order from the Führer or Bormann merely acting on his own authority.

Rosenberg had welcomed Bormann's rise after Hess's flight. He seemed to be "a man of practical reason, robust and determined," and he enthusiastically endorsed Rosenberg's campaign against the Christian churches. Once Bormann even asked him to draft a "directive for a new German conduct of life," a sort of Nazi catechism for schoolchildren to replace religious moral instruction. Every girl and boy, he told Rosenberg, should be taught "the law of bravery, the law against cowardliness . . . a commandment to keep the blood pure."

Their bad blood seemed to start after Bormann compiled some of Hitler's most critical private remarks about the churches and circulated them in a bluntly worded secret notice to the party's regional governors. Soon, a copy had been found in the possession of a Protestant priest. "Just as the deleterious influences of astrologers, seers, and other fakers are eliminated and suppressed by the state," Bormann had written, "so must the possibility of church influence also be totally removed." Rosenberg wrote to Bormann to say that he thought the memo was poorly executed and suggested that he leave such writing to him in the future. "You can't overcome two thousand years of European history with the woodchopper method," Rosenberg wrote in his diary after their exchange. "B. is a practical man, but not suited formally for the analysis of such questions." Rosenberg tried to raise his objections delicately, for Bormann was no trifling power. Bormann replied "that he had never intended to start a big thing" and that of course Rosenberg should be the chief messenger when it came to the churches.

But then, Rosenberg wrote, strange things started to happen, "noticeable efforts to torpedo my party office." He could only assume that Bormann had decided that "certain men were too big for him. Among them, first and foremost, me."

Bormann argued that since Rosenberg should be focused on the work in the East, he needed to shut down many of the offices related to his role as Hitler's ideological deputy. Bormann also tried to strip control of the art-looting program from the Einsatzstab and place it in the hands of staff planning the Führermuseum in Linz, accusing Rosenberg's staff of incompetence and corruption. Rosenberg beat back that attempt, but then one of his close allies was attacked over what Rosenberg considered to be trumped-up charges. Bormann ordered an investigation and demanded the man's dismissal. "Really, the most primitive injustice—an example of the most miserable antechamber politics," Rosenberg wrote. "They attack him, but they mean to attack me."

He thought about demanding a meeting with Bormann to personally insist that Rosenberg's office conduct the investigation. He had been able to change Bormann's mind in the past.

But the whole affair made him disconsolate about the state of the Third Reich under manipulative men like Bormann. "To use court camarillas, with power that was bought with thousands of blood sacrifices, to outrageously defame and dispose of honorable men without giving them a hearing—this is something that the decent Nazi Party and the decent people cannot endure in the long run. . . . To say this straight to the Führer's face, however, is hopeless. He would see this as an attack on seasoned staff, possibly even jealousy of a 'theorist' against 'men of practice.'

"If B.'s methods should prove successful," he added, "then my life's work would be for nothing, too."

The war ground toward the end of its fourth year. Everything seemed to be falling apart.

DETENTION REPORT

File number

I.C. — 1096-14-2-45. — 76456.

SEX (1)

Office use only

(M) F

Ring applicable

Surname : ROSENBERG

First names : ALFRED

Aliases :

Civil Occupation : Author, Architect

Nationality : GERMAN (2)

DATE OF BIRTH (3)   12 JAN 1893

PLACE OF BIRTH (3a) REVAL, ESTONIA

WEIGHT 170 LBS (3b)

HEIGHT (4) 1.80M

Arrested on May 18, 1945, by British forces, Rosenberg was relieved at first that he had not been handed over to the Soviets. *(Yad Vashem)*

22

"A Ruin"

Two years after the invasion of the Soviet Union, in the summer of 1943, the Germans lost the initiative on the eastern front as Stalin threw overwhelming numbers of men onto the battlefield. In July and August, the Red Army lost more than one and a half million men but defeated the Germans in the largest land battle in history, at Kursk, three hundred miles east of Kiev. Hitler considered retreat cowardly, but the Germans had no option but to fall back in the face of relentless Soviet frontal attacks. In Ukraine, the Soviets barreled all the way to Kiev by the end of the year. To leave nothing behind for the Soviet armies to use, the Nazis burned villages and blew up buildings as they evacuated. One soldier wrote home, "It's a horrifyingly beautiful picture."

In the meantime, the British tried to break the German will by aiming directly at the capital city. On a cloudy night in late November 1943, more than seven hundred British airplanes flew over Berlin and emptied their bomb bays.

Rosenberg waited out the attack with his wife, Hedwig, and daughter, Irene, at the bomb shelter on the property of his home on Rheinbabenallee, in Berlin's Dahlem district. When the muffled thunder of the blasts finally ended and the all-clear signal came, the family walked outside in the darkness to see a "burning red sky" to the northeast. Rosenberg decided not to evacuate his family south to his villa in Mondsee, on the edge of the Alps in northern Austria. Instead he took them straight into the maelstrom, to the Hotel Kaiserhof, across the Wilhelmplatz from the Reich Chancellery.

The car raced past flames and devastation on the main roads into the center of Berlin. On Kurfürstendamm, the Kaiser Wilhelm Memorial Church had been struck by bombs. Beyond it, the zoo was aflame. Smoke reduced visibility to almost nothing. The driver zigged and zagged through the apocalyptic streets, dodging craters and fireballs, detouring past avenues blocked by wreckage, picking his way east toward the government center, Tauentzienstrasse. "No way through: a rain of sparks, and heavy smoke," Rosenberg reported. Up onto the sidewalk the car went, the driver honking at terrified, newly homeless Berliners fleeing the bombs. "Left and right, showers of sparks from burning buildings that had become huge torches." He found a route into the Tiergarten. A bus burned at the Victory Column. On Pariser Platz by the Brandenburg Gate, the French embassy was in flames. Finally reaching the Kaiserhof, Rosenberg and his family watched as firemen pumped water on the Ministry of Transport, across the Wilhelmplatz, thick smoke billowing every time the spray hit the inferno.

The wind picked up fiery fragments and flung them across the square, setting fires on the roof of the old Reich Chancellery building.

The phones at the Kaiserhof were out, but Rosenberg's deputy finally appeared, covered in soot and wearing a steel helmet, to report that one of the Rosenberg party offices had been hit.

The next morning, the dust was so thick that people could barely speak. It rose twenty thousand feet into the sky. Survivors covered their eyes and mouths with cloths to breathe. "I just can't understand how the English are able to do so much damage to the Reich's capital during one air raid," Goebbels wrote. The Wilhelmplatz was a scene of "utter desolation."

Many rooms in the Reich Chancellery were burned out. At Goebbels's house, the doors and windows were blown in and the rooms filled with water. Ministers were displaced and could be reached only by way of couriers picking their way through the devastation. The Führerbunker was pressed into service as a shelter for the newly homeless.

Rosenberg rode out to inspect the damage to his party office near Potsdamer Platz. "A ruin," he wrote. "In the smoking rubble lie the safes that crashed down. Entrance to the basement only through a small shaft." Piles of memos burned, as did twenty thousand marks in a steel safe. The headquarters of his eastern ministry on Unter den Linden survived, suffering only some broken windows and a layer of grimy dust.

Rosenberg would quickly realize the foolishness of bringing his family into the war zone. Another night saw a fresh load of bombs, and the Rosenbergs had to hide out in the Führerbunker. Even deep underground, the walls shook from the blasts. Emerging, Rosenberg saw a deep crater: A bomb had struck directly above the shelter. The Hotel Kaiserhof took a direct hit, and no one was fighting the fire because there were no hoses to be had. Dashing through flaming hallways to his room, Rosenberg packed everything he could into suitcases and fled back to Hitler's bunker, where everyone spent the night on cots.

"What has been happening and what will continue to happen in the buildings and basements of our bombarded cities, future dramatists will describe as the most horrible trial to which a population could ever be subjected," Rosenberg wrote in his diary. He likened it to the fall of Magdeburg in 1631 during the Thirty Years' War, when twenty thousand people were massacred and the town set aflame by marauding soldiers of the Holy Roman Empire. "Nowadays," Rosenberg wrote, "that's a day's loss. The twenty large cities that are already in ruins for the most part already have hundreds of thousands of women and children buried beneath them."

He was exaggerating. The raids of 1943 and 1944 would kill more than nine thousand civilians, put more than eight hundred thousand people out of their homes, and terrify the German people.

But it would take more than that—much more—before Hitler blinked.

"To not break down in the face of this is a credit to the National Socialist movement," Rosenberg wrote, "the fortitude that has become the virtue of the entire nation today."

"In the east," Rosenberg wrote in his diary in the dark days of the summer of 1944, "incessant retreat." One hundred twenty thousand Axis soldiers were cut off in the Crimea in the spring as the Soviets pushed mercilessly west. In June, a million and a half soldiers supported by tanks and artillery engulfed the German armies in Belarus, killing or capturing three hundred thousand men before pushing to within five hundred miles of Berlin. In the West, the Allies landed at Normandy on D-Day, June 6, and worked to break the German lines and liberate Paris.

Inside Germany, plotters were again trying to kill Hitler. A number of senior military officials had long been angered by the Führer's handling of the war and his reckless appetite for destruction on a continent-wide scale. Others, including former civilian government officials, were alarmed by the police state under Himmler, by the extermination of the Jews, and by the atrocities against the eastern peoples. Whatever their motives, the conspirators were united in their belief that Hitler was steering Germany toward catastrophe. They wanted to halt Germany's fall, end the war, and save lives.

"The assassination must be attempted at any cost," said one of the leaders of the plot, Henning von Tresckow, a general staff officer in the army. "We must prove to the world and to future generations that the men of the German resistance movement dared to take the decisive step and to hazard their lives upon it."

In March 1943, six weeks after the surrender of the Sixth Army at Stalingrad, Tresckow managed to get a bomb aboard Hitler's airplane during the Führer's visit to an army group headquarters in Smolensk, Russia. But the device, manufactured by military intelligence to look like cognac bottles, did not detonate. A suicide bomb plot failed when Hitler, as he had at the Bürgerbräukeller in Munich six years earlier, left the scene of a public appearance earlier than expected.

Undeterred, the leaders of the intrigue drafted a blueprint for Operation Valkyrie, which would be an assassination followed by a military coup using the reserve army forces stationed in Berlin. The opportunity finally came together on July 20, 1944, at Hitler's field headquarters, the "Wolf's Lair," near Rastenburg. Claus von Stauffenberg, a German army officer, brought a briefcase bomb into a military staff meeting that Hitler was attending. He placed it next to a heavy wooden table near the Führer, excused himself, watched the explosion at the barracks, talked his way out of the compound, then called his allies to tell them the news: Hitler was dead.

In Berlin, complications began almost immediately. Phone contact with Hitler's field headquarters had not been severed, and soon word reached Berlin that the Führer had somehow survived the blast, which blew out the walls of the barracks. The heavy table had deflected the force of the bomb. Hitler walked outside, his pants aflame and his eardrums severely damaged, and set about stamping out the rebellion.

General Friedrich Fromm, chief of the reserve army in Berlin, had known about the plot ahead of time. He was to launch the coup by dispatching his soldiers to occupy key government buildings. Learning of Hitler's survival, he refused to cooperate. When the plotters arrived at army headquarters, Fromm tried to have them arrested; instead, they managed to take him prisoner. But following a gunfight in the army headquarters, Fromm was freed and the conspirators arrested. Fearing he would be implicated, given his prior knowledge of the plot, Fromm had the four key players—including Stauffenberg—taken out to the courtyard and executed. The next morning, Hitler took to the radio to denounce the plotters and thank Providence for saving his life again, just as it had in November 1939 in Munich.

Rosenberg could not understand how military generals—who had not risen up against the hated Weimar Republic—would try to assassinate the founding hero of the Third Reich. "Never before," he claimed, "has an officer wanted to murder the highest commander-in-chief in such a cowardly fashion."

Himmler set about arresting anyone tied to this or other plots against the Führer; some committed suicide by gunshot or grenade or poison to avoid arrest. Prisoners were beaten and tortured for information. Those who survived were put on trial in notorious People's Court proceedings, then hung on Hitler's explicit orders, using ceiling hooks and thin wire to ensure slow, painful deaths. Back in the Wolf's Lair, the Führer watched the gruesome executions on film. Himmler arrested relatives of some of the conspirators, dispatched them to concentration camps, and sent their children to orphanages.

Rosenberg's rage was inflamed by a detail that came out during the trials. Major Ludwig von Leonrod, a Catholic, had gone to an army chaplain who was a friend of his, Father Hermann Wehrle, and asked whether or not church doctrine permitted assassination of a tyrannical despot. The cleric said no, but in court he testified that Leonrod's question seemed theoretical, so he reported it—not to the Nazis, but to his bishop.

"So the Vatican has been in the know for half a year. And waits for the Catholic assassins like Stauffenberg, who always wore a golden cross on his chest," Rosenberg wrote. "Unfortunately, he was shot <u>before</u> an interrogation, so that nothing could be heard about <u>his</u> confessors."

Leonrod and Wehrle, too, were both executed.

In October 1944, Rosenberg slept in his log cabin in the woods of Michendorf for the first time, reveling in the "deepest calm while the surrounding world is raging." Several times that summer he had retreated to the village south of Potsdam, sleeping aboard his own special train, "Gotenland," to get away from the devastation in Berlin. His birthplace of Reval, Estonia, had been pummeled in the fighting, as had Aachen, the spa town, and Cologne—all the places he had visited as a youth. At no time was Rosenberg more shocked than when he visited Munich, the birthplace of Nazism. "We drove in at midnight," he recounted in the diary. "A maze of ruins and wires. The nearby streets destroyed." The city was "shredded . . . mutilated."

The beams that propped up the Third Reich were collapsing all around them. The Soviets had reversed all of the German advances. "Now," Rosenberg wrote, "the biggest battles are taking place on <u>German</u> soil. Near the Führer's headquarters." He remained minister for the occupied eastern territories, but it was an empty title now: as one bitter bureaucrat noted, it was the "Ministry for the no longer Occupied Eastern Territories." His old foe Goebbels gleefully noted that Rosenberg was like a European monarch "without countries or subjects."

Rosenberg spent the last months of 1944 trying to beat back a fundamental—though ultimately meaningless—challenge to his work. It involved Himmler and a Soviet general who had been captured at the front, Andrei Vlasov. For three years, Rosenberg and many others had tried in vain to change Hitler's mind about enlisting the various nationalities in the East to fight against Moscow. The Führer would not do it. Give them arms and they might turn them against the Nazis: This was Hitler's ironclad conviction. It could not be changed.

But in the army, a movement to let Russians fight the Russians coalesced, and in July 1942 they thought they had found just the sort of charismatic leader they needed in Vlasov. He told the Germans that the Red Army was primed and ready to turn against Stalin and overthrow the communists. If the patriotism of the people could be rallied against their dictator, a revolution was possible. All he needed was an army and a political operation. The military's propaganda wing set about turning Vlasov into the paper leader of a fictional Russian liberation committee and hoped that by doing so it could turn its dreams into reality.

Rosenberg was wary. Vlasov was talking about a unified Russia. It sounded as though the Nazis would be helping to set up a powerful new Russia—exactly what they had spent the past twenty years trying to break apart. But at the same time, Rosenberg was desperate. He agreed to go along with the idea of a liberation committee for Russia as long as the other major eastern nationalities—the Ukrainians, the Belarusians, the Estonians—got their own.

In January 1943, a pamphlet signed by Vlasov was dropped over the war zone. It appealed to the Russian people to support his cause: the overthrow of Stalin, peace with Germany, and a "New Russia" free of both communists and capitalists. The fliers were a hit, and Vlasov went on a lecture tour through the occupied East, where he spoke freely. Perhaps too freely. He denounced the Nazi forced labor program and the brutal German administration. "The Russian people lived, lives, and shall live," Vlasov declared. "It will never be possible to reduce it to the status of a colonial people."

The Nazis were furious. This was supposed to be harmless propaganda. Now it sounded threatening. In June 1943, Hitler reeled in the Vlasov operation. Himmler denounced the Soviet general and his lecturing of the Germans. "Herr Vlasov began to tell us stories with his Russian superciliousness," Himmler said in a speech to a group of SS officers later that year. "He said, 'Germany has never yet been able to defeat Russia. Russia can be beaten only by Russians.' You see, gentlemen, this sentence constitutes a mortal danger to a people and an army."

But now, a year later, with the momentum of the war fully against the Nazis, Vlasov had reappeared on the scene, and his sponsor this time was none other than Heinrich Himmler. Worse still for Rosenberg, the SS leader backed Vlasov's idea of a unified Russia, and Hitler gave a nod of approval.

This was one disgrace too many. On October 12, 1944, Rosenberg sent a memo of protest to Hitler. He complained that the Nazi vision for the East was being corrupted. "I beg you, my Führer, to tell me whether you still desire my work in this field," he wrote. "In view of developments, I must surmise that you no longer deem my activity necessary."

Bormann told Rosenberg that Hitler had been bedridden and had not read Rosenberg's report. Rosenberg never heard back from Hitler.

On November 14, Vlasov appeared at Hradčany Castle in Prague to announce the formation of a Committee for the Liberation of the Peoples of Russia. A manifesto was released. Vlasov pledged "equality of all peoples and their genuine right to national development, self-determination, and statehood."

But to Rosenberg these were just empty words. In reality, Himmler had simply reinforced the idea of a new imperialist Russia by backing Vlasov. Rosenberg had known the mission was doomed from the start—it came too late in the war—but it still upset him because he knew that somehow he would be blamed for the debacle.

"If they all fail, the fault lies with the erratic treatment of this matter, then letting it all slide. No seriousness regarding the eastern problem," he jotted in his diary. "I will write later about the painfulness and outrageousness of the personal side of this. The feelings are still too raw. They are also less important given the fate of the Reich. . . . I can only hope that the German Reich won't suffer any more damage than it already has thanks to political fools like Koch."

His bitterness about the Reichskommissar would not abate. The man was "a textbook example of philistinism gone amok in world politics, who may be well-suited for breeding pigs in East Prussia and building settlements in Zichenau"—part of occupied Poland—"but has become a disaster for the Reich's East policy." Koch actually had the gall to say that the Ukrainian people had no history. "Almost impossible to say anything more stupid," Rosenberg foamed. "Several assassinations of his colleagues can most likely be blamed on this and other speeches and actions." Chief among them was the killing of Wilhelm Kube, head of the civilian administration in Belarus, who had been blown up by a time bomb placed under his bed in September 1943 by a maid allied with the Resistance.

"I can definitely understand how a Nietzsche could go crazy in _his_ world," Rosenberg wrote. "He _saw_ it all coming, and he couldn't change it." If only Hitler had listened to Rosenberg. It could have altered the course of the entire war. "An army of a million Ukrainians with a vision of a new country in the east perhaps could have spared us the catastrophe of Stalingrad."

And yet, through all of the rejection and disappointment and failure, Rosenberg refused to turn on Hitler.

He stayed at his post, empty as it was.

At the beginning of December, after sleeping in a hotel for a year, Rosenberg moved back to the Dahlem neighborhood of Berlin, where his home had been restored after the bombings. The next day, he wrote an entry in his diary that would be the last to survive the war. "From the remaining ruins of my house, the remnants of my library were picked out. Torn up, battered, and still full of mortar chunks and glass shards." He picked out a volume by the mystical Austrian poet Rainer Maria Rilke, and it brought him back sharply to his youth, to the carefree days he had spent poring over the pages.

"How much time has passed since my youth," Rosenberg wrote. He could hardly believe it.

The Soviets were at the doorstep. In late 1944, Hitler finally had to flee the Wolf's Lair in East Prussia for the safety of Berlin. In December, he traveled to the Western Front to supervise an attempt to break through the Allied lines with two hundred thousand troops, but in the Battle of the Bulge, British and American forces turned the German armies back. It was to be the last major Nazi offensive of the war.

In January, with defeat all but assured, Hitler returned to the capital. From east and west, millions of Allied troops pressed toward Berlin.

By the dawn of 1945, Rosenberg had not had a private meeting with Hitler in more than a year. He would see the Führer for the final time on February 24, when Hitler delivered a speech to try to rally the party leadership. Hitler was in frighteningly poor condition. He hobbled into the room like an old man. His left hand shook so violently that he could not raise a glass of water to his lips. Rosenberg managed nothing more than to shake the Führer's hand. Time and again, he tried to request a meeting through intermediaries. Word came back that Hitler would be happy enough to see Rosenberg over tea, but he knew the minister would insist on "a technical discussion," and Hitler was in no frame of mind for that.

"What is the head of a state for," Rosenberg asked his chief of staff, "if not a technical discussion?"

One night in March, the Americans launched their largest air raid against Berlin, dispatching a thousand planes over the city during daylight hours. Three thousand Germans were killed, a hundred thousand made homeless, and large parts of the city were left without water and electricity.

The roof of Rosenberg's house collapsed in a raid later in the month, and he moved into the basement with Hedwig and Irene. After the attack, "I did what seemed important," he wrote later in a jailhouse accounting of his life. "The garden was spaded, vegetables and potatoes planted." The attack had ruined plans for Irene's fifteenth birthday party. Rosenberg watched her as she sat at the family's typewriter in the basement drafting something. "What she wrote I don't know, but it was probably about life in Berlin, what she saw of the destruction, and what she heard about death in the heart of the city."

He learned that his friend and close colleague Arno Schickedanz had killed himself, along with his wife and their eight-year-old daughter. Rosenberg considered his own course of action. Cyanide capsules had been distributed to all members of the Nazi leadership, and Rosenberg had stockpiled enough for his family. He would not let his loved ones be taken by the Soviets.

By April, nearly all of the German armies had been destroyed; more than a million German soldiers had died since the beginning of 1945 alone.

Still, Hitler did not surrender.

On April 20, he turned fifty-six, and the Soviets launched their final assault on Berlin.

The next day, a rainy morning, Rosenberg stood in the window and looked over his garden. He was leaving for good. "There, the paths where we used to stroll," he wrote. "In the back, Irene's swing and the half-demolished garden house. On the right, the slender birch recently planted. Everything we still possess must remain behind."

The Soviet soldiers were gutted by the deaths of their comrades, shocked by the extermination camps they had overrun, and intent on revenge.

Wrote one soldier: "They are going to remember this march by our army over German territory for a long, long time." The Soviets plundered everything, from art to industrial machines to bicycles and radios and wristwatches. They burned down German cities and raped women by the hundreds of thousands. "We are taking revenge for everything," another soldier wrote home, "and our revenge is just. Fire for fire, blood for blood, death for death."

Hitler's apartment in the Reich Chancellery had been destroyed, and he took to his bunker belowground with his girlfriend, Eva Braun, and his most loyal supporters: Bormann, his top generals, and his personal aide. Goebbels moved into the shelter with his wife and six children. Two days after Hitler's birthday, in a hysterical outburst that eclipsed anything his inner circle had seen before, he finally admitted that the war was lost, that everyone had betrayed him.

He spurned offers to spirit him out of Berlin to Berchtesgaden. No, he insisted, he would stay and do the right thing: He would shoot himself.

He suggested that Göring, who was in his Bavarian compound in Obersalzberg, could take charge of southern Germany and even negotiate with the Allies. When word of this reached Göring, he pulled out a copy of a 1941 decree setting him up as Hitler's successor should the Führer's "freedom of action" be curtailed.

Göring sent a message to the bunker asking whether the time had come for him to take over. "If by 2200 hours no answer is forthcoming, I shall assume you have been deprived of your freedom of action," Göring wrote. "I will then consider the terms of your decree to have come into force and act accordingly for the good of the people and the Fatherland."

Bormann brought Hitler the message, along with a second one Göring had sent to Ribbentrop, and persuaded the Führer that Göring was staging a coup.

Blind with rage, Hitler promptly stripped Göring of all offices, and Bormann dispatched the SS to place him under immediate house arrest. Robert Ritter von Greim flew to Berlin, dodging antiaircraft fire, to accept his commission as Göring's successor as chief of the Luftwaffe. But when word arrived via a BBC report that Himmler was offering up an unconditional surrender, Hitler ordered Greim to fly back out of the capital and place yet another member of his inner circle under arrest, crying, "A traitor must never succeed me as Führer!"

Meanwhile, the Soviet armies closed in on the government district. A week after Hitler's meltdown in the bunker, the enemy was at Potsdamer Platz: barely a quarter of a mile away.

The following day, April 30, 1945, the generals came to Hitler with sobering news: They could not hold out any longer.

That same week, the American armies reached the towers and turrets of Neuschwanstein Castle, the soaring fairy-tale fortress built for Bavaria's Mad King Ludwig atop a rugged ridge south of Munich. James Rorimer, a curator at New York's Metropolitan Museum of Art and a member of the Allies' Monuments, Fine Arts, and Archives unit, had been hanging around the map room of his army group for weeks, waiting for word that the Allies had taken the castle. He commandeered a Jeep from the Red Cross and—ignoring the fact that he would be driving 130 miles through territory that had not yet been entirely cleared of German fighters—rushed south to investigate.

The Monuments Men, as they would come to be immortalized, were a small band of academics and architects dispatched to protect and secure Europe's treasures as the armies pushed toward Berlin in 1944–1945. Rorimer had spent some time in Paris after its liberation, in August 1944, and there he had met Rose Valland, a French art historian who worked for Rosenberg's operation at the Jeu de Paume. All through the occupation, Valland had surreptitiously recorded what artwork the Nazis had taken and where they had taken it. She guided the American museum official on a tour of the Einsatzstab's storage facilities, invited him to her apartment, and finally, over champagne, shared with him her meticulous lists. She had promised Rorimer that at Neuschwanstein and a few other castles he would find the stolen French art.

Arriving at the fortress, Rorimer learned that the Nazis had disappeared, but the longtime custodian was still there, watching over the treasure. "It was a castle in the air come to life for egocentric and mad thirsters after power," Rorimer would write, "a picturesque, romantic, and remote setting for a gangster crowd to carry on its art looting activities."

Lugging around an enormous ring of keys, the German took Rorimer and his men up staircases pitched almost as steeply as the craggy rocks upon which the castle stood. The curator showed the Americans from room to room, virtually all of them crammed with plunder. They found unopened crates embossed with the initials of Rosenberg's outfit—ERR—as well as tapestries, books, prints, and, of course, many, many paintings. They found, behind a steel door, two chests of jewels taken from the Rothschilds and a thousand pieces of silver belonging to the David-Weill banking family.

"I passed through the rooms as in a trance," Rorimer wrote, "hoping that the Germans had lived up to their reputation for being methodical and had photographs, catalogues, and records of all these things. Without them it would take twenty years to identify the agglomeration of loot."

He was in luck. In another wing of the castle they found eight thousand photo negatives and a card catalog documenting the twenty-two thousand pieces swept up by Rosenberg's staff.

Still, remarkably, the Allies had not found the mother lode. Some of the most priceless pieces were still missing. Two other Monuments Men, Robert Posey and Lincoln Kirstein, had an idea where they might be. At the end of March, they had happened upon a young art historian who'd worked closely with Göring and von Behr in Paris. He told them that they would find Hitler's pilfered collection of art hidden deep inside the tunnels of a salt mine outside a little village east of Salzburg: Alt Aussee.

A few days after American forces took control of the town, Posey and Kirstein sped to Austria to check it out. After navigating the steep, winding road to the mine's entrance, they discovered, to their alarm, that the fleeing Nazis had sealed it with explosives. But the next day they managed to pick their way through a small opening and into the tunnel. It did not take long for them to find what they had come to see, flickering in the glow of their lanterns.

Inside the second room they checked, they discovered panels of the famous Ghent altarpiece, dating to 1432. Deeper inside the mountain, a large chamber held boxes of artwork and, on a dirty mattress, the Bruges *Madonna* carved by Michelangelo. A few days later, still working through the enormous cache, they located Vermeer's *Astronomer*.

Tallying up all the loot, the men estimated that the Nazis had hidden nearly nine thousand pieces of priceless art inside the mine at Alt Aussee—truckloads of paintings, drawings, prints, sculptures, and tapestries.

All told, some 650,000 pieces of art were stolen by the Nazis. The Allies resolved to return the art to their owners, starting with the Ghent altarpiece, which was flown back to Belgium for restoration and display. The Monuments division spent six years cataloging and repatriating objects. But many pieces would remain missing—some for decades, some apparently forever—and many could never be returned, for the rightful owners had perished in the Holocaust. Many other pieces, having been dealt by unscrupulous buyers and sellers taking advantage of wartime chaos, would become the subject of prolonged international disputes.

Some would turn up in strange places over the years, like a safety deposit box in Zurich owned by an art dealer who resurrected his career after serving only a few years in prison for his role in the looting of France. Generations on, in 2012, authorities would find more than fourteen hundred paintings, worth a billion dollars, in the Munich apartment of Cornelius Gurlitt, whose father, though he had Jewish ancestry, had become a buyer for Hitler's museum and in the meantime acquired for himself hundreds of "degenerate" paintings—by Matisse, by Otto Dix, by Picasso—from fleeing Jews at bargain basement prices.

The ripples of Rosenberg's plunder would travel across generations.

On April 21, Rosenberg and his family were driven north, past the ruins and the fleeing refugees, eventually arriving in Flensburg, 275 miles northeast of Berlin on the Denmark border.

He was in Flensburg when the bombshell came. At three thirty in the afternoon on April 30, Hitler and Eva Braun, whom he had married the day before, had closed themselves in his study and ended their lives, he with a gun, she with poison. Five hours later, Goebbels and his wife committed suicide after insisting that the doctors on hand anesthetize and then poison their six children.

Naming a successor in his final orders, Hitler passed over Göring and Himmler and instead selected Grand Admiral Karl Dönitz, chief of the German navy, whose novel strategy of deploying U-boats in packs had helped the Nazis sink some three thousand merchant ships and Allied naval vessels during the war. The appointment served only to hand Dönitz the shame of officially surrendering Germany to the Allies, which he did on May 8, eight days after Hitler's suicide.

Rosenberg, who had been officially relieved by Dönitz of his duties as minister of the occupied eastern territories on May 6, walked the shoreline of the Flensburg Firth, an arm of the Baltic

Sea, and thought about where his life had taken him. He thought of his birthplace in Estonia, six hundred miles to the northeast. He knew he would never see it again. Returning to headquarters, he fell hard, injured his foot, and ended up in the hospital again. He blamed the fall on the foot ailment that had hobbled him for years, but Albert Speer, Hitler's architect and, after 1942, minister of armaments and war production, told a different story.

"He was found almost lifeless," he wrote. "He spoke of having poisoned himself, and a suicide attempt was suspected, but it turned out that he was merely drunk."

On May 18, the British came for him. Rosenberg said he had written a letter to Field Marshal Bernard Montgomery six days earlier, "putting myself at his disposal." By other accounts, soldiers stumbled upon him while they searched for Himmler; the SS leader was captured by the Allies on May 21 while trying to flee in disguise, and committed suicide two days later by biting down on a cyanide capsule.

Rosenberg kissed his weeping wife and daughter and limped off to the cars that would take him to prison. Sitting in his cell, he listened to two Allied guards attempting to sing "Lili Marlene," the song of the times for troops on both sides, a soldier's lament about being separated from his lover.

A few days later, Rosenberg was shackled, taken to an airfield, and flown south. Looking out the window, he spotted the remains of Cologne. "As if trampled down by gigantic beasts, Cologne's rubble lies heaped around the skeleton of the cathedral," Rosenberg wrote later. "Blown-up bridges in the river. A desert giving evidence of the terrible fate of people and Reich."

As he realized that his transport was headed west, a wave of relief passed over him. He was not being handed over to the Soviets.

Instead he was deposited at the Palace Hotel, in the spa town of Bad Mondorf, Luxembourg, just over the border from Germany.

When he arrived, many of the other leading survivors of the Third Reich were already there, including Göring, who had managed to escape from house arrest in Obersalzberg before being detained by the Allies.

The eight-story hotel had been stripped of all its luxuries and converted into a plain holding pen for the century's greatest war criminals. The chandeliers, carpets, curtains, and beds were gone. Bars replaced the windows. The prisoners slept on army cots with straw mattresses and coarse blankets. To prevent suicides, tables were rigged to collapse under a person's weight.

Rosenberg was given a full-body strip search, his clothes were combed for poison capsules and sharp objects, and he was relieved of his shoelaces and belts.

His temporary home was no longer known as the Palace Hotel. The Americans had given it a new name: the Allied Supreme Headquarters Center for Axis Nationals—ASHCAN for short.

Nuremberg in ruins. *(National Archives)*

23

"Loyal to Him to the End"

On March 8, 1945, Robert Kempner and his wife went to the federal courthouse at Ninth and Market in Philadelphia and took their oaths as United States citizens. He wore a suit and a striped tie; she wore a flower in her hat.

Kempner had earned his citizenship. His government work had expanded greatly in the last three years of the war. He was not only providing expert testimony for the Justice Department and intelligence to the FBI but was also reporting to the Military Intelligence Division in the War Department and, with his wife and a team of assistants, producing extensive reports for the Office of Strategic Services, forerunner to the Central Intelligence Agency. For the OSS, the Kempners worked with Henry Field, an anthropologist assigned by Roosevelt to study what the president considered the most pressing postwar issue: the migration and resettlement of international refugees. The top-secret "M" Project resulted in more than six hundred reports of global scope; the

Kempners provided a registry of major and minor German officials and a five-part report on women in Nazi Germany. The studies were distributed to key officials in D.C. and then, with Roosevelt's death, they entered "the twilight zone of file and forget."

Kempner still hoped to shed his status as a special employee and land a full-time post with the FBI. Even though it was unclear whether he had a future with the Bureau, he turned down offers of two well-paid jobs in Washington, one as a $6,200-a-year investigator with the Office of Alien Property Custodian, which oversaw the seizure of enemy property in the United States, and the other as a $5,600-a-year researcher with the War Department, which was preparing for war crimes trials against the Nazis.

But with the Allied armies closing in on Berlin and war crimes prosecutions on the horizon, Kempner had positioned himself for a role in what promised to be the trial of the century. His work against the accused German seditionists had helped him forge important connections. Pitching himself for a job on the prosecution team, he wrote that he thought of the trial as the conclusion of a case he had tried to make back in the 1930s. "It might be a good idea," he wrote, "to have at least one person around with some knowledge of German administration, law and practices, and the right answers to the lies of your defendants."

The Allies had been calling for their enemies to be brought to justice as war criminals since 1942, though they were divided about how to do it. In a twist, Churchill argued for summary executions, while Stalin wanted trials. Henry Morgenthau, Roosevelt's treasury secretary, recommended severe retribution against the country that had dragged Europe and America into two world wars. He wanted the army dismantled. He wanted the permanent destruction of German industry. He wanted the Nazis interned and sentenced to hard labor. He wanted the top leaders shot upon capture. Secretary of War Henry Stimson argued against the vengeful idea. It made no sense to use the Nazis' own tactics against them. "It is primarily by the thorough apprehension, investigation, and trial of all the Nazi leaders and instruments of the Nazi system of terrorism such as the Gestapo," Stimson wrote, "that we can demonstrate the abhorrence which the world has for such a system." Roosevelt backed Stimson, and by 1945 the Allies had agreed that the Second World War would end with the leading Nazis in the dock.

There were endless questions about how war crimes trials would work. No precedent existed, no rules, no mechanism. Stimson set his War Department to studying the problem, and a low-level lawyer, Colonel Murray C. Bernays, drew up a brief memorandum from which the International Military Tribunal, in all its flawed glory, would spring. Bernays argued that the Nazi system was a grand conspiracy, and thus its leaders could be held responsible as criminals. At the same time, the separate components of the Nazi machine—the party, the SS, the Gestapo— were criminal organizations themselves, and each member could be deemed a criminal as well. In six pages, Bernays found a way to bring both top leaders and rank-and-file Nazis to justice in one dramatic trial.

The ideas came in for some criticism. For one thing, the entire indictment would smack of ex post facto law, holding the Nazis accountable for crimes established after they had been perpetrated. And was it just to convict millions of people merely for membership in a vast criminal organization?

But Bernays's plan won the attention of the man named in May 1945 to lead the American prosecution team, Supreme Court Justice Robert H. Jackson. Over the summer, Jackson met with leaders of the British, French, and Soviet delegations to craft a charter for the war crimes tribunal. It generally followed the ideas dreamed up by the War Department lawyer. The Nazis would be tried on four counts of conspiring to commit, and then carrying out, wars of aggression, war crimes—murdering and abusing civilians, employing slave labor, and killing prisoners—and crimes against humanity, including the annihilation of the Jews. Twenty-three men were to be tried as "major war criminals," including Göring, Ribbentrop, Hess, Rosenberg, and, in absentia, Bormann, whose whereabouts after the war were unknown.

Robert Jackson saw the trial not just as an historic opportunity to create a powerful new international legal precedent but as a moral cause. At the same time, he took pains to avoid the impression that the tribunal would be a show trial, revenge in a judicial cloak.

Kempner ended up on Jackson's radar through work Kempner was doing for the War Department. As was his habit, he had sent a few unsolicited suggestions about the planned trials to the department's War Crimes Division. Though he turned down their offer of a full-time job, still pinning his hopes on the FBI, he was quickly hired as a freelance expert consultant producing reports about the "organization, personnel, and activities" of the German government, the history of the Nazi Party, and the particulars of German record-keeping systems. The reports, produced for a fee of $25 a day, were to serve as background material for those arresting and prosecuting the war criminals. Kempner also wrote a series of short biographies of key Nazi figures, including a detailed document on Göring.

The refugee lawyer documented that Göring had founded the Gestapo, the "machinery for illegal arrests, internments, and confiscation of property." He implicated Göring in the Reichstag fire that prompted President Hindenburg to sign the emergency decree suspending civil rights in Germany. That decree led to an immediate national crackdown on communists, pacifists, and other Nazi enemies. "The decree was in force until the defeat of the Third Reich in 1945, and became the main tool for the extermination and expropriation policy of the Nazis throughout Europe. Thus Göring . . . became responsible for all such acts."

The Reichsmarschall would not disagree, Kempner reported: He publicly took responsibility for his subordinates' actions during a speech to officers in the city of Dortmund just after the Nazis took power in 1933. "Every bullet fired from a police pistol is my bullet. If that is called murder, then I have murdered. All this I have ordered; I stand for it; mine is the responsibility for it and I am not afraid of it."

Kempner's brief was not quite an indictment, but it was a start.

The document made the rounds in the War Department, and Kempner caught the attention of Jackson's inner circle, including Bernays. "He is thoroughly familiar with the activities of the Nazis prior to their access to power, did not leave Germany until 1935 or '36, has kept up with their doings since that time, and has had a good deal of experience in the United States working on cases involving Nazi infiltration and subversion," Bernays wrote to Jackson on July 17. "His study on Göring . . . is sound, solid stuff. I think we can use him to advantage." Three days later, Kempner was officially on the team. He told his superiors at the FBI that he would be taking "unpaid leave" for about ten weeks.

The years of writing letters and memos and reports by the hundreds had finally paid off. He was issued the coat of a civilian military officer, with triangular patches on the lapels emblazoned US, and on August 3 he flew from Washington, D.C., to London, by way of Bermuda, the Azores, and Paris. Separately, in two boxes weighing ninety-one pounds, he shipped some of the material he had collected about Germany and the Nazis.

Kempner, a man with an outsize ego, couldn't help but feel like he was returning to his native country as a key player in a conquering army.

"I am finishing something I started sixteen years ago," he told one newspaper correspondent. Years later he would say: "I just wanted to put a little piece of justice back into the world."

Nuremberg was a ruin, a cemetery. Tens of thousands of bodies lay under block after block of bombed-out buildings. Disinfectant hung in the air. Visitors were warned against drinking the water. The Bavarian courthouse, the Palace of Justice, had taken its share of concussions during the war. Its windows were blasted out, its water lines severed, its corridors scorched by fire; one bomb had dropped straight through to the basement. But amazingly, the stone edifice stood tall amid the wreckage, and officials at the International Military Tribunal decided it was there that they would try the Nazi war criminals. First they would need to move out the American soldiers who had converted the main courtroom into a bar. BEER TONIGHT, ½ MARK, read the sign when the lawyers came to vet the place.

Meeting in Nuremberg also had symbolic resonance. It was there that the Nazis had staged their enormous party rallies celebrating Germany's revival. It was there that the Nazis had stripped Jews of their citizenship in 1935. Now, it was at Nuremberg that the men responsible would be held to account for their crimes.

On August 12, Rosenberg and the other Nazi defendants were flown in a C-47 from Bad Mondorf. "Well, my friends," Göring said, looking out the window, "take a good look at the Rhine. It's probably the last time we'll ever see it." The Nazis were moved into the prison behind the Palace of Justice, where they would wait out the trial in what was known as C wing.

Rosenberg was assigned to cell 16 in the lower level, between Albert Speer, Hitler's architect and the man who relied on forced labor to run Germany's war production factories, and Hans Frank, the cruel leader of the General Government in Poland. Each cell had a cot, one chair, a rickety table. A toilet in the corner was the only place to get away from the watchful eyes of the guards, who were instructed to keep a continual suicide watch over the prisoners. At night, a spotlight shone on the inmates. "I imagined them crouching in their cells like wounded beasts," wrote Airey Neave, a member of the British prosecution team, who had escaped from a German prison camp during the war. "I feared to approach them as a man backs from a corpse."

The prisoners were to keep their hands outside their blankets at all times, a rule Rosenberg particularly protested. Every time he tried to warm up his hands by slipping them under the covers, the guard would poke him awake. Contact between the defendants was strictly limited, and they were allowed only a single letter from their family per week. Their only real human interaction came through sessions with prison psychologists and interrogators.

In the months before the trial began, Rosenberg would be questioned more than two dozen times. At the very first session in Nuremberg, on August 14, he was confronted with his diary, which Rosenberg called "notes" and "short impressions." The interrogator accused Rosenberg of being evasive and warned him that his answers would be challenged by the voluminous documentary evidence now in Allied hands.

"You know that we have all of your private papers, do you not?"

"I heard about it," Rosenberg answered. "I do not know."

"Think about these things tonight," the interrogator said, "and if you don't tell the truth more readily than you have today, you will probably end up in plenty of trouble."

One of the lawyers in the room that day was Thomas J. Dodd, a federal prosecutor who had worked with Kempner in 1942 on a Nazi espionage case in Connecticut. He found Rosenberg to be "very keen minded, sly, cagy," but he couldn't help noting that his brown suit showed signs of wear. "I thought how the mighty have fallen," Dodd wrote back to his wife. "Here in this city, where he strutted in his fancy Nazi clothes. He is now a jailbird in the ruins." A month later, Rosenberg tried in vain to explain his philosophies to Dodd and squirmed away from the charge that he and Hitler had plotted the end of the churches after the war.

"Isn't it a fact," Dodd asked, "that it was your purpose to destroy the old established religions?"

"Well—" Rosenberg began to say.

"You don't need to give us a speech to such a question," Dodd interrupted.

"To such a question I am obliged to answer no," he said. The prosecutor suggested Rosenberg read his own book, but the Nazi claimed that he had never been interested in an "official fight" with the clerics.

"You were certainly for a fight against the Jews, weren't you?"

"Yes," Rosenberg said, "for the elimination of the Jews from the political leadership of the Reich."

"You wanted to put them out of Germany altogether."

"Well, this is the simplest solution to the problem."

Rosenberg acknowledged that his theories on the Jews were "very frequently applied" by the Nazis.

"Are you now ashamed of the views which you expressed for many years while you were in power?" Dodd asked. "Answer that yes or no."

"No," Rosenberg replied.

"Are you aware now of any responsibility for the present plight of Germany?"

"In the course of this last month, I often wondered whether I could have done better," Rosenberg said. "Perhaps in the course of these twenty years, I dropped certain words which, with a clear head, I may not use now. But still they were expressed in a moment of struggle. As a member of a movement which is responsible for what has happened, I of course am to a certain extent responsible. Well, the gist of what I was aiming at and driving at and what I wanted to bring about is decent and honest, and even today I can't think about it otherwise."

Then he stopped and, apparently realizing what he had admitted, walked back his remark. "I can only be responsible for what I have done personally."

Hours of questions followed in September and October as interrogator Thomas Hinkel confronted Rosenberg with document after document as the combative Nazi threw up implausible, convoluted defenses.

Rosenberg argued that the Nazi anti-Jewish policies were "defensive" measures against a hostile enemy who wanted to bring Germany to ruin. The Germans deported the Jews, just as the Zionists were said to have forced Palestinians off their land. Rosenberg acknowledged that prisoners of war died of exposure and malnutrition; but so did German soldiers. He tried to deny that the central point of Nazi ideology was that the "Aryan" race was superior to all others. He said that while books and pieces of art had been confiscated by his Einsatzstab, it was possible that Germany would have returned some of them one day. He denied knowledge of the goings-on inside Germany's concentration camps; he had never even been inside one, he said, and "the police kept rather silent on that subject." He denied having anything to do with the killing of the Jews in the eastern lands, though his civil administration had been deeply involved in the Holocaust.

"I had heard that some shooting had been done of the Jews," Rosenberg allowed on September 22.

"What did you do when you heard that?" Hinkel, the interrogator, asked. "Did you make any inquiry?"

"No."

"Why not?"

"I couldn't," Rosenberg said. "It was not under my authority."

He contended that his efforts to learn more had been rebuffed by the SS and that if he had pressed further, "I would have received no reply anyway."

"You knew it was Himmler's policy to exterminate the Jews, didn't you?"

"In this shape or manner, I did not believe it until the end."

"You had been informed of that, had you not?"

"No," Rosenberg claimed, "I was not."

He diminished his ministry's role until it sounded not just powerless but entirely pointless. "I wish to say that my headquarters were in Berlin and I was simply issuing general rules and laws for the administration," he said, "but the regional matters, I didn't go into." He contended that the reports from those on the ground in the East had not gone into great detail.

In fact, he said on October 4, the eleventh session in eight days, he had had nothing to do with the handling of the Jews as minister for the East. "I have never participated in any discussions on the Jewish problem at all," Rosenberg told Hinkel. Personally, he wanted to "reduce the number of Jews in Germany by creating a place where they would be all by themselves in their Jewish homeland." But it wasn't up to him—it had been Himmler's responsibility.

"You have been interested in the Jewish question for years, haven't you?" Hinkel asked.

"But I was so overburdened with the work of establishing my own ministry and the entire Jewish problem was so neatly separate from any of my responsibilities that I did not spend any time on that," Rosenberg said. He assumed that they were being fed and given productive jobs.

"You mean, you never discussed the Jewish problem with anybody from the time you were appointed minister for the occupied eastern territories," Hinkel asked. "Is that your statement? . . . I find it a little difficult to believe, that with all the interest you have had in this problem for so many years, that you would drop it so suddenly when you became minister for the occupied eastern territories, and wouldn't have enough curiosity regarding the treatment of the people under your own jurisdiction, that you wouldn't ask anybody or receive any reports about it."

"It was always our habit," Rosenberg claimed, "that once an assignment was given to a man, nobody else meddled with the man who had the assignment."

Hinkel returned with documents showing that Rosenberg had received reports of eastern atrocities.

On October 19, the indictments were finally handed down against Rosenberg and the rest of the Nazi leaders on cell block C in Nuremberg. Neave, the British prosecutor, was chosen to serve the papers. When he arrived at Rosenberg's cell, he found the Nazi covered with bread crumbs he hadn't bothered to brush off his clothes. "He had the expression of a sick spaniel," he wrote.

"His appearance was that of an off-duty undertaker in a Boris Karloff horror film, for which the yellowish tinge of his complexion was well-suited."

The cell was foul-smelling and littered with papers, and as Rosenberg rose to face his visitor, he was trembling.

Kempner made it to Paris on August 4, 1945, "after a 27½ hour flight minus 2 hours rest," he wrote to his wife, Ruth, and his onetime mistress, Margot Lipton, back in Lansdowne, Pennsylvania. Then he flew to London for his assignment. The city was a wreck after years of German bombing, still pocked with destroyed buildings and craters and piles of rubble.

An American citizen for all of five months, Kempner had come to believe that his adopted land was the greatest of countries and that Europe was a lost cause. He had little hope that the Continent would ever return to its former glory. It made no sense, he told the women, to return to Germany and try to rebuild their old lives. Better to keep doing what they were doing in America. "You cannot imagine how fortunate we have been (and selfish, too, by the way). All the little nuisances are nothing compared with the way of things in Europe. . . . Nothing is more exciting as Lansdowne and I regard this uniformed trip just as a means for my own training and getting a new perspective (besides the job which must be performed)."

A few days later Kempner returned to Paris, where he had been assigned to help analyze German documents pouring into a central processing office set up for the tribunal in a building a block from the Champs-Élysées and the Arc de Triomphe.

The Allies had ordered their armies to look for key archives as they stormed across Europe, and the soldiers turned up a true mother lode of paper. The Paris office was one of three document centers, and its analysts could barely keep up with the flood. There was no time to translate everything, let alone examine it for its evidentiary value. "These Nazis had a mania for writing things down," Jackson's interrogations chief, John Harlan Amen, told a newspaper reporter in September. "So now we are swamped with more documents than can possibly be gone through thoroughly in the time allotted to us, and new batches are being uncovered each day."

The Rosenberg papers that turned up in the castle outside Lichtenfels were only the beginning. The archivist for the German Foreign Office, Heinrich Valentin, showed investigators where to find nearly five hundred tons of diplomatic records hidden away in the rugged Harz Mountains in central Germany. He even helped the Allies order and pack them. Paul Schmidt, the translator who sat in on some of the most important diplomatic meetings of the Nazi era, surrendered his voluminous notes; he had them buried in large tin and wooden boxes in a forest. Göring's Luftwaffe papers were discovered scattered across Bavaria, and they were shipped to England with the official historian, Major General Hans-Detlef Herhudt von Rohden. He had begun a history of the air force, and he was directed to complete it. Sixty thousand files' worth of naval records, which were to be burned in an empty pool at a castle, were instead handed over intact. The archive of Hitler's official photographer, Heinrich Hoffmann, made its way to Nuremberg, where Hoffmann himself cataloged it.

Inside the Paris document center, Kempner got to work going through the captured records. One day, he was paging through Rosenberg documents when he was ordered to fly to Germany immediately. It would be his first trip back to his homeland in nearly a decade.

He boarded a military plane for the short flight to Frankfurt, and as he watched the plane pass over the ruins of his native country, he would write years later in his memoir, he was strangely unmoved. He could only think about how familiar it all looked. He felt as if he had been transported to 1918, when he'd made his way back to Germany through devastated Belgium and France.

But then the plane landed and Kempner was driven to Fechen-heim, where he leafed through captured military documents. Here before him were the orders for the destruction of Europe, written by the perpetrators themselves. Confronted by the hand-writing of the men responsible for the crimes of the Third Reich, Kempner was finally moved to emotion.

Later during that trip, he visited the cellar of the Reichsbank in Frankfurt. There he saw dozens of boxes the Nazis had hidden in the salt mines of central Germany at the end of the war. Inside the wooden crates were gold fillings the Nazis had extracted from the teeth of their victims. Thousands and thousands of pieces— each, Kempner thought, a testament to a murder and a final theft.

"I never dreamed in all my life," he wrote, "I would ever see something like this."

Robert Jackson decided that the tribunal should convict the Nazis using their own words. But it would be no easy task to sift through the mass of papers and make sense of these German atrocities on a continental scale.

Interrogations went hand in hand with document analysis, and to Kempner's great satisfaction, he was getting the chance to question witnesses and defendants. "For the criminals," Kempner wrote later, "my participation in the work in Nuremberg was very unpleasant. Now, they were facing someone who knew of their sins." One day he found himself face-to-face with one of his old adversaries.

"Good morning, Herr Göring," he said to the man who had fired him back in 1933. "I wonder if you remember me. It is a long time since we last met."

The week before, interrogators had questioned Göring about the Reichstag fire and reports that he had been behind a plot to burn the German legislature so the Nazis would have a pretext for clamping down on their communist opponents in 1933.

"This is absolute nonsense," Göring insisted. He was Reichstag president at the time—why would he ever burn down his own house?

Kempner was brought in to challenge that contention. According to Kempner, Göring remembered the disenfranchised lawyer well, and was surprised to see him enter the room. At first, Göring refused to submit to Kempner's questions. Surely, the man could not be fair. Kempner just smiled. "Reichsmarschall, I am not biased against you, I am very happy you threw me out on February 3, 1933. If you hadn't done it, I would have been smoke through a chimney."

With that, the interrogation began.

Kempner confronted Göring with information he had heard in 1933 from Rudolf Diels, Göring's Gestapo chief and Kempner's friend, who survived the war and was brought to Nuremberg as a potential witness. "Diels says you knew exactly that the fire was to be started in some manner," Kempner said, "and that he had prepared the arrest lists already." Göring told Kempner it was true that lists had been prepared. The Nazis had long been ready to crush the communists. But that was of no consequence. Even if the Reichstag had not burned, "they would have been arrested anyway."

Again he denied knowledge of the fire plot, saying it would have been "lunacy." He also told Kempner that he would like to hear his accusers make their allegations "to my face."

Göring was asked how it was that his press officer could tell Kempner, one hour after the fire, that Göring had declared that the communists were to blame. "Wasn't it too early to say without any investigation that the communists started the fire?"

"Yes, that is possible," Göring admitted, "but the Führer wanted it this way."

Kempner repeatedly circled back, pressing for details, challenging Göring's statements. He asked why Social Democrats and pacifists had been arrested. He asked why Göring had not followed up on reports that storm trooper leaders were involved in the fire. He asked about the passageway running between the

Reichstag and Göring's official residence, and why it had not been locked that night.

Through it all, Göring stuck to his line and challenged the idea that the Nazis had needed to set the building aflame to get Hindenburg to sign his infamous order stripping Germans of their civil rights.

In any case, Göring told Kempner, if he had conspired to burn down the Reichstag, it would have been for a different reason: The place was so ugly.

Kempner sent a steady stream of letters home. In one, he remarked that he was getting the chance to satisfy his tireless curiosity about the Nazi regime for hours each day. "Isn't that a wonderful life?" One day he mailed romantic postcards to both Ruth and Lipton; they were still living together in the house outside Philadelphia. Ruth's read, "My heart only belongs to you for life!" Lipton's read, "Nothing in the world is as sweet as you!" They sent him letters and telegrams and care packages of chocolate and soap. He sent complaints. "Today I have been in Europe for five weeks," he wrote from Frankfurt on September 9, "and it seems terribly long, too long." He sounded depressed. The whole tribunal was poorly organized, and "the result is that I sit around a lot. . . . The days pass by in loneliness." He was asked to go along on a fact-finding mission in Essen but tried to get out of it. "More ruins, and therefore, even more crazy dust. And only English food." He hung around with other lawyers on the prosecution team, but downtime boredom started to get to him.

That might explain why, in October, he mailed home a draft press release for the Lansdowne women to pass along to the *Philadelphia Record*. Heavy on coy intimations, it was Kempner the public relations showman at the top of his game. "Rumors that new traces of Adolf Hitler and Eva Braun might have been discovered started in Nuremberg in connection with the arrival from the United States of Dr. Robert M W Kempner, foremost American expert on Hitler and the Nazi Party machinery. Dr. Kempner arrived by plane from Washington DC but left Nuremberg for an undisclosed mission after a short visit in the Palace of Justice."

Sure enough, wild stories began appearing in papers back home. PHILADELPHIAN HUNTING HITLER, DEAD OR ALIVE, ON WHITE HOUSE ORDERS, one headline screamed. The gist of the tall tale was that Kempner had "shadowed" Hitler for years and was one of the few Nazi fighters anywhere in the world "who possesses detailed knowledge of Hitler's physical appearance, even his skeleton structure. He could point his finger at a Hitler disguised by plastic surgery, or at a cadaver that had been cremated, and say with certainty: 'That is the Führer.'"

One of the journalists wrote, "It was learned yesterday that he left this country for Germany four weeks ago under a special White House traveling priority." The stories reported that during his years as an official with the Prussian Interior Ministry, Kempner had led a team of twelve secret agents who, from 1928 to 1933, regularly tailed Hitler. "Kempner has said in interviews that Hitler had certain physical characteristics he could never obliterate if he were in hiding or in disguise," *Stars and Stripes* reported. "He described them as a sharply pointed right ear, abnormally long right thumb, jaw with receding teeth, and habitually stooped shoulders."

The whole thing was absurd, of course, but the stories appeared on October 22 and 23, at the moment Kempner was moving to Nuremberg from Paris. "Radio brought item on Hitler hunting," Kempner wrote back to Lansdowne. "Had some fun."

The news generated enough interest that the White House assistant press secretary was asked about it. He said the White House had not dispatched the lawyer to Germany. The stunt publicly separated Kempner from the pack of prosecutors swarming Nuremberg. Correcting the bad information he had spread, Kempner wrote one broadcaster to say he was not hunting for Hitler "right now" but was instead helping put on the trial against the Nazis.

Jackson had brought Kempner to Nuremberg to direct the seventh of seven sections: a unit of lawyers who would anticipate what defenses the Nazis would throw up to fight the charges against them. So it was that on the morning of November 20, a Tuesday, six months after the war ended, Kempner found himself near—if not at—the prosecution table as the trial opened to a crowded courtroom in the Palace of Justice. Kempner sat in the last row of chairs behind Jackson's table. If he turned around, he could sling an arm over the wooden barrier separating the lawyers from the press, whose packed gallery stretched for more than a dozen rows on risers.

He thought back to his parents, the two bacteriologists who had traveled throughout Europe trying to rid the Continent of infectious diseases. His mission in Nuremberg was not so very different. He had returned to Germany to drain the swamp that had bred the Nazi menace.

He clipped out a page from the December 3 issue of *Time* magazine with a wide shot of the courtroom, circled his tiny head in the back, and mailed it off to Lansdowne.

Rosenberg and the other defendants made their way into the courtroom in suits and ties or military uniforms for the first day of the trial. Handcuffed to guards, they passed through a covered wooden chute from the cell block to the basement of the Palace of Justice, then rode an elevator up to the courtroom. Taking his seat in the front row, Rosenberg watching the proceedings with hooded eyes, his arms crossed, looking small and, as always, grimly sober.

The courtroom, rebuilt and finished with dark paneling and fluorescent lights, was packed. Across the courtroom, the judges—representing the United States, the Soviet Union, Britain, and France—watched on a dais bedecked with the flags of the four Allied victors. A row of guards wearing white hats and belts surrounded the two rows of accused. Defense lawyers sat in front of their clients at banks of brown wooden tables. To the left, translators worked behind glass partitions; to the right were the prosecution teams, the press gallery, the film and radio booths, and a balcony for 150 spectators. Nuremberg felt like the absolute center of the world.

The first day was given over to the reading of the indictment against the twenty-two Nazi leaders and seven organizations. The next day, the defendants entered their pleas, and after the court blocked Göring's efforts to hijack the proceedings with an opening statement of his own, Jackson took the podium and turned to face the four judges. He set the stage with an opening address that reminded everyone in the chamber that history would be watching over their shoulders.

"The wrongs which we seek to condemn and punish have been so calculated, so malignant, and so devastating, that civilization cannot tolerate their being ignored, because it cannot survive their being repeated," Jackson told the court. His left elbow rested on the podium, and his right thumb was tucked into the pocket of his striped pants. The defendants listened to a translation through earphones. "That four great nations, flushed with victory and stung with injury, stay the hand of vengeance and voluntarily submit their captive enemies to the judgment of the law is one of the most significant tributes that power has ever paid to reason."

The American chief prosecutor was responding to German attacks on the legitimacy of the tribunal; one defense lawyer called the trials the "continuation of war by other means." Jackson argued that the prosecutors were not exacting victors' retribution against the Nazis, but seeking justice under international law. "To pass these defendants a poison chalice is to put it to our own lips as well."

In his opening statement, Jackson promised to take advantage of the Germans' "Teutonic passion for thoroughness in putting things on paper," and over the coming weeks and months, the prosecution confronted witnesses with document after incriminating document.

In November, the court watched films showing scenes of concentration camps and SS atrocities. Some of the Nazi defendants could hardly bear to watch as images of mass graves and stacked bodies flashed on the screen. Two weeks later, the prosecution screened a film called *The Nazi Plan* that dramatized their case, using footage the Germans had shot during their years in power. It opened with Rosenberg, sitting at a chair in Nazi uniform, discussing the early years of the party, when he played such an influential role in the formation of Hitler's thinking.

In December, the prosecution introduced a volume produced by Major General Jürgen Stroop of the SS on the destruction of the Warsaw ghetto. "This finest example of ornate German craftsmanship, leather bound, profusely illustrated, typed on heavy bond paper," the American prosecutor said, "pays tribute to the bravery and heroism of the German forces who participated in the ruthless and merciless action against a helpless, defenseless group of Jews, numbering, to be exact, 56,065, including, of course, the infants and the women."

In January 1946, the leader of one of the Einsatzgruppen killing units testified that his men had shot ninety thousand people between the summers of 1941 and 1942.

As the evidence piled up of atrocities and slave labor and mass extermination, the prison psychologist, Gustave Gilbert, moved from cell to cell, speaking with the Nazis about what they were hearing in the courtroom. Rosenberg seemed to be trying out his defense on Gilbert. Absurdly, he said Nazism had nothing to do with racial prejudice. The Germans simply wanted their own racially pure land, and for the Jews to have theirs. He himself had never wanted the Jews killed. "I didn't say that the Jews are inferior," he claimed. Racial enmity had arisen in countries all around the world. "Now it has suddenly become a crime, just because Germans have done it!" He allowed that the Nazi Party ought to be abolished. But as for the war crimes at issue in the trial, the real guilty parties were Hitler, Himmler, Bormann, and Goebbels. "We are not to blame."

The prosecution disagreed, of course, and on January 9 and 10, 1946, a lawyer named Walter Brudno slowly and methodically outlined the reasons that Rosenberg should be found guilty of war crimes. Charged on all four counts, Rosenberg was accused of aiding the Nazi rise to power by developing and spreading party doctrine against the churches and the Jews; with preparing Germany psychologically and politically for its wars of aggression; and with participating in war crimes and crimes against humanity as Reich minister for the occupied eastern territories.

"It will be seen that there was not a single basic tenet of the Nazi philosophy which was not given authoritative expression by Rosenberg," Brudno said while the defendant in the dock studiously took notes. "As the apostle of neo-paganism, the exponent of the drive for *Lebensraum*"—living space—"and the glorifier of the myth of Nordic superiority, and as one of the oldest and most energetic Nazi proponents of anti-Semitism, he contributed materially to the unification of the German people behind the swastika." Brudno recited passages from Rosenberg's writing on race. He repeated Rosenberg's infamous declaration in 1941 that the Jewish question would be solved only when "the last Jew has left the European continent." He explained how Rosenberg was Hitler's delegate for indoctrinating party members with the Nazi ideology.

He quoted so liberally from *The Myth of the Twentieth Century* that the president of the tribunal asked him to stop. "We really don't want to hear any more about it."

Brudno moved on to describe Rosenberg's collaborative role in the eastern occupied lands. How he helped plan and execute the savage occupation. How he supported the uprooting of other races to make room for ethnic Germans. How he had no objections to the German plans for starving the Soviet Union. How he cooperated with the deportation of more than a million forced laborers to Germany. How he received periodic reports of "unspeakable brutality."

A few days after Brudno presented the case against Rosenberg, damning evidence came from a doctor who had been arrested and imprisoned at Dachau, where he witnessed horrific medical experiments conducted on his fellow prisoners. Asked by Dodd which defendants he had seen pass through the camp, he named four. Rosenberg, despite his claims to the contrary, was one of them.

With the trial in full swing, Kempner was busy with a team of people producing dossiers on every prosecution and defense witness, preparing trial briefs for the prosecutors, and mapping out the cases against individual defendants. Much of the staff stayed at the Grand Hotel, "the finest in the city," Dodd wrote, even though it had no hot water, and to pass through the corridor he was forced to walk over a plank laid over a three-story chasm. "My room is quite comfortable. The walls are all ripped out—bullet holes in them—no glass in the windows. The ceiling is half gone, but compared to some rooms it is in good shape." Staffers capped long hours inside the courthouse with after-hours drinks in the hotel's Marble Room, where they danced to American music played by German musicians and tried to forget for a while the atrocities they were uncovering and the utter devastation outside on the streets.

On the thirty-fifth day of the trial—the last day of the American prosecution case—Kempner finally got a chance to step into the klieg lights. Although his story would need no gilding this time, that did not stop him from notifying the press ahead of time. "He is the only direct victim of Nazi persecution," a correspondent wrote in the New York City tabloid newspaper *PM*, "who is getting a chance during these trials to get up in open court and say what he thinks of them out loud."

"To be at the prosecutor's stand here was, briefly, to be at the center of the legal universe," one historian would write. On January 16, 1946, Kempner took to the podium and, wielding piles of documents, presented the prosecution case against the "manager of the Nazi conspiracy," Wilhelm Frick, minister of the interior from 1933 to 1943.

Kempner argued that Frick had paved the way for the war by helping Hitler win German citizenship. The Austrian automatically became naturalized when Frick orchestrated his appointment to a civil service post as government councilor in the Office of State Culture and Measurement in the German city of Braunschweig. If not for Frick, Kempner argued, Hitler could never have become chancellor of Germany. As interior minister, Frick oversaw state and local government, elections, racial law, health policy, even, technically, the police. Kempner showed that Frick had enacted Nazi racial legislation, not least by signing the Nuremberg Laws, which stripped Jews of their citizenship in 1935.

"He was the administrative brain who devised the machinery of state for Nazism, who geared that machinery for aggressive war," the prosecutor told the court. Frick not only knew about the T4 euthanasia program but actually signed the secret order putting it in motion. Later, Kempner charged, he was Reich protector of Bohemia and Moravia during a period when Czechoslovakia's Jews were being deported to the death camps.

Kempner, ever the self-promoter, found an opening to read from his own interrogation of Göring about the Reichstag fire, which he knew would make the newspapers. (It landed in the *New York Times* the following morning.)

His recitation prompted the president of the tribunal, Sir Geoffrey Lawrence, to ask, "What has that got to do with Frick?"

"He signed the decree, as I said before, abolishing civil liberties on the morning after," Kempner said lamely.

The presentation offered a break from the usual dry American statements. Making the most of his moment, Kempner delivered a baroque performance. The Nazis in the dock could not help smirking at his dramatic moralizing. Rudolf Hess, an English speaker himself, quietly lampooned the prosecutor's accent, while Hans Frank mocked Kempner's florid, theatrical gestures.

The British team, though, welcomed an American prosecutor with a full grasp of Nazi history. It was, they thought, something sorely lacking among the other nearly seven hundred members of Jackson's staff.

Kempner worried how well the trial was playing with the German public, which was learning about the proceedings from radio broadcasts, newsreels, and blanket newspaper coverage. The prosecutors wanted to change German attitudes. After years of Nazi propaganda, there was some doubt among the people that trials were really and truly under way at Nuremberg. So Jackson invited politicians, professors, teachers, clerics, judges, and lawyers to Nuremberg to watch the proceedings in person. Afterward, Kempner would bring them to a theater and show them film of Germany's infamous People's Court, which had tried those arrested by Himmler following the attempted assassination of Hitler in 1944. The contrast was marked. The president of the People's Court, Roland Freisler, was shown berating and bullying the defendants, who looked foolish holding up their pants because they were not allowed to wear belts, even in the courtroom. "You dirty old man," Freisler shouted at one defendant. "Why do you keep fiddling with your trousers?" Goebbels had filmed the proceedings to strike terror in potential dissidents within Germany. Now the prosecution turned it against the Nazis themselves.

On April 15, Rudolf Höss, the commandant of Auschwitz, took the stand and testified that millions of men, women, and children were killed in the gas chambers of his extermination camp. Höss had gotten his start at the Dachau and Sachsenhausen concentration camps before being transferred to Auschwitz in May 1940. He said that he was summoned to Berlin by Himmler in 1941 and given secret orders. "He told me something to the effect—I do not remember the exact words—that the Führer had given the order for a final solution of the Jewish question. We, the SS, must carry out that order. If it is not carried out now, then the Jews will later on destroy the German people."

On the stand, he confirmed the details of an affidavit he had signed for the prosecution, in which he described how the trains arrived, how those fit for work were issued striped uniforms and sent to the camp barracks, how the rest were told to strip and go to chambers that were disguised as showers, how the chambers held two thousand people at a time, how the people died in less than fifteen minutes, how the workers knew the victims were dead when the screaming stopped.

"Did you yourself ever feel pity with the victims, thinking of your own family and children?" he was asked.

"Yes."

"How was it possible for you to carry out these actions in spite of this?"

"The only one and decisive argument was the strict order and the reason given for it by the Reichsführer Himmler."

Afterward, Gilbert, the prison psychologist, ventured up to Höss's prison cell. He wanted to know why the commandant had pursued the extermination policy with such bureaucratic single-mindedness. Did he really believe the Jews deserved death? Höss told the man that he had never heard anything in his life but that Jews were subhuman and deserved to be exterminated. He said he had read Rosenberg's *Myth*, Hitler's *Mein Kampf*, and Goebbels's newspaper editorials. "For me as an old fanatic National Socialist, I took it all as fact—just as a Catholic believes in his church dogma," he said. "It was just truth without question; I had no doubt about that. I was absolutely convinced that the Jews were the opposite pole from the German people, and sooner or later there would have to be a showdown." From the books, he said, he learned that though the Jews were a minority, they controlled the press, the radio, the films. "And if anti-Semitism did not succeed in wiping out this Jewish influence, the Jews would succeed in bringing about a war to wipe out Germany. But everybody was convinced of this; that was all you could hear or read."

So when Himmler told him his duty was to exterminate Jews, "it fitted in with all that had been preached to me for years."

The very same day Höss testified, Rosenberg finally had his chance to defend himself. He took the stand on the 108th day of the proceedings and testified over the course of three days. To the frustration of everyone—including his court-appointed lawyer, Alfred Thoma, a district judge who had never joined the Nazi Party—Rosenberg refused to simply answer questions. Instead he took off on tedious monologues about tangential matters.

As he had in his books and memos, as he had in speeches, as he had in the interrogation room, Rosenberg led his followers into the deepest of thickets. "It would take time and patience," one analyst wrote after encountering the Nazi philosopher at ASHCAN, "for an ordinary mortal to get a footing in the world of Alfred Rosenberg."

Setting the tone for testimony that would strain credulity, Thoma argued that his client had made a career of advocating "respect for all races," "freedom of conscience," and "a sensible solution to the Jewish problem." Rosenberg set about a detailed explanation and defense of his sprawling philosophy and the Nazi Party's political theories, as if he could throw up a smoke screen of bogus erudition to cover up the murder of millions. "Industrialization and the clamor for profit dominated life and created the industrial state and the metropolis with all its backyards and estrangement from nature and history," Rosenberg told the court. "At the turn of the century, many people who wanted to regain their homeland and its history turned against this one-sided movement." It was a youth movement, he said, that nodded to the past while charging forward into a modern future.

"Dr. Thoma," interrupted Lawrence, president of the tribunal, "would you try to confine the witness to the charges which are against him?"

Dodd rose to his feet to concur. "No one in the prosecution has made any charge against this defendant for what he has thought," the American lawyer said. "I think we are all, as a matter of principle, opposed to prosecuting any man for what he thinks."

Personally, Rosenberg said, he wanted people to be allowed to believe whatever they wanted to believe about God. He laid the blame for measures against the churches at the feet of Bormann, who was still believed to be missing. (In fact, he had died while trying to flee the Führerbunker in the final days of the war. His remains were discovered by a Berlin construction crew in 1972 and positively identified by DNA testing in 1998. Fragments of glass embedded in his jawbone led historians to deduce that Bormann, his escape cut off by the Soviets, bit down on a poison capsule.)

Rosenberg denied any plot to plunder Europe. When the Nazis arrived in Paris, they found that the Jews had fled and their properties were now unoccupied. They took it upon themselves to protect the treasures, which Rosenberg's staff meticulously cataloged and packed with great care. "We were dealing with an unforeseen situation," he said. In any case, the Nazis were justified in repatriating art that had been removed from Germany in past wars, and they were justified in seizing archives so they could investigate the enemies who had been agitating against them.

He addressed a secret memo from December 1941 that prosecutors had found, in which Rosenberg made a deadly suggestion about how Hitler should respond to an escalating round of attacks against German officers in France. In October, the dictator had ordered the execution of one hundred French hostages in response to the murders of a pair of German officials in Nantes and Bordeaux. But the way Rosenberg saw it, the goal of the Resistance had been to spark Nazi reprisals against the French and thereby stir up renewed animosity against the Nazis. "I suggest to the Führer that instead of executing 100 Frenchmen, we substitute 100 Jewish bankers, lawyers, etc. It is the Jews in London and New York who incite the French communists to commit acts of violence, and it seems only fair that the members of this race should pay for this," he wrote. "It is not the *little* Jews but the *leading* Jews in France who should be held responsible. That would tend to awaken the anti-Jewish sentiment." On the stand, Rosenberg said he had written the memo in a moment of excitement, and that Hitler had not followed through on his recommendation. In his typically muddled way, Rosenberg said he regretted making the suggestion while contending that in wartime, shooting hostages was not illegal.

Continuing his defense, Rosenberg said he had nothing to do with the planning of Operation Barbarossa; it was a fait accompli by the time Hitler called him in to prepare a civil administration in the occupied lands. It had never been his plan to decimate the eastern people. Once he was appointed minister, he had no power over economic or police matters, and Koch, the Reichskommissar in Ukraine, ignored his orders.

Rosenberg acknowledged approving plans to bring eastern children to Germany in the summer of 1944, though he tried to give it a positive spin. This "Heuaktion," or hay-harvesting operation, involved arresting forty to fifty thousand children between the ages of ten and fourteen. Some of the children had been left behind when their parents were rounded up for forced labor on fortifications; others were simply taken from their homes. The idea was to hand over the kidnapped children to serve as apprentices in German factories. One of the long-term rationales for the abductions was to destroy the "biological potentialities" of the eastern people. Rosenberg told the court that he'd objected to the plan at first, although he was willing to let the army seize older teenagers. He relented, he said, because the army was going to deport them with or without his consent. Rosenberg said he thought that if he took on the job, his "youth department" could make sure the children were treated well. He claimed he wanted them housed in villages or small camps and returned to their parents after the war.

His lawyer asked about reports that reached Rosenberg in June

1943 about atrocities outside Minsk, Belarus. A prison warden
wrote that the police were removing the gold dental work of Jewish captives before handing them over, and Wilhelm Kube, the
top civilian administrator in Belarus, reported the killings of
women and children in a "police action" against partisans.

"The fact that Jews receive special treatment requires no further discussion. However it appears hardly believable that this is
done in the way described," read a letter from Lohse's office
addressed to Rosenberg. How could they pacify and exploit the
occupied territories if the population was terrorized? "It should be
possible to avoid atrocities and to bury those who have been liquidated. To lock men, women, and children into barns and to set
fire to these does not appear to be a suitable method of combatting
bands, even if it is desired to exterminate the population. This
method is not worthy of the German cause and hurts our reputation severely. I am asking you to take the necessary action."

Confronted with this letter in court, Rosenberg said that it had
arrived soon after Hitler sided with Koch in 1943 and ordered the
minister to stop frivolous meddling in the East. "I was dejected,"
Rosenberg claimed, "and I did not read this document."

He testified that he knew about the concentration camps but
assumed the arrests were "politically and nationally necessary." He
claimed to have asked Himmler about foreign reports of atrocities
in the camps and said that the Reichsführer-SS invited him to
come to Dachau and see the camp with his own eyes. "We have a
swimming pool there, we have sanitary installations," Himmler
said. "Irreproachable. No objections can be raised." Rosenberg
told the court he had declined the invitation "for reasons of good
taste; I simply did not want to look at people who had been
deprived of their liberty."

As for the murder of Europe's Jews, Rosenberg claimed ignorance. Yes, he had read the reports of "terrible harshness" in the
East. Yes, he had heard about shootings of Jews. "But that there
was an order for the individual annihilation of the entire Jewry, I

could not assume," he said, "and if, in our polemics, the extermination of Jewry was also talked about, I must say that this word of course must make a frightful impression in view of the testimonies we think are available now, but under conditions prevailing then, it was not interpreted as an individual extermination, an individual annihilation of millions of Jews."

The man whose unrivaled anti-Semitism had paved the way for the Holocaust now insisted that he had advocated a "chivalrous" treatment of the Jews, though he did not elaborate on what this supposed alternate plan would have entailed. "That it turned out otherwise is a tragic destiny," he said. "Things occurred which were regrettable and I must say robbed me of the inner strength to continue petitioning the Führer for the method I favored."

But he insisted that he did not know about mass shootings and the death camps.

"I would not have believed it even if Heinrich Himmler himself had related it to me," he said. "There are things which, even to me, appear beyond the humanly possible, and this is one of them."

On April 17, Thomas Dodd came to the podium to cross-examine Rosenberg. Working slowly and methodically, he picked away at Rosenberg's defenses until he came to the question of the Jews.

"Did you ever talk about the extermination of the Jews?" Dodd asked.

"I have not in general spoken about the extermination of the Jews in the sense of this term," Rosenberg replied. "One has to consider the words here."

Dodd confronted Rosenberg with the memo about the Reich minister's December 14, 1941, meeting with Hitler, the one at which the two men decided that Rosenberg should not mention the extermination—"*Ausrottung*"—of the Jews in a speech he planned to deliver.

"That word does not have the sense which you attribute to it," Rosenberg argued.

Dodd offered a German–English dictionary and asked Rosenberg to look it up. Rosenberg refused and proceeded to lecture the prosecutor.

"I do not need a foreign dictionary in order to explain the various meanings 'Ausrottung' may have in the German language," he said. "One can exterminate an idea, an economic system, a social order, and as a final consequence, also a group of human beings, certainly. Those are the many possibilities that are contained in that word. Translations from German into English are so often wrong."

Dodd persisted. "Are you very serious in pressing this apparent inability of yours to agree with me about this word or are you trying to kill time?"

Rosenberg said his planned speech at the Sportpalast was to be nothing more than "a political threat." It was not an announcement of the final solution.

"Well, actually," Dodd said, "the Jews were being exterminated in the eastern occupied territories at that time and thereafter, weren't they?"

"Yes."

"Yes, and after that . . . you wanted the tribunal to believe that that was being done by the police and without any of your people involved."

Next, Dodd confronted Rosenberg with the letter from Lohse, the Reichskommissar of the Ostland, protesting "the wild execution of Jews" in a city in his territory, and the reply from the ministry that Lohse was not to interfere with the SS mission on the Jewish question. Dodd also showed Rosenberg the letter to Lohse from another civilian administrator, in July 1942, reporting that fifty-five thousand Jews had been "liquidated" in Belarus in the past ten weeks and that others shipped to their district would meet the same fate.

Rosenberg said he had never seen the letters, though both were found among the papers in his Berlin office. Pressing the matter, Dodd pointed out that at least five top people in his ministry knew what was happening—certainly Rosenberg must have known.

Rosenberg tried to go off on a tangent, but the president of the tribunal broke in. "Will you answer the question first? Do you agree that these five people were engaged in exterminating Jews?"

"Yes, they knew about a certain number of liquidations of Jews. That I admit," Rosenberg said, "and they have told me so, or if they did not, I have heard it from other sources."

With that damning admission, Dodd took his case for Rosenberg's guilt a step further. "The witness Höss, you were in the courtroom when he testified?"

"Yes, I heard him," Rosenberg replied.

"You heard that terrible story of two and a half to three million murders which he told from the witness stand, very largely of Jewish people?"

"Yes."

"You know that he was a reader of your book and of your speeches, this man Höss?"

No, Rosenberg said, he had not been aware of that.

Dodd sent a letter home that day about the Rosenberg cross-examination. "He was most difficult to examine—an evasive lying rogue, if ever I saw one. I actually dislike him—he is such a faker, such a complete hypocrite."

After the prosecution rested, the American prosecutors left Nuremberg en masse. But Kempner was persuaded to stay behind with Dodd. He oversaw a section responsible for rebutting arguments raised by the defendants and their attorneys. "I am still here—so to speak, one of the last survivors," he wrote to a friend. "Most of the old crowd are gone." The tribunal had set up a separate commission to hear testimony from members of the organizations on trial, such as the SS, the Gestapo, the storm troopers, and the military. Kempner was the chief liaison between the American prosecution team and this ancillary commission, and he was none too happy about it. "It is pretty difficult from all points of view," he wrote. "There are too many angles and the cases of the organizations have never been thoroughly investigated and analyzed, and in the last moment a lot has to be done."

He wanted to go home to Lansdowne. There, that very month, his son Lucian had finally arrived safely after years on the run.

From 1941 through 1943, Lucian had attended schools in Düsseldorf and Berlin. For a time he worked as a night watchman to support himself. He always knew that, as a half-Jew, he could be arrested by the Gestapo at any time, and in September 1943 they finally came for him.

First he was dispatched to a forced labor camp in Westerland, on the island of Sylt, which jutted out into the North Sea near the border of Denmark. The Luftwaffe had an air base there, and twelve hundred prisoners were put to work building fortifications in anticipation of Allied assaults. In February 1944, Lucian was sent to a camp in Arnheim, Holland, to work on the expansion of another air base, and eventually he ended up at the Amersfoort concentration camp, where thousands of Jews, conscientious objectors, and political prisoners were held.

He tried many times to get away. Finally, in April 1945, as he was being transported to a new camp in Berlin, he escaped, slipped through German lines, and rode a stolen bicycle to the Allied lines, nearly a hundred miles west at the Elbe River near Madgeburg. He surrendered to the American Ninth Army, and after an interrogation he was kept with the unit as an interpreter. (He spoke four languages.) Later that year he volunteered as a soldier with the British Royal Norfolk Regiment C Company. He spent some of the time working to reeducate German youth indoctrinated by the Nazis.

He spent the second half of 1945 trying to reconnect with his father, even writing to the Voice of America. "Please help me to find my father," he wrote. "You are my last hope." They finally found each other at the end of 1945, and exchanged letters. "I risked my life," Lucian wrote, "and miraculously, won it back."

But it was a strange sort of freedom. He was still in Germany, stationed in Solingen, halfway between Düsseldorf and Cologne, and he still did not have the papers he needed to leave. He was still a man buffeted by the forces of history. "I am equated with today's Germans," he wrote his father, "and since they are notorious to the entire world—and rightly so—I, too, am a pariah to the world public, i.e., an outcast, just like I was before and during the war to these German Aryans. I am not a German, not British, and also not an American. So, what am I, then?" Lucian was desperate. "Is it possible for you to get me out of this horrible country?"

The British treated him well enough, but he was miserable. There was nothing to read, and his fellow soldiers spoke single-mindedly about "German women, drinking, and smoking." Lucian didn't even get a ration card, so he was bumming off his company-mates.

His demands were basic. "I want to live in a free country as a human with equal rights."

Father and son had a chance to reunite briefly in February, at the Grand Hotel in Nuremberg. Kempner helped his son acquire a U.S. visa, and in May 1946 Lucian landed in America on the *Marine Perch* cargo ship and took a bus to the Kempner house in Lansdowne. He dispatched a telegram of thanks to the White House and gave interviews to reporters in Philadelphia. "He was persecuted and pursued and beaten and starved," the *Philadelphia Inquirer* reported. "Yesterday his modern Odyssey came to an end in Lansdowne." Ruth had decorated the house with flowers. She was described as Lucian's mother in the story; his actual mother, Helene, who had abducted him from Italy, died in Germany before the end of the war. "From the newspaper clippings," Robert Kempner's old journalist friend, Kurt Grossman, wrote to Nuremberg, "I would say that he is a real Kempner."

Lucian, emaciated following his captivity, had gained back fifty pounds since reaching the Allied lines a year earlier. He said he planned to join the U.S. Army. "There were many boys who fell and died on the European battlefield to save me," he told the newspaper. "If it had not been for them, I would not be here today. I want to try to repay them in the only way I know."

André, meanwhile, would arrive in Lansdowne in the early 1950s after his formal adoption by the Kempners, and eventually marry and settle in Sweden.

On July 17, Kempner received a letter from a surprising correspondent: Emmy Göring, the Reichsmarschall's wife.

"May I ask a great favor of you?" she wrote. "Do you think that you might have time within the next 14 days, for ½ hour?" Kempner agreed, and though it is unclear what she wanted, it is likely that she sought his help gaining permission to visit her husband in jail, or to simply sit in the courtroom—neither of which was permitted for defendants' wives. In September, the former actress breezily walked into the Palace of Justice wearing a fur coat, but she was quickly recognized and removed.

After the war, she had been tracked down in a lodge in Bavaria, where she was hiding out with stores of champagne, liquor, and Cuban cigars and a trunk full of jewelry and gold. She was arrested and imprisoned for five months, and after her release, in February 1946, she lived a life of impoverishment in a house with no running water or heat. She was still angry that, in those crazed final days in the bunker, Hitler had ordered her husband's arrest. One of the military psychologists at Nuremberg visited her in March, hoping she could persuade the Reichsmarschall to drop his loyal support of the Führer. She sent Göring a letter, but he was unmoved. "Nothing," Göring told the psychologist, "can sway me."

Kempner began visiting Emmy regularly, bringing her food and chocolate. He knew how to cultivate valuable sources of information, and this was a relationship worth nurturing.

Kempner had a more complicated relationship with another Nazi interned at Nuremberg: Rudolf Diels, the former Gestapo chief. In the 1930s, Kempner had helped Diels avoid an embarrassing situation with a prostitute; Diels may have helped spring Kempner from the Columbia-Haus concentration camp after his 1935 arrest. A decade later in Nuremberg, British prosecutors declared that the founding head of the secret police had been "responsible for the grossest of brutalities and barbarisms," and argued for his indictment. Kempner helped prevent that from happening. Diels, who insisted that he had done what he could to stop the worst abuses in the days and months after the Nazis took power, agreed to give prosecutors a series of sworn statements about the defendants, including Göring and Rosenberg. He became an important early informant. "We wanted to find out as much as possible as quickly as possible," Kempner said many years later about his relationship with Nazis like Diels. "That meant talking to certain people with whom one might not otherwise have shared a cup of tea." As Kempner wrote in his memoir, "Murderers can tell the truth about their murderous colleagues—never mind what their motives for doing so are."

Kempner and Diels saw a fair amount of each other during the trial. As a witness, Diels was required to stay at a witness house set up by the Americans. Remarkably enough, the place housed Nazis alongside concentration camp survivors. But Diels also won permission to visit a hunting lodge south of Nuremberg owned by friends of his, the Count and Countess Faber-Castell. The lodge became the hub of a small social scene; Kempner was also a regular visitor there.

Diels, as was his way, struck up an affair with the countess. When she gave birth to her first child, Kempner said Diels was the father. Presumably, he would have known: He stood in as one of the child's godparents.

On July 26, Robert H. Jackson returned to Nuremberg to deliver his final statement. When he came to Rosenberg, Jackson dismissed him as "the intellectual high priest of the 'master race,'" saying it was he who had "provided the doctrine of hatred which gave the impetus for the annihilation of Jewry, and who put his infidel theories into practice against the eastern occupied territories. His woolly philosophy also added boredom to the long list of Nazi atrocities."

A month later, the defendants stood in the center of the dock and made brief final statements.

Rosenberg denied any and all responsibility for the Nazi massacres. "I know my conscience to be completely free from any such guilt, from any complicity in the murder of peoples." He had wanted to lift up the eastern peoples against Moscow. He had wanted the Jews resettled to a nation of their own. "The thought of a physical annihilation of Slavs and Jews—that is to say, the actual murder of entire peoples—has never entered my mind, and I most certainly did not advocate it in any way." His labor in the service of Nazi ideology was no conspiracy, no crime. "I ask you to recognize this as the truth."

The four judges spent September deliberating. The arguments revolved around the peculiar points of improvised international law that had guided the Nuremberg trials from the beginning, as well as, of course, the political interests of the four Allies. Göring and Ribbentrop were easy enough to convict. Rosenberg required some debate. When the judges took up the Nazi ideologue on September 2, they were reluctant to convict a man of conspiracy simply on the grounds that his ideas had given ideological cover to Nazi persecution and mass murder. On the other hand, the charges against Rosenberg went beyond mere words. He had participated in the continent-wide plunder, the forced labor program, and a murderous and brutal eastern occupation. He had also played a role in the invasion of Norway in 1940.

The first round of deliberations revealed disagreements among the judges about whether to convict Rosenberg on all or only some of the counts, and about whether he should hang or go to prison for life. By September 10, three of the four judges were in favor of a full conviction—but while the Soviets and British wanted a death sentence, the French judge opted for life in prison. That left Rosenberg's fate in the hands of the American judge, Francis Biddle, the former U.S. attorney general.

Biddle remained undecided. He told the others that he wanted to consider the case overnight before casting his vote.

On October 1, the defendants sat in the dock together for the last time to hear the verdicts against them. Göring: guilty. Hess: guilty. Ribbentrop and Keitel: guilty. And Rosenberg: guilty. Of the twenty-two men tried, three were acquitted: former vice chancellor Franz von Papen, who brokered Hitler's rise to power in 1933; Propaganda Ministry official Hans Fritzsche; and banker Hjalmar Schacht. At 1:45, the court took a recess.

After the break, the men returned, one by one, to hear their sentences. Rosenberg's turn came sixth, and he rode the elevator upstairs, flanked by two guards. The sliding door opened and he stepped out into the courtroom. The chambers were dimly lit for the first time; because the sentencings would not be filmed, the fluorescent lights had been flicked off. Rosenberg slipped on his headphones to hear the brief words of the tribunal president translated for him.

"*Tod durch den Strang.*" Death by the rope. Biddle had come down on the side of execution. In their verdict, the judges convicted him not for his ideas, only for his actions.

Rosenberg said nothing as he removed his headphones and stepped back into the elevator heading down.

. . .

The chaplain who ministered to the Nazi defendants, Henry Gerecke, wrote later that more than half of them had repented at the end and begged forgiveness. Rosenberg "remained the sophisticate. He had no use for his childhood faith." He was one of four who declined the ministrations of the prison clerics. After the sentences, the defendants' wives and children were allowed to visit the cells. Gerecke moved among the children, and when he approached Rosenberg's teenage daughter, Irene, she said, "Don't give me any of that prayer stuff."

Gerecke, taken aback, asked, "Is there anything at all I can do for you?"

"Yes," she shot back. "Got a cigarette?"

During his months in prison, Rosenberg wrote a memoir in which he retold his version of the history of the Third Reich. "What Hitler did, what Hitler ordered, how he burdened the most honorable men, how he dragged into the dust the ideals of a movement created by himself, all this is of such ghastly magnitude that no everyday adjective is adequate to describe it," Rosenberg wrote. It was as close as he came to disowning his hero and idol. He wrote that Hitler had succumbed in the end of his life to a "paroxysm of self-intoxication," making wild remarks that were "the explosions of a man who no longer seriously bothers to seek counsel from anyone but still believes he is listening to his inner voice; they are soliloquies, in part still logical, in part merely extravagant."

He had decided that Hitler's great fault was that he had not listened more to men like Rosenberg and instead took the counsel of Himmler and "the Mephisto of our once straightforward movement," Goebbels.

"These two were able to do the most unbelievable things without being restrained," Rosenberg wrote, working at the flimsy table in the quiet of his prison cell. "Here, in this purely human soil, is the root of Adolf Hitler's great sins of omission which resulted in such ghastly consequences—that indefinable element of inconsistency, muddleheadedness, negligence, and in the long run, injustice that so frequently nullified his own considerations, plans and activities."

He described a moment when, he claimed, it hit him that Himmler wanted complete power in the Third Reich. He was having a glass of wine with one of Himmler's allies when he spotted a photo of the Reichsführer-SS hanging on a wall in the other room. "I couldn't keep my eyes off it," Rosenberg wrote. "And then it occurred to me that I have never had the opportunity to look Himmler straight in the eyes. His were always concealed by his pince-nez. Now, from the photograph, they stared at me unblinkingly, and what I thought I saw in them was malice."

Still, he continued, "How could anyone believe Himmler capable of these proven cruelties?"

He remembered how a fellow Nazi leader had visited him in Berlin and spoken about making a last stand against the Allies in the mountains. Rosenberg could hardly see the point. The man asked a question that had been bothering him: Had the very idea of Nazism been wrong from the start?

No, no, Rosenberg replied. "A great idea had been misused by small men."

Rosenberg thought he was writing for a future when his ideas and the ideals of the Nazi Party would be fully vindicated, when he would be held up as a hero. "The day will come when the grandchildren of the present generation will be ashamed of the fact that we have been accused of criminals for having harbored a most noble thought."

To the end, Rosenberg held fast to the righteousness of the Nazi cause and to Hitler's greatness, for all his flaws.

"I venerated him, and I remained loyal to him to the end," Rosenberg wrote. "And now Germany's destruction has come with his own. Sometimes hatred rises in me when I think of the millions of Germans who have been murdered and exiled, of the unspeakable misery, the plundering of the little that remained, and the squandering of a thousand-year-old wealth. But then again there rises in me the feeling of pity for a man who also was a victim of fate, and who loved this Germany as ardently as any of us."

Hans Frank found religion. The leader of the General Government had lived in luxury in Wawel Castle, in Krakow, while the Nazis brutally destroyed occupied Poland during the war. At Nuremberg, he repented for all that he and his fellow Nazis had said and done. After listening to the testimony from Höss, the death camp commandant, Frank told a prison psychologist that his father's closest friend had died at Auschwitz. He held himself responsible—himself, he said, and Rosenberg. "No, I didn't kill him myself," Frank said. "But the things I said, and the things Rosenberg said, made those horrors possible." When Frank took the stand, he confessed his guilt in the annihilation of the Jews. "A thousand years will pass and still Germany's guilt will not have been erased."

Rosenberg recanted nothing. To the very end, the Nazis' chief ideologue couldn't, or wouldn't, accept the notion that the ideas he had trumpeted had led to genocide.

"What will become of me?" he asked his lawyer one day.

The man replied with a famous poem by Goethe, "Wanderer's Night Song II," giving it a fateful twist for the Baltic native:

> Over every crest
> Is rest,
> In all the trees
> The breeze
> Scarce touches you.
> Hushed is the wood-bird's song.
> Wait, Balt: before long,
> You will rest too.

An hour after lights-out on October 15, the guard watching over Göring's cell saw the Reichsmarschall bring a hand to his face. Three minutes later, he began choking as froth poured from his mouth. He was dead before anything could be done. On his chest, prison officials found two envelopes, one containing four letters, the other containing an empty cyanide vial. The executions were on for that very night; Göring had been tipped off.

After midnight, the sentences were read to the other ten condemned Nazis, and they were served a last meal of sausage, potato salad, and fruit.

A little after one in the morning, the guards came for the men, one by one. Rosenberg was fourth in line. Gerecke, the chaplain, asked if he might say a prayer for him. "No, thank you," he replied.

Rosenberg, his hands cuffed, made the short walk across the yard from the cell block and entered the prison gymnasium at 1:47 a.m. Inside, witnesses sat at tables or stood in the back. His hands were tied behind him with a leather belt and he was led up the thirteen steps to the gallows, where his feet were bound.

"Rosenberg was dull and sunken-cheeked as he looked around the court," wrote Kingsbury Smith, who witnessed the executions for the International News Service. "His complexion was pasty-brown, but he did not appear nervous and walked with a steady step to and up the gallows. . . . Despite his avowed atheism he was accompanied by a Protestant chaplain who followed him to the gallows and stood beside him praying. Rosenberg looked at the chaplain once, expressionless."

Alone among the condemned, the most prolific writer in the history of the Third Reich had no final words.

A hood was pulled over his head. The trap opened, and Rosenberg fell. A few hours later, his body was driven with the others to Munich, where they were incinerated. The ashes were dumped into a river.

The men who tracked down the pilfered diary: Homeland Security Investigations special agent Mark Olexa, assistant U.S. attorney Dave Hall, Robert Wittman, the Holocaust museum's Henry Mayer, and Robert's son, Jeff. *(Author collection)*

Epilogue

T his historical document, from another continent in another century, is now, we think, in its proper home," Sara Bloomfield, director of the United States Holocaust Memorial Museum, said on December 17, 2013. That morning, the National Archives—which technically owned the diary—officially granted the pages to the institution that had spent so much time and effort hunting them down. The journal took its place in the museum archive alongside thousands of other government documents, letters, photographs, and recordings telling the story of the Nazi genocide. At the museum's Center for Advanced Holocaust Studies, scholars using those resources were still researching the history of the killings, still laboring to explain the unexplainable, still trying to make sense of what happened.

In the months after the handover, the Holocaust museum arranged for Mayer to speak to local and regional Jewish groups, where his work was hailed as a prime example of the institution's mission to preserve important documents about the crimes of the Nazis—so they would not be forgotten, or repeated.

One night, Mayer took the stage at the National Museum of American Jewish History, on Independence Mall in Philadelphia, for a question-and-answer session before a packed room of listeners. He spoke about the long, tangled hunt for the papers, and their significance to historians of the Third Reich.

Toward the end, somebody asked him what it felt like to hold Rosenberg's lost pages in his hands.

"Unfortunately," Mayer said dryly, "it goes with the territory."

Then he paused a beat.

He was not one to talk much about his ancestors who suffered during the Holocaust. Theirs were just a few tragedies among many millions. His father had not even considered himself a survivor, although the museum does, because he was a Jew who had to flee persecution in Germany.

And yet Mayer could not deny that the terrible deaths of his people—in the mud at Gurs, in the gas chambers at Auschwitz, and in the forests of Latvia—gave his work at the museum a deeper purpose.

Mayer looked over at the questioner and smiled.

"I've derived great satisfaction," he said, "from the fact that this Jew discovered this guy's diary."

Though he was no longer an undercover agent who needed to hide from the cameras, Wittman was in his usual spot for events like these: at the back of the room. Mayer publicly recognized him from the stage. The audience craned their necks to look, and a few walked over to shake his hand.

It was hard to describe the feeling Wittman got at the end of a successful hunt for a piece of art or a priceless manuscript. That first moment of success was a flash of euphoria. Maybe that was a testament to the ineffable power of these sorts of unique cultural artifacts. For Wittman, something about this one felt different. Alfred Rosenberg was not just another diarist, and the Holocaust museum was not just another museum. By helping to recover the Nazi's papers, by helping to save one piece of the unsolvable puzzle that is the Nazi genocide, Wittman had done his small part to advance the museum's mission—not just to honor the millions of innocents who lost their lives, but to remind another generation of a horror that must never happen again.

Acknowledgments

M any thanks to Henry Mayer and Jürgen Matthäus at the United States Holocaust Memorial Museum; Tim Mulligan at the National Archives and Records Administration; David Hall at the U.S. attorney's office in Delaware; and Mark Olexa at U.S. Immigration and Customs Enforcement for their crucial roles in bringing the Rosenberg diary into the public domain.

We also want to thank Mayer for generously sharing his time and his stories with us; librarians Ron Coleman, Megan Lewis, and Vincent Slatt, in the Holocaust museum's archives, for pointing us in the right direction time and again; freelance researcher Satu Haase-Webb for mining the Kempner Collection in search of letters and personal papers; and translators Natascha Hoffmeyer, Nika Knight, and Chris Erb for helping us decipher German documents, not least the Rosenberg diary itself. We're grateful to Jonathan Bush, Allan Stypeck, and Edward Jesella for their time. The deep German history collection at the University of Pennsylvania's Van Pelt Library put answers at our fingertips. Thanks also to the many helpful aides at the National Archives and Records Administration, in College Park, Maryland, and the Library of Congress, in Washington, D.C.

Cheers to Katie Shaver and Bob Barnard for the D.C. lodging, the wine, and the company.

Special appreciation to John Shiffman for making introductions; to our agents, Larry Weissman and Sascha Alper, for putting together another great deal; and to Jonathan Burnham, Claire Wachtel, Hannah Wood, Jonathan Jao, Sofia Ergas Groopman, Brenda Segel, Juliette Shapland, Heather Drucker, and everyone else at HarperCollins who helped launch the book out into the world.

As always, much love to our families: Donna, Kevin, Renee, Jeffrey, and Kristin; and Monica, Jane, and Owen.

Appendix A:
A Third Reich Timeline

December 1918: Alfred Rosenberg arrives in Germany from his native Estonia and settles in Munich; he is twenty-five years old.

January 5, 1919: The German Workers' Party, which will evolve into the Nazi Party a year later, is founded in Munich. Rosenberg and Hitler both join later that year.

December 1920: The Nazis purchase a newspaper, the *Völkischer Beobachter*, and Rosenberg becomes a chief writer and editor.

November 8–9, 1923: In an attempted coup at the Bürgerbräukeller in Munich, the Nazis try to overthrow the Bavarian government. Hitler is wounded in gunfire and arrested. Rosenberg escapes unscathed and is chosen by Hitler to lead the party until his release.

January 30, 1933: Hitler is appointed chancellor of Germany, and the Nazis quickly take full control of the state. Rosenberg moves to Berlin.

February 1933: Robert Kempner is dismissed from his post as a senior government official in the Prussian Interior Ministry.

April 1, 1933: The Nazis launch a boycott of Jewish businesses.

May 10, 1933: Books deemed offensive are burned at universities across Germany.

January 24, 1934: Hitler appoints Rosenberg his delegate for the entire intellectual and ideological indoctrination and education of the National Socialist party.

June 30, 1934: On the Night of the Long Knives, Hitler purges his enemies from the Nazi Party, including Ernst Röhm, the storm trooper chief.

August 2, 1934: President Paul von Hindenburg dies; Hitler establishes himself as Germany's dictator.

March 12, 1935: Kempner is arrested by Gestapo; he is released after two weeks in Berlin's Columbia-Haus concentration camp.

September 15, 1935: The Nuremberg Laws make Jews second-class subjects.

March 7, 1936: Germans reoccupy the demilitarized Rhineland region.

Summer 1936: Kempner flees to Italy, where he works at a boarding school for Jewish exiles in Florence.

March 12, 1938: Austria is annexed to Germany.

April–May 1938: Kempner and other Jewish teachers and students from his boarding school in Florence are jailed for three weeks during Hitler's visit to Italy.

September 3, 1938: Italian officials close Kempner's boarding school; he flees to France with his wife and his mistress.

September 30, 1938: In Munich, Britain and France agree to the surrender of a piece of Czechoslovakian territory, the Sudetenland, to Germany.

November 9–10, 1938: On Kristallnacht, the Night of Broken Glass, Jewish synagogues, shops, and homes are destroyed all across Germany.

January 30, 1939: Hitler, in a speech before the Reichstag, promises the destruction of the Jews of Europe.

March 15, 1939: Germany invades Czechoslovakia.

August 23, 1939: Hitler concludes a non-aggression pact with Soviet leader Joseph Stalin, in which the two powers also agree to carve up Poland.

September 1, 1939: Germany invades Poland and the Second World War begins. Kempner, after landing a job in America, arrives in New York.

November 8, 1939: A bomb explodes at the Bürgerbräukeller, in Munich, minutes after Hitler finishes a speech.

April 9, 1940: The Germans invade Norway and Denmark.

May 10, 1940: The Germans attack the Netherlands, Belgium, Luxembourg, and France.

June 22, 1940: France surrenders and signs armistice with Germany. Rosenberg opens a task force, the Einsatzstab Reichsleiter Rosenberg, that orchestrates the plunder of books and artwork all across occupied Europe.

June 22, 1941: Launching Operation Barbarossa, Germany invades the Soviet Union and occupies the Baltics, Belarus, and Ukraine.

July 17, 1941: Hitler appoints Rosenberg to oversee the civilian administration of the former Soviet lands as minister for the occupied eastern territories.

December 7, 1941: Japan attacks United States naval base at Pearl Harbor.

December 8, 1941: The first Nazi extermination camp, Chelmno in Poland, begins operation.

January 20, 1942: Nazi leaders meet at Wannsee to discuss the extermination of the Jews.

February 15, 1942: Mass extermination of Jews begins at Auschwitz.

January 31, 1943: General Friedrich Paulus surrenders his troops to the Russians at Stalingrad; the rest of the German Sixth Army follows suit on February 2, turning the tide of the war.

May 16, 1943: In Poland, a ghetto uprising in Warsaw is finally crushed by the Germans after a monthlong battle.

June 6, 1944: The Allies invade Normandy on D-Day.

July 20, 1944: In Operation Valkyrie, German officers launch a failed plot to assassinate Hitler.

August 25, 1944: The Allies liberate Paris.

January 25, 1945: Putting an end to the Battle of the Bulge, the Allies turn back the last major German offensive.

January 27, 1945: The Russian advance reaches Auschwitz, where more than one million people have been murdered in the preceding three years.

April 30, 1945: With the Russians surrounding Berlin, Hitler commits suicide.

May 8, 1945: Germany surrenders.

May 18, 1945: Rosenberg is arrested.

November 20, 1945: In Nuremberg, trial begins on war crimes charges against Rosenberg, Hermann Göring, Rudolf Hess, and other surviving Nazis; Kempner serves as part of the American prosecution team.

October 16, 1946: Convicted of war crimes, Rosenberg and nine others are hung.

Appendix B:
Cast of Characters

BIDDLE, FRANCIS: U.S. attorney general, 1941–1945; chief American judge at the Nuremberg war crimes trials, 1945–1946.

BORMANN, MARTIN: Chief of staff to Rudolf Hess, 1933–1941; chief of the Nazi Party Chancellery, 1941–1945; personal secretary to Hitler, 1943–1945.

BRAUN, EVA: Hitler's girlfriend and, at the end, his wife.

DIELS, RUDOLF: Gestapo chief, 1933–1934.

ECKART, DIETRICH: Editor of *Völkischer Beobachter*, the Nazi newspaper, from 1920 to 1923; introduced Rosenberg to Hitler in 1919.

FAULHABER, MICHAEL: Roman Catholic archbishop of Munich, 1917–1952; led opposition to Rosenberg's writings against the Church.

FROMM, BELLA: Diplomatic correspondent for Berlin's *Vossische Zeitung* newspaper.

GOEBBELS, JOSEPH: Reich minister of public enlightenment and propaganda.

GÖRING, HERMANN: Chief of the German air force, the Luftwaffe; Reich economic director; until April 1945, Hitler's chosen successor.

HALL, DAVID: Assistant United States attorney in Delaware; worked with Robert Wittman to recover Rosenberg diary.

HANFSTAENGL, ERNST: Nazi foreign press chief, 1922–1933; known as "Putzi."

HESS, RUDOLF: Deputy Führer of the Nazi Party from 1933 to 1941.

HEYDRICH, REINHARD: Director of the Reich Security Main Office, which oversaw Germany's security apparatus, from 1939 to 1942; delegated to address the "final solution of the Jewish question" and led the Wannsee conference; assassinated in 1942.

HIMMLER, HEINRICH: Reichsführer-SS and architect of the Holocaust.

HINDENBURG, PAUL VON: First World War general; president from 1925 to 1934; appointed Hitler chancellor in 1933.

JACKSON, ROBERT: U.S. attorney general, 1940–1941; Supreme Court justice, 1941–1954; chief U.S. prosecutor at the Nuremberg war crimes trial, 1945–1946.

KEITEL, WILHELM: Chief of the Supreme High Command of the German Armed Forces, 1938–1945.

KEMPNER, ANDRÉ: Son of Robert Kempner and his legal secretary, Margot Lipton; spent the war years as an infant in a children's home in Nice, France.

KEMPNER, LUCIAN: Son of Robert and his first wife, Helene; trapped in Germany during the war and sent to forced labor camps; escaped in 1945; joined U.S. Army.

KEMPNER, ROBERT: Lawyer; fled Nazis in 1936; arrived in the United States in 1939; worked for the FBI and the OSS; member of the American prosecution staff during war crimes trials in Nuremberg, 1945–1949.

KEMPNER, RUTH: Robert Kempner's second wife; author.

KOCH, ERICH: Reichskommissar of Ukraine, 1941–1944.

KREBS, ALBERT: Early Nazi Party leader in Hamburg and editor of a newspaper aligned with the Nazis, the *Hamburger Tageblatt*; dismissed from the party in 1932.

KUBE, WILHELM: Generalkommissar of Belarus, 1941–1943.

LAMMERS, HANS: Chief of the Reich Chancellery, 1933–1945.

LESTER, JANE: Robert Kempner's aide and legal secretary in Germany after the war.

LEY, ROBERT: Reich organization leader and head of the party's Main Training Office; oversaw German Labor Front and Strength Through Joy program, 1933–1945.

LIPTON, MARGOT: Robert Kempner's mistress and secretary in Italy and the United States; changed her surname from Lipstein after emigrating to America in 1939.

LOHSE, HINRICH: Reichskommissar of the Ostland, the German designation for occupied Estonia, Latvia, Lithuania, and Belarus, 1941–1943.

LÜDECKE, KURT: Early Nazi supporter and fund-raiser.

LUDENDORFF, ERICH: First World War general who marched with the Nazis during the attempted Beer Hall Putsch in 1923.

MAYER, HENRY: Chief archivist at the United States Holocaust Memorial Museum, 1994–2010; later became the museum's senior adviser on archives; spearheaded the search for the Rosenberg diary.

OLEXA, MARK: U.S. Homeland Security Investigations special agent; worked with Robert Wittman to recover the Rosenberg diary.

PAPEN, FRANZ VON: German chancellor in 1932 and vice chancellor, 1933–1934; played a pivotal role in Hitler's appointment as chancellor.

PEISER, WERNER: Founder of Istituto Fiorenza boarding school in Florence, Italy, 1933–1938.

QUISLING, VIKDUN: Nationalist politician in Norway; colluded with Rosenberg and the Nazis before Germany invaded his country in 1940.

RIBBENTROP, JOACHIM VON: German foreign minister, 1938–1945.

RICHARDSON, HERBERT: Former professor; author; publisher of Edwin Mellen Press; befriended Kempner's secretaries, Lester and Lipton; turned Rosenberg diary over to federal authorities in 2013 after he was served with a federal subpoena.

RÖHM, ERNST: Chief of the Sturmabteilung, the Nazi storm troopers, from 1931 to 1934; executed by Hitler following the Night of the Long Knives, in 1934.

SHIRER, WILLIAM: Berlin correspondent for Hearst wire services and CBS Radio before and during the war.

STRASSER, OTTO: Left-wing Nazi Party leader in Berlin until his ouster in 1930; his brother, Gregor, was murdered on the Night of the Long Knives, in 1934.

TAYLOR, TELFORD: Chief counsel for the U.S. military tribunals in Nuremberg, during which 185 accused Nazi war criminals were prosecuted in twelve trials between 1946 and 1949.

VON BEHR, KURT: Chief of the Paris headquarters of Nazi art-and-library-looting operation, the Einsatzstab Reichsleiter Rosenberg, from 1941 to 1942; later directed Operation Furniture, the removal of furnishings from thousands of Jewish homes in Western Europe.

VON GALEN, CLEMENS: Roman Catholic bishop of Münster; critic of Nazi euthanasia program.

VON KAHR, GUSTAV RITTER: Bavarian general state commissioner who put down the attempted Nazi coup in 1923; murdered during the Night of the Long Knives, in 1934.

WEIZSÄCKER, ERNST VON: State secretary in the German Foreign Office, 1938–1943.

WITTMAN, JEFF: Robert Wittman's son, who assisted in the hunt for the Rosenberg diary.

Notes

Prologue

2 charged across the western reaches of the battered country: *After Action Report, Third US Army, 1 August 1944–9 May 1945*, vol. I: *The Operations*, p. 337.

2 spent the war in Paris: Dreyfus and Gensburger, *Nazi Labour Camps*, p. 9, p. 130

2 had grown accustomed to living like royalty: Marguerite Higgins, "Americans Find Nazi Archives in Castle Vault," *New York Herald Tribune*, April 24, 1945.

3 G-2 military intelligence unit: *After Action Report, Third US Army, 1 August 1944–9 May 1945*, vol. II: *Staff Section Reports*, p. G-2 47.

3 a vintage rich in symbolism: Higgins, "Americans Find Nazi Archives."

4 left behind such diaries: Himmler's surviving diaries end in 1924. Many lesser figures in the Third Reich left behind diaries.

5 "racially infecting germs": Office of the U.S. Chief of Counsel for the Prosecution of Axis Criminality, *Nazi Conspiracy and Aggression*, vol. 5, pp. 554–57.

5 collaborated with Himmler's genocidal crusaders: See Ernst Piper, "Vor der Wannsee-Konferenz: Ausweitung der Kampfzone," *Der Tagesspiegel*, December 11, 2011.

6 "material for the battle": Rosenberg diary, August 23, 1936.

6 Rudolf Höss: Gilbert, *Nuremberg Diary*, pp. 267–68.

6 "swept up in a rage": Rosenberg diary, August 23, 1936.

6   "the main guilt": Goldensohn, *The Nuremberg Interviews*, pp. 73–75.
6   "intellectual high priest of the 'master race'": Closing statement of Robert
    Jackson, chief American prosecutor, *Trial of the Major War Criminals*, vol. 19,
    p. 416.

1: The Crusader

13   "Better to shoot two Poles too many": Maguire, *Law and War*, p. 128.
13   finally coming to a close: Ibid., pp. 151–58.
13   "the entire criminal fresco": Kempner, *Ankläger einer Epoche*, p. 348.
13   "a fortress of faith in international law": Ibid., p. 369.
14   "make martyrs out of the common criminals": Charles LaFollette to Lucius
    Clay, June 8, 1948, Frei, *Adenauer's Germany and the Nazi Past*, pp. 108–10.
14   "a most Gestapo-like man": Eivind Berggrav, Lutheran bishop in Oslo,
    quoted in Wyneken, "Driving Out the Demons," p. 368.
14   bent on vengeance: One of the newspapers was *Die Zeit* under Richard Tün-
    gel, a right-wing journalist. See Pöppmann, "The Trials of Robert Kemp-
    ner," p. 41, and Pöppmann, "Robert Kempner und Ernst von Weizsäcker im
    Wilhelmstrassenprozess," pp. 183–89.
15   "what type of morons": Maguire, *Law and War*, pp. 160–61.
15   "Today I want to go on record with a warning": Jack Raymond, "Krupp to
    Get Back Only Part of Plant," *New York Times*, February 2, 1951.
15   nearly all of the war criminals had been freed: Of the seven major war crim-
    inals who were sent to prison by the International Military Tribunal in 1946,
    three were released early on grounds of ill health. Admiral Karl Dönitz (ten
    years), Albert Speer (twenty years), and Baldur von Schirach (twenty years)
    served their entire prison terms. Rudolf Hess, sentenced to life, committed
    suicide in 1987.
16   "more or less outspoken nostalgia": Robert M. W. Kempner, "Distorting
    German History," *New York Herald Tribune*, January 13, 1950.
16   borrowed five documents and not returned them: Administrative memos,
    National Archives, Record Group 238, Correspondence with European Doc-
    ument Centers Relating to the Receipt and Return of Documents 1945–1946.
17   the Wannsee Protocol: Roseman, *The Villa, The Lake, The Meeting*, pp. 1–2.
18   "Which nobody believed": Ben Ferencz to Kempner, December 15, 1989,
    Telford Taylor Papers, Series 20, Subseries 1, Box 3. The letter continued:
    "All's well that ends well. This is not to suggest that there aren't other people
    who consider you an S.O.B. and bastard and would be happy to kill you. I'm
    sure that many former Nazis and their sympathizers would gladly agree."
    Thanks to Taylor biographer Jonathan Bush for sharing this letter.
18   "private journalistic instincts": Eckert, *The Struggle for the Files*, pp. 58–59.
18   awash in paper: Memorandum on document disposal, August 27, 1948,
    National Archives, Record Group 260, Records of the Office of the Chief of
    Counsel for War Crimes.
19   "I don't want to know anything": Kempner, *Ankläger*, pp. 400–7.
19   "The undersigned authorizes": Fred Niebergall, memorandum, April 8, 1949,
    Kempner Papers.

20 "Hitler and His Diplomats": Kempner correspondence with Dutton, 1949–
    50, Kempner Papers, Box 55.
20 "I had my documents": Kempner, *Ankläger*, p. 408.
20 twenty-nine boxes weighing more than eight thousand pounds: Pennsylva-
    nia Railroad notice, Kempner Papers, Box 3.
20 Nazi victims suing for restitution: Kempner, *Ankläger einer Epoch*, p. 380;
    Lester oral history.
21 a flurry of books: See bibliography for Kempner's publishing history.
22 "It is mathematically impossible": Hans Knight, "Anthology of Hell," *Sunday*
    (Philadelphia) *Bulletin Magazine*, May 9, 1965.
22 Margot Lipton: She changed her name from Margot Lipstein after emigrat-
    ing to the United States.
23 "Simpler . . . for Dr. Kempner": Lipton deposition in *Lipton v. Swansen*, June
    23, 1999.
23 "it was not my business": Lucian Kempner deposition in *Lipton v. Swansen*,
    December 8, 1999.
23 "never underestimate the love and understanding I have for you and your
    work": André Kempner to Robert Kempner, September 14, 1969, Kempner
    Papers, unfiled as of March 2015.
25 "horror, grief, and disbelief": Jane Lester testimony in *Lipton vs. Swansen*,
    January 31, 2001.

2: "Everything Gone"

27 keep his legacy alive: Lester oral history.
28 "what can I do???": Richardson to Kempner, April 8, 1982, Kempner Papers,
    Box 69.
28 asked about donating "a small quantity" of Kempner's papers: Henry Mayer,
    memorandum, "Re: Alfred Rosenberg 'Tagebuch,'" June 12, 2006.
28 elaborate ceremony: Video of dedication of the Robert Kempner Collegium,
    September 21, 1996, Kempner Papers, Videobox #1.
30 Farmers were pressured: Levine, *Class, Networks, and Identity*, pp. 37–41;
    Kaplan, *Between Dignity and Despair*, p. 23; Evans, *The Third Reich in Power*,
    p. 574.
32 Gurs: Details of the October 1940 deportations and life at Gurs come from
    Browning, *The Origins of the Final Solution*, pp. 89–91; Zuccotti, *The Holo-
    caust, the French, and the Jews*, pp. 65–80; Poznanski, *Jews in France During
    World War II*, pp. 171–95; Schwertfeger, *In Transit*, pp. 137–62; Frank, *The
    Curse of Gurs*, pp. 229–67; and Gutman, *Encyclopedia of the Holocaust, Vol. 2*,
    pp. 631–32.
33 "atmosphere of human hopelessness": American Friends Service Committee
    report, quoted in "Misery and Death in French Camps," *New York Times*,
    January 26, 1941.
33 "a morass": Dr. Ludwig Mann, quoted in Frank, *The Curse of Gurs*, p. 239.
33 "stench of urine": Poznanski, *Jews in France*, p. 180.
33 "It would take a master poet": Professor A. Reich, quoted ibid., p. 182.
33 arrived at their final destination: Details found in two online databases, the

Bundesarchiv Memorial Book at bundesarchiv.de/gedenkbuch and the Yad Vashem Central Database of Shoah Victims' Names at db.yadvashem.org/ names. See also Klarsfeld, *Memorial to the Jews Deported from France, 1942–44*, pp. xxvi–xxvii.

37 In his years as a teacher: Details of Richardson's life are drawn from Charles Trueheart, "Publish AND Perish?" *Washington Post*, July 13, 1994, and Jake New, "Herbert Richardson v. the World," *Chronicle of Higher Education*, April 15, 2013. Richardson did not respond to calls from the authors to his office and to his lawyer seeking an interview.

39 "This public humiliation has been the most extraordinary embarrassment": Trueheart, "Publish AND Perish?"

39 "self-serving half-truths": *University of St. Michael's College v. Herbert W. Richardson*, p. 5.

40 she sued: *Lipton v. Swansen*.

40 believed Herbert Richardson . . . was behind the legal maneuvering: Motion of the Estate of André Kempner and Lucian Kempner for Permanent Injunction, September 20, 1999, filed in *Lipton v. Swansen*.

40 "I don't remember": Lipton deposition in *Lipton v. Swansen*, June 23, 1999.

42 Investigators tracked Richardson down in Lewiston: Timothy Logue, "History Uncovered," *Delaware County Times*, August 26, 1999.

3: "To Stare into the Mind of a Dark Soul"

46 The former prosecutor did not hide the truth: Correspondence between Kempner and Seraphim, 1955–56, Kempner Papers, Boxes 53, 58.

46 "in my own archive": Kempner, *SS im Kreuzverhör*, p. 228.

47 "One million, two million?": This account of Mayer's conversation is drawn from a memorandum Mayer wrote to his file, "Re: Alfred Rosenberg 'Tagebuch,'" June 12, 2006. Walt Martin did not return calls from the authors for comment.

49 "There were no more documents": Ralph Vigoda, "Nazi Papers in Custody Fight," *Philadelphia Inquirer*, March 25, 2003.

50 the entire affair ended up in federal court: *United States of America v. William Martin*, United States District Court for the Eastern District of Pennsylvania.

51 Richardson had persuaded Lipton to add his name to her bank accounts: Edward Jesella, interview with author, April 20, 2015.

58 "like my mother": This account of Richardson's interview is drawn from the special agent's Report of Investigation, dated March 1, 2013, which was released to the authors under the Freedom of Information Act by U.S. Immigration and Customs Enforcement.

58 federal grand jury subpoena: Though they are assigned to a particular district, U.S. attorneys may open investigations into criminal activity anywhere in the United States. It is routine for federal prosecutors to send subpoenas outside their districts.

60 "I was glad to meet with them and cooperate with their efforts": Patricia Cohen, "Diary of a Hitler Aide Resurfaces After a Hunt That Lasted Years," *New York Times*, June 13, 2013.

4: "Stepchildren of Fate"

66 "So dense were the masses": "Berlin Welcomes Army," *New York Times*, December 10, 1918. See also the British Pathé newsreel "German Troops Return 1918," at britishpathe.com.

66 "No enemy has conquered you!": Stephenson, *"Frontschweine* and Revolution," pp. 287–99.

67 "are not afraid of life": Unnamed correspondent to Evelyn Blücher, the English wife of a German prince who spent the war in Germany, quoted in Blücher von Wahlstatt, *An English Wife in Berlin*, p. 305.

67 "the great sorrow of the German people": Lang and Schenck, *Memoirs of Alfred Rosenberg*, p. 29.

67 a standard German joke: Piper, *Alfred Rosenberg*, p. 208.

68 "'only Aryan Rosenberg'": Neave, *On Trial at Nuremberg*, p. 103.

68 "This kneeling down": Cecil, *The Myth of the Master Race*, p. 11; see Rosenberg, "How the *Myth* Arose," National Archives, T454, Roll 101.

68 would fondly remember his art teacher: Details of Rosenberg's early life come from Lang and Schenck, *Memoirs*, pp. 1–30.

69 "man of profound half-culture": Fest, *The Face of the Third Reich*, pp. 163–74.

69 "the Philosopher": Cecil, *Myth of the Master Race*, p. 15.

70 "the psychosis had gripped millions": From Rosenberg's *Pest in Russland!*, quoted in Cecil, *Myth of the Master Race*, p. 17.

70 noisily led his compatriots out of the hall: Cecil, *Myth of the Master Race*, p. 20.

71 "I left my homeland": Lang and Schenck, *Memoirs*, p. 29.

72 "Athens on the Isar": Large, *Where Ghosts Walked*, pp. xii–xvii.

72 "preferred cafés to beer halls": Ibid., pp. 3–5.

72 unfathomable turmoil: Evans, *The Coming of the Third Reich*, pp. 156–61.

72 "stepchildren of fate": Lang and Schenck, *Memoirs*, p. 40.

73 "fighter against Jerusalem?": Layton, "The *Völkischer Beobachter*, 1925–1933," pp. 58–59; see Alfred Rosenberg, *Dietrich Eckart: Ein Vermächtnis* (Munich: n.p., 1927).

73 "a *Who's Who*": Kershaw, *Hitler: A Biography*, p. 82.

74 rejected by the Thule Society: Evans, *Coming of the Third Reich*, p. 160.

74 DOWN WITH BOLSHEVISM!: Rosenberg describes this scene in Lang and Schenck, *Memoirs*, p. 43.

5: "The Most Hated Paper in the Land!"

77 Born in Braunau: Details of Hitler's early life come from Kershaw, *Hitler: A Biography*, pp. 1–46.

78 "The city was as familiar to me": Hitler, *Mein Kampf*, p. 126.

78 had not yet coalesced into the ideology that would change the face of Europe: Kershaw, *Hitler: A Biography*, p. 27.

78 seemed to get along exceptionally well: Reinhold Hanisch, "I Was Hitler's Buddy," *The New Republic*, April 5, 12, and 19, 1939.

79 anti-Semitism based on "reason": Kershaw, *Hitler: A Biography*, pp. 74–75.

80 "I would be lying": Lang and Schenck, *Memoirs of Alfred Rosenberg*, pp. 47–50.

80   "no great admirer of the Hitler intellect": Lüdecke, *I Knew Hitler*, p. 510.

80   "Here I saw a German front-line soldier": Cecil, *The Myth of the Master Race*, p. 30.

80   "changed my entire personal fate": Lang and Schenck, *Memoirs*, pp. 47–50.

81   "the most ruthless weapon for Germandom": Layton, "The *Völkischer Beobachter*, 1920–1933," p. 354.

81   "the most hated paper in the land!": Ibid., p. 360.

81   *Völkischer Beobachter*: The name of the newspaper has been variously translated as "People's Observer" or "Racial Observer."

81   "full of confusion": Paula Schlier diary entry, quoted in Layton, "The *Völkischer Beobachter*, 1925–1933," pp. 87–88.

82   "had difficulty in understanding it": Trevor-Roper, *Hitler's Table Talk*, p. 490.

82   far more than Rosenberg's opaque musings: Layton, "The *Völkischer Beobachter*, 1920–1933," pp. 369–80.

82   "The babbler (!!!) Hitler": Layton, "The *Völkischer Beobachter*, 1925–1933," p. 256.

83   "the more sales increased!": Trevor-Roper, *Hitler's Table Talk*, p. 490.

83   "such an unappetizing fellow": Hanfstaengl, *Hitler: The Missing Years*, p. 91.

83   "intrinsically illiterate": Ibid., p. 122.

84   lifted from writers and thinkers: Rosenberg, *Race and Race History*, p. 14.

84   comparative linguistics: This summation of the Aryan idea and its development is drawn from Pringle, *The Master Plan*, pp. 27–36.

85   "gospel of the Nazi movement": Shirer, *The Rise and Fall of the Third Reich*, pp. 104–9.

85   "yes, yes, and yes again": Bollmus, "Alfred Rosenberg," p. 185.

85   "anti-Jewish polemicist": Nova, *Alfred Rosenberg*, p. 103.

86   "Jewish trickery": Alfred Rosenberg, *The Track of the Jew Through the Ages*, excerpted in Rosenberg, *Race and Race History*, p. 178.

86   "a poison": Ibid., p. 189

86   "are chosen as a plague": Quoted in Nova, *Alfred Rosenberg*, p. 118.

87   brought it to Hitler's attention: Kellogg, *The Russian Roots of Nazism*, pp. 70–73. Others have argued that Rosenberg brought the book to Hitler, but evidence is lacking.

87   accurate outline of global Jewish strategy: Ibid., p. 75.

87   "the undisputed brain behind Adolf Hitler": Strasser, *The Gangsters Around Hitler*, pp. 21–23.

87   "always listen to": Lüdecke, *I Knew Hitler*, p. 79. Lüdecke later fell out with Hitler.

88   "Germany's coming 'great leader'": Kershaw, *Hitler: A Biography*, pp. 37–42.

88   the tenor of church revival meetings: Evans, *The Coming of the Third Reich*, pp. 171–75.

88   "racial tuberculosis": Ibid., p. 174.

88   "the symbol of the race high over the world": Baynes, *The Speeches of Adolf Hitler*, p. 73.

89   His Russian-speaking acolyte quickly filled him in: Kershaw, *Hitler: A Biography*, pp. 92–93; Kellogg, *Russian Roots*, p. 242.

89 in his very first published piece: Alfred Rosenberg, "The Russian Jewish Revolution," *Auf Gut Deutsch* 21 (February 1919), reproduced in Lane and Rupp, *Nazi Ideology Before 1933*, pp. 11–16.

89 "Russia = Bolshevism = Jewry": Dallin, *German Rule in Russia*, p. 9.

89 "That will secure the scaffold for you": Baynes, *Speeches of Adolf Hitler*, p. 12.

89 "It is a gigantic fraud": Hitler's July 28, 1922, speech is reprinted ibid., pp. 21–41.

90 "God have mercy on you!": Evans, *Coming of the Third Reich*, pp. 174–75.

90 Weimar Republic: Ibid., pp. 78–96.

91 stage a coup and take power: Ibid., pp. 176–94; Shirer, *Rise and Fall*, pp. 68–75; Read, *The Devil's Disciples*, pp. 85–102.

91 his childhood: Read, *Devil's Disciples*, pp. 26–38.

92 "cherish hatred": Ibid., p. 38.

92 "Bring your pistols": Hanfstaengl, *Hitler: The Missing Years*, p. 92.

93 "or we are dead": Layton, "The *Völkischer Beobachter*, 1925–1933," p. 91.

93 "awakens from her wild feverish dream": Layton, "The *Völkischer Beobachter*, 1920–1933," p. 359.

95 "you will lead the movement": Lang and Schenck, *Memoirs*, p. 73.

95 unsuited for executive leadership: Kershaw, *Hitler: A Biography*, p. 140.

95 "Secret!": Piper, *Alfred Rosenberg*, p. 98.

95 Rolf Eidhalt: Lang and Schenck, *Memoirs*, p. 76.

95 "He could do little to direct us": Lüdecke, *I Knew Hitler*, p. 184.

96 he was ousted: Rosenberg wrote later that he asked Hitler to allow him to resign. Lang and Schenck, *Memoirs*, p. 78.

96 "I won't take part in that comedy": Lüdecke, *I Knew Hitler*, p. 279.

96 "*Ja, ja*, we'll see": Ibid., p. 278.

97 "When the heart is full": Cecil, *Myth of the Master Race*, pp. 50–51.

97 a black, six-seat Mercedes: The car cost more than his annual earnings: 20,000 *Reichsmarks*. Hitler said a bank loan financed the purchase. Kershaw, *Hitler, 1899–1936: Hubris*, p. 685.

97 "he did not like me": Cecil, *Myth of the Master Race*, p. 52.

98 "I cannot give up the cause": Lüdecke, *I Knew Hitler*, p. 288.

98 sarcastic and combative: Layton, "The *Völkischer Beobachter*, 1920–1933," pp. 367–68.

98 "our opponents spared us absolutely nothing": Lang and Schenck, *Memoirs*, pp. 260–61.

99 "Here's a Jew!": Piper, *Alfred Rosenberg*, p. 240.

99 "doing in Paris during the war": Ibid., p. 244.

99 "You want me to box your ears?": Ibid., p. 240. When the Nazis took power the following year, the offending politician, Christian Heuck, would face punishment more severe than that. Swept up with the rest of the leading communists and political unreliables, Heuck was charged with treason and sent to prison, where he would be murdered by the SS.

99 "had not yet discovered what his real fatherland was": Ibid., p. 243; Cecil, *The Myth of the Master Race*, p. 107.

99 divorced in 1923: Lang and Schenck, *Memoirs*, pp. 70–71.

100 more prose than all the other leading Nazis—combined: Piper, *Alfred Rosenberg*, p. 74.

6: Night Descends

103   It all happened so quickly: See Evans, *The Coming of the Third Reich*, pp. 310–54.

104   A reporter spotted him there, watching: Delmer, *Trail Sinister*, pp. 185–86.

105   "two sorts of men": Read, *The Devil's Disciples*, p. 282.

105   "young revolution": Fromm, *Blood and Banquets*, p. 88.

105   "destroy and exterminate": Shirer, *The Rise and Fall of the Third Reich*, p. 195.

105   "a farce": Report from U.S. Ambassador Frederic M. Sackett, March 3, 1933, reproduced in *Foreign Relations of the United States*, 1933, vol. 2, pp. 201–4.

106   "may never recover": Report from Sackett, March 9, 1933, reproduced in *Foreign Relations of the United States*, 1933, vol. 2, pp. 206–9.

106   "Full powers, or else!": Shirer, *Rise and Fall*, p. 199.

106   "done quite legally": Ibid., p. 188.

107   loyal opposition: Kempner, *Ankläger einer Epoche*, p. 16.

107   "skepticism played a great role": Ibid., p. 205.

107   "Waiting for the plague": Ibid., pp. 13–14.

107   Lydia Rabinowitsch: Biographical details in Creese, *Ladies in the Laboratory II*, pp. 129–38.

107   Robert Koch: "Robert Koch," Nobelprize.org, http://www.nobelprize.org/ nobel_prizes/medicine/laureates/1905/koch-bio.html.

108   in honor of their hero, Koch: Kempner, *Ankläger*, pp. 11, 19.

108   he might need them: Ibid., pp. 22–26.

108   faced an insurrection: This account is drawn from Watt, *The Kings Depart*, pp. 247–73.

109   "street fighting": Kempner to Büro für Kriegsstammrollen, May 9 and September 3, 1934, Kempner Papers, Box 41.

109   "marched out of sheer curiosity": Kempner, *Ankläger*, pp. 25–26.

110   according to his military records: Certified copy of Kempner Landsturm-Militärpass, Kempner Papers, Box 76.

111   pro bono legal work: Kempner, *Ankläger*, p. 71.

111   comprehensive investigation: Memorandum detailing Kempner's planned testimony in *United States v. McWilliams*, Kempner Papers, Box 154.

111   outlawing the party: The report was published as Kempner, "Blueprint of the Nazi Underground—Past and Future Subversive Activities."

112   "139,900 mistakes": "Hitler Ridiculed as a Writing Man," *New York Times*, February 9, 1933.

113   "Heads will roll!": Shirer, *Rise and Fall*, p. 141.

114   "pretty hard to believe": Fromm, *Blood and Banquets*, p. 73.

114   "in two thousand years": *Foreign Relations of the United States*, 1933, vol. 2, p. 320.

114   "Little self-appointed posses": Frederick T. Birchall, "Nazi Bands Stir Up Strife in Germany," *New York Times*, March 9, 1933.

114   eat his manuscript: "Charge Terrorism by Nazi Troopers," *New York Times*, March 15, 1933.

115   "unidentified suicides": "German Fugitives Tell of Atrocities at Hands of Nazis," *New York Times*, March 20, 1933.

115 "The whole city seemed to be an army camp": Brandt, *My Road to Berlin*, p. 58.

115 massacre of Jews and Nazi enemies: Report from Sackett, March 21, 1933, reproduced in *Foreign Relations of the United States*, 1933, vol. 2, p. 212.

115 "incurable optimist": "Reviews Nazi Rise in Talk Over Radio," *New York Times*, March 13, 1933.

116 "detach the Jew from Germany": Report from Consul General George Messersmith, "Present Status of the Anti-Semitic Movement in Germany," September 21, 1933, George S. Messersmith Papers, Item 305.

116 "There remains the question": Quote from *Der Deutsche*, ibid.

116 "mental cruelties": Report from Messersmith, November 1, 1933, reproduced in *Foreign Relations of the United States*, 1933, vol. 2, p. 363.

116 Diels had grown close to Göring: Kempner, *Ankläger*, pp. 26–37; Read, *The Devil's Disciple*, p. 280.

117 "Are there any decent men here at all?": Hett, *Burning the Reichstag*, p. 34.

117 "Get out of my sight": Mosley, *The Reich Marshal*, p. 151.

118 political unreliability: Kempner, *Ankläger*, pp. 88–90. See also "Police Counsel on Leave of Absence," *8 Uhr-Abendblatt*, February 23, 1933; Kempner dismissal and pension documents, Kempner Papers, Box 95.

118 "racially handicapped": This quote, and details of Kempner's relationship with Diels, are drawn from Kohl, *The Witness House*, pp. 43–47, 152–53.

118 "played the lead in an American western": Leni Riefenstahl, quoted in Hett, *Burning the Reichstag*, p. 28.

118 Kempner intervened: Kempner, *Ankläger*, pp. 111–12.

118 scandalized the diplomatic community in Berlin: Larson, *In the Garden of Beasts*, pp. 116–19.

119 "I have to put together lists": Kempner, *Ankläger*, p. 110.

119 "finding out things": Hett, *Burning the Reichstag*, p. 79.

119 burned the organization's membership lists: Kempner, *Ankläger*, pp. 68–72.

120 They *felt* German: Kaplan, *Between Dignity and Despair*, pp. 62–66.

120 enthusiastically embraced their new freedom: Dippel, *Bound Upon a Wheel of Fire*, 1–20.

120 worse attacks were still to come: Ibid., p. 140.

120 "even opportunism": Ibid., p. xxiii.

121 some Jewish businesses even thrived: Ibid., p. 139.

121 "faithfully German, patriotic": Kempner, *Ankläger*, p. 176.

7: "Rosenberg's Path"

123 "a sedentary life": Henry C. Wolfe with Heinrich Hauser, "Nazi Doctor of Frightfulness," *Milwaukee Journal*, July 6, 1940.

123 "A block of ice!": Lüdecke, *I Knew Hitler*, pp. 83–85.

125 "wrapped up in his own opinions": Allen, *The Infancy of Nazism*, p. 217.

125 "unreal, phantasmagoric imaginings": Ibid., p. 184.

125 "the incomprehensible and the nonsensical": Ibid., p. 220.

126 "as thoroughly as a learned man": Rosenberg interrogation, September 21, 1945, 14:30–16:40, National Archives, M1270, Roll 17.

126 "undergraduate ninny!": Allen, *Infancy of Nazism*, pp. 220–21.

126 "clever": Cecil, *The Myth of the Master Race*, p. 101.

127 a treatise on his philosophy: Rosenberg interrogation, September 21.

127 "Every race has its soul": Rosenberg, *Der Mythus des 20. Jahrhunderts*, p. 116.

127 a lengthy glossary: Cecil, *Myth of the Master Race*, p. 82.

127 "alien blood": Rosenberg, *Der Mythus*, p. 105.

128 "ideological belch": Fest, *The Face of the Third Reich*, p. 168.

128 put him to sleep: Goldensohn, *The Nuremberg Interviews*, pp. 108–9; Piper, *Alfred Rosenberg*, p. 494.

128 "glanced cursorily": Trevor-Roper, *Hitler's Table Talk 1941–1944*, p. 318. It should be noted that these remarks were recorded by an avowed Rosenberg enemy, Martin Bormann.

128 "It is tripe": Hanfstaengl, *Hitler: The Missing Years*, p. 122.

128 privately ridiculed the book and its author: Papen, *Memoirs*, p. 261.

128 "A true German cannot condemn them": Strasser, *Hitler and I*, p. 96.

128 "you would understand these things": Baynes, *The Speeches of Adolf Hitler*, p. 988.

129 "the path of German youth": Bollmus, "Alfred Rosenberg," p. 187. Later, von Schirach would tell Nuremberg prison psychiatrist Douglas Kelley that while his Hitler Youth leaders all had copies, none of them could get through it. "Rosenberg should go down in history as the man who sold more copies of a book no one ever read than any other author." But Schirach's remarks were belied by the fact that Rosenberg's files were filled with letters from readers. See Kelley, *22 Cells in Nuremberg*, p. 44, and Piper, *Alfred Rosenberg*, p. 213.

129 more than a million copies: Piper, *Alfred Rosenberg*, p. 293. In 1934 alone, his publishing income was forty-two thousand reichsmarks, the equivalent of $300,000 in today's currency.

129 "your work will endure": Rosenberg diary, August 10, 1936.

129 no place captured Berlin's true nature more than Potsdamer Platz: Ladd, *The Ghosts of Berlin*, pp. 115–25.

130 "extra-legal government": Report from Consul General George Messersmith, April 10, 1933, reproduced in *Foreign Relations of the United States, 1933*, vol. 2, p. 223.

131 "plot it mathematically": Kelley, *22 Cells*, p. 38. Douglas Kelley was one of the psychiatrists who interviewed Rosenberg during his incarceration at Nuremberg before the war crimes trials.

131 "indulges in more bunk": Dodd and Dodd, *Ambassador Dodd's Diary*, p. 190.

131 "a word of English!": Lüdecke, *I Knew Hitler*, pp. 642–43.

131 "looked like cold cod": Vansittart, *The Mist Procession*, p. 475.

131 turned out to be spies: Winterbotham, *The Nazi Connection*, pp. 32–81.

132 "My dear party comrade Rosenberg!": Piper, *Alfred Rosenberg*, pp. 293–94.

133 Robert Ley: Evans, *The Third Reich in Power*, pp. 457–60.

133 The ideologue would design curriculum: Rothfeder, "A Study of Alfred Rosenberg's Organization for National Socialist Ideology," pp. 72–76.

134 "only just beginning": Cecil, *Myth of the Master Race*, p. 113.

134 "cheerfully cut the throat": Fromm, *Blood and Banquets*, p. 164.

134 Goebbels grew up: Details of Goebbels's early life are drawn from Read, *The Devil's Disciples*, pp. 126–34, and Lochner, *The Goebbels Diaries*, pp. 12–14.

135 "we are not really enemies": Read, *Devil's Disciples*, p. 142.

135 "A reactionary?": Lochner, *Goebbels Diaries*, p. 19.

136 "What one calls a genius": Kershaw, *Hitler: A Biography*, p. 171.

136 "hydrochloric acid": Fest, *Face of the Third Reich*, p. 333, n. 44.

136 "a mask of urbanity": Lochner, *Goebbels Diaries*, p. 20.

137 "Mephistopheles": Ibid., p. 22.

137 "over the whole field of spiritual indoctrination of the nation": "Decree Concerning the Duties of the Reich Ministry for Public Enlightenment and Propaganda," June 30, 1933, reproduced as 2030-PS in Office of the U.S. Chief of Counsel for the Prosecution of Axis Criminality, *Nazi Conspiracy and Aggression*, vol. 4, pp. 653–54.

137 "the New Yorkers of Central Europe": Otto Friedrich, *Before the Deluge: A Portrait of Berlin in the 1920s* (New York: Harper Perennial, 1995), p. 6.

137 modernism of all shades flowered: Ladd, *Ghosts of Berlin*, pp. 110–15.

138 "a melting pot of everything that is evil": *Völkischer Beobachter* article, quoted ibid., p. 82.

138 "infecting the Volk": Rosenberg article from 1925 issue of *Der Weltkampf*, quoted in Rosenberg, *Race and Race History*, p. 173.

138 Goebbels . . . appreciated modern art: Petropoulos, *Art as Politics in the Third Reich*, pp. 23–25.

139 "little half-idiotic admixtures of indefinable human types": Rosenberg article in *Völkischer Beobachter*, July 1933, quoted in Rosenberg, *Race and Race History*, p. 161.

139 tried to assuage the critics: Evans, *Third Reich in Power*, pp. 164–66.

140 "to prevent worse misfortunes": Ibid., p. 189.

140 "to be confused, let alone intimidated, by their twaddle": Nicholas, *The Rape of Europa*, pp. 15–16.

140 "Horrible examples of art Bolshevism": Evans, *Third Reich in Power*, p. 171.

141 Office for the Protection of Art: Rothfeder, "A Study," pp. 136–38, 215–18.

141 sent the Gestapo memos: Petropoulos, *Art as Politics*, p. 45.

141 "the entirety of German literature": Barbian, *The Politics of Literature in Nazi Germany*, p. 118.

142 "undesirable literature": Ibid., p. 121.

142 Offices spawned offices: Rothfeder, "A Study," pp. 199–207.

142 "'almost' Rosenberg": Allen, *Infancy of Nazism*, p. 202.

143 "whoring after strange gods": Cecil, *Myth of the Master Race*, p. 4.

143 "Our revolution . . . has an abscess": Rosenberg diary, February 6, 1939.

143 "remained <u>alone</u>": Ibid., May 7, 1940.

144 agitated for a "second revolution": Shirer, *Rise and Fall of the Third Reich*, pp. 204–6.

144 "Military uniforms, elaborate gowns, sparkling jewels": Fromm, *Blood and Banquets*, pp. 134–35.

144 "debauchers and parasites": Rosenberg diary, July 7, 1934.

144 "Look at that Baltic pig": Fromm, *Blood and Banquets*, p. 135.

8: The Diary

147 preparations for another war: "Reich to Be Armed in Air with Mighty Fleet by 1936," *New York Times*, May 11, 1934; "Britain Alarmed by Reich Planes," *New York Times*, May 12, 1934; "Aviation Exports to Reich Mounting," *New York Times*, May 12, 1934. The American manufacturers defended themselves by saying that the exports were for commercial, not military, applications, and that they were not selling directly to the German government but to businesses.

147 twenty thousand German Americans turned out: "20,000 Nazi Friends at a Rally Here Denounce Boycott," *New York Times*, May 18, 1934.

148 Heinz Spanknöbel: Rogge, *The Official German Report*, pp. 17–21; Bernstein, *Swastika Nation*, pp. 25–37; Diamond, *The Nazi Movement in the United States*, pp. 113–24.

149 ready to fight, there and then: "Reds Riot in Court After Nazi Rally," *New York Times*, May 18, 1934.

150 "let them be warned": "Goebbels Utters Threats to Jews," *New York Times*, May 12, 1934.

150 "grumblers and faultfinders": Details of the campaign are drawn from Longerich, *Goebbels*, pp. 258–59; Read, *The Devil's Disciples*, p. 361; Evans, *The Third Reich in Power*, pp. 28–29.

151 "Every day is better already": Otto D. Tolischus, "Grumblers Face Arrest in Reich," *New York Times*, May 19, 1934.

151 "I haven't kept a diary": Rosenberg diary, May 14, 1934.

152 private notes: Matthäus and Bajohr, *Alfred Rosenberg: Die Tagebücher von 1934 bis 1944*, p. 20.

153 "shrink like a <u>mimosa</u>": Rosenberg diary, May 22, 1934.

153 "In view of recent rumours that Herr Rosenberg has been 'shelved'": "The German Jigsaw: Herr Hitler as Helmsman," *The Times* (London), May 9, 1934.

154 "this pig?": Rosenberg diary, May 15, 1934.

154 "sudden and bitter": Ibid., May 17, 1934; Bernstorff, who in the 1930s helped Jews escape Germany, was one of the "Solf circle" anti-Nazi intellectuals arrested in 1944 after a Gestapo spy infiltrated a tea party at which guests made critical comments about the regime. He was executed a few weeks before the end of the war.

154 "We shall ruthlessly get rid of them": This account of the Night of the Long Knives is drawn from Evans, *Third Reich in Power*, pp. 30–41; Shirer, *The Rise and Fall of the Third Reich*, pp. 204–25; Read, *Devil's Disciples*, pp. 343–74; and Noakes, *Nazism: A History in Documents*, vol. 1, pp. 172–85.

155 steeped in Germanic history: Details of Himmler's early life and career are drawn from Read, *Devil's Disciples*, pp. 39–49, 93–95.

156 fearsome army: Ibid., pp. 168–69, 179–81.

158 pulp fiction: Rosenberg diary, July 7, 1934.

159 as the bloodbath came to be known: The origin of the name is unclear, though the use of the phrase "long knives" to describe treachery has roots in Anglo-Saxon mythology.

161 "will want to make acquaintance with <u>that</u>": Rosenberg diary, August 2, 1934.

161 "A great one is lost": Ibid.

9: "Clever Workings and Lucky Coincidences"

164 "speedy settlement": Kempner flyer, "Emigration and Transfer to Palestine and Other Countries," Kempner Papers, Box 41; correspondence on Kempner legal work from 1933 to 1935, Kempner Papers, Box 95. See also Nicosia, "German Zionism and Jewish Life in Nazi Berlin," and Schmid, *Lost in a Labyrinth of Red Tape*, p. 71.

164 to flee the country: Evans, *Third Reich in Power*, pp. 555–60.

164 bribes, gifts, even sex: Kaplan, *Between Dignity and Despair*, p. 72.

165 money to be made: Kempner interview, Records of the Emergency Committee in Aid of Displaced Foreign Scholars.

165 One false move: Kempner to Ernst Hamburger, February 17, 1939, Kempner Papers, Box 2. See also Kempner to Alfred S. Abramowitz, November 16, 1938, and Kempner to Carl Misch, November 28, 1938, both in Kempner Papers, Box 2.

165 $5,000 to $8,000: Kempner Application for Federal Employment, Kempner personnel files from Department of Justice and Department of the Army; in a draft application, he lists his annual income during that period as $10,000 to $30,000 per year, Kemper Papers, Box 41.

165 Lydia: Creese, *Ladies in the Laboratory II*, p. 137.

166 "their Jewish stock": Copy of affidavit by Sidney Mendel, dated 1944, and copy of divorce ruling, March 9, 1932, in Kempner Papers, Box 76. See also Evans, *Third Reich in Power*, p. 566.

166 "pogroms will start": Kempner, *Ankläger einer Epoche*, p. 135.

166 Berthold Jacob: Barnes, *Nazi Refugee Turned Gestapo Spy*, p. 76.

167 "This is the end": Kempner, *Angläger*, p. 134.

167 What frightened Kempner most: Kempner to Misch, November 28, 1938, Kempner Papers, Box 2.

168 "Ossietzky was not exactly a first reference": Kempner, *Ankläger*, p. 133.

169 "lucky coincidences": Kempner to Misch, November 28, 1938, Kempner Papers, Box 2. In *Ankläger*, Kempner says that Hitler released him, along with Jacob and the other prisoners, after international pressure.

169 ordered the journalist freed after six months: Palmier, *Weimar in Exile*, p. 432. In 1941, Jacob was rearrested in Portugal while trying to flee overseas. He died three years later in a Berlin prison.

169 his mother died: Creese, *Ladies*, p. 137.

170 "Set in the Tuscan countryside": Advertisement reproduced in *Dial 22-0756, Pronto*, p. 11.

170 "it is not difficult": Ibid., p. 15.

170 "there was no Jewish question": Kempner, *Ankläger*, pp. 137–40.

10: "The Time Isn't Ripe for Me Yet"

174 "sacrificial altars": Otto D. Tolischus, "Hindenburg Rests on Site of Victory After Hero's Rites," *New York Times*, August 8, 1934.

174 "assailed us with Bible quotes": Rosenberg diary, August 19, 1934.

175 "holy ground": Ibid., May 29, 1934.

175 "We are only Germans": Cecil, *The Myth of the Master Race*, p. 112.

176 "one superstition after another": Rosenberg, *Der Mythus des 20. Jahrhunderts*, p. 79.

176 "falsified history": Ibid., p. 73.

176 "inwardly false and dead": Ibid., p. 133.

176 "religion of the blood": Ibid., p. 258.

176 "fifth gospel": Ibid., p. 603.

176 "horrible crucifixes": Ibid., p. 701.

176 "angry man in the temple": Ibid., p. 604.

176 "slim, tall, blond": Ibid., p. 616.

176 "the myth of the blood": Ibid., p. 114.

177 "horrible, distorted": Rosenberg diary, August 19, 1934.

177 "lay the foundations of this holy order of Germany": Dodd and Dodd, *Ambassador Dodd's Diary*, p. 199.

177 "Ashanti religion": Rosenberg diary, January 19, 1940.

177 "we would never fathom": Ibid., December 14, 1941.

178 syphilis and Christianity: Ibid., April 9, 1941.

178 "the Christian poison to face its end": Ibid., June 28, 1934.

178 "by fools or by criminals": Hitler, *Mein Kampf*, p. 267.

179 spreading the Nazi gospel: Evans, *The Third Reich in Power*, pp. 220–24.

179 "stark dementia": Arendzen, foreword to *"Mythus,"* p. 4.

180 "religious delusion": Lewy, *The Catholic Church and Nazi Germany*, p. 8.

180 "national morality": Baynes, *The Speeches of Adolf Hitler*, pp. 369–70.

180 urged the flock to obey: Lewy, *Catholic Church*, pp. 40–41.

181 vociferously opposed: Ibid., p. 258.

181 fundamental misunderstanding: Ibid., pp. 53, 132.

181 Renaissance cathedral: Descriptions of the church are drawn from Jeffrey Chipps Smith, *Infinite Boundaries: Order, Disorder, and Reorder in Early Modern German Culture*, vol. 40 of *Sixteenth Century Essays & Studies*, edited by Max Reinhart (Kirksville, Mo.: Sixteenth Century Journal Publishers, 1998), p. 154.

182 every life was precious—pointedly including the Jews': Lewy, *Catholic Church*, p. 274.

182 "The Jews . . . can help themselves": Griech-Polelle, *Bishop von Galen*, p. 52.

182 "May God preserve the Reich Chancellor": Lewy, *Catholic Church*, p. 104.

182 "not a Jew at all but an Aryan": Faulhaber, *Judaism, Christianity and Germany*, pp. 2–5.

183 "scorns all dogmas": Bonney, *Confronting the Nazi War on Christianity*, p. 127.

183 "best of company on the Index": Office of the U.S. Chief of Counsel for the Prosecution of Axis Criminality, *Nazi Conspiracy and Aggression*, vol. 6, pp. 240–41.

183 "no use for that book": Ryback, *Hitler's Private Library*, p. 122.

184 a fine distinction: Lewy, *Catholic Church*, p. 152.

184 "a nullity": Evans, *Third Reich in Power*, pp. 234–38.

184 "sub-humanity": Rosenberg, *Der Mythus*, pp. 577–78.

184 "upbreeding": Ibid., p. 596.

184 "old maids who have been robbed of their vital right?" Ibid., p. 593.

184 factual errors: Krieg, *Catholic Theologians in Nazi Germany*, p. 53.

185   intelligence reports: Cecil, *Myth of the Master Race*, p. 121.

185   "his most dangerous colleague": Rosenberg diary, February 24, 1935.

185   Alban Schachleiter: Ibid., January 18, 1937.

185   Faulhaber responded by censuring Schachleiter: Hastings, *Catholicism and the Roots of Nazism*, pp. 171–73.

186   "great upheaval has begun": Rosenberg diary, December 26, 1936.

186   Niemöller: Evans, *Third Reich in Power*, pp. 231–32.

187   "following me in this": Rosenberg diary, August 11, 1936.

187   "like wildfire": Letter from Canon Vorwerk, reproduced in Anonymous, *Persecution of the Catholic Church*, pp. 121–24.

187   protested as never before: Bonney, *Confronting the Nazi War*, pp. 132–35; Evans, *Third Reich in Power*, pp. 240–241.

188   ran very long: Kershaw, *Hitler: A Biography*, pp. 375–76; Longerich, *Goebbels*, pp. 251–52.

188   "corpse eaters": Rosenberg diary, February 2, 1941.

189   "The church is losing its power": Ibid., January 18, 1937.

190   "If there is a heaven": Anonymous, *Persecution of the Catholic Church*, p. 278.

190   "blood is stronger than any documents of mere paper": Evans, *Third Reich in Power*, pp. 623–37.

191   "isn't ripe for me yet": Rosenberg diary, August 11, 1936.

11: Exile in Tuscany

193   a simple precaution: Kempner, *Ankläger einer Epoche*, p. 141.

194   a small but steady stream of Jews entering Fascist Italy: Felstiner, "Refuge and Persecution in Italy, 1933–1945," p. 4.

194   forced out of the public schools: Evans, *The Third Reich in Power*, p. 562.

194   "You smell like a Jew": Ernst Levinger, quoted in *Dial 22-0756, Pronto*, p. 96.

195   "wanted to see the last of us": *Dial 22-0756, Pronto*, p. 15.

195   sent ahead . . . as "pioneers": Kempner to the Council of German Jewry in London, May 5, 1937, Kempner Papers, Box 2.

195   applications to the school spiked: Kempner, *Ankläger*, p. 142.

195   "like a beautiful woman: constantly changing": Eva Keilson-Rennie, quoted in *Dial 22-0756, Pronto*, p. 59.

196   "There was a little mist": *Dial 22-0756, Pronto*, p. 61.

196   "singular beauty of the landscape": Henry Kahane, quoted ibid., p. 28. See also Ruth Kempner to Otto Reinemann, August 13, 1938, Kempner Papers, Box 95.

196   "spoiled brats of the bourgeoisie": *Dial 22-0756, Pronto*, p. 18.

197   "transit facility": Ibid., p. 47.

197   "like a detective": Ibid., p. 107. Manasse left the school after a dispute with Kempner.

197   "a crook": Wasow, *Memories of Seventy Years*, pp. 176–86.

198   fell in love: *Dial 22-0756, Pronto*, pp. 88–95.

198   "carnival, cake, and sport": Robert Kempner to Lucian Kempner, July 4, 1938, Kempner Papers, Box 71.

198   dream of being aboard: *Dial 22-0756, Pronto*, p. 93.

198 "relieved to have escaped": Manasse quoted ibid., p. 102.

198 at Duke University: Walter Kempner earned fame as the inventor of the Rice Diet, for treating patients with diabetes and kidney and cardiovascular disease.

199 Nuremberg Laws: Noakes, *Nazism: A History in Documents*, vol. 1, p. 535.

199 mobs were nowhere to be seen: Evans, *Third Reich in Power*, pp. 570–75.

199 "Berlin offered magnificent scenery": Brandt, *My Road to Berlin*, p. 79.

200 "My deep regards for his deed": Rosenberg diary, August 21, 1936.

200 preparing for departure: Unknown friend in The Hague to Kempner, June 4, 1938, Kempner Papers, Box 2.

200 smoothed the way for an alliance of convenience: Evans, *Third Reich in Power*, pp. 638–41.

200 arrived in Rome: Details of Hitler's visit are drawn from Baxa, "Capturing the Fascist Moment," pp. 227–42.

201 "worthy of Nero": Leo Longanesi quoted in Baxa, *Roads and Ruins*, p. 150.

201 wandered through the Uffizi galleries: Deirdre Pirro, "The Unwelcome Tourist," *The Florentine*, May 7, 2009.

202 "without a scratch": *Dial 22-0756, Pronto*, pp. 50–52.

202 identify and investigate: Felstiner, *Refuge and Persecution*, pp. 12–14.

202 As if by osmosis: Bosworth, *Mussolini*, pp. 334–44; Zimmerman, *Jews in Italy under Fascist and Nazi Rule*, p. 3; Felstiner, *Refuge and Persecution*, p. 15.

203 his time in Italy was up: Kempner, *Ankläger einer Epoche*, p. 147.

203 cut off tuition transfers from parents: Ruth Kempner to Otto Reinemann, August 13, 1938, Kempner Papers, Box 95.

203 "coming to an end": Moura Goldin Wolpert, quoted in *Dial 22-0756, Pronto*, p. 86.

203 "the last minute": Kempner to Erich Eyck, October 21, 1938, Kempner Papers, Box 2.

203 "contrary to fascist doctrine": Closure decree, Kempner Papers, Box 94.

204 "thunder-struck": *Dial 22-0756, Pronto*, p. 95.

204 "Neither of us got much sleep": Ibid., pp. 89–92.

204 made her nauseous: Beate Davidson to Margot Lipton, October 23, 1938, Kempner Papers, Box 2.

205 "*Judenweiber*": Peiser and Kempner to Beate Davidson, October 26, 1938, Kempner Papers, Box 94.

205 three thousand lire: Informational notice from Peiser and Kempner, Kempner Papers, Box 94.

205 "If we had been alone, we would have never been arrested": Kempner to Carl Misch, November 28, 1938, Kempner Papers, Box 2.

206 "the last station of our earthly pilgrimage": Kempner to Rudolf Olden, December 12, 1938, Kempner Papers, Box 2.

206 "at a small Italian mountain resort": Robert Kempner to Helene Kempner, November 20, 1937, Kempner Papers, Box 71.

206 abducted: Lucian Kempner application to company commander, September 29, 1945, Kempner Papers, Box 71.

206 challenging Helene's fitness to be a parent: Kempner memorandum in response to letter from lawyer Adolf Arndt, March 17, 1938, Kempner Papers, Box 2.

207 "an anti-German attitude": Villingen district court ruling, July 1, 1939, Kempner Papers, Box 71.

207 "the Germans only made it worse": Lucian Kempner to Robert Kempner, January 9, 1946, Kempner Papers, Box 71.

207 "still have a dad": Robert Kempner to Lucian Kempner, September 29, 1938, Kempner Papers, Box 71.

207 "still in beautiful Nice": Robert Kempner to Lucian Kempner, October 7, 1938, Kempner Papers, Box 71.

12: "I Had Won Over the Old Party's Heart"

209 the biggest rally to date: Burden, *The Nuremberg Party Rallies*, pp. 137–47.

209 visit one of the hundred or so prostitutes: Vice squad report quoted in Täubrich, *Fascination and Terror*, p. 76.

210 wealthiest and most important cities in Europe: Burden, *Nuremberg Party Rallies*, pp. 3–9.

210 "manly power and fighting spirit": Ibid., p. 8.

211 feed the Führer cult: Evans, *The Third Reich in Power*, pp. 123–24.

212 convoy of black Mercedes-Benzes: Frederick T. Birchall, "Duty Is Stressed at Nazi Congress," *New York Times*, September 8, 1937.

212 "more than a gorgeous show": Shirer, *Berlin Diary*, pp. 18–19.

213 National Prize: Frederick T. Birchall, "Labor Has Its Day at Nazi Congress," September 9, 1937.

213 "tangible jolt": Entry titled "After the party congress. 1937," Rosenberg diary, September 1937.

213 "realm of ideas": Stephen Kinzer, "Exonerations Still Eludes an Anti-Nazi Crusader," *New York Times*, January 13, 1996.

213 "preposterous and fatal": "Germany Enraged by Ossietzky Prize," *New York Times*, November 25, 1936.

213 "precious star": Rosenberg diary, January 31, 1938.

213 "rejoice with deep satisfaction": Bonney, *Confronting the Nazi War on Christianity*, p. 247, n. 47.

214 ego swelling: Entry titled "After the party congress. 1937," Rosenberg diary, September 1937.

214 "radical anti-Roman heretic being received like a king by the people": Entry titled "At the beginning of October," Rosenberg diary, October 1937.

214 forty-fifth birthday: Undated entry, Rosenberg diary, January 1938.

215 grown ever more affluent: Read, *The Devil's Disciples*, pp. 384–85.

215 "while I fight the battle": Entry titled "At the end of July 1936," Rosenberg diary, July 1936.

216 "Niggerstep!": Ibid.

216 "declare us dumb": Fritz Sauckel, quoted in Rosenberg diary, July 20, 1938.

216 "plays a minister": Rosenberg diary, July 29, 1943.

217 "the vanity of Dr. G": Ibid., November 25, 1937.

217 It had to do with Goebbels's marriage: Details of his affairs and marital woes are drawn from Read, *Devil's Disciples*, pp. 421–22, 443, 484, 491–92.

217 "hard and cruel": Quoted ibid., p. 492.

218   "most hated man in Germany": Undated entry, Rosenberg diary; Matthäus, in *Alfred Rosenberg: Die Tagebücher von 1934 bis 1944,* dates this entry to late November or December 1938.

218   "seediness of Dr. G.": Rosenberg diary, March 1, 1939.

219   "a question of space": Evans, *Third Reich in Power,* p. 359.

220   bristling with manic energy: Shirer, *Rise and Fall,* p. 326. See also Schuschnigg, *Austrian Requiem,* pp. 12–19.

220   99.75 percent of Austrians: Evans, *Third Reich in Power,* pp. 111–13.

221   "peace for our time": Ibid., p. 674.

221   a series of new discriminatory measures: Meyer, Simon, and Schütz, *Jews in Nazi Berlin,* pp. 98–100.

221   shot a diplomat: On Kristallnacht, see Evans, *Third Reich in Power,* pp. 580–86.

222   "must be repudiated": Read, *Devil's Disciples,* p. 510.

222   potato hoe: Descriptions of Kristallnacht in Oberlustadt are drawn from two documents in the Irma Gideon collection at the U.S. Holocaust Memorial Museum: a copy of Landau criminal court records from a 1948 trial against five Germans who organized the assault, and an account by Gideon, who witnessed the events.

224   thirty thousand sent to concentration camps: Evans, *Third Reich in Power,* p. 591.

224   "Bravo!": Ibid., p. 590.

224   "hadn't destroyed such valuable property": Ibid., p. 593.

224   "For everything G. does, we must pay": Undated entry, Rosenberg diary; Matthäus and Bajohr, in *Alfred Rosenberg: Die Tagebücher,* dates this entry to late November or December 1938. See also Lang and Schenck, *Memoirs of Alfred Rosenberg,* pp. 171–72.

13: Escape

227   a realistic attitude, helpful friends, and luck: Henry Kahane, quoted in *Dial 22-0756, Pronto,* pp. 28–29.

227   "bitter and distraught": *Dial 22-0756, Pronto,* p. 92. Hirsch did not make it out; he perished in Auschwitz.

227   stripped of their German citizenship: List published in the official government newspaper, *Deutscher Reichsanzeiger,* October 21, 1938, Kempner Papers, Box 41.

228   "courage in meeting the challenge": Copy of recommendation letter from Hans Simons at the New School for Social Research, undated, Kempner Papers, Box 76.

228   "honorarium": Stephen B. Sweeney to Roland Morris, December 1, 1938, Kempner Papers, Box 95.

228   "several hundred thousand francs": Kempner to Alexandre Besredka, September 8, 1938, Kempner Papers, Box 2.

228   "awaiting your answer with great impatience": Kempner to Stephen B. Sweeney and Kempner to Martha Tracy, December 19, 1938, Kempner Papers, Box 95.

229   financial aid: Peiser and Kempner to American Jewish Joint Distribution Committee, September 13, 1938, Kempner Papers, Box 2.

229 twenty-one thousand francs: Grossman to Kempner, November 25, 1938, Kempner Papers, Box 2.

229 took months: Kempner to Carl Misch, November 28, 1938, Kempner Papers, Box 2.

229 "tortured in the most horrible ways": Kempner to Milly Zirker, December 6, 1938, Kempner Papers, Box 2.

229 "the reward will not fail to appear!": Kempner to Grossman, December 16, 1938, Kempner Papers, Box 2.

230 to teach and shelter children: Kempner correspondence with Emil Gumbel, November 8–December 19, 1938, Kempner Papers, Box 2.

230 British and French refugee committees: Kempner correspondence with Jewish Assistance Committee in Strasbourg, France, Assistance Médicale aux Enfants de Réfugiés in Paris, and Alliance Israélite Universelle in Paris, December 1938, and with the British Committee for the Jews of Germany, January 12, 1939, Kempner Papers, Box 2.

230 "ten Jewish children": Who these ten students were and what became of them is unclear. According to *Dial 22-0756, Pronto*, a memoir about the school, at least four former students of the Istituto Fiorenza perished in the Holocaust, but the majority of the alumni made it to safety in the United States, Britain, Israel, and South America.

230 "is probably very expandable?": Kempner to Ernst Hamburger, February 17, 1939, Kempner Papers, Box 2.

230 knuckled under: Shirer, *The Rise and Fall of the Third Reich*, pp. 444–48.

231 agitating against Poland: Ibid., pp. 462–75.

232 "if I cannot get to the United States within a short time": Kempner to Stephen B. Sweeney, May 1, 1939, Kempner Papers, Box 95.

232 "friends of mine": Ibid.

233 Wilbur Thomas: Reinemann to Kempner, May 29 and June 6, 1939, Kempner Papers, Box 95.

233 THOUSAND THANKS: Cables between Reinemann and Kempner, June 9–10, 1939, Kempner Papers, Box 95.

233 "a new epoch in our lives": Kempner to Reinemann, June 21, 1939.

233 "I think that everything is alright": Talking points, Kempner Papers, Box 76.

234 children's home in Nice: Margot Lipton deposition in *Lipton v. Swansen*, June 23, 1999.

234 "no future in the Third Reich in the long term": Carl Misch to Kempner, December 10, 1938, Kempner Papers, Box 2.

234 "Dear Lucian": Transcript of handwritten Robert Kempner letter to Lucian Kempner, July 1939, Kempner Papers, Box 71. The letter appears to have been produced by his ex-wife as part of their custody fight.

235 SS *Nieuw Amsterdam*: Kempner to Immigration and Naturalization Service, July 1, 1969, Kempner Papers, Box 76.

14: "The Burden of What's to Come"

239 "Jewish criminality": Rosenberg diary, August 22, 1939.

240 "common bloodstained criminals": Hitler, *Mein Kampf*, p. 660.

240 "You cannot drive out the Devil with Beelzebub": Ibid., p. 662.
240 "a moral loss of face": Rosenberg diary, August 22, 1939.
241 "not a secret": Ibid., August 12, 1936.
241 cultured upbringing: Details of Ribbentrop's early life are drawn from Read, *The Devil's Disciples*, pp. 392–98.
241 midwife the deal: Ibid., pp. 246, 264–70.
241 "he feels extraordinarily indebted to Ribbentrop": Rosenberg diary, August 12, 1936.
242 "the seed of confidence between Hitler and myself": Read, *Devil's Disciples*, p. 379.
242 Büro Ribbentrop: Ibid., pp. 400–3.
242 "they know Ribbentrop": Ibid., p. 413.
242 the Brits would not go to war: Ibid., p. 555.
243 cut a deal: Evans, *The Third Reich in Power*, pp. 691–95.
243 talks and telegrams: Shirer, *The Rise and Fall of the Third Reich*, pp. 520–28.
243 Ribbentrop flew to Moscow: Ibid., pp. 538–44.
244 "joke of world history": Rosenberg diary, September 24, 1939.
244 "an idiot?": Ibid., May 21, 1939.
245 "dire consequences": Ibid., August 25, 1939.
246 "pitilessly and remorselessly": Shirer, *Rise and Fall*, p. 532; Evans, *The Third Reich at War*, p. 11.
246 roared across the border: Evans, *Third Reich at War*, pp. 3–8.
247 "Such humanity": Rosenberg diary, September 29, 1939.
247 "old, intense arthritis": Ibid., August 19, 1936.
247 excessively overweight: Piper, *Alfred Rosenberg*, p. 310.
247 "Other men": Rosenberg diary, September 24, 1939.
247 The Poles were to blame: Details of the negotiations between England and Germany are drawn from Shirer, *Rise and Fall*, pp. 548–49, 574–76.
248 "bombs will be met with bombs": Ibid., pp. 598–99.
248 "deliberately underestimated": Rosenberg diary, September 24, 1939.
248 "crush them like lice": Shirer, *Rise and Fall*, p. 592.
249 "What now?": Ibid., p. 613.
249 "Stunned": Shirer, *Berlin Diary*, p. 200.
249 Britain's bullheadedness: Rosenberg diary, September 24, 1939.
249 "horribly hammered in": Ibid., November 1, 1939.
249 "ruin them by all available means": Ibid., September 29, 1939.
249 unleashed their radical worldview: Evans, *Third Reich at War*, pp. 9–23.
250 SS that did much of the killing: Read, *Devil's Disciples*, p. 371.
250 "this black uniform": Burleigh, *The Third Reich: A New History*, p. 192. See also Heinrich Himmler, *Die Schutzstaffel als antibolschewistische Kampforganisation* (Munich: Franz Eher Nachfolger, 1937).
250 a sort of religious order: Evans, *Third Reich in Power*, pp. 50-52, 252.
250 "Nazi sadism": Shirer, *Berlin Diary*, p. 110.
250 consolidated his sweeping, all-powerful police operation: Read, *Devil's Disciples*, pp. 608–11.
250 cynically efficient: Evans, *Third Reich in Power*, pp. 53–54.
251 "depopulated and resettled with Germans": Evans, *Third Reich at War*, p. 11.

252 "last thing on earth I care about": Longerich, *Holocaust*, p. 154.

252 "a horrible substance": Rosenberg diary, September 29, 1939.

252 "Painted today": Ibid., January 7, 1940.

252 "revolutionized by my work": Ibid., January 19, 1940.

15: On the Make

255 good fortune: Ruth Kempner postcard to Otto Reinemann, September 2, 1939, Kempner Papers, Box 95.

256 They would be deported: Kempner, *Ankläger einer Epoche*, p. 143.

256 "politically free country": Kempner interview, Records of the Emergency Committee in Aid of Displaced Foreign Scholars.

256 "mentally disturbed individual": Ibid.

257 "cannot discuss politics": "Ex-Advisor to Germany's Police Comes Here to Begin New Life," *Evening Public Ledger* (Philadelphia), September 29, 1939.

257 "German is German": Kempner, *Ankläger*, p. 158.

258 "My Scrapbook Begins with My Death": Kempner speaker's profile, Kempner Papers, Box 1.

258 "Cemper or Cempen": Kempner to FBI, March 16, 1942, Kempner Papers, Box 1.

259 "'frozen' faces": Kempner to F. P. Foley, October 8, 1941, Kempner Papers, Box 1.

259 *Blueprint for the Nazi Underground as Revealed in Confidential Police Reports*: The report was later published under a slightly different title by *Research Studies of the State College of Washington.*

259 would be a bestseller: Kempner to Knopf, December 10, 1941, and Curtice Hitchcock to Kempner, November 11, 1941, Kempner Papers, Box 1.

260 "render very good services to your country": Kempner to Hoover, December 21, 1938, Kempner Papers, Box 43.

260 had become famous: Material on Hoover is drawn from Weiner, *Enemies,* pp. 3–6, 13–46, 60–70.

261 "the treatment they received in Germany was nothing": Olson, *Those Angry Days*, p. 240.

261 "Lindbergh is a Nazi": Charles, *J. Edgar Hoover and the Anti-Interventionists*, p. 30.

262 Nazis really were here: Weiner, *Enemies*, pp. 78–79.

262 "Gestapo methods": Ibid., pp. 83, 106.

262 no words of encouragement: Hoover to Kempner, January 16 and July 24, 1939, and Kempner to Hoover, July 10 and September 25, 1939, Kempner Papers, Box 43.

16: Thieves in Paris

265 The plotters scattered: Kershaw, *Hitler: A Biography*, pp. 541–43.

265 "your old saints": Rosenberg diary, November 14, 1936.

266 a time bomb ticked away: Kershaw, *Hitler: A Biography*, pp. 544–47.

266 "back to Berlin": Rosenberg diary, November 11, 1939.

267 turned their sights on Denmark and Norway: Evans, *The Third Reich at War*, pp. 117–22; Shirer, *The Rise and Fall of the Third Reich*, pp. 673–83, 697–712.

268 "named Quisling": Rosenberg diary, December 20, 1939.

268 "great day in German history": Ibid., April 9, 1940.

269 "decisive for the war": Ibid., April 27, 1940.

269 probed Allied fortifications: G. H. Archambault, " 'Violent' Nazi Fire Pounds Key Points," *New York Times*, March 31, 1940; Torrie, *"For Their Own Good": Civilian Evacuations in Germany and France*, p. 33.

269 "no man's land": Rosenberg diary, April 11, 1940.

270 "The final battle begins": Ibid., May 10, 1940.

270 drew up for the invasion: Evans, *Third Reich at War*, pp. 122–36.

270 the woods of Compiègne: Shirer, *Rise and Fall*, pp. 741–46.

271 "coordination": Evans, *The Coming of the Third Reich*, pp. 386–90.

271 Hitler Youth: Evans, *Third Reich in Power*, pp. 271–81.

272 "put into the hands of Germans a weapon": Anonymous, *The Persecution of the Catholic Church in the Third Reich*, p. 360.

272 indoctrination camps: Cecil, *The Myth of the Master Race*, p. 143.

272 "must be eliminated": Anonymous, *Persecution of the Catholic Church*, p. 364.

272 "are now looking": Rosenberg diary, September 24, 1939.

273 "art nouveau philosophers": Ibid., November 1, 1939.

274 "vaudeville performances": Ibid., November 11, 1939.

274 "fought faithfully for the party's trust": Ibid., November 1, 1939.

274 Hitler suddenly vetoed the idea: Rosenberg did win permission to handle the ideological education of German soldiers. His office provided libraries of politically appropriate literature and dispatched speakers to the war zone to reiterate key Nazi themes. Predictably, Goebbels didn't think very much of Rosenberg's work. "There are always ideologists in our midst who believe a man of the submarine crews on emerging from the machinery compartment dirty and oil-bespattered, would like nothing better than to read *The Myth of the Twentieth Century*," he wrote in his diary. "That, of course, is sheer nonsense. . . . After the war we can talk again about ideological education. At present we are living our ideology and don't have to be taught it." Lochner, *The Goebbels Diaries*, p. 122.

274 "before the beginning of the great offensive": Rosenberg diary, March 3, 1940.

274 a new library: Weinreich, *Hitler's Professors*, pp. 98–99.

274 an imposing slab of a main building: Hermand, *Culture in Dark Times*, p. 49.

275 elite ideological educational system: Evans, *Third Reich in Power*, pp. 285–86.

275 build collections for the Hohe Schule: Details of the looting of libraries and archives are drawn from Collins, "The Einsatzstab Reichsleiter Rosenberg and the Looting of Jewish and Masonic Libraries During World War II," pp. 24–34, and Grimsted, *Reconstructing the Record of Nazi Cultural Plunder*, pp. 25–35.

276 "fighting organizations": Rosenberg interrogation, September 25, 1945, 14:15–16:30, National Archives, M1270, Roll 17.

276 large, secret research library of its own: Starr, "Jewish Cultural Property

under Nazi Control," pp. 45–46; Grimsted, "Roads to Ratibor," pp. 409–10. The RSHA cache held an estimated two million volumes.

276 filled eleven railcars: Petropoulos, *Art as Politics in the Third Reich*, p. 128.

276 "doubtlessly unique": Rosenberg diary, March 28, 1941.

276 "will <u>have</u> to go to Frankfurt": Ibid., February 2, 1941.

277 a grand museum complex in Linz, Austria: Nicholas, *The Rape of Europa*, pp. 41–46; James S. Plaut, "Hitler's Capital," *The Atlantic*, October 1946.

277 as a plunderer had no equal: Nicholas, *Rape of Europa*, pp. 35–37; James S. Plaut, "Loot for the Master Race." *The Atlantic*, September 1946.

277 pillaged Vienna: Nicholas, *Rape of Europa*, pp. 37–41.

277 The crown jewels of the Holy Roman Empire: Ibid., p. 40.

278 Nazi dragnet: Ibid., pp. 101–2.

278 veneer of legality: Ibid., pp. 104–9.

278 "impede it": Ibid., p. 107.

279 "ownerless Jewish possessions": Keitel order, September 17, 1940, reproduced as 138-PS in Office of the U.S. Chief of Counsel for the Prosecution of Axis Criminality, *Nazi Conspiracy and Aggression*, vol. 3, p. 186.

279 love letters: Diels, *Lucifer Ante Portas*, p. 76. See also Lüdecke, *I Knew Hitler*, pp. 650–51. Historians discount Diels's statement for lack of corroborating evidence. See Piper, *Alfred Rosenberg*, p. 699, n. 360.

280 seemed like a blessing: Petropoulos, *Art as Politics in the Third Reich*, pp. 133–34.

280 "all were taken away to Germany": Rosbottom, *When Paris Went Dark*, p. 71.

280 "seized all Jewish art collections": Rosenberg letter and report to Hitler, April 16, 1943, reproduced as 015-PS in Office of the U.S. Chief of Counsel, *Nazi Conspiracy*, vol. 3, pp. 41–45.

280 trapdoor in a secret cellar: Rosenberg diary, September 6, 1940.

280 "The owners were all away": Rosenberg interrogation, September 25, 1945, 14:15–16:30, National Archives, M1270, Roll 17.

281 Imperious and vain: Dreyfus, *Nazi Labour Camps in Paris*, pp. 9–10.

281 "such as furs, jewelry, and silver": OSS Art Looting Investigation Unit Consolidated Interrogation Report No. 1, Activity of the Einsatzstab Rosenberg in France, August 1945, National Archives, M1782, Roll 1.

281 Göring came to Paris to shop: Nicholas, *The Rape of Europa*, pp. 127–28.

282 "I have no intention of attacking": Rosbottom, *When Paris Went Dark*, pp. 30, 66–67.

283 six hundred pages: Ibid., p. 101. Historian Cécile Desprairies conducted the census.

283 "The name of Paris evokes something special": Ibid., p. 11.

283 "A strange feeling": Rosenberg diary, February 2, 1941.

284 Rosenberg could have been killed: Ibid.

285 wresting away control of the art-looting operation: OSS Consolidated Interrogation Report No. 1; Nicholas, *Rape of Europa*, pp. 130–32.

286 "even a trifle object as a souvenir": Rosenberg interrogation, September 25, 1945, 14:15–16:30, National Archives, M1270, Roll 17.

287 three valuable paintings taken from the Netherlands: See Davidson, *The Trial of the Germans*, p. 139. Rosenberg said they were gifts.

287 "some joy for your birthday": Rosenberg letter and report to Hitler, April 16,
      1943, reproduced as 015-PS in Office of the U.S. Chief of Counsel, *Nazi
      Conspiracy*, vol. 3, pp. 41–45.
287 burned with the trash: Nicholas, *Rape of Europa*, p. 170.

17: "Rosenberg, Your Great Hour Has Now Arrived"

289 "a cleansing biological world revolution": Report on Rosenberg speech in
      Völkischer Beobachter, March 29, 1941, reproduced as 2889-PS in Office of the
      U.S. Chief of Counsel for the Prosecution of Axis Criminality, *Nazi Conspir-
      acy and Aggression*, vol. 5, pp. 554–557
290 ten European nations: The foreign officials were Nazi supporters from Nor-
      way, Denmark, the Netherlands, Belgium, Romania, Bulgaria, Hungary,
      Slovakia, and Italy. Among them were an anti-Semitic newspaper editor in
      Belgium, the solicitor general in occupied Holland, and Vikdun Quisling,
      who had collaborated with the Nazis during the invasion of Norway.
290 turn their words into deadly action: Rosenberg diary, March 28, 1941.
291 "the world will hold its breath": Dallin, *German Rule in Russia 1941–1945*,
      pp. 13–19
291 "in case of a Russian attack": Rosenberg diary, August 12, 1936.
291 paid close attention: Kay, *Exploitation, Resettlement, Mass Murder*, pp. 18–22.
292 suffering endured by the people of Ukraine, Belarus, and western Russia:
      Descriptions of Soviet rule in the 1930s are drawn from Snyder, *Bloodlands*,
      pp. 21–105.
293 "their kin!": Ibid., p. 72.
293 plotted yet another round of horrors: Details on planning for the Soviet occu-
      pation are drawn from Kay, *Exploitation*, pp. 68–95, 120–98, and Dallin, *Ger-
      man Rule*, pp. 20–58.
293 "What India was for England": Trevor-Roper, *Hitler's Table Talk 1941–1944*,
      p. 21.
294 Ukrainians in 1932?: Kay, *Exploitation*, pp. 39, 141.
294 "no false pity!": Dallin, *German Rule*, pp. 39–40.
295 "absolute clarity must reign": *Trial of the Major War Criminals*, vol. 36, p. 145;
      Kay, *Exploitation*, p. 134.
295 "Nazi dolt": Shirer, *The Rise and Fall of the Third Reich*, p. 832. Shirer contin-
      ued: "Rosenberg's voluminous files were captured intact; like his books, they
      make dreary reading and will not be allowed to impede this narrative."
295 "undesirable elements of the population": Rosenberg memorandum, "The
      USSR," April 2, 1941, reproduced as 1017-PS in Office of the U.S. Chief of
      Counsel, *Nazi Conspiracy*, vol. 3, pp. 674–81.
296 "your great hour has now arrived": Rosenberg diary, April 2, 1941.
297 "I will <u>never</u> forget it": Ibid. Rosenberg did not elaborate later in the diary,
      and historians are left to speculate about whether Hitler spoke of the extermi-
      nation of the Jews at this meeting. Rosenberg could just as easily have been
      stunned by the millions of Slavic people who would face death under Nazi
      plans. See Piper, *Alfred Rosenberg*, p. 510.
297 "Greedily, childishly": Dallin, *German Rule*, p. 26.

297 "only theorize . . . not organize": Goebbels diary, May 9 and June 16, 1941, quoted in Kay, *Exploitation*, p. 81.

297 "entrusted with special tasks": Keitel top-secret order, March 13, 1941, reproduced as 447-PS in Office of the U.S. Chief of Counsel, *Nazi Conspiracy*, vol. 3, p. 409.

298 "cannot take over this assignment": Rosenberg diary, April 20, 1941.

298 "a glorious place in the middle of paradise": Ibid., February 2, 1941.

299 "this will end differently": Ibid., April 20, 1941.

299 hosted a key meeting: Kay, *Exploitation*, p. 125. There is some disagreement among historians about whether Rosenberg attended the meeting, but in any case his memos show that he incorporated its conclusions into his planning. See Browning, *The Origins of the Final Solution*, p. 237.

299 "x million people": "Memorandum on the Result of Today's Discussion with the State Secretary Regarding Barbarossa," May 2, 1941, reproduced as 2718-PS in Office of the U.S. Chief of Counsel, *Nazi Conspiracy*, vol. 5, p. 378. See also Kay, *Exploitation*, p. 124.

299 "general staff work": Rosenberg diary, May 6, 1941.

299 excited about the job: Ibid., April 11, 1941.

299 "a great positive assignment": Ibid., May 6, 1941.

300 "very hard years will certainly be in store": Speech by Rosenberg, June 20, 1941, reproduced as 1058-PS in *Trial of the Major War Criminals*, vol. 26, pp. 610–27. See also Kay, *Exploitation*, pp. 171–72; Dallin, *German Rule*, p. 109.

300 Hess greeted him: Rosenberg diary, May 14, 1941.

300 could hardly get in to see Hitler: Details of Hess's flight are drawn from Evans, *The Third Reich at War*, pp. 167–70.

302 "Machiavelli of the office desk": Fest, *The Face of the Third Reich*, p. 127.

302 "he began to make himself indispensable": Lang and Schenck, *Memoirs of Alfred Rosenberg*, p. 192.

303 involve Rosenberg's ministry where necessary: See Longerich, *Holocaust*, pp. 260–61, and Kay, *Exploitation*, p. 109.

303 intractable conflicts of interest: Mulligan, *The Politics of Illusion and Empire*, p. 22.

303 "political leadership by police officers!": Rosenberg diary, May 1, 1941.

303 "I am keen on his reaction": Ibid., May 6, 1941.

304 "most difficult thing in the Nazi Party": Dallin, *German Rule*, p. 37.

304 "free of all obstacles": Breitman, *The Architect of Genocide*, p. 160.

304 "unparalleled chaos": Kay, *Exploitation*, p. 168.

304 began their assault on the Soviet Union: Evans, *Third Reich at War*, pp. 178–90.

304 "Everything's lost": Ibid., p. 187.

305 "They looked like starved animals": Zygmunt Klukowski, quoted in Evans, *Third Reich at War*, p. 183.

305 the headquarters caught fire: Snyder, *Bloodlands*, p. 179.

305 "the Russian nation as a whole will thus have to pay": Rosenberg diary, September 12, 1941.

306 long meeting at Wolfsschanze: Ibid., July 20, 1941; Martin Bormann's minutes of the meeting, July 17, 1941, reproduced as L-221 in Office of the U.S. Chief of Counsel, *Nazi Conspiracy*, vol. 7, pp. 1086–93; Kay, *Exploitation*, pp. 180–85.

308 operate independently on Rosenberg's turf: Kay, *Exploitation*, p. 184.
308 a fig leaf of German regulatory order?: Ibid., pp. 191–93; Mulligan, *Politics of Illusion*, p. 10.
308 could control, or at least ignore: Dallin, *German Rule*, p. 35.
308 "gigantic task": Rosenberg diary, July 20, 1941.

18: "Special Tasks"

311 in the most cheerful of spirits: Rosenberg diary, January 27, 1940.
312 an important supporting role in the killings: See Matthäus, *Alfred Rosenberg: Die Tagebücher von 1934 bis 1944*, p. 61; Browning, *The Origins of the Final Solution*, pp. 293–97, 301; Lower, *Nazi Empire-Building and the Holocaust in Ukraine*, pp. 139–42; and Lower, "On Him Rests the Weight of Administration," p. 239.
313 a clash of two irreconcilable worldviews: Longerich, *Holocaust*, pp. 198–99; Steinberg, "The Third Reich Reflected," p. 634.
313 "special tasks": Keitel top-secret order, March 13, 1941, reproduced as 447-PS in Office of the U.S. Chief of Counsel for the Prosecution of Axis Criminality, *Nazi Conspiracy and Aggression,* vol. 3, p. 409.
313 "snipers, assassins, agitators, etc.": Longerich, *Holocaust*, p. 190.
313 "shoot them down without pity and compassion": Breitman, *The Architect of Genocide*, p. 177.
314 covered with dirt: Browning, *Origins*, p. 261.
314 "the count is what remains": Snyder, *Bloodlands*, pp. 201–3.
315 "the people are coming alive again": Rosenberg diary, September 14, 1941.
315 taken to a camp established in an open field: Mikhail Grichanik account in Rubenstein, *The Unknown Black Book*, pp. 235–43; Arad, *The Holocaust in the Soviet Union*, pp. 151–158.
316 "they do this mercilessly": Arad, *The Holocaust in the Soviet Union*, p. 152.
316 dance for them on a table: Rubenstein and Altman, *The Unknown Black Book*, p. 244.
317 "The howls of mortal fear and horror": Ibid., pp. 250–51.
318 fifteen thousand Jews: Arad, "The 'Final Solution' in Lithuania," p. 241.
318 "the Jews should be totally removed from this area": Browning, *Origins*, p. 284.
318 "a temporary solution": Memorandum, "General organization and tasks of our office for the general handling of problems in the Eastern territories," April 29, 1941, reproduced as 1024-PS in Office of the U.S. Chief of Counsel, *Nazi Conspiracy*, vol. 3, p. 685.
319 "which cannot be discussed in writing": Browning, *Origins*, pp. 285–86.
319 "provisional . . . minimum measures": Memorandum, "Provisional directives on the treatment of Jews in the area of Reichskommissariat Ostland," reproduced as 1138-PS in Office of the U.S. Chief of Counsel, *Nazi Conspiracy*, vol. 3, pp. 800–5.
319 the SS had Lohse's full support: Browning, *Origins*, p. 287.
319 "emphasize the jurisdiction of the SS": Steinberg, "The Third Reich Reflected," p. 647.
319 set in motion a fateful step: Kershaw, *Hitler: A Biography*, pp. 683–84.
319 "Hatred of Moscow": Rosenberg diary, September 12, 1941.

320 they were not pleased: Browning, *Origins*, pp. 303, 332–33.

320 "gassing apparatus": Ibid., pp. 304.

320 There is no evidence the letter went out: Ibid.; Historians have not found a signed, delivered copy of the document.

321 pressed for cooperation: Ibid., p. 301.

321 liquidate every Jew in the city: Heinrich Carl memorandum to Wilhelm Kube, October 30, 1941, reproduced as 1104-PS in Office of the U.S. Chief of Counsel, *Nazi Conspiracy*, vol. 3, p. 785.

322 "necessary to liquidate children": Arad, "'Final Solution' in Lithuania," p. 249.

322 "Tell Lohse it is my order": Breitman, *Architect*, pp. 208, 217.

322 "I have forbidden the wild executions of Jews": Arad, "'Final Solution' in Lithuania," p. 250.

322 "Clarification of the Jewish question": Letter dated December 18, 1941 from Rosenberg's ministry to Lohse, reproduced as 3666-PS in Office of the U.S. Chief of Counsel, *Nazi Conspiracy*, vol. 6, pp. 402–3.

322 Rosenberg and Himmler: Arad, "Alfred Rosenberg and the 'Final Solution' in the Occupied Soviet Territories," pp. 279–80.

324 "biological eradication of the entire Jewry of Europe": Browning, *Origins*, p. 404.

324 smoothed the path to murder: Longerich, *Holocaust*, pp. 345–56.

324 Lohse watched without objection: Gerlach, "The Wannsee Conference," p. 768.

325 lay down in trenches: Breitman, *Architect*, p. 219.

325 would have happily killed them too: Arad, "'Final Solution' in Lithuania," p. 252.

325 *after* Lohse arrived: Ibid., p. 247.

325 800,000 Jewish civilians were already dead: Matthäus, "Controlled Escalation," p. 219.

325 "having their heads removed": Rosenberg diary, October 1, 1941.

325 priestly protests: Greich-Polelle, *Bishop von Galen*, pp. 78–80; Evans, *The Third Reich at War*, p. 95–101.

327 "keeping the idiots": Rosenberg diary, December 14, 1941.

327 internal political ramifications: Greich-Polelle, *Bishop von Galen*, pp. 89–92.

327 von Galen said nothing: Ibid., p. 92.

327 "The Führer is determined": Gerlach, "Wannsee Conference," p. 785. Gerlach argues that this is Hitler's announcement of a decision to exterminate all the Jews of Europe, but other historians disagree.

328 He had planned to say: Ibid., p. 784.

328 "the extermination of the Jews should not be mentioned": Rosenberg, "Memorandum about discussions with the Führer on 14 December 1941," reproduced as 1517-PS in Office of the U.S. Chief of Counsel, *Nazi Conspiracy*, vol. 4, p. 55. See also Browning, *Origins*, p. 410, and Gerlach, "Wannsee Conference," in which he argues that Rosenberg is referring to a recent decision to begin implementing the final solution.

328 Hitler hosted a separate meeting: Trevor-Roper, *Hitler's Table Talk 1941–1944*, p. 112. See Piper, *Alfred Rosenberg*, p. 589. A full accounting of their discussion does not survive.

329 "They have to be gotten rid of": Gerlach, "Wannsee Conference," p. 790.

329 "Those were the gentlemen who knew the things you had to know": Roseman, *The Villa, the Lake, the Meeting*, p. 57.

330 "In large, single-sex labor columns": Ibid., p. 113.

331 "And here was genocide, going through, on the nod": Ibid., pp. 87–88.

331 "I feel like the Robert Koch of politics": Kershaw, *Hitler, 1936–45: Nemesis*, p. 470.

19: "Our Own Tragic Special Destiny"

333 a small black notebook: Frieda and Max Reinach diary, United States Holocaust Memorial Museum.

334 sold to the Jews for ten pfennigs apiece: Meyer, Simon, and Schütz, *Jews in Nazi Berlin*, p. 111.

334 ever more harsh: Ibid., pp. 102–4.

335 "annihilation of the Jewish race in Europe!": Kershaw, *Hitler: A Biography*, p. 469.

335 no longer allowed to emigrate: Meyer, Simon, and Schütz, *Jews in Nazi Berlin*, pp. 184–85.

336 firewood: Ibid., p. 107.

336 contributing to the war effort: Ibid., p. 187.

337 coerced into helping the Nazis: Ibid., p. 321.

337 coming for them as well: Ibid., p. 327.

338 stray valuables: Ibid., p. 185.

339 taken into the forest and shot: Bundesarchiv memorial book for the victims of Nazi persecution of Jews in Germany (1933–1945), bundesarchiv.de/gedenkbuch.

339 eight thousand Berlin Jews: Meyer, Simon, and Schütz, *Jews in Nazi Berlin*, p. 189.

339 "careful erasure": Longerich, *Holocaust*, p. 288.

339 agreed to keep the diary: Trude and Walter Koshland to their grandchildren, December 1972, letter on file with the Reinach diary.

339 Alfred Kerr: Coincidentally, Kerr was born Alfred Kempner and was a distant cousin of Robert Kempner. When Kempner wrote to him in 1942, Kerr replied with a bit of verse: "Times are grim, but let's be gay. Hang the Huns, on Judgment Day." Kerr to Kempner, July 13, 1942, Kempner Papers, Box 1.

20: Nazis Next Door

341 wanted no part of city life: Kempner, *Ankläger einer Epoche*, pp. 177–79.

341 "The question of whether I am really an enemy alien": Kempner to Gerald Gleeson, January 5, 1942, Kempner Papers, Box 1.

342 "Is that a German?": Kempner, *Ankläger*, p. 183.

342 "eliminate subversive activity": Gary, *The Nervous Liberals*, p. 199.

343 made contact: Special Defense Unit prosecutor Charles Seal to Kempner, July 29, 1941, Kempner Papers, Box 1.

343 "Can you get documents for us?": Kempner, *Ankläger*, pp. 149–50.

344 Nazified psychological warriors: Gary, *Nervous Liberals*, pp. 175–79.

344 one of the regular paid independent experts in these cases: Thomas G. Spencer memorandum to FBI special agent in charge, October 28, 1942, Kempner Papers, Box 43.

345 Among those Kempner helped prosecute: *Report of the Attorney General to Congress on the Foreign Agents Registration Act, 1942–44* (Washington, D.C.: Department of Justice, 1945), www.fara.gov/reports/Archive/1942-1944_FARA.pdf.

345 "work out the theory of a very difficult case": Rogge to U.S. Immigration and Naturalization Service, January 10, 1945, Kempner Papers, Box 76.

345 "lunatic fringe characters": James Wechsler, "Sedition and Circuses," *The Nation*, May 6, 1944.

345 "neither worth defending nor fighting for": Rogge's opening statement is reproduced in St. George and Lawrence, *A Trial on Trial*, p. 129.

346 obsequious dispatches: Kempner to Hoover, January 1, May 30, October 28, and December 19, 1942, and February 21, September 2, and September 26, 1943, Kempner Papers, Box 43.

347 eighteen thousand names: Gary, *Nervous Liberals*, p. 201.

347 replies to his letters: In his autobiography, Kempner wrote that he did meet Hoover once in connection with a case, and the FBI director advised him that in America it was best not to admit to being a lawyer. Kempner, *Ankläger*, p. 180.

347 the FBI's Philadelphia office: Hoover to Kempner, June 10, 1942, Kempner Papers, Box 43.

348 "on the side of the losers": Kempner to Hoover, December 19, 1942, and Hoover to Kempner, December 28, 1942, Kempner Papers, Box 1 and Box 43.

348 a small team of German-speaking researchers and translators: Kempner memorandum to FBI special agent in charge, January 8, 1945, Kempner Papers, Box 43.

348 provided intel: Kempner invoice memos, Kempner Papers, Box 43.

21: The Chaostministerium

351 brief flickering of nationhood: Dallin, *German Rule in Russia 1941–1945*, p. 121, n. 5. See also Berkhoff, *Harvest of Despair*, p. 52.

352 "Appetite comes with eating": Rosenberg diary, September 1 and September 7, 1941.

352 "if we gave in": Ibid., September 7, 1941.

352 "just what's needed to conduct a revolution!": Trevor-Roper, *Hitler's Table Talk 1941–1944*, p. 28.

352 Over Rosenberg's vociferous objections: Dallin, *German Rule*, pp. 120–22.

353 "isn't worth being regarded as independent by others": Rosenberg diary, September 1, 1941.

353 "i.e. the current primitiveness": Ibid., October 1, 1941.

354 "a Garden of Eden": Lower, *Nazi Empire-Building and the Holocaust in Ukraine*, p. 99.

354 "does as he likes": Lochner, *The Goebbels Diaries*, p. 409.

354 "too few practical men": Ibid., p. 229.

354 Erich Koch: Buttar, *Battleground Prussia*, p. 5; Berkhoff, *Harvest of Despair,* pp. 36–37; Dallin, *German Rule*, p. 125.

355 "A first-rate demagogue": Gisevius, *To the Bitter End*, pp. 200–201.

355 "work, work, and work": Dallin, *German Rule*, p. 439.

355 "a thousand times more valuable": Berkhoff, *Harvest of Despair*, p. 47.

356 "Negroes": Lower, *Nazi Empire-Building*, p. 131.

356 "shot for sabotage": Koch memorandum to Rosenberg, March 16, 1943, reproduced as 192-PS in *Trial of the Major War Criminals*, vol. 25, pp. 255–88; quoted in Dallin, *German Rule*, p. 157.

356 "loud provocative behavior": Rosenberg to Koch, May 13, 1942, quoted ibid., pp. 134–35.

356 "not open contempt": Rosenberg diary, December 18, 1942.

357 memos from afar: Dallin, *German Rule*, p. 133.

357 "haven't yet understood": Rosenberg diary, December 18, 1942.

357 "liquidated about fifty-five thousand Jews": Kube to Lohse, July 31, 1942, reproduced as 3428-PS in Office of the U.S. Chief of Counsel for the Prosecution of Axis Criminality, *Nazi Conspiracy and Aggression*, vol. 6, pp. 131–33.

358 Heydrich's assassination: Evans, *The Third Reich at War*, pp. 275–78.

359 put to death more than three million people . . . in the six camps: Ibid., pp. 282–302.

359 "can never be written": Himmler speech, October 4, 1943, reproduced in Noakes, *Nazism: A History in Documents*, vol. 2, p. 1199.

359 Stalingrad: Evans, *Third Reich at War*, pp. 409–23.

360 partisan movements: Ibid., p. 402.

360 severed the tracks: Cecil, *The Myth of the Master Race*, p. 213.

360 plans to assassinate Rosenberg: Rosenberg diary, November 30, 1942.

360 "barricaded himself at home": Ibid., November 20, 1942.

360 find forced laborers: Berkhoff, *Harvest of Despair*, pp. 255–72.

361 "liberated from the Ukrainians": Quoted ibid., p. 264.

361 "it is the hardest blow": Rosenberg diary, October 12, 1942.

362 "terrible conditions": Rosenberg memorandum, "Concerning: Jewish Possessions in France," December 18, 1941, reproduced as 001-PS in Office of the U.S. Chief of Counsel, *Nazi Conspiracy*, vol. 3, p. 1.

362 Möbel Aktion: Dreyfus, *Nazi Labour Camps in Paris*, pp. 1–33, 56–82.

362 sixty-nine thousand residences: Ibid., p. 120.

362 One saw a photograph of his own daughter: Ibid., pp. 66–67.

363 "sheets, towels, and other accessories": Ibid., p. 69.

363 request the arrest of more Jews: Ibid., p. 32.

363 homes were obliterated: Ibid., pp. 16–17.

363 the plunder of art and priceless archives: Details of the looting by Rosenberg's Einsatzstab in the East are drawn from Collins, "The Einsatzstab Reichsleiter Rosenberg and the Looting of Jewish and Masonic Libraries During World War II," pp. 24–34, and Grimsted, *Reconstructing the Record of Nazi Cultural Plunder*, pp. 25–35.

364 of special meaning to the Russian people: Nicholas, *The Rape of Europa*, pp. 192–200.

365 "most precious works of literature": Rosenberg diary, February 2, 1943.

365 "I have never swayed in my faith": Entry titled "After January 12, 1943," ibid.

366 He offered an alliance: Mulligan, *The Politics of Illusion and Empire*, pp. 65–70.

366 Rosenberg met with Himmler: Rosenberg diary, January 25–26, 1943.

366 happily agreed to the Berger appointment: Dallin, *German Rule*, pp. 168–176. The deal would not come together until June.

366 had long questioned Leibbrandt's trustworthiness: Ibid., p. 88.

366 "If the war is lost": Cecil, *Myth of the Master Race*, p. 212.

367 "speak at length about all things": Mulligan, *Politics of Illusion*, p. 70.

367 "straight off into a concentration camp!": Trevor-Roper, *Hitler's Table Talk*, p. 466.

367 soundly defeated: Dallin, *German Rule*, pp. 157–63.

368 merely acting on his own authority: Rosenberg diary, August 7, 1943.

368 "a commandment to keep the blood pure": Bormann memorandum to Rosenberg, February 22, 1940, reproduced as 098-PS in Office of the U.S. Chief of Counsel, *Nazi Conspiracy*, vol. 3, pp. 152–57.

368 "also be totally removed": Memorandum, "Relationship of National Socialism and Christianity," undated, reproduced as D-75 in Office of the U.S. Chief of Counsel, *Nazi Conspiracy*, vol. 6, pp. 1036–39.

368 "woodchopper method": Rosenberg diary, September 7, 1941.

369 "torpedo my party office": Ibid., August 7, 1943.

22: "A Ruin"

371 "horrifyingly beautiful picture": Evans, *The Third Reich at War*, pp. 490, 618.

371 emptied their bomb bays: Ibid., pp. 459–66.

372 Rosenberg waited out the attack: Rosenberg diary, December 31, 1943.

373 "utter desolation": Lochner, *The Goebbels Diaries*, p. 586.

373 Piles of memos burned: Piper, *Alfred Rosenberg*, p. 612.

373 shook from the blasts: Lochner, *Goebbels Diaries*, p. 588.

374 "incessant retreat": Rosenberg diary, July 29, 1944.

374 Soviets pushed mercilessly: Evans, *Third Reich at War*, p. 618.

374 trying to kill Hitler: Ibid., pp. 632–46.

376 "such a cowardly fashion": Rosenberg diary, July 30, 1944.

376 question seemed theoretical: Shirer, *The Rise and Fall of the Third Reich*, p. 1060, note.

377 "Catholic assassins": Rosenberg diary, August, 27, 1944.

377 "shredded . . . mutilated": Ibid., October 22, 1944.

377 "Ministry for the no longer Occupied Eastern Territories": Dallin, *German Rule in Russia 1941–1945*, p. 639.

377 "without countries or subjects": Petropoulus, *Art as Politics in the Third Reich*, p. 157.

377 Andrei Vlasov: Ibid., pp. 553–86.

378 "Russian superciliousness": Ibid., p. 594.

379 reappeared on the scene: Ibid., pp. 613–40.

379 "No seriousness regarding the eastern problem": Rosenberg diary, November 12, 1944.

380 "philistinism gone amok": Ibid., October 22 and 26, 1944.

380 "go crazy in his world": Ibid., November 12, 1944.

380 "could have spared us the catastrophe of Stalingrad": Ibid., October 26, 1944.
381 "How much time has passed since my youth": Ibid., December 3, 1944.
381 The Soviets were at the doorstep: Evans, *Third Reich at War*, pp. 657–58, 681–83.
381 frighteningly poor condition: Ibid., pp. 718–20.
381 "technical discussion": Lang and Schenck, *Memoirs of Alfred Rosenberg*, pp. 294–95.
381 largest air raid: Evans, *Third Reich at War*, p. 699.
382 sat at the family's typewriter: Lang and Schenck, *Memoirs*, pp. 295–96.
382 more than a million German soldiers had died: Evans, *Third Reich at War*, p. 682.
382 "must remain behind": Lang and Schenck, *Memoirs*, p. 297.
383 "for a long, long time": Evans, *Third Reich at War*, p. 708.
383 "our revenge is just": Ibid., p. 710.
383 took to his bunker: Ibid., p. 722–27; Kershaw, *Hitler: A Biography*, pp. 951–55, 960.
383 "If by 2200 hours no answer is forthcoming": This account of Göring's message and Himmler's treachery is drawn from Read, *The Devil's Disciples*, pp. 899–905.
384 The Monuments Men: Edsel, *The Monuments Men*, pp. 348–52.
385 "It was a castle in the air": Rorimer, *Survival*, pp. 183–85.
386 sped to Austria to check it out: Edsel, *Monuments Men*, pp. 382–84.
387 in the Munich apartment of Cornelius Gurlitt: Alex Shoumatoff, "The Devil and the Art Dealer," *Vanity Fair*, April 2014.
387 walked the shoreline: Lang and Schenck, *Memoirs*, p. 299.
388 "He was found almost lifeless": Speer, *Inside the Third Reich*, p. 496.
388 "putting myself at his disposal": Lang and Schenck, *Memoirs*, pp. 300–2.

23: "Loyal to Him to the End"

391 took their oaths as United States citizens: Kempner memorandum to FBI, March 8, 1945, Kempner Papers, Box 43; "Searching For Hitler?" *Philadelphia Record*, October 22, 1945.
391 extensive reports for the Office of Strategic Services: See Kempner Papers, Box 44.
392 "the twilight zone of file and forget": Field, quoted in Sandy Meredith and Bob Sanders, "Refugees on Mars: FDR's Secret Plan," *Mother Jones*, February–March 1983.
392 two well-paid jobs in Washington: Kempner memorandum to FBI special agent in charge, April 5, 1945, Kempner Papers, Box 43.
392 "lies of your defendants": Kempner to Sam Harris, July 9, 1945, Kempner Papers, Box 43.
393 leading Nazis in the dock: Tusa and Tusa, *The Nuremberg Trial*, pp. 52, 63.
393 one dramatic trial: Ibid., p. 54. See also Persico, *Nuremberg*, p. 17.
394 revenge in a judicial cloak: Ibid., pp. 26–27.
394 background material: Ruth S. Bentley memorandum, "Reappointment of Robert Max W. Kempner as Consultant," June 9, 1945, National Archives at St. Louis, Kempner personnel papers, Department of the Army/Air Force.

395 Kempner's brief: "The Guilt of Herman Goering," June 11, 1945, National Archives, Record Group 238, Security-Classified General Correspondence 1945–1946, Container 18. In the brief, Kempner noted that it was Göring's agents who abducted Berthold Jacob in 1935 and brought him from Switzerland to the Columbia-Haus concentration camp. "Aquaintances of Jacob were arrested and tortured in Berlin at the same time," Kempner wrote, though he did not explicitly mention that he had been one of them.

395 "I think we can use him to our advantage": Bernays memorandum to Jackson, July 17, 1945, Robert H. Jackson Papers, Box 106, Roll 12.

395 ninety-one pounds: Daniel Noce memorandum on shipping details, August 7, 1945, National Archives at St. Louis, Kempner personnel papers, Department of the Army/Air Force.

395 "sixteen years ago": "Yanks Sing for Newsmen at Nuremberg," clipping from unknown newspaper, Kempner Papers, Box 418.

395 "put a little piece of justice back into the world": Thom Shanker, "Despite Nuremberg Trials, War Crimes a Murky Issue," *Chicago Tribune*, June 30, 1993.

395 Nuremberg was a ruin: Persico, *Nuremberg*, p. 39; Neave, *On Trial at Nuremberg*, p. 42.

396 "Well, my friends": Andrus, *I Was the Nuremberg Jailer*, p. 52.

396 "crouching in their cells like wounded beasts": Neave, *On Trial at Nuremberg*, p. 45.

396 poke him awake: Persico, *Nuremberg*, p. 151.

397 "you will probably end up in plenty of trouble": Rosenberg interrogation, August 14, 1945, National Archives, M1270, Roll 26.

397 Thomas J. Dodd: Both Dodd and his son Christopher J. Dodd represented the state of Connecticut in the U.S. Senate, from 1959 to 1971 and from 1981 to 2011, respectively.

397 "jailbird in the ruins": Dodd, *Letters from Nuremberg*, p. 92.

397 "established religions": Rosenberg interrogation, September 21, 1945, 14:30–16:40, National Archives, M1270, Roll 17.

398 "defensive" measures: Ibid., September 22, 1945, 14:15–16:00.

399 so did German soldiers: Ibid., September 24, 1945, 10:30–12:00.

399 superior to all others: Ibid., September 22, 1945, 11:00–12:00.

399 would have returned some of it one day: Ibid., September 24, 1945, 14:30–15:30.

399 "police kept rather silent on that subject": Ibid., September 24, 1945, 10:30–12:00.

399 killing of the Jews: Ibid., September 22, 1945, 14:15–16:00.

399 "my headquarters were in Berlin": Ibid., September 24, 1945, 10:30–12:00.

400 "a little difficult to believe": Ibid., October 4, 1945, 10:30–12:15.

400 "a sick spaniel": Neave, *On Trial at Nuremberg*, pp. 102–4.

401 "how fortunate we have been": Kempner letter, "Dear Folks," August 11, 1945, Kempner Papers, Box 418; Kempner interview, Records of the Emergency Committee in Aid of Displaced Foreign Scholars.

401 "a mania for writing things down": Tusa and Tusa, *Nuremberg Trial*, pp. 96–101.

403 "see something like this": Kempner, *Ankläger einer Epoche*, pp. 251–52.

403   "knew of their sins": Ibid., p. 253.

403   "since we last met": Kempner interview, quoted in Mosley, *The Reich Marshal*, p. 325.

404   "smoke through a chimney": Kempner interview, quoted in Maguire, *Law and War*, p. 117.

404   confronted Göring: Göring interrogation, October 13, 1945, National Archives, M1270, Box 5.

405   Göring stuck to his line: Despite ongoing attempts to implicate the Nazis in the burning of the Reichstag, many historians have come to conclude that Marinus van der Lubbe, the Dutch communist executed in 1934 for the crime, acted alone that night. In the 1970s and '80s, Kempner, working on behalf of van der Lubbe's surviving brother, unsuccessfully sought to have the conviction overturned. In 2008, van der Lubbe was posthumously pardoned by the German state.

405   "a wonderful life?": Robert Kempner to Ruth Kempner, September 21, 1945, Kempner Papers, Box 418.

405   romantic postcards: Kempner postcards, September 13, 1945, Kempner Papers, Box 418.

405   "terribly long, too long": Kempner letter, September 9, 1945, Kempner Papers, Box 418.

406   "undisclosed mission": Kempner letter, October 10, 1945, Kempner Papers, Box 418.

406   in papers back home: Newspaper clippings in Kempner Papers, Box 418.

406   "Had some fun": Kempner postcard to "Der Folks," October 23, 1945, Kempner Papers, Box 418.

407   anticipate what defenses: Office of U.S. Chief of Counsel memorandum, Kempner Papers, Box 418.

407   to drain the swamp that had bred the Nazi menace: Kempner, *Ankläger*, p. 252.

407   circled his tiny head: Marked clipping from *Time* magazine dated December 3, 1945, Kempner Papers, Box 418.

407   made their way into the courtroom: Persico, *Nuremberg*, pp. 131–34.

408   "The wrongs which we seek to condemn": *Trial of the Major War Criminals*, vol. 2, p. 99.

408   "war by other means": Otto Kranzbühler, quoted in Maguire, *Law and War*, p. 88.

408   "Teutonic passion": *Trial of the Major War Criminals*, vol. 2, p. 102.

409   "ornate German craftsmanship": Ibid., vol. 3, p. 553.

409   "We are not to blame": Gilbert, *Nuremberg Diary*, pp. 97, 120, 354.

410   Charged on all four counts: *Trial of the Major War Criminals*, vol. 5, pp. 41–66.

411   he named four: Ibid., pp. 176, 181–82. The circumstances of this visit are otherwise unknown.

411   mapping out the cases against individual defendants: Robert G. Storey memorandum to Kempner, November 28, 1945, Kempner Papers, Box 418.

411   "finest in the city": Dodd, *Letters from Nuremberg*, p. 90.

411   after-hours drinks in the hotel's Marble Room: Neave, *On Trial at Nuremberg*, pp. 43–44.

411 "say what he thinks of them out loud": Victor H. Bernstein, "Kempner Will Have His Day in Court," *PM*, January 11, 1946; clipping in Kempner Papers, Box 263.

411 "center of the legal universe": Persico, *Nuremberg*, p. 175.

412 Kempner argued that Frick: *Trial of the Major War Criminals*, vol. 5, pp. 352–67.

412 florid, theatrical gestures: Raymond Daniell. "Goering Accused Red Baselessly," *New York Times*, January 17, 1946.

412 full grasp of Nazi history: Persico, *Nuremberg*, p. 226.

413 how well the trial was playing with the German public: Robert M. W. Kempner, "Impact of Nuremberg," *New York Times*, October 6, 1946.

413 "You dirty old man": Shirer, *Rise and Fall*, p. 1070; Evans, *The Third Reich at War*, p. 643.

413 "destroy the German people": *Trial of the Major War Criminals*, vol. 11, pp. 396–422.

414 "It was just truth without question": Gilbert, *Nuremberg Diary*, pp. 267–68.

415 "for an ordinary mortal to get a footing in the world of Alfred Rosenberg": OSS memorandum on Rosenberg, July 11, 1945, National Archives, Record Group 238, German Dossiers 1945–1946, Container 41.

415 testimony that would strain credulity: *Trial of the Major War Criminals*, vol. 11, pp. 444–529.

416 died while trying to flee: Evans, *Third Reich at War*, p. 728; Graeme Wood, "Martin Bormann has a Stomachache," *Atlantic*, July 20, 2009.

416 secret memo: Rosenberg memorandum, "Concerning: Jewish Possessions in France," December 18, 1941, reproduced as 001-PS in Office of the U.S. Chief of Counsel for the Prosecution of Axis Criminality, *Nazi Conspiracy and Aggression*, vol. 3, p. 1.

416 execution of one hundred French hostages: Laub, *After the Fall*, p. 46.

417 "Heuaktion": Memorandum, "Re: Evacuation of youths," June 12, 1944, reproduced as 031-PS in Office of the U.S. Chief of Counsel, *Nazi Conspiracy*, vol. 3, pp. 71–74.

418 "The fact that Jews receive special treatment": Letter from Lohse's office to Rosenberg, June 18, 1943, reproduced as R-135 in Office of the U.S. Chief of Counsel, *Nazi Conspiracy*, vol. 8, pp. 205–8.

419 to cross-examine Rosenberg: *Trial of the Major War Criminals*, vol. 11, pp. 529–64.

421 "two and a half to three million murders": Höss estimated that 2.5 million people were gassed at Auschwitz, but historians have put the number at 1.1 to 1.5 million; see Evans, *Third Reich at War*, p. 304.

421 "such a complete hypocrite": Dodd, *Letters from Nuremberg*, p. 287.

422 none too happy about it: Kempner to Murray Gurfin, June 17, 1946, Kempner Papers, Box 262; Thomas Dodd memorandums on assignments, May 16 and 18, 1946, Kempner Papers, Box 263.

422 arrested by the Gestapo: Lucian Kempner application letter to company commander, September 29, 1945, Kempner Papers, Box 71.

422 dispatched to a forced labor camp: Lucian Kempner draft Application for Federal Employment, Kempner Papers, Box 41; camp details drawn from Weinmann, *Der Nationalsozialistische Lagersystem*, p. 69; Megargee, *The United*

States Holocaust Memorial Museum Encyclopedia of Camps and Ghettos 1933–1945, p. 820; and the Web site of the Amersfoort National Monument, www.kamp amersfoort.nl/p/start.

422 rode a stolen bicycle to the Allied lines: In another account, Lucian said he was "liberated by U.S. forces." Lucian Kempner deposition in *Lipton v. Swansen*.

423 "help me to find my father": Lucian Kempner to Voice of America radio station, July 1945, Kempner Papers, Box 71.

423 "I risked my life": Lucian Kempner to Robert Kempner, January 9, 1946, Kempner Papers, Box 71.

423 reunite briefly: Lucian Kempner deposition in *Lipton v. Swansen*.

423 "He was persecuted and pursued and beaten and starved": "Refugee and Mother Reunited After Decade," *Philadelphia Inquirer*, May 27, 1946; "Kempner's Son, Victim of Nazis, Rejoins Mother," *Philadelphia Record*, May 27, 1946.

424 "a real Kempner": Grossman to Robert Kempner, June 18, 1946, Kempner Papers, Box 262.

424 "May I ask a great favor of you?": Kempner memorandum to Thomas Dodd, July 17, 1946, Kempner Papers, Box 262.

424 she was quickly recognized and removed: Persico, *Nuremberg*, p. 367; Tusa and Tusa, *Nuremberg Trial*, p. 455.

424 "Nothing . . . can sway me": Persico, *Nuremberg*, pp. 294–98; Gilbert, *Nuremberg Diary*, pp. 212–14.

425 food and chocolate: Kempner interview quoted in Mosley, *The Reich Marshal*, pp. 325, 347.

425 helped prevent that from happening: Hett, *Burning the Reichstag*, pp. 194, 220. Kempner declared Diels's testimony at Nuremberg to be "assistance especially deserving of thanks."

425 "shared a cup of tea": This quote and details of Kempner's relationship with Diels are drawn from Kohl, *The Witness House*, pp. 43–47, 152–53.

426 he would have known: Hett, *Burning the Reichstag*, p. 183.

426 "added boredom to the long list of Nazi atrocities": *Trial of the Major War Criminals*, vol. 19, p. 416.

426 "conscience to be completely free": Ibid., vol. 22, pp. 381–83.

426 spent September deliberating: Smith, *Reaching Judgment at Nuremberg*, pp. 190–94; Persico, *Nuremberg*, pp. 388–94.

427 to hear the verdicts against them: Persico, *Nuremberg*, pp. 395–405.

428 "Got a cigarette?": Henry F. Gerecke and Merle Sinclair, "I Walked to the Gallows with the Nazi Chiefs," *Saturday Evening Post*, September 1, 1951.

428 "dragged into the dust the ideals of a movement": Lang and Schenck, *Memoirs of Alfred Rosenberg*, p. 201.

428 a "paroxysm of self-intoxication": Ibid., p. 248.

428 "the Mephisto": Ibid., p. 161.

429 "great sins of omission": Ibid., p. 104.

429 "stared at me unblinkingly": Ibid., pp. 184–85.

429 "proven cruelties": Ibid., p. 189.

429 "A great idea had been misused": Ibid., p. 197.

429 "a most noble thought": Ibid., p. 113.

429 "loyal to him to the end": Ibid., p. 266.

430 "Germany's guilt will not have been erased": Persico, *Nuremberg*, pp. 322–23.

430 "You will rest too": Kempner, *Ankläger*, p. 236.

431 four letters: One of the letters, or part of it, ended up in Kempner's possession; Taylor, *The Anatomy of the Nuremberg Trials*, p. 619.

431 "Rosenberg was dull and sunken-cheeked as he looked around the court": Kingsbury Smith, "The Execution of Nazi War Criminals," International News Service, October 16, 1946.

431 Rosenberg fell: Burton Andrus memorandum, October 17, 1946, Jackson Papers, Box 101, Roll 7; Persico, *Nuremberg*, pp. 423–29.

Selected Bibliography

Archival Materials

High-quality scans of the Rosenberg diary are posted on the Web sites of the National Archives and the United States Holocaust Memorial Museum. Entries from 1934 to 1935 can be found by searching for "Alfred Rosenberg diary" at archives.gov/research/search and navigating to scans of Nuremberg documents labeled 1749-PS. Entries from 1936 to 1944 can be found at collections.ushmm.org/view/2001.62.14.

American Friends Service Committee Refugee Assistance Case Files, Ruth Kempner file, United States Holocaust Memorial Museum, Washington, D.C.
Correspondence with European Document Centers Relating to the Receipt and Return of Documents 1945–1946, Record Group 238, National Archives, College Park, Md.
Einsatzstab Reichsleiter Rosenberg correspondence (microfilm M1946), Record Group 260, National Archives, College Park, Md.
German Dossiers 1945–1946, Record Group 238, National Archives, College Park, Md.
Interrogation Records Prepared for War Crimes Proceedings at Nuernberg 1945–1947 (microfilm M1270), Record Group 238, National Archives, College Park, Md.

Irma Gideon collection, United States Holocaust Memorial Museum, Washington, D.C.

Jackson, Robert H., Papers. Boxes 14, 101, and 106. Library of Congress, Washington, D.C.

Kempner, Robert M. W., files from Department of Justice and Department of the Army. National Archives, National Personnel Records Center, St. Louis, Mo.

Kempner, Robert M. W., and Ruth Benedicta Kempner Papers, Record Group 71.001, United States Holocaust Memorial Museum, Washington, D.C.

Lester, Jane, oral history. USC Shoah Foundation Institute for Visual History and Education (sfi.usc.edu), Los Angeles.

Lipton, Margot, probate and estate records. File 2006-80096. Niagara County Surrogate's Court, Lockport, New York.

Margot Lipton v. Samuel T. Swansen, et al. Case no. 98-12106, Delaware County Court of Common Pleas, Office of Judicial Support, Media, Pa.

Messersmith, George S., Papers. University of Delaware Library, Newark, Del.

OSS Art Looting Investigation Unit reports, 1945–46 (microfilm M1782), Record Group 239, National Archives, College Park, Md.

Records of the Emergency Committee in Aid of Displaced Foreign Scholars, Robert Kempner file, Record Group 19.051, United States Holocaust Memorial Museum, Washington, D.C.

Records of the Office of the Chief of Counsel for War Crimes, Record Group 260, National Archives, College Park, Md.

Records of the United States Nuernberg War Crimes Trials Interrogations 1946–1949 (microfilm M1019), Record Group 238, National Archives, College Park, Md.

Reinach, Frieda and Max, diary, Record Group 10.249, United States Holocaust Memorial Museum, Washington, D.C.

Rosenberg, Alfred, diary, 1936–1944, Record Group 71, United States Holocaust Memorial Museum, Washington, D.C.

Security-Classified General Correspondence 1945–1946, Record Group 238, National Archives, College Park, Md.

Taylor, Telford, Papers, 1918–1998. Columbia University Library, Rare Book and Manuscript Library, New York.

Third Army After Action Reports. U.S. Army Combined Arms Center, Combined Arms Research Library Digital Library (cgsc.contentdm.oclc.org).

United States Evidence Files 1945–1946, Record Group 238, National Archives, College Park, Md.

United States v. William Martin, Civil Action No. 03-01666. United States District Court for the Eastern District of Pennsylvania, Philadelphia.

Journal Articles

Arad, Yitzhak. "Alfred Rosenberg and the 'Final Solution' in the Occupied Soviet Territories." *Yad Vashem Studies* 13 (1979): 263–86.

———. "The 'Final Solution' in Lithuania in the Light of German Documentation." *Yad Vashem Studies* 11 (1976): 234–72.

Baxa, Paul. "Capturing the Fascist Moment: Hitler's Visit to Italy in 1938 and the Radicalization of Fascist Italy." *Journal of Contemporary History* 42, no. 2 (2007): 227–42.

Collins, Donald E., and Herbert P. Rothfeder. "The Einsatzstab Reichsleiter Rosenberg and the Looting of Jewish and Masonic Libraries During World War II." *Journal of Library History* 18, no. 1 (Winter 1983): 21–36.

Felstiner, Mary. "Refuge and Persecution in Italy, 1933–1945." *Simon Wiesenthal Center Annual* 4 (1987): n.p. Online archive.

Gerlach, Christian. "The Wannsee Conference, the Fate of German Jews, and Hitler's Decision in Principle to Exterminate All European Jews." *Journal of Modern History* 70, no. 4 (December 1998): 759–812.

Grimsted, Patricia Kennedy. "Roads to Ratibor: Library and Archival Plunder by the Einsatzstab Reichsleiter Rosenberg." *Holocaust and Genocide Studies* 19, no. 3 (Winter 2005): 390–458.

Kempner, Robert M. W. "Blueprint of the Nazi Underground—Past and Future Subversive Activities." *Research Studies of the State College of Washington* 13, no. 2 (June 1945): 51–153.

Layton, Roland V., Jr. "The *Völkischer Beobachter*, 1920–1933: The Nazi Party Newspaper in the Weimar Era." *Central European History* 3, no. 4 (December 1970): 353–82.

Matthäus, Jürgen. "Controlled Escalation: Himmler's Men in the Summer of 1941 and the Holocaust in the Occupied Soviet Territories." *Holocaust and Genocide Studies* 21, no. 2 (Fall 2007): 218–42.

Starr, Joshua. "Jewish Cultural Property under Nazi Control." *Jewish Social Studies* 12, no. 1 (January 1950): 27–48.

Steinberg, Jonathan. "The Third Reich Reflected: German Civil Administration in the Occupied Soviet Union." *English Historical Review* 110, no. 437 (June 1995): 620–51.

Books

Allen, William Sheridan, ed. *The Infancy of Nazism: The Memoirs of Ex-Gauleiter Albert Krebs 1923–1933.* New York: New Viewpoints, 1976.

Andrus, Burton C. *I Was the Nuremberg Jailer.* New York: Tower Publications, 1970.

Anonymous. *The Persecution of the Catholic Church in the Third Reich: Facts and Documents.* Gretna, La.: Pelican, 2003.

Arad, Yitzhak. *The Holocaust in the Soviet Union.* Lincoln: University of Nebraska Press, 2009.

Arendzen, Rev. John. Foreword to *"Mythus": The Character of the New Religion*, by Alfred Rosenberg. London: Friends of Europe, 1937.

Baedeker, Karl. *Southern Germany (Wurtemberg and Bavaria): Handbook for Travelers.* Leipzig: Karl Baedeker, 1914.

———. *Berlin and Its Environs: Handbook for Travelers.* Leipzig: Karl Baedeker, 1923.

Barbian, Jan-Pieter. *The Politics of Literature in Nazi Germany: Books in the Media Dictatorship.* Translated by Kate Sturge. New York: Bloomsbury Academic, 2013.

Barnes, James J., and Patience P. Barnes. *Nazi Refugee Turned Gestapo Spy: The Life of Hans Wesemann, 1895–1971.* Westport, Conn.: Praeger, 2001.

Baxa, Paul. *Roads and Ruins: The Symbolic Landscape of Fascist Rome.* Toronto: University of Toronto Press, 2010.

Baynes, Norman H., ed. *The Speeches of Adolf Hitler, April 1922–August 1939.* 2 vols. London: Oxford University Press, 1942.

Berkhoff, Karel C. *Harvest of Despair: Life and Death in Ukraine Under Nazi Rule.* Cambridge, Mass.: Harvard University Press, 2004.

Bernstein, Arnie. *Swastika Nation: Fritz Kuhn and the Rise and Fall of the German-American Bund.* New York: St. Martin's, 2013.

Biddle, Francis. *In Brief Authority.* New York: Doubleday, 1962.

Blücher von Wahlstatt, Evelyn Mary. *An English Wife in Berlin: A Private Memoir of Events, Politics, and Daily Life in Germany Throughout the War and the Social Revolution of 1918.* New York: Dutton, 1920.

Bollmus, Reinhard. "Alfred Rosenberg: National Socialism's 'Chief Ideologue'?" In *The Nazi Elite,* edited by Ronald Smelser and Rainer Zitelmann, pp. 183–93. New York: NYU Press, 1993.

Bonney, Richard. *Confronting the Nazi War on Christianity: The Kulturkampf Newsletters, 1936–1939.* New York: Peter Lang, 2009.

Bosworth, R. J. B. *Mussolini.* New York: Oxford University Press, 2002.

Brandt, Willy. *My Road to Berlin.* New York: Doubleday, 1960.

Breitman, Richard. *The Architect of Genocide: Himmler and the Final Solution.* New York: Knopf, 1991.

Browning, Christopher R. *The Origins of the Final Solution.* Lincoln: University of Nebraska Press, 2004.

Burden, Hamilton T. *The Nuremberg Party Rallies: 1923–39.* London: Pall Mall, 1967.

Burleigh, Michael. *The Third Reich: A New History.* New York: Hill & Wang, 2000.

Buttar, Prit. *Battleground Prussia: The Assault of Germany's Eastern Front 1944–45.* Oxford: Osprey, 2012.

Cecil, Robert. *The Myth of the Master Race: Alfred Rosenberg and Nazi Ideology.* New York: Dodd, Mead, 1972.

Ciano, Galeazzo. *Ciano's Diplomatic Papers.* Edited by Malcolm Muggeridge. London: Odhams, 1948.

Charles, Douglas M. *J. Edgar Hoover and the Anti-Interventionists: FBI Political Surveillance and the Rise of the Domestic Security States, 1939–1945.* Columbus: Ohio State University Press, 2007.

Creese, Mary R. S. *Ladies in the Laboratory II: West European Women in Science, 1800–1900: A Survey of Their Contributions to Research.* Lanham, Md.: Scarecrow Press, 2004.

Dallin, Alexander. *German Rule in Russia 1941–1945: A Study in Occupation Politics.* New York: Macmillan, 1957.

Davidson, Eugene. *The Trial of the Germans: An Account of the Twenty-Two Defendants Before the International Military Tribunal at Nuremberg.* New York: Macmillan, 1966.

Delmer, Sefton. *Trail Sinister: An Autobiography.* London: Secker and Warburg, 1961.

Dial 22-0756, Pronto: Villa Pazzi: Memories of Landschulheim Florenz 1933–1938. Ottawa: n.p., 1997.

Diamond, Sander A. *The Nazi Movement in the United States 1924–1941*. Ithaca, NY: Cornell University Press, 1974.

Diels, Rudolf. *Lucifer Ante Portas: Zwischen Severing und Heydrich*. Zurich: Interverlag, [1949?].

Dippel, John V. H. *Bound Upon a Wheel of Fire: Why So Many German Jews Made the Tragic Decision to Remain in Nazi Germany*. New York: Basic Books, 1996.

Dodd, Christopher J., with Lary Bloom. *Letters from Nuremberg: My Father's Narrative of a Quest for Justice*. New York: Crown, 2007.

Dodd, William Jr., and Martha Dodd, eds. *Ambassador Dodd's Diary 1933–1938*. New York: Harcourt, Brace, 1941.

Dreyfus, Jean-Marc, and Sarah Gensburger. *Nazi Labour Camps in Paris: Austerlitz, Lévitan, Bassano, July 1943–August 1944*. New York: Berghahn, 2011.

Eckert, Astrid M. *The Struggle for the Files: The Western Allies and the Return of German Archives After the Second World War*. New York: Cambridge University Press, 2012.

Edsel, Robert M., with Bret Witter. *The Monuments Men: Allied Heroes, Nazi Thieves, and the Greatest Treasure Hunt in History*. New York: Back Bay, 2009.

Ehrenreich, Eric. *The Nazi Ancestral Proof: Genealogy, Racial Science, and the Final Solution*. Bloomington: Indiana University Press, 2007.

Evans, Richard J. *The Coming of the Third Reich*. New York: Penguin, 2004.

———. *The Third Reich in Power*. New York: Penguin, 2005.

———. *The Third Reich at War*. New York: Penguin, 2009.

Farago, Ladislas. *The Game of the Foxes: The Untold Story of German Espionage in the United States and Great Britain During World War II*. New York: David McKay, 1971.

Faulhaber, Michael von. *Judaism, Christianity and Germany*. Translated by Rev. George D. Smith. New York: Macmillan, 1934.

Fest, Joachim. *The Face of the Third Reich: Portraits of the Nazi Leadership*. London: I. B. Tauris, 2011.

Frank, Werner L. *The Curse of Gurs: Way Station to Auschwitz*. Lexington, Ky.: n.p., 2012.

Frei, Norbert. *Adenauer's Germany and the Nazi Past: The Politics of Amnesty and Integration*. New York: Columbia University Press, 1997.

Fromm, Bella. *Blood and Banquets: A Berlin Social Diary*. New York: Harper, 1942.

Gary, Brett. *The Nervous Liberals: Propaganda Anxieties from World War I to the Cold War*. New York: Columbia University Press, 1999.

Gilbert, G. M. *Nuremberg Diary*. New York: Farrar, Straus, 1947.

Gisevius, Hans Bernd. *To the Bitter End*. New York: Da Capo Press, 1998.

Goldensohn, Leon. *The Nuremberg Interviews*. New York: Knopf, 2004.

Griech-Polelle, Beth A. *Bishop von Galen: German Catholicism and National Socialism*. New Haven, Conn.: Yale University Press, 2002.

Grimsted, Patricia Kennedy. *Reconstructing the Record of Nazi Cultural Plunder*. Amsterdam: International Institute of Social History, 2011.

Gutman, Israel. *Encyclopedia of the Holocaust*. 4 vols. New York: Macmillan, 1990.

Hanfstaengl, Ernst. *Hitler: The Missing Years*. New York: Arcade, 1994.

Hastings, Derek. *Catholicism and the Roots of Nazism*. New York: Oxford University Press, 2010.

Hermand, Jost. *Culture in Dark Times: Nazi Fascism, Inner Emigration, and Exile.* New York: Berghahn, 2013.

Hett, Benjamin Carter. *Burning the Reichstag: An Investigation into the Third Reich's Enduring Mystery.* New York: Oxford University Press, 2014.

Hitler, Adolf. *Mein Kampf.* Translated by Ralph Manheim. Boston: Mariner, 1999. First published 1925 by Franz Eher Nachfolger.

Kaplan, Marion A. *Between Dignity and Despair: Jewish Life in Nazi Germany.* New York: Oxford University Press, 1998.

Kay, Alex J. *Exploitation, Resettlement, Mass Murder: Political and Economic Planning for German Occupation Policy in the Soviet Union, 1940–1941.* New York: Berghahn, 2006.

Kelley, Douglas M. *22 Cells in Nuremberg: A Psychiatrist Examines the Nazi Criminals.* New York: Greenberg, 1947.

Kellogg, Michael. *The Russian Roots of Nazism: White Émigrés and the Making of National Socialism 1917–1945.* Cambridge, UK: Cambridge University Press, 2005.

Kempner, Robert M. W. *Eichmann und Komplizen.* Zurich: Europa Verlag, 1961.

———. *SS im Kreuzverhör.* Munich: Rütten + Loening, 1964.

———. *Edith Stein und Anne Frank: Zwei von Hunderttausend.* Freiburg im Breisgau, Germany: Herder-Bücherei, 1968.

———. *Das Dritte Reich im Kreuzverhör: Aus den Vernehmungsprotokollen des Anklägers.* Munich: Bechtle, 1969.

———. *Der Mord an 35000 Berliner Juden: Der Judenmordprozess in Berlin schreibt Geschichte.* Heidelberg, Germany: Stiehm, 1970.

———. *Ankläger einer Epoche: Lebenserinnerungen.* Frankfurt: Verlag Ullstein, 1983.

———. *Autobiographical Fragments.* Translated by Jane Lester. Lewiston, N.Y.: Edwin Mellen Press, 1996.

Kershaw, Ian. *Hitler, 1889–1936: Hubris.* New York: Norton, 2000.

———. *Hitler, 1936–1945: Nemesis.* New York: Norton, 2000.

———. *Hitler: A Biography.* New York: Norton, 2008.

Klarsfeld, Serge. *Memorial to the Jews Deported from France, 1942–1944: Documentation of the Deportation of the Victims of the Final Solution in France.* New York: B. Klarsfeld Foundation, 1983.

Kohl, Christine. *The Witness House: Nazis and Holocaust Survivors Sharing a Villa During the Nuremberg Trials.* New York: Other Press, 2010.

Krieg, Robert A. *Catholic Theologians in Nazi Germany.* New York: Continuum, 2004.

Ladd, Brian. *The Ghosts of Berlin: Confronting German History in the Urban Landscape.* Chicago: University of Chicago Press, 1997.

Lane, Barbara Miller, and Leila J. Rupp, eds. and trans. *Nazi Ideology Before 1933: A Documentation.* Manchester, UK: Manchester University Press, 1978.

Lang, Serge, and Ernst von Schenck, eds. *Memoirs of Alfred Rosenberg.* Chicago: Ziff-Davis, 1949.

Large, David Clay. *Where Ghosts Walked: Munich's Road to the Third Reich.* New York: Norton, 1997.

Larson, Erik. *In the Garden of Beasts: Love, Terror, and an American Family in Hitler's Berlin.* New York: Broadway, 2011.

Laub, Thomas J. *After the Fall: German Policy in Occupied France, 1940–1944.* Oxford, UK: Oxford University Press, 2010.

Layton, Roland Vanderbilt, Jr. "The *Völkischer Beobachter*, 1925–1933: A Study of the Nazi Party Paper in the *Kampfzeit.*" Dissertation, University of Virginia, 1965.

Lester, Jane. *An American College Girl in Hitler's Germany: A Memoir.* Lewiston, N.Y.: Edwin Mellen Press, 1999.

Levine, Rhonda F. *Class, Networks, and Identity: Replanting Jewish Lives from Nazi Germany to Rural New York.* Lanham, Md.: Rowman & Littlefield, 2001.

Lewy, Guenter. *The Catholic Church and Nazi Germany.* New York: Da Capo, 2000.

Lochner, Louis P., ed. *The Goebbels Diaries.* Garden City, N.Y.: Doubleday, 1948.

Longerich, Peter. *Holocaust: The Nazi Persecution and Murder of the Jews.* New York: Oxford University Press, 2010.

———. *Goebbels: A Biography.* New York: Random House, 2015.

Lower, Wendy. *Nazi Empire-Building and the Holocaust in Ukraine.* Chapel Hill: University of North Carolina Press, 2005.

———. "On Him Rests the Weight of the Administration: Nazi Civilian Rulers and the Holocaust in Zhytomyr." In *The Shoah in Ukraine: History, Testimony, Memorialization,* ed. Ray Brandon and Wendy Lower, pp. 224–27. Bloomington: Indiana University Press, 2008.

Lüdecke, Kurt G. W. *I Knew Hitler: The Story of a Nazi Who Escaped the Blood Purge.* New York: Charles Scribner's Sons, 1937.

Maguire, Peter. *Law and War: International Law and American History.* Rev. ed. New York: Columbia University Press, 2010.

Matthäus, Jürgen, and Frank Bajohr, eds. *Alfred Rosenberg: Die Tagebücher von 1934 bis 1944.* Frankfurt: S. Fischer, 2015.

Megargee, Geoffrey P., ed. *The United States Holocaust Memorial Museum Encyclopedia of Camps and Ghettos, 1933–1945.* Vol. I. Bloomington: Indiana University Press, 2009.

Meyer, Beate, Hermann Simon, and Chana Schütz, eds. *Jews in Nazi Berlin: From Kristallnacht to Liberation.* Chicago: University of Chicago Press, 2009.

Morris, Jeffrey. *Establishing Justice in Middle America: A History of the United States Court of Appeals for the Eighth Circuit.* Minneapolis: University of Minnesota Press, 2007.

Mosley, Leonard. *The Reich Marshal: A Biography of Hermann Goering.* London: Pan Books, 1977.

Mulligan, Timothy Patrick. *The Politics of Illusion and Empire: German Occupation Policy in the Soviet Union, 1942–1943.* New York: Praeger, 1988.

Neave, Airey. *On Trial at Nuremberg.* Boston: Little Brown, 1979.

Nicholas, Lynn H. *The Rape of Europa: The Fate of Europe's Treasures in the Third Reich and the Second World War.* New York: Knopf, 1994.

Nicosia, Francis R. "German Zionism and Jewish Life in Nazi Berlin." In *Jewish Life in Nazi Germany: Dilemmas and Responses,* ed. Francis R. Nicosia and David Scrase, pp. 89–116. New York: Berghahn, 2010.

Noakes, J., and G. Pridham, eds. *Nazism: A History in Documents and Eyewitness Accounts, 1919–1945.* 2 vols. New York: Schocken, 1983–1988.

Nova, Fritz. *Alfred Rosenberg: Philosopher of the Third Reich.* New York: Hippocrene, 1986.

O'Brien, Kenneth Paul, and Lynn Hudson Parsons. *The Homefront War: World War II and American Society.* Westport, Conn.: Greenwood Press, 1995.

Office of the U.S. Chief of Counsel for the Prosecution of Axis Criminality. *Nazi Conspiracy and Aggression.* 8 vols. Washington, D.C.: U.S. Government Printing Office, 1946.

Olson, Lynne. *Those Angry Days: Roosevelt, Lindbergh, and America's Fight Over World War II, 1939-1941.* New York: Random House, 2013.

Palmier, Jean Michel. *Weimar in Exile: The Antifascist Emigration in Europe and America.* New York: Verso, 2006.

Papen, Franz von. *Memoirs.* New York: Dutton, 1953.

Papen-Bodek, Patricia von. "Anti-Jewish Research of the Institut zur Erforschung der Judenfrage in Frankfurt am Main between 1939 and 1945." In *Lessons and Legacies VI: New Currents in Holocaust Research,* ed. Jeffry Diefendorf, pp. 155– 189. Evanston, Ill.: Northwestern University Press, 2004.

Persico, Joseph E. *Nuremberg: Infamy on Trial.* New York: Penguin, 1994.

Petropoulos, Jonathan. *Art as Politics in the Third Reich.* Chapel Hill: University of North Carolina Press, 1996.

Piper, Ernst. *Alfred Rosenberg: Hitlers Chefideologe.* Munich: Karl Blessing Verlag, 2005.

Pöppmann, Dirk. "Robert Kempner und Ernst von Weizsäcker im Wilhelmstrassenprozess." In *Im Labyrinth der Schuld: Täter, Opfer, Ankläger,* ed. Irmtrud Wojak and Susanne Meinl, pp. 163–197. Frankfurt: Campus Verlag, 2003.

———. "The Trials of Robert Kempner: From Stateless Immigrant to Prosecutor of the Foreign Office." In *Reassessing the Nuremberg Military Tribunals,* ed. Kim C. Priemel and Alexa Stiller. New York: Berghahn, 2012.

Posnanski, Renée. *Jews in France During World War II.* Hanover, N.H.: University Press of New England, 2001.

Prange, Gordon W., ed. *Hitler's Words.* Washington, D.C.: American Council on Public Affairs, 1944.

Pringle, Heather. *The Master Plan: Himmler's Scholars and the Holocaust.* New York: Hyperion, 2006.

Read, Anthony. *The Devil's Disciples: Hitler's Inner Circle.* New York: Norton, 2003.

Reinemann, John Otto. *Carried Away . . . Recollections and Reflections.* Philadelphia: n.p., 1976.

Ribuffo, Leo P. *The Old Christian Right: The Protestant Far Right from the Great Depression to the Cold War.* Philadelphia: Temple University Press, 1983.

Rogge, O. John. *The Official German Report: Nazi Penetration 1924–1942, Pan-Arabism 1939–Today.* New York: Thomas Yoseloff, 1961.

Rorimer, James. *Survival: The Salvage and Protection of Art in War.* New York: Abelard, 1950.

Rosbottom, Ronald C. *When Paris Went Dark: The City of Light Under German Occupation, 1940–1944.* New York: Back Bay, 2014.

Roseman, Mark. *The Villa, the Lake, the Meeting: Wannsee and the Final Solution.* London: Allen Lane, 2002.

Rosenberg, Alfred. *Der Mythus des 20. Jahrhunderts.* Munich: Hoheneichen-Verlag, 1934.

————. *Race and Race History and Other Essays by Alfred Rosenberg.* Edited by Robert Pois. New York: Harper & Row, 1970.

Rothfeder, Herbert Phillips. "A Study of Alfred Rosenberg's Organization for National Socialist Ideology." Dissertation, University of Michigan, 1963.

Rubenstein, Joshua, and Ilya Altman, eds. *The Unknown Black Book: The Holocaust in the German-Occupied Soviet Territories.* Bloomington: Indiana University Press, 2008.

Ryback, Timothy W. *Hitler's Private Library: The Books That Shaped His Life.* New York: Knopf, 2008.

Safrian, Hans. *Eichmann's Men.* Cambridge, UK: Cambridge University Press, 2010.

Schmid, Armin. *Lost in a Labyrinth of Red Tape: The Story of an Immigration That Failed.* Evanston, Ill.: Northwestern University Press, 1996.

Schuschnigg, Kurt von. *Austrian Requiem.* New York: Putnam, 1946.

Schwertfeger, Ruth. *In Transit: Narratives of German Jews in Exile, Flight, and Internment During "The Dark Years" of France.* Berlin: Frank & Timme, 2012.

Seraphim, Hans-Günther, ed. *Das politische Tagebuch Alfred Rosenbergs: 1934/35 und 1939/40.* Munich: Deutscher Taschenbuch Verlag, 1956.

Sherratt, Yvonne. *Hitler's Philosophers.* New Haven, Conn.: Yale University Press, 2013.

Shirer, William L. *Berlin Diary: The Journal of a Foreign Correspondent, 1934–1941.* Baltimore: Johns Hopkins University Press, 2002. First published 1941 by Alfred A. Knopf.

————. *The Rise and Fall of the Third Reich: A History of Nazi Germany.* New York: Simon & Schuster, 2011. First published 1960 by Simon & Schuster.

Smith, Bradley F. *Reaching Judgment at Nuremberg: The Untold Story of How the Nazi War Criminals Were Judged.* New York: Basic Books, 1977.

Snyder, Timothy. *Bloodlands: Europe Between Hitler and Stalin.* New York: Basic Books, 2010.

Speer, Albert. *Inside the Third Reich: Memoirs.* New York: Macmillan, 1970.

St. George, Maximilian, and Dennis Lawrence. *A Trial on Trial: The Great Sedition Trial of 1944.* Chicago: National Civil Rights Committee, 1946.

Stein, George H. *The Waffen SS: Hitler's Elite Guard at War, 1939–1945.* Ithaca, N.Y.: Cornell University Press, 1966.

Steinweis, Alan E. *Studying the Jew: Scholarly Antisemitism in Nazi Germany.* Cambridge, Mass.: Harvard University Press, 2006.

Stephenson, Donald. "*Frontschweine* and Revolution: The Role of Front-Line Soldiers in the German Revolution of 1918." Dissertation, Syracuse University, 2007.

Strasser, Otto. *Hitler and I.* Boston: Houghton Mifflin, 1940.

————. *The Gangsters Around Hitler.* London: W. H. Allen, 1942.

Täubrich, Hans-Christian, ed. *Fascination and Terror: Party Rally Grounds Documentation Center, The Exhibition.* Nuremberg, Germany: Druckhaus Nürnberg, n.d.

Taylor, Frederick. *The Downfall of Money: Germany's Hyperinflation and the Destruction of the Middle Class.* New York: Bloomsbury, 2013.

Taylor, Telford. *The Anatomy of the Nuremberg Trials: A Personal Memoir.* New York: Knopf, 1992.

Tomasevich, Jozo. *War and Revolution in Yugoslavia, 1941–1945*. Stanford, Calif.: Stanford University Press, 2001.

Torrie, Julia S. *"For Their Own Good": Civilian Evacuations in Germany and France, 1939–1945*. New York: Berghahn, 2010.

Trevor-Roper, H. R., ed. *Hitler's Table Talk 1941–1944*. New York: Enigma, 2008.

Trial of the Major War Criminals Before the International Military Tribunal. 42 vols., 1947–1949; http://www.loc.gov/rr/frd/Military_Law/NT_major-war-criminals.html.

Trials of War Criminals Before the Nuernberg Military Tribunals Under Control Council Law No. 10. 15 vols., 1946–1949; http://www.loc.gov/rr/frd/Military_Law/NTs_war-criminals.html.

Tusa, Ann, and John Tusa. *The Nuremberg Trial*. New York: Atheneum, 1986.

University of St. Michael's College v. Herbert W. Richardson. Toronto: Hearing Committee, St. Michael's College, 1994.

U.S. Department of State. *Foreign Relations of the United States: Diplomatic Papers, 1933*. Vol. II: *The British Commonwealth, Europe, Near East and Africa*. Washington, D.C.: U.S. Government Printing Office, 1949.

Vansittart, Robert. *The Mist Procession: The Autobiography of Lord Vansittart*. London: Hutchinson, 1958.

Wasow, Wolfgang R. *Memories of Seventy Years: 1909 to 1979*. Madison, Wis.: n.p., 1986.

Watt, Richard. *The Kings Depart: The Tragedy of Germany; Versailles and the German Revolution*. New York: Simon & Schuster, 1968.

Weinberg, Gerhard L. *The Foreign Policy of Hitler's Germany: Diplomatic Revolution in Europe 1933–36*. Chicago: University of Chicago Press, 1970.

Weiner, Timothy. *Enemies: A History of the FBI*. New York: Random House, 2012.

Weinmann, Martin. *Das Nationalsozialistische Lagersystem*. Frankfurt: Zweitausendeins, 1990.

Weinreich, Max. *Hitler's Professors: The Part of Scholarship in Germany's Crimes Against the Jewish People*. New York: Yiddish Scientific Institute, 1946.

Winterbotham, F. W. *The Nazi Connection*. New York: Dell, 1978.

Wittman, Robert K., with John Shiffman. *Priceless: How I Went Undercover to Rescue the World's Stolen Treasures*. New York: Crown, 2010.

Wyneken, Jon David K. "Driving Out the Demons: German Churches, the Western Allies, and the Internationalization of the Nazi Past, 1945–1952." Dissertation, Ohio University, 2007.

Zimmerman, Joshua D., ed. *Jews in Italy under Fascist and Nazi Rule, 1922–1945*. Cambridge, UK: Cambridge University Press, 2005.

Zuccotti, Susan. *The Holocaust, the French, and the Jews*. Lincoln: University of Nebraska Press, 1999.

Index

About the Authors

ROBERT K. WITTMAN created the FBI's Art Crime Team and was the Bureau's national expert on cultural property theft. He is the author of the *New York Times* bestseller *Priceless: How I Went Undercover to Rescue the World's Stolen Treasures* and president of Robert Wittman, Inc.

DAVID KINNEY is a Pulitzer Prize–winning reporter whose journalism has appeared in numerous publications, including the *New York Times*. He is the author of *The Big One: An Island, an Obsession, and the Furious Pursuit of a Great Fish* and *The Dylanologists: Adventures in the Land of Bob*.